California Bankers Association

Proceedings of the California Bankers Association

Held at Los Angeles, March 11, 12 and 13, 1891

California Bankers Association

Proceedings of the California Bankers Association
Held at Los Angeles, March 11, 12 and 13, 1891

ISBN/EAN: 9783337111946

Printed in Europe, USA, Canada, Australia, Japan

Cover: Foto ©Suzi / pixelio.de

More available books at **www.hansebooks.com**

PROCEEDINGS

OF THE

CALIFORNIA BANKERS ASSOCIATION

HELD AT

Los Angeles, March 11, 12 and 13, 1891.

CONSTITUTION AND BY-LAWS

OF THE

CALIFORNIA BANKERS ASSOCIATION

NOTE—THE CONVENTION AND ASSOCIATION DO NOT NECESSARILY
ENDORSE THE OPINIONS EXPRESSED IN ANY ADDRESS OR PAPER
PRINTED HEREIN, AND DISCLAIM ANY RESPONSIBILITY THEREFOR.

LOS ANGELES:
THE TIMES-MIRROR PRINTING AND BINDING HOUSE.
1891.

OFFICERS

OF THE

California Bankers Association.

1891

President: THOMAS BROWN,
                    Bank of California, San Francisco
First Vice-President. ISAIAS W. HELLMAN,
                    Nevada Bank, San Francisco
Secretary. GEO. H. STEWART,
                    Los Angeles County Bank, Los Angeles
Treasurer: G. W. KLINZ,
                    First National Bank, San Francisco

Executive Council: Chairman: A D. CHILDRESS

   One Year Term:
        W. M. EDDY, Santa Barbara County National Bank, Santa Barbara.
        T. S. HAWKINS, Bank of Hollister, Hollister
        W. D. WOOLWINE, First National Bank, San Diego

   Two Year Term:
        A. D. CHILDRESS, City Bank, Los Angeles
        N. D. RIDEOUT, California State Bank, Sacramento.
        LOVELL WHITE, San Francisco Savings Union, San Francisco.

   Three Year Term:
        C. E. PALMER, Union National Bank, Oakland
        W. W. PHILLIPS. Farmers Bank of Fresno, Fresno.
        A. L. SELIGMAN, Anglo-Californian Bank, San Francisco

List of Vice-Presidents will follow later on

*To the Bankers of California:—Greeting:—*To induce harmony and promote the welfare and usefulness of banks and banking institutions of California, and to secure the proper consideration of questions regarding the financial and commercial usages, customs and laws affecting the banking interests of our great state, and especially to adopt such rules and methods as will insure uniformity of action in the conduct of our institutions, the Los Angeles Clearing House extends an invitation to assemble at Los Angeles on the 11th day of March, proximo, for the purpose of organizing a State Bankers Association.

Papers on live subjects will be arranged for, and voluntary contributions will be given place if practicable.

As the State Citrus Fair opens in this city on March 10th, (Tuesday,) continuing through the week, hotel accommodations should be secured at the earliest date practicable. Any assistance desired in this or other particulars will be rendered on application.

Your acknowledgment is requested.

Very Respectfully,

GEO. H. STEWART, Secretary.

A. D. CHILDRESS,
W. F. BOSBYSHELL,
H. W. HELLMAN,

Clearing House Committee.

In response to the forgoing invitation the following banks and bankers were registered in attendance at the convention :

BANKS REPRESENTED AT THE CONVENTION

EACH BANK BEING ENTITLED TO ONE VOTE

LOCATION	NAME OF BANK.	REPRESENTATIVE.
Anaheim,	Bank of Anaheim,	Piez James, President.
Auburn.	Placer County Bank,	N. D. Rideout, President.
Chico,	Bank of Butte County,	N. D. Rideout, "
Colton,	First National Bank,	John W. Davis, "
Elsinore,	Consolidated Bank,	M. A. Baird.
Eureka,	Bank of Eureka,	Geo. H. Stewart, (proxy.)
Fallbrook.	Fallbrook Bank,	J. A. Pruett, President.
Fresno,	Farmers' Bank,	W. W. Phillips, Vice-Pres.
Fresno,	Fresno National Bank,	H. D. Colson, President.
Fresno,	Bank of Central California,	Louis Einstein, President
Fresno,	First National Bank,	Louis Einstein,
Fresno,	People's Savings Bank,	Louis Einstein.
Hollister,	Bank of Hollister,	T. S. Hawkins, President.
Los Angeles,	Farmers and Merchants Bank,	H. W. Hellman, V.-Pres.
Los Angeles,	Farmers " " "	John Milner, Cashier
Los Angeles,	Los Angeles County Bank,	John E. Plater, President.
Los Angeles,	Los Angeles " "	Geo. H. Stewart, Cashier.
Los Angeles,	First National Bank,	E. F. Spence. President.
Los Angeles,	First National Bank,	J. M. Elliott, Cashier.
Los Angeles,	Los Angeles National Bank,	Geo. H. Bonebrake, Pres.
Los Angeles,	Los Angeles National Bank,	F. C. Howes, Cashier.
Los Angeles,	Southern California National Bank.	L. N. Breed. President.
Los Angeles.	Southern " " "	W. F. Bosbyshell, V.-Pres.
Los Angeles,	University Bank,	R. M. Widney, President.
Los Angeles,	University Bank,	Geo. L. Arnold, Cashier.
Los Angeles,	The City Bank,	A. D. Childress, President.
Los Angeles,	The City Bank,	John S. Park, Cashier.
Los Angeles,	California Bank,	T. J. Weldon. Cashier.
Los Angeles,	California Bank,	J. Frankenfield, Vice-Pres
Los Angeles,	National Bank of California.	J. M. C. Marble, President
Los Angeles,	National " " "	Perry Wildman, Ast. Cash.
Los Angeles,	German American Savings Bank.	W. M. Sheldon, V.-Pres.
Los Angeles,	German " " "	M. N. Avery, Secretary.
Los Angeles,	Broadway Bank,	H. Sinsabaugh, President.
Los Angeles,	State Loan and Trust Company.	John Bryson, Sr., V.-Pres.
Los Angeles,	State " " " "	J. F. Towell, Manager.
Los Angeles,	Los Angeles Savings Bank,	W. M. Caswell, Sec.
Los Angeles,	East Side Bank,	W. J. Washburn, Pres.
Los Angeles,	Main Street Savings Bank,	J. B. Lankershim. Pres.
Los Angeles,	Citizens' Bank,	T. S. C. Lowe, President.
Los Angeles,	Citizens' Bank,	T. W. Brotherton. V.-Pres.
Los Angeles,	Security Savings Bank and T. Co.,	F. N. Myers, President.
Los Angeles.	Security " " " "	J. F. Sartori, Cashier.
Los Angeles,	Savings Bank of Southern California,	John N. Hunt, Secretary.

Madera,	Bank of Madera,	M. A. Baird, Vice-Pres.
Monrovia,	Granite Bank,	E. F. Spence, President.
Monrovia,	First National Bank,	J. F. Sartori, Vice-Pres.
Marysville,	The Rideout Bank,	Norman Rideout, V.-Pres.
National City,	Bank of National City,	C. B. Whittelsey. Ast. Cash.
Oakland,	Union National Bank,	C. E. Palmer, Cashier.
Oakland,	First National Bank,	Geo. J. Ainsworth.
Ontario.	Ontario State Bank,	G. T. Stamm, President
Orange,	Bank of Orange,	B. G. Balcom, Cashier.
Oroville,	Bank of Rideout, Smith & Co.,	N. D. Rideout, Pres.
Pasadena,	First National Bank,	A. H. Conger, Cashier.
Pasadena,	Pasadena National Bank.	T. P. Lukens. Cashier
Pasadena,	San Gabriel Valley Bank,	H. W. Magee, President.
Perris,	Perris Valley Bank,	Jas. Patterson, Jr. Cashier.
Pomona,	First National Bank,	Stoddard Jess, Cashier
Pomona,	People's Bank,	John V. Dole, Cashier
Red Bluff,	Bank of Tehama County,	J. S. Cone, Vice-President
Redlands,	First National Bank,	F. P. Morrison. President
Riverside,	First National Bank,	A. H. Naftzger, President
Santa Ana,	First National Bank,	M. M. Crookshank, Cash
Santa Ana.	Commercial Bank,	W. K. James. Cashier
Santa Ana	Commercial Bank,	D. Halladay. President
Santa Barbara,	First National Bank,	A. L. Lincoln, Cashier
Santa Barbara,	The Commercial Bank	W. B. Metcalf, Cashier
Santa Barbara,	Santa Barbara County National Bank,	W. M. Eddy. President
San Bernardino,	Farmers' Exchange Bank,	Richard Gird. Vice-Pres.
San Bernardino,	Farmers' " "	S. F. Zombro, Cashier.
San Bernardino	San Bernardino National Bank,	J. W. Davis, President
San Diego,	First National Bank,	W. D. Woolwine, Cashier
San Diego.	Bank of Commerce,	G. W. Jorres, Cashier
San Francisco,	Anglo-Californian Bank,	A. I. Seligman, Ast. Cash.
San Francisco,	Bank of California,	Thomas Brown, Cashier
San Francisco,	First National Bank,	G. W. Kline, Ast. Cashier
San Francisco,	Nevada Bank,	I. W. Hellman. President
San Francisco,	San Francisco Savings Union,	Lovell White, Cashier
San Francisco,	Pacific Bank,	R. H. McDonald, Pres.
Santa Monica,	First National Bank,	E. J. Vawter, Cashier
Santa Paula,	First National Bank,	C. H. McKevett. Pres.
San Pedro,	Bank of San Pedro,	Wm. G. Kerckhoff, Pres.
Sacramento,	California State Bank,	N. D. Rideout, President.
Sacramento,	People's Savings Bank,	Wm. Beckman, President
Sanger,	Bank of Sanger,	W. W. Phillips, (proxy.)
Selma,	Bank of Selma,	D. S. Snodgrass, Cashier
Tustin,	Bank of Tustin,	W. S. Bartlett, Vice-Pres.
Ventura,	Bank of Ventura,	E. P. Foster, President
Ventura,	Bank of "	J. A. Walker, Cashier
Ventura,	Bank of "	L. C. McKeeby, Vice-Pres.
Ventura,	Wm. Collins & Sons,	J. S. Collins, Cashier
Visalia,	Harrell & Son,	A. J. Harrell, Manager
Watsonville,	Pajaro Valley Bank,	Thomas Brown, (proxy)

BY INVITATION.

A. Gerberding, State Bank Commissioner.
C. H. Dunsmoor, State Bank Commissioner.
J. E. Farnum, Ex-State Bank Commissioner.
W. H. Chamberlain, National Bank Examiner.

RECEPTION.

COUNCIL CHAMBER, NEW CITY HALL, }
WEDNESDAY EVENING, MARCH 11TH, 8 O'CLOCK. }

The meeting was called to order by Geo. H. Stewart, Secretary of the Los Angeles Clearing House, who said:

Bankers of California—Ladies and Gentlemen :—For years the bankers of California have recognized the desirability of an organization on this coast, similar in character to the "American Bankers Association," particularily adapted, however, to the customs and business methods of our people, but until recently no effort has been made to reduce the opinion to practice.

In December last the banks, members of the Los Angeles Clearing House, determined to undertake the preliminary work of forming the "Bankers Association of California."

In response to their invitation you have come to deliberate with us and to-night we are here to bid you welcome.

This will be expressed in words more appropriate than I command, and I beg to introduce to you our speaker, on behalf of the city, Hon Henry T. Hazard, Mayor of Los Angeles.

Mayor Hazard spoke in his usual happy vein. He said that Los Angeles had of late been honored with many conventions, but none had the important and vital matters to deal with that this one had. It was a sincere pleasure for him to welcome all of the visiting bankers, having, as they did, the financial interests of the country to discuss and handle. The Mayor thought that in the struggle for life all should know something about the science of financiering. This convention he thought would be fraught with many benefits to all concerned. He was glad to meet the distinguished gentlemen in attendance upon it, and again, on behalf of the city, he welcomed them.

The Mayor's remarks were applauded.

Mr. Stewart next introduced Hon. E. F. Spence, President of the Los Angeles Clearing House, who delivered the following address of welcome on the part of the local bankers:

GENTLEMEN : It gives me unfeigned pleasure to have the honor of welcoming the bankers of the Pacific Coast to the California State Bankers Convention at Los Angeles.

As Chairman of our local Clearing House Association and Vice-President for California of the American Bankers Association, gentlemen. I bid you welcome. welcome, thrice welcome, to this our loved city, the City of the Angels.

May your stay here be attended with cheerful associations. May the impressions you receive whilst among us be pleasant and lasting. As a city we are young and growing, and hope you will not expect to find wisdom and maturity here crystalized as in other and older cities further east.

We hope the result of our deliberations will be conducive of good to all.

Bankers are only the agents of the people; a banker is the trusted friend of the depositor. The man of means, as well as the laboring man, the servant girl and the servant boy who save a few dollars a month are comparatively as much interested in the character of our banking institutions and have as much at stake in the strength and stability of our financial fabrics as the richest in the land.

During our deliberations let the impress be made that thrift, prudence, economy, industry, intelligence, temperance and loyalty are the true avenues to wealth and prosperity; and still further let the impress be made that genuine wealth does not consist in the possession of gold and silver, as these are only the standards by which wealth or property is measured.

Let the bankers impress upon each other the fact that their duty is first to be in full sympathy with the people whom they serve, viz., their customers; and secondly, the entire community around them; to sympathize with those whom adversity has temporarily overtaken, and to rejoice with those whose lines have fallen in pleasant places and whose heritage is goodly; yet sympathy should not be foolishly overflowing, nor rejoicing obsequiously exuberant.

Should not the bankers of the country stand as sentinels upon the watchtowers of the nation and sound the alarm of approaching danger? Nay, not only to give the alarm, but be ready with brain and mental brawn to ward off attacks caused by communistic ideas generated abroad, and the foolish vagaries of well-meaning men at home?

It is expected that questions of varied import will be presented before the Association and discussed fairly and freely on all sides.

Would it be out of place to ask our Federal Government to make an appropriation to the State of California of an amount equal to the amount of gold that the miners extract from the mountains of the State? Such an appropriation to be used for the protection of our agricultural lands, the impounding and solidifying of the tailings from the mines, the control of our internal rivers, creating illimitable power for machinery, giving employment to thousands and thousands of laboring men, and furnishing water for irrigating every acre of land from the mountains to the sea.

I believe it is a pertinent question, because unfriendly legislation and adverse legal decisions have forced our richest gold mines to be abandoned, and, should not we, as *bankers*, do everything possible to be done in order to add to the world's supply of gold? Such action by our Government would be of inestimable value to this State, to the Nation, and to the world at large.

The idea may appear wild, but no harm can result from discussing it.

Gentlemen, these is a feeling of uneasiness abroad in the land; there is an element of disturbance pervading the financial world. Russia, England and France seem to have felt the full force of the tidal wave; our own country, of course, had to sympathetically respond to the perturbation, and happily the Pacific Coast was only imperceptibly affected, and now, my fellowbankers, will our voices be heard, or have we of the wild and rugged west any suggestions to offer?

Let us ask the question, as the earth continues in a greatly increased ratio to yield her productions, and the consequent reproductions by arts and manufacture, have we standards of value enough to weigh, measure, determine and represent the increase? If I were asked to answer the question I would reply in the negative.

To whom shall we apply for a remedy? What nation shall we immitate? Whose policy shall we adopt? We may ask the South, the North, or the East, yet no satisfactory answer comes. We may look to the nations of the old world, but receive no new light. Then what new mine of knowledge shall we open, or where is it to be found? I do not know, I cannot tell.

It may be in California, or somewhere on the Pacific Coast, and I will give my reason for thinking it may be here.

Away back, back beyond the time that memory or history penetrates—ere the mind of man began its onward march, we can fancy the struggling, the throbbing, the commencement of its existence, and, when human thought was still in a nebulous condition, we, in imagination, may behold its gathering forces; we, in imagination, may see the beginning of that progressive journey that shall never end while time endures; and tracing it from its dim outlines in the far-away past, we now see it a mighty, irresistable power.

We have always been taught, and so believe, that the trend of advanced thought has been and is in the wake of the setting sun.

Friends, were you seated some still evening in a quiet nook on one of the lovely hillsides near our city, you could hear in the distance the waves of the majestic Pacific breaking upon the shore. You ask what and whence the sound. You would be told it is the voice of the watchman placed upon the barriers of the West, warning the picket line of the advancing millions of the army of civilization that thus far they may come, but no farther.

We now behold the tide of enterprise, aggression, thought: I might say civilization, turned back upon itself, and the field of conjecture that this opens to the enquiring mind is so large that I will not for a moment attempt to enter, only for the purpose of asking a question.

Will it not fall to the lot of some Californian to devise a plan that will be enacted into a law that will be enforced by the nation and adopted by the other commercial nations of the world whereby the two precious metals that we produce so abundantly may be used as co-standards of value of commodities the world over, and, at the same time, one may not surpass the other.

We acknowledge the power of gold; we admit that it is and has been the yardstick by which our wealth is and has been measured; we have conceded to it the first place in the world's racecourse, but is it not possible to place a silver steed in harness with the golden in such a manner that both may strongly and smoothly pull together, shoulder to shoulder and side by side? I ask, is it not possible for the genius of the far western man to evolve a scheme whereby this double team may work together in such a manner that our western country may yield its millions upon millions of now hidden precious metals, our common country become enriched, and the world at large benefited?

Gentlemen, again I greet you in the name of the bankers of Los Angeles and hope that the State Association, which at this convention will be formed, will last always, and grow in influence and be a great power for good to all.

A. D. Childress, president of the City Bank, was then introduced, and read the following paper on the "Scope of a State Bankers Association."

"SCOPE OF A STATE BANKERS ASSOCIATION."

In accord and harmony with the idea that "in the multiplicity of counsellors there is wisdom," the propriety and necessity of a State Association to bring bankers together for the discussion of matters pertinent to general business; of vital importance to their own welfare and success; the States' advancement, and the prosperity of all classes cannot for a moment be questioned or gainsaid. And too, while we may meet for the first time as strangers, our continued intercourse will imperceptibly ripen many sympathies, and beneath the inexorable form of business will be born many cordial friendships which will change the usual "Yours truly" correspondent into "Sincerely your friend."

Nothing so softens and smooths down the hard places in the rough and rugged paths, which all business men travel during their lives of varied up and down experiences as frequent intercourse and good-fellowship. I might lay down as a very broad and incontrovertible proposition that the genus homo was not created to live alone either as bachelor or business man. Contact with one's fellows brightens the wits, broadens the soul, and, in fact, expands the scope of one's thoughts and feelings until everything 'round takes on a roseate hue of cheerfulness and contentment, the opposite of that cheerless gloom and despondency which inevitably envelops and environs the secluded hermit. We meet them as friends in a common cause but burdened with no selfish interests and purposes. We greet each other hailing from and in the interest and furtherance of every section of this, the grandest and greatest State of all the galaxy of our most glorious Union, from Red Bluff to National City; from the base of the snow-capped and hoary Sierras to the placid but ever-rolling waters of our Western sea. It is truly said that the banking fraternity represents the most powerful factor of civilization; the highest type of property the centuries have evolved and that is *money*.

The operations of the banking system underlie and permeate all business interests.

The system stands in relation to the people pre-eminent and different from all other business pursuits. It is, to a large degree, the foundation stone upon which our trade and commerce rest; it multiplies the means of development; facilitates a rapid and profitable exchange of products, and promotes alike the best interests of capital and labor.

The recent disturbance in financial circles shows conclusively that a well organized banking system is not only the life-spring of commerce, but in times of emergency and financial panic proves the savior of the whole business world. Twice in the United States within the past decade have we seen "Black Fridays" and wide-spread disaster averted by prompt action and co-operation of New York Clearing House Banks, which enjoy the most splendidly equipped banking system known in financial history. We have only to look backward a few years when one-half the shock received by American banks on account of the suspension of the great house of the Barings and other European troubles coupled with our own congested Public Treasury and panicky money market would have precipitated a financial crisis utterly paralyzing in its effects, and from the serious consequences of which we would not have recovered for many long and weary years.

In co-operation as well as union there is untold strength. It is becoming therefore, that the bankers of California assemble first of all for California's good, to unify and harmonize our efforts by the consideration and discussion of the financial questions and problems of the day, and devise ways and means of escape from the existing stringency all over the union caused by a contracted currency, as is now universally conceded by thinkers regardless of political complexion, whether by the free and unlimited coinage of tne white metal of our coast, the perpetuation and multiplicity of National Banks, or the increased issue of legal tender notes with the credit of our Nation as security.

Whatever must be the remedial means they must emanate from those, who make a specialty of finance, and from whom more naturally than from the bankers of California, who, like their great commonwealth in the sisterhood of States should rank them all.

In enumerating those things that will come within the scope of a State Bankers' Association for California, I would mention the great good to be accomplished by our united action in petitioning Congress in behalf of interests beneficial to our State.

Never in the history of California was there so auspicious a period for us to convene and labor for the great good of our people as the present time and opportunity afford. Numerous matters of great moment, both State and National, are pending, which *must* arrest and command our earnest attention. Chief of all, even taking precedence of the currency question, in my humble opinion, so far as the interests of this coast are concerned, is the Senate Committee's report on the Nicaragua Canal bill pending in the United States Senate.

With the history of the projected canal all are doubtless familiar, but I will be pardoned, I trust, for refreshing your memories as to the present bill and the attitude of the matter before Congress, as recently published.

In reply to the application of the Maritime Canal Company asking that the government endorse the company's bonds so that they could be sold at or near par, though bearing a low rate per cent, in view of the vast and incalculable advantage which the canal would confer on our mercantile interesrs, the Senate Committee on Foreign Relations recommended a reorganization of the company so that its capital stock shall stand at one hundred millions of dollars, and that it shall issue bonds to the amount of another hundred millions—the bonds to bear 3 per cent interest, running twenty years, and be endorsed by the National government. The whole issue of bonds is to be deposited in the treasury of the United States, and as construction proceeds, on presentation of certificate from a board of government engineers to be appointed by the President, the bonds are to be delivered to the company and by it sold in open market at the best price obtainable. In order to secure the government against loss through possible inability of the company to meet the interest or principal of the bonds when they mature, seventy-five millions or stock are to remain in the custody of the Government as collateral ; and on these the government holds an option to buy at any time at par; of the remaining twenty-five millions of stock, five millions are to go to Nicaragua and Costa Rica, in payment for the concession ; seven millions are to be given to the company to pay for expenditures already made, and the remaining thirteen millions are to be held in the treasury of the company as a reserve,'and are not to be sold without the permission of the government.

The Engineer's estimate of the cost of the work is 65 million dollars, but unforseen difficulties and expenses may doubtless swell the actual cost to 100 millions by the time the 'canal is opened. As the bonds, being U. S. 3 per cent. would probably sell at par, the whole expense of the canal would thus be defrayed by the sale of bonds, without having recourse to sales of Stock. But as the Stock would represent the earning capacity of the canal,-the bonds only requiring a fixed annual appropriation of 3 millions of dollars,-the shares would possess a real market value.

The Company's Statisticians reckon on a tonnage amounting annually to ten millions, and they propose a uniform rate of tolls of Two Dollars and-a-half per ton. This would realize an annual gross income of 25 million dollars, and, even allowing liberally for cost of maintenance and working expenses, the net encome, after payment of interest on bonds, would necessarily be large. The Stock would doubtless be so good an investment that the Government might be tempted to exercise its option and take the 75 million dollars deposited in escrow at par, thereby rivaling ifnot excelling its purchase of Alaska, whose munificent revenues and intrinsic value are historic and of world-wide repute, but whose sources of wealth are not yet even guessed at. much less developed.

And what would be the effect of the opening of Nicaragua Canal upon our Coast trade as well upon the Nation's traffic?

It would diminish, by over two-thirds, the distance between San Francisco and New York, and nearly one-half between San Francisco and Liverpool. From San Francisco to New York, via Cape Horn, the distance is 14,840 miles; by the Nicaragua Canal it would be 4,946 miles; an astounding difference and saving of 9,894 miles. From San Francisco to Liverpool, via Cape Horn, the distance is 14,690 miles; via the Nicaragua Canal it would be 7,694 miles—a saving of 6,996 miles.

Such a saving in distance--it requiring less than one-third the time—for vessels to go to New York via the Canal than by the Horn, and but half the time to Liverpool, would imply so large a saving in time, cost of transportation and insurance that it would revolutionize our commercial intercourse with the East and Europe, restore the American flag to the trackless deep, and hasten the happy day when all the nations of the earth will yield the palm and join in praises of our Golden State, the richest in climate and productions of all the nations of the earth, and the paradise of the world.

Truly the Canal would be worth more to California than a new Gold discovery rivaling the Comstock in its palmiest days, and it behooves us as Bankers in Convention assembled having the interests of our great State at heart to memorialize Congress and extendour influence for the passageof the bill. Concerted action on the part of the Banks, their Customers and friends will materially assist and hasten, if not accomplsh, this great undertaking, thereby marking another epochin our Commercial history; prove a glorious monument to American enterprise and energy and a be benison and blessing to all mankind.

Second to this great National undertaking, which will redound more particularly to the advancement and prosperity of the Pacific Coast, there is a broad field of labor spread out before us in the enactment and repeal of State laws. Such stumbling blocks and barriers to progress, the investment of foreign Capital and general prosperity as the Chattle Mortgage and Mortgage tax laws should not cumber out Statute books.

The improvement and perfecting of methods of assessment and collection of Taxes, County and Municipal, should not be delayed. Demoralized credit as the direct result of the Law's dalays, cost of legal proceedings, Homesteads, Exemptions, &c., is a problem, which should receive our greatest consideration, and the solution of which means prosperity to all business interests. The urgent need of a simple, practical, economical, National Bankrupt law and the Future of National Banks are subjects which commend themselves to our sober, serious attention. Apart from Subjects of National and State Legislation are those relative to the Government of our own Banking Institutions, due consideration and discussion of which are just as assential and important to preserve, maintain and increase their usefulness. The list of suggestive topics submitted by the Clearing House Committee, together with many others not mentioned therein come within the scope of our proposed Association.

In fact our consideration of all questions and issues of a public character in the solution of which, all classes are vitally interested will necessarily strengthen the trust of our people in Banking Institutions; restore that degree of confidence we really merit and to which we are entitled by the relation we sustain and the vital assistance rendered to the business world in the hour of darkest gloom as well as the brightest sunshine, and utterly annihilate and destroy the baseless charge of monopoly so frequently hurled at Banking Institutions.

At the conclusion of the addresses, and after a pleasant half-hour spent in social converse, the reception closed. The chamber had been decorated with bunting and presented a handsome appearance. The Harmony Orchestra composed of fifteen talented young musicians, discoursed most agreeable music during the evening.

Chamber of Commerce Rooms,

THURSDAY, MARCH 12th, 1891.

MORNING SESSION.

Hon. E. F. Spence, President Los Angeles Clearing House:—
Gentlemen of the Bankers Convention: The hour for convening this Convention has arrived, it being now ten o'clock, and it becomes my duty in carrying out the the program to call the Convention to order, and proceed with the business before us.

A. L. Seligman, of the Anglo-Californian Bank, San Francisco, moved that a committee of five on credentials be appointed by the chair. Carried.

The chairman appointed the following members as such committee on credentials:—

A. L. Seligman, of the Anglo-Californian Bank, San Francisco,

W. F. Bosbyshell, of South. California National Bank, Los Angeles,

W. D. Woolwine, of First National Bank, San Diego,

Norman Rideout, of The Rideout Bank, Marysville,

W. W. Phillips, of Farmers Bank, Fresno, and

Lovell White, of San Francisco Savings Union, San Francisco.

A. D. Childress. of the City Bank, Los Angeles, moved that the chair appoint a committee of five on organization. Carried.

The chair appointed as such committee the following:—

A. D. Childress, City Bank, Los Angeles,

G. W. Kline, First National Bank of San Francisco,

J. S. Cone, Bank of Tehama County, Red Bluff,

Stoddard Jess, First National Bank, Pomona, and

T. S. Hawkins, Bank of Hollister, Hollister.

Upon motion of W. W. Phillips, of Fresno, duly seconded, E. F. Spence, First National Bank, Los Angeles, was elected temporary chairman, and Geo. H. Stewart, Los Angeles County Bank, temporary secretary of the convention, pending the report of Committte on permanent organization.

C. E. Palmer, of Union National Bank, Oakland, moved that the chair appoint a committee of five on consiitution and by-laws. Carried.

The chair appointed as such committee on constitution and by-laws:

C. E. Palmer, Cashier Union National Bank, Oakland,

R. H. McDonald, President Pacific Bank, San Francisco,

R. M. Widney, President University Bank, Los Angeles,

Wm M. Eddy, Pres. Santa Barbara Co. Nat. Bank, Santa Barbara,

Geo. H. Bonebrake, Pres. Los Angeles Nat. Bank, Los Angeles.

H. D. Colson, of Fresno National Bank, moved that while waiting for reports of the various committees, some of the papers mentioned on the program be read, as they might suggest ideas for the Convention to discuss. Carried.

The Secretary, Geo. H. Stewart, then read the following paper, written by Mr. Frank Miller, of the National Bank of D. O. Mills, Sacramento, entitled

NOTES VERSUS ACCOUNTS.

Banks are usually considered the especial agents of rich men; the contrary is the fact. A banker who has only two deposits of one million dollars each is not so happy as he who has one thousand deposits of $2,000 each. The first would have to keep on hand the entire sum awaiting demand at any moment, whereas the latter would find his deposits standing at an average the year through and thus be enabled to lend out part of that money.

It is equally well known that one thousand loans of $2,000 each will be better for any bank than two loans of one million each. The national bank statutes which limit a borrower to a sum equal to one tenth of the capital of a bank are good laws and the State laws should be amended to read likewise.

Bankers are common carriers of credits; and they are much like the great pipes and reservoirs which collect water from many small sources and distribute it in as many different directions and quantities. They can give out no more than they have received, and should ever retain a reserve for emergencies.

From reliable sources we can get three sets of figures which will state the financial situation in simple terms; these figures are not accurate but will lead to correct comparisons and conclusions.

Here they are:

For each man, woman and child in the United States there is—

  $20 of money,

  $200 of annual products,

  $2,000 of annual transfers.

In other words, to every family of five souls there should be found $100 cash, and $1,000 annual productions and $10,000 annual exchanges.

In ordinary times there is no demand for more money per capita than this pro rata of $20. In hard times the clamor for more is loud but it is like the call of a fever patient for water; the remedy for the disease is not indicated by the demand. True it is that cash and water are temporary alleviators of distress but the permanent relief must come from other sources. While we give water and quinine to the sick what remedy may we give to those oppressed by hard times?

The furnishing of more cash is difficult and sometimes leaves a dangerous complication in the financial system. To increase or diminish the annual product is equally difficult, and, indeed, the cry of over-production is seldom worth listening to. Nature regulates that better than man.

When we look at the item of annual transfers of $2,000 per capita we approach a subject where, in a limited way, bankers can do much good and can do no harm.

Most of these transfers are finally made through banks, and if we can improve our machinery and keep it well oiled and do twice the amount of exchanging at the present cost, we shall help stagnant trade to move and make the nimble sixpence fly on its rounds still more swiftly. We shall win the same praise as he who makes two blades of grass grow where only one has before been seen.

Our methods are still largely the same as one hundred years ago. True, we do not use quill pens and we do use envelopes instead of sealing the tail end of a letter over upon the top. In California we do not have the same economy in the use of coin and money as in the Eastern States and in England. There payments at bank are made by check to the extent of 98 per cent, and but 2 per cent of money is used of which much is paper money. Here we doubtless require five times as much coin to make transfers.

There bills of exchange and promissory notes promptly close out ledger accounts, and being negotiable the fabric of credit is quickly adjusted among those able and willing to carry such burdens, leaving to the producer his own task of dealing with men and materials and not with accounts.

In short, we bankers must extend the note system and try to make ourselves the bookkeepers and cashkeepers and the collectors of the community.

To produce this result there should be united action.

If the annual products are $200 per capita, and the annual transfers are $2,000 per capita, a rough guess may be made that these products are turned over (that is re-bought and re-sold) say six times each year and on thirty days credit for each turnover, thus giving an estimate of a continuous line of debt of $100 per capita the year through. It is known that the debts of the governments and the railroads and the mortgageors much exceeds $50 per capita, so that the burden of total debt per capita may be about $200. Anyhow, in a State of one million souls the commercial indebtedness may be something like one hundred million dollars, and much of this recorded on ledgers where its handling is an infinite source of trouble and expense. Larger profits are necessarily charged by the owner of a ledger, yet he finds himself unable to negotiate a loan on the book in case of his own distress.

If the accounts were frequently drafted into the form of notes the amount of circulating medium would be increased at will according to the demands of business.

There is a great deal of delay and friction in the keeping of book accounts, even in the best form, as will be seen from the following illustration:

The national banks publish reports for the same instant of time all over the country; these are collated by the comptroller and show debit item "Due from National Banks" and a credit item "Due to National Banks." The items should offset but as a matter of fact the amount charged against banks is usually some twenty millions greater than the other and this sum represents the remittances in the mails etc. The sender charged them when they left his hand and of course the consignee has no knowledge of them.

At the present time notes of hand payable at a future date are not so generally used in this state as they should be. Competition in business is responsible for much laxity in our rules of business.

Another reason exists in the fact that the holder of unmatured paper is at some disadvantage in case of fraud or insolvency as compared with the holder of book account.

An attempt is making before the present legislature (1891) to remedy this, but through the apathy of the Boards of Trade, no result is likely to follow.

At the risk of appearing revolutionary, the following legislation is suggested as the remedy for some of the things which should be improved, and as good for both debtors and creditors.

Let the codes be so amended that interest shall not be collectable on debts, save where security is given, and then only to the limit of the security in hand; but permit discounting.

Governmental debts would have to be excepted also; but for debts between individuals, unsecured, allow no interest to be collectable at law.

The result of such legislation would be the closing of long and indefinite accounts by the writing of non-interest bearing notes due on definite dates. Interests for the delay would, by agreement, be made a part of the principal and the note thus written would sell from hand to hand at current rates of discount.

The good fashion of drawing sight drafts or drafts due on definite dates would be enlarged. As legislation is not to be expected, the same result could be had largely by public agreement between banks to charge no interest on over-drafts and past due notes.

Under these plans the field of money loaning would be vastly increased, and a currency of negotiable paper would be available according to the varying volume of trade, and more ease and benefits would follow than from any proposed free coinage of silver. The necessity for some expansibility of credits was clearly stated by a merchant of Hong Kong who said that the future of California was limited by reason of her financial system and for other reasons; he knows that the finances of China and Japan are managed in London which is farther away than San Francisco.

It is the true principle of commercial banking to buy paper made by the purchaser of a definite lot of goods and given to the seller and endorsed by him to the banker.

The security of the lender is increased because the maker uses the goods to pay the note; if the wisdom of the seller in selecting his risks is found to be reliable, then the banker will take as much of that kind of paper as possible. Dull and improvident merchants will be drilled into better habits by the open quotation of their demerits in the market for negotiable paper.

Bankers stand between their depositors and their borrowers. They promise much to their creditors and must demand much from their debtors. Twenty

five years of experience have led me to agree with the words of an old banker
which are used as a motto by a bankers magazine and which runs as follows:

" No expectation of forbearance or indulgence should be encouraged. Favor
and benevolence are not the attributes of good banking. Strict justice and the
rigid performance of contracts are the proper foundation."

After the conclusion of paper and some discussion upon it the Committee on Credentials appeared, made partial report and asked for
further time to complete their work. Leave granted without objection.

I. W. Hellman, President of the Nevada Bank, San Francisco,
moved to adjourn until one o'clock to give the Committee an opportunity to report and several representatives an opportunity to be
present at time of report who have not as yet arrived in the city.
Carried. Adjourned to one P. M.

AFTERNOON SESSION.

The convention was called to order by the Chairman promptly at
one o'clock, and the committee on permanent organization made their
report. Adopted as follows:

Your committee on permanent organization beg leave to submit the following
report, to-wit:

We would respectfully recommend the formation of an association to be known
as THE CALIFORNIA BANKERS ASSOCIATION. Officers of said association shall be
hereafter agreed on by the convention, and we recommend that the present temporary officers be declared the permanent officers of this convention.

Respectfully submitted,

A. D. CHILDRESS, Chairman.
G W. KLINE.
T. S. HAWKINS.
STODDARD JESS.
J. S. CONE.

Upon the motion of R. M. Widney, of Los Angeles, the report of the
committee on Constitution and By-laws was taken up and acted upon
seriatim, after which it was adopted in its entirety.

[See Constitution at end of Proceedings.]

R. M. Widney then gave notice that he would to-morrow introduce
the following resolution :

Resolved, That this convention respectfully request Congress at its next session
to devise a uniform money system for the people of the United States, with the
gold dollar as the standard unit of value ; using gold, silver and currency for a
circulating medium, in a sufficient volume to fully meet and keep pace with the
growing wants of the business of the country ; founding the issue of currency upon

the wealth of the whole nation, making gold, silver and currency a legal tender and exchangeable at par on demand; fixing by a constitutional amendment the legality of such a circulating medium, and preventing the dangers of inflation, contraction, repudiation, or change in the standard of values.

A. Gerberding, Bank Commissioner, here read a paper on

"THE DUTIES OF A BANK COMMISSIONER."

It has been said that a bankers convention is a clearing house of experiences and opinions, relating to the financial interests of the state.

The clearing house, for checks, is recognized as indispensable, and now, after our Eastern sisters have long set the fashion, you are about to establish a clearing house for ideas.

It his high time, and the query naturally arises, why does it take California so long to adopt modern methods?

Your freight crosses the country between two Sundays; your news annihilates space, and yet it takes years for an idea to come from the older to the younger.

Is this because the Rocky mountains are a natural barrier between us and a more enlightened civilization, where are concentrated the great capital and reserves of thought, incident to age, population and wealth? Is it because we are so dull that we cannot absorb new ideas, or have we a natural pioneer abhorrence of anything new, simply because it is new?

Why should not California, more blessed than any other part of God's domain, be the leader, rather than the follower?

Perhaps we have had too much done for us, and are loth to do for ourselves.

Here nature bends to the smallest effort, while beyond our borders everything must almost be torn from her resisting embrace, and yet, see what has been accomplished in the great Northwest by the effort of a people whose main weapons have been modern methods and advanced ideas.

At last you assemble in bankers convention, and where? not in the metropolis, (where in the minds of many, the water still comes up to Montgomery street), but in the one city of California, where there is enough public spirit to undertake a new and large proposition, and where the citizens are willing to lay aside personal affairs; to relinquish for a moment the individual battle; to forget the great I, and join hands in some effort for the general welfare.

You are to be congratulated, citizens of Los Angeles, that you have taken the lead, and it is to be hoped that your good intentions will be accepted in the spirit in which they have been extended, and that you inaugurate here a useful and long-lived institution.

A suggestion of the desirability of a bankers convention appeared in the last report of the bank commissioners, and a few observations from that branch of the service may therefore be in order.

"The ideal bank commissioner has been described as a man of intelligence, integrity and experience. His habits and character should be such as to make him a welcome visitor to the banks managed by officers most exacting in these regards.

"He should be firm as well as courteous, exacting proof without expressing doubt, and withall so discreet, as to be safely trusted with the knowledge of those confidential relations, existing between the bank and its customers. Upon occassions he must be firm, prompt and self-reliant, not hesitating to assume grave responsibilities, and he should be capable of imparting information, without seeming officious, and to so conduct himself at all times, as to establish the most agreeable relations between the banks and himself."

I would add to all these rare qualifications, that he should be a broad-minded business man, which implies tact and that most uncommon attribute, common sense. (It is to be hoped that the ideal banker will be as fully described during these proceedings.)

Could you find, in one individual, all these qualities; you would have a perfect Bank Commissioner.

But alas, men are not made perfect and even good men are scarce, and so long as the office is subject to the methods of our political system, we cannot expect men to be selected solely for fitness, as other qualifications are unfortunately too often deemed paramount.

The law requires that no two commissioners be appointed from the same county, which may be upon the supposition that no one county could produce more than one man fit for the office. This hypothesis is perhaps borne out by the fact that this County of Los Angeles has twice furnished a commissioner.

The law further provides, that at least one-third of the commission shall be an expert of accounts, a somewhat vague requirement, which probably also implies the keen scent of a detective.

We are neither experts nor detectives.

If such work is required it is for the bank directors to furnish.

The general public, however, views us in this light, and the threadbare question is "did you find the cash all right?"

When the cash is alas too often but a very small percentage of the total resources, how little bearing has it upon the one great question, the *solvency* of the bank.

While its quantity may often affect the immediate condition, it is but a small factor in the ability of a concern to meet its liability, which is the main desideratum for the consideration of a commissioner.

We have been asked, if we knew of any method to prevent defalcations; as well ask us if we knew how to make all men honest.

To this question we answer, let the directors do their duty.

Many bank directors are guilty of criminal negligence wilfully remaining in the fullest ignorance of the bank's affairs, having no appreciation of their responsibility and never aware until disaster overtakes them, that they are morally and legally liable, first to depositors and next to stockholders.

These two parties to a bank often confound their positions; the depositor believes he owns the bank and the stockholder thinks it is his.

Neither is correct. The stockholder says to the world, I have put my money where it is safe; now you put yours in and I will take care of it for you.

But in the great law books, hidden in thousands of calf-bound pages, there is written, the Bank Commissioner shall care for the depositor and see that the stockholder does what he promises to do and if he does not, he shall repay to said depositor all of the sheckels he has received.

For this reason does the Commissioner go wandering about the face of the earth, examining, who? the owners of the bank, the stockholders. He examines their work as done for them by the directors, through the bank officers.

Stockholders often say "we are glad to meet you, gentlemen, for now we know everything is O. K." And perhaps it is, but there are solvent banks, whose stock you or I would not buy.

The stockholder may say, "what then is the bank commission for, if not for me? To protect my interests?" He forgets that his business is the caring for other people's money, for which service they pay him, and how well they pay him, you know, and the bank commissioner is entrusted with the grave responsibility of seeing that the banker does what he advertises to do, take care of his patron's money.

The funds of the stockholder, however, being so identified with those of the depositor, the commissioner in his service to the latter, incidentally assists the former, although the capital and reserve of a bank are the fortifications between danger and the depositor; the greater they are the safer is the depositor.

The whole duty then of a bank commissioner pertains solely to the solvency of a bank, and the law certainly does not intend that he shall pry into petty details or meddle with peculiar methods of book-keeping.

The law requires at least one examination annually, and this is perhaps sufficient, for within that time objectionable practices can be stopped and bad business cancelled, or unloaded upon some ambitious competitor and thus assume the form of new business, with the natural strength of youthful vigor.

A very marked improvement in the services of the commission could be effected, by abolishing the semi-annual statements, required by law January and July 1st, and adopting the national plan, of requiring them for some past date, but only twice annually.

The main feature of this change would be, that it would eliminate the extraordinary and somewhat unnecessary accumulation of funds in order to make a grand showing Jan. 1st, that annual congestion for which our legislative quacks have been prescribing in vain.

It would also assist in the general work of the Commission, by necessitating the constant maintenance of a proper condition, as any day might bring forth a public statement.

In pursuing his duties, the Commissioner has as his main aid the honesty and ability of bank managers, and in most cases these elements render the work pleasant and easily accomplished .

If perchance the former be lacking, the work of the best Commission may go for naught, but an absence of the latter, while perhaps bringing equally serious results, can be supplied in one way or another.

While the banks of California are all in good condition and fulfilling their functions in a proper way, satisfying depositors and pleasing stockholders, the law is technically violated, the bankers and commissioners know it, and yet the question arises "what are you going to do about it?"

If the commissioner insists upon the actual letter of the law, he may bring unnecessary hardship; he may drive business from the state banks whose servant he is, and he may render himself disagreeable and accomplish no good.

These are not his functions and his excuse, if indeed be need any, is that many laws made under other circumstances and conditions, are not applicable or practicable for to-day.

However, there are many questions, not legally stated or defined, arising in the pursuit of the Commissioner's work, which are difficult to answer. A Com -

missioner's knowledge of the exact status, the people and conditions in any given locality is of nece ssity far inferior to that of the local banker, whose business it is to know the character, value and even the pedigree of all his customers.

The Commissioner may find first-class directors and stockholders borrowing heavily; he may note certain parties apparently accommodated too generously ; the cash reserve may be too low; dividends may have been declared out of funds that might have been better applied to the surplus; banks may be rediscounting, all of which must be admitted are undesirable practices, but any one or more of them may be encountered in the best of banks, and yet who can determine as between the honest and capable banker who knows his locality, is in touch with all his immediate surroundings, and who takes the risk, and the Commissioner who drops in casually.

A proper examination and final comprehension of all the attending circumstances is the duty of the Commissioner.

The cordial relations existing between the bankers and this commission, warrant the possible egotistical remark, that the services of the board are recognized as a useful factor in our state system, and that the purposes of the law have been faithfully and honestly executed.

When the public clamor, in their just indignation, that the political household is overcrowded with servants, that extravagance is fostering destruction, it is indeed a gratification, even a privilege, to be identified with a department against which no word of complaint rests, and which we believe and hope has the unqualified endorsement of that most potent element in the development and progress of our state, "The Bankers of California."

A. D. Childress then read a paper written by Mr. James A. Thompson, Cashier Mutual Savings Bank, San Francisco, entitled,

"COMMERCIAL NOTE SYSTEM VS. OPEN ACCOUNTS."

In nearly all the State commercial banks it is usual to allow the regular customers to borrow money by overdrawing their accounts. In National banks the practice is prohibited by statute. In the former the officers consent to the method, if indeed they do not actually invite it—in the latter to tolerate it is to commit a felony. It is true the revised statutes passed to control the National associations in this particular, were caused by and directed against flagrant abuses in some of the New York banks, but the laws are there, like the sun, shining on the just and the unjust alike.

The legislative opposition was caused by a custom of certifying the checks of stock brokers for sums not at the time to the credit of their accounts, but to be made good during banking hours. With these checks enormous blocks of stocks were handled, a clearance, as it were, settling matters at the close of each day. A volume of business, impossible if actual money had been used, was transacted, finally reaching dangerous quantities, and causing the Government to interfere, and hence, because abused, the privilege of offering to customers a convenient form of facilitating everyday business transactions was abolished by law. It has been stated that certain National banks have retired in consequence, adopting the State form of banking.

In the National system the law prohibits the certification of the customer's check unless the amount be actually at his credit on the books. To so certify even a check drawn inadvertently in the ordinary course of business is a violation of law. An attempt to evade by "accepting" checks that could not be "certified," was prosecuted and condemned. Assuming that checks that cannot be certified nor accepted cannot be paid, it follows that any over-drafts are unlawful. Notwithstanding the interdiction of the Government, the banks repeatedly report them, it is true, almost without exception in sums that are inconsequential, showing that the banks prefer to infringe the law rather than refuse to pay the checks of customers.

What is there in the legitimate use of the system of overdrafts to condemn it?

Confining our attention to the granting of overdrafts in reasonable amounts to acceptable borrowers, instead of calling for their respective notes of hand, the persons chiefly interested in banks and their practices are the bankers, the depositors, and the borrowers. It is sometimes hard to decide which of the three classes is of the most importance in considering the welfare of the concern, but we will begin courteously with the depositors. The overdraft system is a benefit to the depositors, for, as we will attempt to show hereafter, the toleration of overdrafts compels the bank to keep larger reserves than if confined to the promissory note system, decidedly an advantage to all the creditors of the institution. Another point claimed to be favorable to overdrafts, is that all sums so advanced are call loans, and subject to payment on demand, and this circumstance has the tendency to create confidential relations between banker and customer not so likely with promissory notes. The argument is used that the nervous, shifting character of overdrafts quickens the apprehension and intensifies the relations between banker and borrower, far less likely when promissory notes constitute the only way of raising money, for they may be offered to comparative strangers and in numbers of places.

As opposed to these alleged facts, it is hard to point out any imperilment necessarily incidental to the use of overdrafts as opposed to promissory notes.

It is true, in the minds of many people the feeling prevails that the former is a loose and unbusiness like method of transacting banking, and the expression "over drafts without security," has passed into circulation to an extent sufficiently great, possibly, to effect in occasional instances, the minds of some depositors. But all this is modified when subjected to analysis and comparison, for, as a matter of fact, "promisory notes without security," are no better off, and no worse than overdrafts. In other words, a discussion between the two systems is a question of manner, not matter, and if the security of depositors is assured, the way of doing business may be safely left to the banker.

Turning next to the borrower, the overdraft is advantageous for many reasons. He is charged interest for his actual drafts on the bank, getting the full benefit of his unpresented checks until the last moment, while his deposits go to his credit instantly, diminishing the amount he has at interest. The books at the bank rarely show the full amount he owes the bank, and he really borrows more than he pays for. Often he obtains an accommodation which he does not use, the money lies idle, and the bank bears the inconvenience or the strain. To such an extent is the method an advantage, that many operators refuse to do business with a bank that declines to pay their checks overdrawing without notice, even carrying the point so far as to secure the privilege in different towns, and in banks in which they never leave deposits.

The objections to overdrafts must exist, if they exist at all, among the bankers, and that is precisely where we will find them. With the banker there is absolutely nothing to recommend the system, unless it be the wish to be accommodating, while there is much to condemn it.

Cash reserves must be maintained in careful proportion to the number of overdrawing "patrons" and the amount each is likely to want. This means a state of uncertainty that can only be made tolerable by extraordinary cash balances, and at all times demanding a vigilance that may be called eternal. Loans are not negotiated at the cashier's desk, and completed by the note clerk, but materialize through the paying teller. It lies beyond the power of mortal man to tell what a day may bring forth. Just as the various red ink figures becomes familiar they disappear, only to come again, until the manager wonders if the bookkeepers are all right, and if forged and other irregular checks are not creeping into the business. Money borrowed by overdraft is certainly worth as much as one per cent more per annum, but the banker is not always so fortunate as to get it. From a bank bookkeeping point of view, the overdraft is objectionable, highly so, for loans obtained in that way must pass through the depositor's account in the ledger, thus mixing up the bank's creditors and debtors, or, if we may use the expression, its depositing depositors with its borrowing depositors, and as balances only appear the true liability to depositors is obscure in many banks, disappearing altogether in those where the overdrawing depositors exceed the depositing, presenting the curious feature of depositors, as depositors, owing the bank money.

The overdraft system does not present the securities of a bank in such a shape that re-hypothecation is possible, while the promissory notes can be readily transferred. Whether this be an advantage or a disadvantage, depends entirely upon the way you look at it.

It is often suggested that the open account operates to permit borrowers to encroach upon the bank, obtain more than the amount originally intended to be loaned, finally ending in disaster, not likely under the short note system. Possibly, but this depends rather on the temper of the management than on the form employed to accommodate the customer.

As between open accounts and promissory notes, it may be concluded that depositors are indifferent, and that the advantages to the borrowers are more than an offset to the disadvantages to bankers. When the protecting arm of the Government interfered in the National associations it was supposed, doubtless, that the interests of the public were involved, but as a matter of fact the enactment seems more especially calculated to benefit the banker, if it results in abolishing overdrafts. In the State banks, no laws operate to prevent them. That the bankers would like to stop the practice may be taken for granted. Two causes render efforts in that direction weak if not actually useless, namely, the deep-rooted hold the system has upon a large number of valuable customers, and secondly, the want of unity of purpose as among the bankers themselves, due, undoubtedly, to the competitions of business.

A paper was next read by **W. W. Phillips**, of Fresno, entitled

GRATUITOUS WORK DONE BY BANKS.

Upon this subject much may be said, but I shall not attempt to enumerate the many things done by Banks without remuneration.

Were I to ask the many bankers present for their individual experiences in this kind of work, no doubt we should all be much surprised.

I shall point out what I consider the most important items of this gratuitous work done. For instance, I do not believe that a Banking institution in the State, gets sufficient pay for the collections it makes. In many cases it gets no pay at all. As an illustration of this fact, a bank receives a sight draft, drawn on a merchant with exchange who happens not to be a client of that particular bank. The collection clerk after registering the collection, starts out to collect it.

Possibly he has made two visits before he has found the merchant in his office. The merchant upon examination of the draft, declines to pay, for the reason that he does not pay exchange, as he gets that free of charge at the bank with which he has his account.

The collection is returned after the two repeated efforts to collect, with the reason of non-payment, the bank being loser the time of its collection clerk, postage and stationery.

And again, how many collections are received, and an effort made to collect, and finally returned unpaid at the bank's expense.

Now if it is proper to charge for those collected, why should it not be proper to make a charge for those uncollected? If the Bank has performed its duty, it has made an earnest and strenuous effort to make the collection. In fact, more actual work has been done than in the collection of those which were promptly paid.

For this work a proper charge should be made, otherwise at the end of the year the bank has lost money in the collection business.

A promissory note is left by a client for collection; it is usually one of the doubtful kind and no doubt the holder has exhausted his individual powers to collect. To hand it to an attorney would cost him ten per cent of the amount of the note but his banker will make the collection for a nominal fee, possibly not charge him anything at all.

If he is charged more than one or two dollars for collecting a note of one thousand dollars, he complains, and thinks it too much. There should be some regular charge for services of this kind, equitable and fair.

Collections of checks received from the San Francisco banks and correspondents are made for nothing.

Why should this be so? I have never had a satisfactory reason given.

It cannot be argued that the city correspondent does similar service without remuneration, as such work is not in proportion; besides, the city bank has the benefit of the deposit of all sums collected, and no interest allowed on credit balances.

I think it within the power, and one of the duties of this Convention to consider these matters, and if possible to arrive at some method of correcting this condition of affairs. I think it a proper time to call a halt on the gratuitous work done by Banks.

By consent of the Convention, and out of the regular order of the program, J. M. C. Marble, National Bank of California, Los Angeles, read a paper entitled,

"GOVERNMENT LOANS ON REAL ESTATE AND PERSONAL PROPERTY."

GENTLEMEN:—The assembling of business men to consider what relates to business interests is a hopeful sign, leading as it does to a comparison of views, and thoughtful consideration of subjects, which accomplishes much good, because subject to the friction that comes from difference in views. If commendable in any profession, it certainly is in that of the banker, who is the custodian of that, which has so much to do with the development and well being of a people,

Bankers usually care to have little to do with politics, yet when questions relating to finance become prominent, and fallacies are promulgated, that might prove, if received, a general misfortune, they are hardly excusable for remaining silent.

The press of the day is full of propositions based upon the idea of the Federal Government turning general pawn-broker, and embarking in the loaning of money to all comers at two per cent. on land or personal property.

Such schemes, favored by men of influence, high in the councils of the nation, and powerful in politics, may gain the impetus of a movement to build up a new party, that in the flush of its first victories might carry them on to success. The spasms in politics, that cause attempts to build up new parties, usually soon run their course, the harbinger of success being in the enthusiasm of the first effort, therefore the necessity of early and careful consideration of measures thus brought prominently before the people, before the small streams of public opinion have united to carry everything before them.

Why the government should in its favors, give preference to those, who by incompetency, imprudence, waste or over-speculation become involved in debt and give or loan money for a small part of its value of its use, rather than grant its favors to the large and deserving class of people, who need work and will suffer and perish without it, by supplying them work at a loss, or selling them them the necessities of life for one-fourth or one-half their value, is a question to consider.

The impolicy of the government going into the cedula business and becoming a national pawn-broker, needs no better illustration, than the object lesson presented by the recent events in the money markets of the world, and especially of London. The states of the Argentine Republic of South America were rich in fertile lands that, in the opinion of the people of that country, only needed the fructifying effect of wealth, to bring to them greater prosperity. To their minds no plan seemed better to accomplish this end than that of securing plenty of money at low rates of interest, through government co-operation; hence the cedula scheme, by which a man possessed of real estate, could make his mortgage at a moderate rate of intesest, with a proper margin, and after so doing, turn his mortgage into the government, and borrow the money at low government rate. The government, to recoup itself, would issue its own obligations against such cedulas. The scheme, on its face, looks feasible or more feasible than any hitherto presented, and yet the results have proven very disastrous, bringing on a crisis that shook England to her center, and vibrated through the whole commercial world.

They, like us, have the gold and silver standard, and have evidently endeavored to meet the clamor of the people for more money in the issue of their currency. As a result, their paper money is now worth only thirty-four cents on the dollar in gold, which causes articles worth a dollar in gold to sell for three. Labor is scarce and the wages of artisans have not been increased in the same ratio, so that those depending on their labor for a living find it very difficult to buy even the necessities of life.

We can get some hint of what would come to this great country were she to enter into this sort of speculation, when so far reaching a crisis was produced in a country of much less importance. The whole trend of such legislation would be, to tax the frugal, industrious, successful and saving people, to pay for the losses to the government, from the extravagance of that large class of people, who have not the faculty of living within the means they create, but Micawber-like, are always ready with their bills, living on the hope that something will turn up to help them out, rather than to help themselves.

Another illustration of the impolicy of the government loaning its credit, comes nearer home, viz; the large loans to the so-called Pacific roads.

After receiving a large subsidy in lands, they were granted a credit of $16,000 per mile in government bonds on the valley sections, and as high as $96,000 per mile in the mountain sections. This magnificent grant was soon abused, and we had early the scandal of lengthening the lines, in cheap construction localities and certifications of mountain sections, too near the bottom of the valley or the sea. The original bill provided that the government should be secured by a first mortgage on the property; but influences were early brought to bear to change this to a second mortgage. While their builders have arisen to be among the wealthiest people of the earth, we see them refusing to provide for the credits by which they arose, striving by all means to repudiate or stave off, or compromise these credits. Does not such a history raise the thought that if we are to make such advances, it is hardly worth while to make the interest two per cent. That for all practical purposes, the loans might just as well be considered bonuses, as it would hardly be worth while to spend any good money in endeavoring to collect them.

Another question, bankers should consider, that is prominent in politics, is free coinage of silver on a ratio of sixteen to one in comparison with gold, when the markets of the world say that the difference is twenty to one. This has narrowly escaped becoming a law, in a republican congress, and it remains to be seen, whether the next congress, a democratic one, will adhere to the principles of the former great lights of that great party, or succumb to the clamor of the silver mill owners, who want the government to buy their product above the market value.

I take it, all are in favor of plenty of money, and yet, I question whether any would favor its being so plenty as to drop to the value of base metals. In such a discussion it is well to consider what money is, a measure of value, acknowledge that, and it follows that the measure, to be just, should be as stable as any measure of quantity or injustice will follow. All, I take it, are willing to admit that a frequent change in size of the bushel or pound would not be a thing to commend, and yet the bushel or the pound measure but few things, while money really measures all things; by so much, therefore, the impolicy of this measure.

Money without full intrinsic value is fiat money. Of course to those that believe in fiat or imaginary money, the argument advanced will have little weight; but the fiats of the Continental Congress of the Southern Confedracy or, for that matter, of our own most powerful government, whose notes, while declared by law the equal of gold as legal tender, dropped to 33 on this coast, show that, no difference whence derived, it is about as effective a means of maintaining values, as the Chinese method of pounding gongs to dispel eclipses.

So long as silver and gold maintain a parity of value, and are readily interchangeable at their declared ratios, little objections will be found, but when the United States, which only contains probably 1--25 of the population of the world, shall say to the remaining 24--25 that the two metals shall be equal in value on a basis of 16 to 1, whilst the opinion of that much larger number is, that it is 20 to 1, your fiats will fail, and the preferred metal emigrate to other climes, where it is better appreciated. This, I take it, would hardly be acceptable to a state that has always given the preference to the yellow metal, and last year produced from her mines $9,896,851 of gold and but $1,865,263 of silver.

All understand that the present silver legislation is very valuable to the producing localities, Colorado and Montana, which produce over 3-5 of the out put of the United States. All are willing to do them full justice, but why should the great mass of the people be forced to buy their product above its real value in the markets of the world, and build ware-houses to store it in? If desirable to popularize the silver dollar more as money, why not put into it sufficient weight of the metal to make it the equivalent of the gold dollar, which is the favored metal, not only of California, but of the most enlightened nations of the world.

We have an illustration of this preference in this city. It is understood that taxes are not gold contracts, and I understand that some certifications of checks have been in silver. Why? Because it is the cheaper and less desirable metal, it being an axiom in finance, that, in time, the poorer money will drive out the better, when the endeavor is to circulate them at even value.

Further—I think the gentlemen present will bear me out in the assertion, that should any bank of this city turn out silver generally over its counter instead of gold, it would soon find its business departed, unless all adopted the silver standard. What I wish to emphasize especially, now, is, that if we are to have for our measure of value, a thing that we must handle by the ton, and that is the favored metal of the Chinese and Asiatics only (whom this coast does not otherwise seem to greatly appreciate or affiliate with) that we should not place on it a value, which every other intelligent people says is wrong. Let us act on the grandly Democratic principle, that the voice of the mass of the most intelligent people of the world, is the voice of Omnipotence and Right, and not permit ourselves to be misled by the term dollar. Were it dropped from our vocaulary, and in its stead were we to speak of so many grains of silver, or so many grains of gold, a better appreciation of the situation would be likely to follow.

This is a more serious question to California than to any other country. Here the rule has always been to use the real thing—gold—rather than its representative. Legislating gold into hoards, or out of the country, would, necessitate a change in monetary modes, or cause contraction of the circulating medium that would greatly reduce values.

The latest statistics I have before me show that there was on Nov. 1, 1890, $634,010,286 gold coin, and $458,134.057 silver coin in the United States.

A very slight premium will cause the entire volume of gold coin to disappear from circulation. This is much the larger as well as the preferred part of our metallic money, and this is a time when there is such a general cry for an increase of our circulating medium. Is it wise to take any chances in contracting the best part of our money, by driving it into hoards or out of the country, in exchange for our securities, held by people of other countries, who will fear our dropping to silver payments? Germany alone, could return to us enough of our securities to about exhaust our entire stock of gold, and she is but one of many countries, holding our securities in large volume, that believe and prefer to believe, an ounce of gold worth more than 16 ounces of silver.

This silver agitation has already given us some experience in what we may expect from hoarding. On July 31st, 1890, there was in the United States treasury and New York Banks $264,259,000 in gold coin. On December 27th, 1890 there was but $227,252,000 gold coin in these depositories. Between these dates there was very little loss by exports, proving that this large sum of our gold coin amounting to $37,304,000 had passed out of circulation and into hoards. If the disappearance of such a sum, not 14 per cent of the holding of the New York banks and United States Treasury, aggravate a pressure such as we had last fall, what is likely to be the result if, by bad legislaton, we drive all our gold coin out of circulation? Continue such a drain as I have referred to, but a short time, with no limit on silver coinage, and you bring the country to silver payments. This means that instead of using the golden yard measure of plump thirty-six inches, as now, we will drop our standard by introducing the silver one representing less than twenty-eight inches.

The production of silver is very rapidly increasing. In 1873 the entire production of the world was 63,267,000 ounces, at the present time, the United States is producing over 50,000,000 ounces, a quantity nearly as large as the world's production in 1873. At this time the world is producing over 124,769,000 ounces of this metal annually.

Montana alone, is expected, by some of her sanguine friends, to soon reach a much larger production, as large as the present output of the whole country. Over-production in the metals, whether precious or base, has the same result as over-production in other things. Their value is depressed, and the difference between gold and silver widened. The cause of this great increase is the large profit made in its production.

The average cost of silver from best authorities attainable is :

     In the United States not to exceed...................52 4-10 per ounce
     In Mexico not to exceed ....37 per ounce
     In South and Central America........................34 5-8 per ounce

The Broken Hill mines of New South Wales produced in nine months last year 17,000,000 ounces of silver at a cost of 16 cents per ounce. If we were to take this large production of their silver at the price proposed by free coinage we would pay those subjects of Great Britain fully $20,000,000 gold for what cost them some $3,000,000.

The government of Roumania has sold 25,000,000 ounces of silver recently to New York brokers, and has much more to sell. The Netherlands are also known to have sold 25,000,000 ounces to us. Europe is full of it, and they are ready to dump it on us, at every favorable opportunity, and take our gold.

The increased production of silver has been so great, that, to keep it in circulation, at the par of gold on old ratios, has caused all mints of Europe for the past twelve years to be closed to the coinage of full legal tender silver.

We hear much about France in these silver arguments. The fact is, that if we make no change in our coinage laws, but continue as at present, we shall soon have more gold and silver money in this country, than that favored land posessess.

The latest statistics I have seen place the gold coin of France at $900,000,000 and of the United States at $702,018,869. The United States stands next to France in the amount of its gold gold and ahead of any other nation.

At the same time France possessed of silver coin $700,000,000 and the United States, $482,051,346. No country possesses more silver money than France, except India, which has $900,000,000. China ranks with France, the United States standing next.

France for twelve years has coined no full legal tender silver, and limits the legal tender quality of her silver to fifty francs, (about ten dollars) between individuals, and 100 francs to the government. She finds this regulation necessary to retain the two coins in circulation, as money, on a gold basis.

If such precautions are necessary to France, the most successful country, in using the two metals interchangeably as money, is it not absurd to expect that we can maintain gold payments, and our gold coin if we embark in free coinage of silver in unlimited quantities, making it redeemable in treasury notes, that are legal tender for all debts public and private?

I have heretofore referred to the disposition shown in this vicinity to pay taxes in silver. No man will pay gold, when it is more profitable to pay otherwise. He will buy silver, coin it, and pay treasury notes, a legal tender for all debts.

The money circulation of this country was increased last year $100,000,000 and is now being increased at the rate of $5,000,000 per month. To the extent that this is silver, the government is making the difference between the cost of the metal and its coin value.

The profits to the government from coining silver for the twelve years prior to June 30th last, have been $65,698,057.41. This large profit goes to the people, and to that extent lessens taxation.

If free coinage had been in existence, this large sum would have gone to the comparatively few men, who own silver mines, and to their Wall Street partners, who are booming their stocks. Are not the profits of the silver producers sufficiently large already?

By their own showings their products in the United States average a cost of but little more than fifty-two cents per ounce, which they are now able to sell at nearly double that price. Is there any good reason that the people should be compelled to buy all the silver-men can possibly produce, whether they want it or not, at about two and a half times what it cost them? Are their profits not large enough without asking the people to give them such a bonus as taking all they can by any possibility mine at 129 20--100 per ounce, when no other par of the earth want their product at 100!

All history shows that the market value is determined by the judgment of the world, and not by the laws of any one nation. There is no good reason that the people of Colorado and Montana, aided by Nevada, that produces but little, but two senators one, representative and silver sentiment, should ask the government of the United States to pay a higher than the market price for the commodity which the government wishes to purchase for common use. If it is not the desire to treat the metallic money as at present, by so regulating it, that the government can maintain its interchangeability, we should protect the standard by the other mode, that is by making the coin equal in intrinsic value by changing the ratios, so that the dollar, whether gold or silver, would be of equal value in the markets of the world.

History has but one tale to tell of the effect of lowering standards of value. The purpose is defeated, leading to bankruptcy, distress and at times overthrow of governments.

Of gold, 240 tons was operated on by our mints in 1889, and of silver, the last fiscal year, 4817 tons. Our present silver dollar contains 371¼ grains of silver. The markets of 1889 would have required that it contained 512 18--100 grains of silver to have been the equal of gold, while at present it contains but 371¼ grains, and the simple question is, whether this great difference between legal value and market value shall go to a few wealthy silver producers or to the whole people.

The last fiscal year our excess of exports over imports of gold and silver was $12,798,502.

There was consumed in manufacture $25,464,000.

Our production of gold was..	$32,800,000
Our production of silver was...............	64,446,464
Total production..................................	97,246,464

Leaving off our home products $58,243.902 to annually increase our metallic money without drawing on the mines of other countries.

Our coinage of gold last year was.............................	$22,021,748
And of other coins	38,232,688
Total coinage for the year...................................	60,254,436

On November 1st, we had a metallic circulation outside the treasury or $23 80 per capita, and our paper circulation was $1,004,200,553, nearly double that of the bank of France, which had $579,593,765 on December 31st 1889.

Money is simply a standard of value—a measure—as we have said. The impecunious will always be railing at its scarcity, and thus make public opinion. The popular sentiment on any subject, is, if not an argument, at least an influence not easily overcome, and if wrong in a land where public sentiment makes the law, causes imminent danger.

The real fact is that where legislation has yielded to such clamor, it has been found that money was never scarcer than when required by the cord, to purchase the common necessities.

No one objects to the silver pool keeping up a bureau at Washington. "But while the National Executive Silver Committee" sends its printed matter broadcast over the land, at a large expense, to popularize its views, and create a market for its product, the conservative people of the land should see to it, that no one product or business receives an advantage to the detriment of all other products or businesses.

What we want, is a sound and stable currency, of acknowledged value everywhere, not cheap and inferior money.

The larger part of the business of the country, estimated at eight-ninths, is transacted on credit. The Clearing House will show how little money is really needed. What we really need is better credits.

When you disturb the monetary standard of value, that measured credits, you cripple and demoralize business.

The government has no power to create money. Its saying a thing is what it is not, does not change the fact. Its duty is to certify the weight and purity of the metal contained in its coin.

The principle is false, that anyting the government stamps becomes money at what is expressed on its face, but many, so believing, create a cry for more money in almost every form but gold.

If the government can create money, why not create all that everybody wants, and thus save all from working for a living?

The attempts of governments to make money valuable beyond the intrinsic value of which it was composed, has always failed. The statistics of the nations are full of attempts to make paper, silver, copper, nickle, iron, leather and other things under the name of money, have an intrinsic value they had not. They always failed and always will, as there is but one power, and that Omnipotence alone, that can create something from nothing.

Stoddard Jess, of Pomona, moved that a committee of five, of which the Chairman of the Convention shall be one, be appointed as a nominating committee, to report to the convention tomorrow morning, to nominate officers of the Association for the first year and also the Executive Committee of the Association. Carried.

The Chairman appointed to act with him as such committee, the following: Stoddard Jess, of First National Bank, Pomona; A. L. Lincoln, of First National Bank, Santa Barbara; T. S. Hawkins, of Bank of Hollister, Hollister; Norman Rideout, of the Rideout Bank, Marysville.

Moved that the delegates from each county represented, be requested to select a vice-president from their county between now and tomorrow morning at 10 o'clock and that they present the names to the Committee on Nominations. Carried.

On motion the Convention adjourned until tomorrow morning, Friday, March 13th, at 10 A. M.

FRIDAY, MARCH 13TH, 1891.

The convention was called to order by the chairman at 10:30 A. M. with a full attendance of delegates.

R. M. Widney, of Los Angeles, offered the following:

Resolved: That it is the sense of this convention that the construction of the Nicaragua Canal would materially aid in the commercial and financial prosperity of the Pacific coast, and that we request congress to enact such legislation for the construction thereof, as will secure the construction of the canal, in the interests of the people of this coast as well as of the United States. Adopted.

Wm. Beckman, of Sacramento, at this time introduced the following motion:

" That we take up the question of the mortgage tax at our next general meeting as to whether it should be abolished or maintained." Carried.

At this time the nominating committee appeared and made the following report:

The committee on nominations beg leave to submit the following report:
For President, Thomas Brown, of the Bank of California, San Francisco.
For Vice-President, I. W. Hellman, of the Nevada Bank, San Francisco.
For Secretary, Geo. H. Stewart, of the Los Angeles County Bank, Los Angeles.
For Treasurer, G. W. Kline, of the First National Bank, San Francisco.
For Members of the Executive Council:
    A. D. Childress, of the City Bank, Los Angeles.
N. D. Rideout, of the California State Bank, Sacramento.
Wm. M. Eddy, of the Santa Barbara County National Bank, Santa Barbara.
T. S. Hawkins, of the Bank of Hollister, Hollister.
A. L. Seligman, of the Anglo-California Bank, San Francisco.
C. E. Palmer, of the Union National Bank, Oakland.
Lovell White, of the San Francisco Savings Union, San Francisco.
W. D. Woolwine, of the First National Bank, San Diego.
W. W. Phillips, of the Farmers Bank, Fresno.

The committee would recommend that the members of the executive council determine the length of their respective terms of office, whether for one, two or three years.

J. B. Lankershim, of Los Angeles, moved that the officers named be elected by acclamation. Carried.

Upon motion the report of nominating committee, as read, was adopted by acclamation and the officers named above declared elected.

R. M. Widney, of Los Angleles, now read his paper entitled:

INCREASED VOLUME OF CURRENCY.

Mr. President and Gentlemen of the Convention :—

In addressing you on the subject of this resolution I wish to say in beginning that the statistics presented in my address are gathered from official reports and public sources. You are at liberty to draw your own conclusions from them.

BANKING.

Banking is a science based on natural laws. There is very little chance in it Carried on pursuant to these laws it succeeds: If these laws are violated to that extent, loss and failure occur. It is as much one of the d partments of civilized society as law, medicine or statesmanship. It is under obligations to society to keep this department of the social fabric in good working order. It is not a robber of society, nor a machine to transfer the property of the many to the few. It should so handle money as to enrich humanity, as well as the bankers. In fact the law is that bankers flourish best when the whole community or nation is most prosperous. Banking should be a great power to build up the industries of the people, in establishing manufactories, planting vineyards and orchards, cultivating and improving farms, building cities and railroads and establishing commerce for the nation.

Banks should be a place where the unused money of the people can be safely kept and under safe rules of business, loaned to those who want it for legitimate safe use. Among these should be classified as of first importance, time loans to develop the industries and productive enterprises of a community.

No system of call loans or thirty or ninety day loans can develop the resources of a country. Who can plant a farm, vineyard, orchard or start a manufacturing enterprise, or build a railroad on a call loan or on ninety day paper?

Such loans can only be used in stock or speculation and to a limited extent in established retail business. Speculative enterprise should rarely receive loans from depositors' money. By such I mean all cases where property is bought on a margin or on part payment, to sell on a rise of the market. Persons thus dealing should be confined to the use of their own money.

As society delegates this financial power to bankers, and pays them for using it, they in return should scientifically, historically and systematically study the subject and solve the money problems of society so as to upbuild the Interests of society and protect its property.

Would not society cry out against its doctors and lawyers, and statesmen if they failed to solve the problem of their department?   Can we not here find the real ground for popular complaint against banks?

STORMS.

Financial storms periodically sweep over not only our own country, but over the nations of the earth.   They seem to come locally about every ten years, and internationally and generally about every thirty years.   In recent decades, as the world increases the rapidity of its growth and development, the storms increase in intensity and frequency.

The wreck of the last financial storm in the United States was frightful.

The failures were over.....................	$190,000,000
The shrinkage in New York stocks and bonds was over.....	300,000,000
Shrinkage of values in the United States over..........	10,000,000,000
Because the banks wanted more money they forced in loans to an amount of over.....................	100,000,000
The United States Treasury paid out over...........	200,000,000
The banks then issued panic certificates to the amount of....	30,000,000
And the United States Treasury deposited with banks to help the situation	30,047,118

Gold was also shipped from England and California to help the situation in the east.   Yet on top of all this one of the National Bank Examiners told me in the early part of last December, while in an eastern city, "*That they did not dare to examine the Banks as they could not show the required reserve.*"

In the face of this condition of affairs eastern bankers and financiers opposed any effort to increase the circulating medium of the nation.

Our eastern banking brethren treat with supercillious, and caustic airs of politeness, our western efforts at banking and our views on finances. But I take pleasure in congratulating you bankers of the Pacific coast, for so managing your finances and forecasting coming events that it has not to be said of you that the government had to come to the rescue to prevent a general suspension of the banks under your care.   Your banks furnished milllons of money to help your eastern brethren through the crisis.

There eastern banks were all solvent.   Their assets were greater than their liabilities, but they did not have circulating medium enough for themselves and for the legitimate industries of their localities.

There was not enough money to go around by hundreds of millions. While the people had the money the banks were hard up, and when the banks got it, then the people were hard up.   And now that the banks have it failures are constantly occurring in long established firms for want of more money.

The cause of this insufficient supply of money is

GROWTH OF CIVILIZATION.

The world has been progressing in civilization, in commerce, industries and in business with wonderful rapidity during the past century and especially during the past fifty years.

Russia has broken its lethargy, and is restless with energy. Asia has thrown off its isolation and its population half awakened from a dream of a thousand years is stretching forth its hands. India is contending for its ancient glory. Africa is showing to the world its rich fertile soil, its rivers, its gold and diamonds, and treasures for commerce and agriculture. All South America is organizing for civilized growth and work with its wealth of soil and mines to tempt the industry of man.

The islands of the sea from the almost continent of Australia to the little islands are becoming active struggling centers for their part of commerce. The business area of the United States in less than a century has spread from the small territory east of the Alleghanies, to an empire extending across a continent from some 3,000,000 to 6 ,000,000 people now scattered over 3,400,000 square miles and overflowing with business, energy and push, eager to develop the resources of their continent and prepare it for the habitation of the coming hundreds of million. The whole earth is rapidly being prepared for the comfortable occupation of man.

The world is constantly outgrowing its appliances for civilization. The circulating medium of exchange is no exception to the rule. All hitherto adopted forms of money have been outgrown in kind and in volume.

The skins of wild animals at an early age were the money of exchange. This was outgrown and they stored the skins, cutting off the ears and passing them as a more convenient form of money, the owner being entitled at any time to call for the corresponding pelts. This was the first bank of deposit. At a later age stamped pieces of leather were the evidences of value, gold and silver not being enough in volume. The Chinese have used paper money for thousands of years past.

Drafts, certificates of deposits, promisory notes and orders for money were used by the ancients to increase the volume of the medium of exchange.

Because we do not know what others have done, we frequently believe that what we are doing or propose to do is a novelty in the world.

In this process of evolution the financiers of the present day may learn two things. *First* that money is a compact representative form of values, without regard to what the money is made of for the purpose of exchange.

Second, That the world periodically outgrows both the kind and volume of its money.

THE WORLD'S DEMAND FOR MONEY.

As a result of this outgrowth there must be periodical contractions of values from a scarcity of money. That is, business must be killed off until it is reduced to correspond with the volume of money, unless the volume of money is increased to take care of the business. The volume is constantly expanding, but not as rapidly as the growth of the world requires.

The demand is far in excess of the supply, as shown by the following calls for loans.

Austro-Hungary	$100,000,000.
France,	182,000,000.
Mexico,	40,000,000.
Argentine Republic	500,000,000.
Other South American States	725,000,000.
African mines, Trust Companys, Etc	350,000,000.
	$1,897,000,000.

Other nations want as much more. The debt of the nations of the earth was, in 1889, over $28,000,000,000.

The volume of business in the United States alone last year is computed at some $130,000,000,000, while the business of exchange of the whole world was many times that amount. You see from this the work put upon money to make exchange.

The value of gold and silver in the United States is about $1,153,194,404. Of this $128,622,489 are locked up in bank reserves. The sum of $652,905,727 are reserved in the United States treasury; another $100,000,000 is locked up as state, county and city taxes, leaving the small sum of $272,666,188 in coin to do the work of the nations' business of $130,000,000,000. If gold alone were used, there would be only about $200,000,000 in circulation. This would be only $3.50 per capita, and could not possibly move the business of the nation. Add to this gold and silver the paper money in circulation outside of the treasury and bank reserves, and there are only about $900,000,000. This sum fell so far short of being able to do the work that the December, 1890, report of the Comptroller of Currency shows that checks, drafts, certificates, and such evidences of money, to the amount of over 92 per cent of the business, were used in 1890, aggregating the enormous sum of $18,000,000,000, *in banks alone, to supplement the use of our legal money*. Book credits and notes were several times this amount.

This eighteen billions was the worst form of inflation. Back of it was only personal and corporate responsibility, and only a deciminal of a cent on the dollar in lawful money to meet them.

People lost confidence in this vast volume of checks, drafts, etc., and then the panic came. People did not lose confidence in the legal tenders of the nation. This was accepted on sight, and a demand existed for millions more. Confidence was not lost in the lands, and cities, and industries of the people. It does seem to me that financiers who talk against government paper money should, in view of these facts, forever hold their peace. If there had been in circulation millions more of United States paper money the panic would never have been heard of.

A GLUT OF $20,000,000 !

Another evidence of the insufficiency of the money supply is the condition of the New York banks at this date, March, 1891. They claim to have a glut of money—a surplus of $20,000,000 over the required legal reserve. This is the result of calling in loans from the channels of trade. It is not money returned voluntarily by the users of money. It can all be absorbed in a day by the places from which it was called in.

But the most startling fact disclosed by this boasted glut, is that there is not enough money in all these banks over the legal reserve, to even *start one railroad* company. The best railroad enterprise with gilt edge security would absorb this boasted $20,000,000, in building its first few miles of track.

On December 19th, 1890, the secretary called a report from all national banks in the United States. They average less that 2 per cent above the legal reserve. Which leaves in the *whole national banking system of the United States only about $50,000,000 for use*. Of this sum $30,000,000, is United States Treasury money deposited in banks to help them make the December showing, and to relieve the financial change. No wonder the business of the nation is paralyzed. It becomes apparent from these results obtained from official reports, that the banks in the United States dare not loan any money on time loans to develop or maintain the industries and business of the people.

CALL LOANS

Can only be used on short speculation. What business man in the United States can start a manufacturing industry, build a railroad, plant out an orchard, or raise a crop on a *call loan*? The $50,000,000 surplus in the United States or the $20,000,000 surplus glut in the New York banks, is only so because the banks dare not loan it except on call, and no legitimate industry can use it on call. A loan for 30, 60 or 90 days is but a trifle better than a call loan. It can only be used by merchants and traders to tide over while collections are being made, or for stock speculation. The industries and productions and large enterprises of the people can only be met by time loans, and not by short loans.

The alarming fact is that if the money was returned to the United States Treasury that belongs there by law, and if from the banks also was returned the tax money that legally belongs in the public vaults, there would not be enough cash in the banks to meet the required reserve. They would not have a dollar to loan *even on call*, but would have to force in millions more of money from already cramped enterprises.

Nothing but the cool level headed sense of the American today prevents a run on the banks in the United States. If it gets started what will be the results in view of these facts?

In the trouble of the Baring Bros. Lord Salisbury refused to give the government consent to allow the Bank of England to furnish aid. Thereupon the Governor (President) of the bank said to him, "*My Lord, I am instructed to tell you, in case you refuse, that unless the government comes to the rescue, there is hardly a bank in the united kingdom that can be relied upon to meet the demand of its creditors twenty-four hours after the disaster we apprehend.*" Lord Salisbury jumped from his chair as if shot and at once consented to the relief.

The banks of the United States are in a condition bearing too strong an analogy to the above incident. Not only today but for a long time past they have been powerless to carry the time business of the nation, and with only call or 60 day loans to offer it became a mockery to those wanting to use money.

No wonder the people say kill off the banks, of what use are they. And too true, of what use are they except to keep matters from being worse.

Yet they are not to blame. They have not the money with which to carry the business. It is not in the country. The remedy is not to destroy the banks, but for the nation to furnish enough money to carry on the business of the growing country.

CALLING IN MONEY.

Because Russia wanted her money she called $80,000,000 from the Bank of England; and she needing more money called in and borrowed over $700,000,000. The banks in the United States needing more money called in hundreds of millions of dollars, issued $30,000,000 panic certificates, and borrowed of the United States and of each other millions more.

THE CRASH.

Because this money was called in from the channels of use and trade people could not make payments in money. The result was a crash of unheard of extent.

The failures reported	$190,000,000
Shrinkage in stock, New York	300,000,000
Estimated shrinkage of values in the United States in other property	10,000,000,000

In addition to this the business enterprises of the United States are to a large extent crippled or closed down. Over 160,000 are out of employment in New York city alone.

THE SITUATION

at present as to the 8055 banking institutions in the United States, national, state, private and savings is as follows:

Due depositors	. . $4,603,844,157
Total cash in all the banks at same date;	
Gold coin	99,811,011
Silver, nickle, etc., ...	28,811,478
Paper momey	349,694,405
Total, ...	$478,316,694

Ten cents on the dollar on hand to pay depositors !

In gold only about 2 cents, or in gold and silver about 3 cents on the dollar.

At this same time the banks had loaned out to the people $3,893,957,799. Among 62,000,000 people scattered over 3,400,000 square miles of the United States were only $957,746,248 with which to pay this loan Only about 25 cents on the dollar. Most of this money was in the hands of those who do not owe the banks, and is held by the owners to run their current expenses. Probably not 10 cents on the dollar available to pay banks. Yet the wealth of the people is some $71,000,000,000 in property.

THE DEMAND.

Some idea of the demand for money may be had from the fact that over $10,-000,000 were used in 1893 to start new banks in the South; as much more in the .

West. The cotton crop was valued at $400,000,000. Over 17,000 *new* enterprises started in the South last year, embracing every variety of industry. Over 32,800 miles of railroad were built the last four years, at a cost of $3,000,000,000. New New York city used $300,000,000 in new buildings, while the West used money by the millions for its new enterprises, many of which are shut down for want money.

This wonderful growth and energy is not to be condemned. It is the preparing of this continent for homes, and for the support of the generations. All of these aids for civilization are to uplift humanity to its high and peerless destiny.

It furnishes labor, food and clothing for the poor; it furnishes use for raw material, and results in industry, home and happiness for millions.

The principal non-productive use of money in the United States is stock and other speculations growing out of call loans. Were this stock speculation constitutionally destroyed, as California destroyed it, and its operators forced to embark in some legitimate calling, it would be a lasting benefit to the country.

TO PAY LABOR.

He who carries on any farm, orchard, dairy, manufacturing, or any other productive enterprise, must have a circulating medium with which to do it. The owner of an enterprise cannot pay laborers daily in portions of an interest in the products.

He can borrow money on his property, and in this way produce, and sell, and repay the principal and be free of debt. But he must have money and time.

VOLUME REQUIRED.

This question cannot be accurately determined, but we are not therefore to leave it wholly undetermined. Approximation is all that can be attained.

Generally the volume should be such that the United States treasury could hold a safe reserve of say twenty-five per cent of the volume issued. So, also, that the banks could hold a twenty-five per cent reserve of deposits, and also that tax money could go into its legal vaults. An estimate might be added for hoarding and loss by accident. In addition to the above reserves there should be a full volume in circulation among the people for the business of the nation. A volume such that time loans could be abundantly supplied.

More specific figures would be suggested by the following statistics:

State and National banks have deposits . . . . $2,516,179,807.
    Take this as the volume of issue and we have, say:
Twenty-five per cent for United States treasury . . . . . 629,044,951.
    "   "   " Bank reserves . . . . 629,044,951.
For tax money . . . . 114,072,288.

    Total reserve . . . . $1,372,162,190.

Taking this sum from the proposed volume there would be left $1,144,017,617. If the above reserves were deducted from the present volume of $2,082,568,942 it would leave only $710,406,734. The increase for active circulation under the proposed volume is $433,610,883. In other words, the country would hold the last amount named to protect business, instead of the present paltry $50,000,000, From this volume the business requiring time loans could be safely supplied.

This is not an experimental volume. It would represent about forty dollars per capita for our population, while France uses from forty-two to forty-four dollars per capita. We could safely use a larger volume than France does.

NOT ENOUGH GOLD AND SILVER.

The gold in the United States represents only $694,869,680 or $11 per capita. The annual increase is about 25 cents per capita.

The total amount of silver is about $485,370,497 or $8 per capita. The annual increase is about 74 cents per individual. Gold and silver would therefor give only $19 per capita and about 85 cents per capita annual increase. The total volume of gold and silver in the world is only about $5.75 per capita of the world's population.

THE SILVER QUESTION.

Free coinage of silver therefor cannot accomplish the desired results. The annual increase of our population is such that the coinage of our entire national silver product would only give $20 per capita for our increase. It will in no manner relieve the standing need.

The great objection to free coinage is that our annual product is worth in the market $46,000,000. When coined it represents $64,000,000 or $18,000,000 profit added by the Government agreeing to pay that difference on demand. This makes a present of $18,000,000 annually to the producers of silver.

This is too great a local benefit to a class of persons for this to be adopted as a law, and it is wholly inadequate to meet the demand.

50 YEAR 2 PER CENT. BONDS.

This is simply a scheme to aid banks at the expense of the people, and seems to have had its origin and backing in the secret councils of those who wish to monopolize the money system of the United States.

Look at it! Its advocates say, issue these bonds and sell them, and redeem the 4 per cent bonds, and let the national banks buy the 2 per cent bonds as a basis of circulation. How will it work? Will the owner of 4 per cent bonds exchange even for 2 per cent bonds? Certainly not. Then if you sell the 2 per cent bonds at par and pay a premium on the 4 per cent bonds you will have to pay all the 4 per cent ones will earn up to maturity. We will then be paying 6 per cent instead of 4 per cent as now, *and that does not increase our circulating medium a dollar.* The people are simply saddled with *more interest.*

The sale of 2 per cent bonds to banks as a basis of circulation is a robbery of the people. To illustrate: The United States issues say $100,000 in 2 per cent bonds, you wishing to open a bank take $100,000 cash, *now in circulation,* and pass it over to the United States for the $100,000 in bonds. Next, you hand back your bonds, as *a deposit,* to the United States and get back your $100,000 cash for a bank capital, and *for fifty years the tax payers through the government pay you 2 per cent per year,*

$100,000 interest on the bonds for doing a banking business on your original $100,000. If you use the semi-annual interest to buy more bonds, so as to make it compound, you will at the maturity of the bonds have your original $100,000 plus $100,000 interest plus about $70,895 bonds bought with interest on interest, making a total profit of $170,895 for doing business on your own money. But during this fifty years your original $100,000 will be loaned out to the same tax payers who are paying 2 per cent interest on the bonds to you. This loaned out capital will bring in ruling rates which by the scarcity of money will be high. This with the profits arising from the periodical wrecking of the people ought to satisfy the owners of money. It will, however, engender the thought among the masses that the banks should be killed off. Our present banking capital is some $700,000,000. At the end of fifty years operating under this bond scheme the banks would own their capital stock $700,000,000 plus $1,196,265,000 interest on bonds, plus over $3,000,000,000 interest on the capital stock for fifty years. That is the banks will own all the money in the United States and have the people in debt to them nearly $3,000,000,000. You perceive at once that this scheme will not increase our circulating medium.

CLEARING HOUSE PLAN.

Another plan is embodied in a proposed national clearing house system to be incorporated under an Act of Congress, by which a confederation of banks can put up approved collateral with the clearing house and receive clearing house notes, to be legal tender, the combined clearing house being responsible for redemption in case the individual bank fails to redeem. This system is put forth by a prominent eastern banker who asserts that we need no more money. Yet this whole scheme is to increase the circulating medium, but *giving the banks a monopoly of issuing and controlling it.* Its weak point is in placing back of our currency no greater responsibility than the banks and their property. It also gives the banks the right to obtain money without interest and loan it on interest.

Better let the government issue the money with the resources and wealth of the whole people of the United States, valued at $71,000,000,000, back of it for redemption. If the property of a combination of banks back of a money issue is good, then the wealth of the nation back of the issue is better.

As a nation we want no money for the people which is only backed by the responsibility of a small part of the people having absolute control of it for selfish ends.

The circulating medium should be issued by authority of the whole population and should be backed by the entire wealth of the nation, and should be controlled for the common benefit of all. The 2 per cent bond system—the free coinage system—the national bank increased issue and sub-treasury plans fail because they are in the interest of localities and minorities. If temporarily successful they would soon be destroyed by the majority as unjust. Justice and equity to all must be at the foundation of any system adopted by our nation.

A NATIONAL SYSTEM

should be based upon a constitutional amendment prescribing what shall constitute our circulating medium, fixing its volume, establishing one standard of value and vesting in Congress authority to issue such money, making it a legal tender and backing it with the wealth, power and resources of the nation, making it exchangeable for gold at par at any time.

An amendment worded about as follows would cover the ground:

CONSTITUTIONAL AMENDNENT.

ARTICLE XVI. SECTION 1. A National Currency Circulating Medium shall be issued to the amount of twenty dollars percapita, as shown by the census of 1890 and by each succeeding census, for the proper redemption of which when required, the resources, the property and the faith of the nation are pledged; for which redemption, Congress, by a two-thirdsvote of each House, may provide for the collection of Government revenues and taxes, in gold or silver coin.

SEC. 2. Said currency, with gold and silver coin of the United States of present weight and fineness, the gold dollar being the standard or unit of values, and such notes as may be issued in lieu of gold or silver coin and bullion, held exclusively for the redemption thereof, shall constitute the only legal money of these United States, and shall be received at par in satisfaction of all obligations for the payment of money within the jurisdiction of the United States. Said gold and silver coin and currency shall be exchangeable at par value.

Sec. 3. Congress shall have power to enforce this Article by appropriate legislation, but shall have no power to increase or decrease said issue; provided that after the issue of 1900, Congress may, by a two-thirds vote of each House, reduce the rate of any further issue per capita from time to time.

This amendment, underlying our national system of finances would give us the best foundation and safeguards ever yet adopted by any nation.

The volume is protected against inflation, contraction or repudiation. It represents about two cents on the dollar of our national wealth of some 3,400,000 square miles of land and national wealth of $71,000,000,000. This is in legal effect a first mortgage given by the nation to secure redemption. With such security the national currency would be considered *gilt edge paper in any market in the world*. It would be received with greater confidence than Bank of England notes.

The gold dollar is today the standard by which all values in the United States are rated or measured, and as an abstract standard of values, this amendment removes from controversy or doubt that disturbing element by fixing the gold dollar as the standard of measure. It at the same time does full justice to silver, by making it and paper money a legal tender, with gold at the par value. In this way the whole people make the difference, if any, between the market value and the coined value, and when exchanged for gold, repay the difference.

This amendment would protect the currency against the dangers of the John law, or Argentine Republic scheme, and from the dangers that beset the Continental money. It is a greater safeguard than is thrown around the Bank of England notes.

No nation can place back of its issues such security as this would give to American money. England cannot place back of an issue the resources of Canada, Australia, India or her African possessions, for at any time they might leave England and set up for themselves, leaving only the little island to redeem the currency issued. France and Germany are to small. Russia is too insecure in her form of government. But the United States with its vast area, its peaceful and stable form of government, and its citizens, each an owner in the currency, is in position to issue a currency that would be received at once by any nation as a medium of exchange—a representative of gold at par.

Such a legal tender note is, in money effect, the clearing house certificate of the nation, backed by the national wealth, good in any clearing house in the United States, instead of a certificate backed by any number of banks, and only good where they wish to accept it by courtesy. It is a check signed by authority of the people of the United States, backed by over $71,000,000,000 of the people's wealth, good at any counter of any bank, instead of an individual's check, only good at his own bank and in his own locality. It is the promissory note of the nation, secured by a constitutional mortgage on over 2,500,000,000 acres of land and the cities, railroads and civilization thereon, payable to bearer and good from any debtor to any creditor, instead of the private note of a citizen, secured by a mortgage on a few acres of land, and only good at a discount to those who wish to buy it. It is a representative of value for exchange purposes, mutually agreed upon by 62,000,000 of people for their joint benefit, backed by their constitutional bond to secure redemption when required, on which bond the people pay no interest.

Such a currency circulating medium possesses all the elements of safety offered in all other proposed systems combined, and many others that cannot be introduced into any other system.

Confidence would never be lost in this medium, for the amendment would prevent Congress or politicians or political parties from disturbing the foundations, as at present.

AN ACT OF CONGRESS

to put this in operation would be substantially as the present law of June 3, 1864. The department of the controller of currency, the bureau of printing and engraving would remain the same.

The system adopted should be complete in itself, it should be as broad as the United States in its effects, it should be planned to extend through the centuries.

While by one department it gathered in the money annually by taxation and revenues, it should annually return the money to the people equitably in all parts of the nation, seeking to collect taxes and revenues from the rich, and largely returning it, through the laboring classes, to circulation.

This would be a system, whereas it is now chaos.

PRESERVE THE NATIONAL BANK SYSTEM.

A bank system in the United States is a commercial necessity. Every individual cannot erect burglar and fire-proof vaults to protect his money. Neither could he employ a set of clerks to keep his accounts and financial exchanges.

The banks to-day use the smallest floor space on which the business could be transacted, and also have their working force reduced to the lowest number. The work could not be done by the government with any less floor space, or with any less number of persons than are at present employed.

Nothing could be gained by destroying the present system, with all its organized and trained forces, and replacing it with any government scheme for commercial banking or loaning.

The scope and flexibility of the present system could be vastly improved by some arrangement, as the following :

Allow states, counties and cities, of say five thousand population or over, where they need money for public improvements, to issue 2 per cent bonds for twenty or thirty years to the amount of 5 per cent of the assessed value of the real estate. Allow the United States to buy these bonds, prohibiting any contest as to their validity after receipt of the money therefor. Let the Treasurer sell these bonds to any national bank wishing to purchase them, and allow them, or any United States bonds to be used as a deposit security with the United States Treasury on which to draw money when additional sums are required by the bank. The large reserve always held by the United States Treasury would be the fund from which this would be drawn, and to which this would be returned when not needed. This would give a perfect elastic currency to meet all contrac-ions and expansions of season trade. Real estate could also be safely used as a reserve, as shown under the head of Farmers' Alliance Scheme hereafter.

The economies of this plan are that states, counties and cities wanting to bor-row money and pay interest could borrow of the people who have the national money to loan, and banks could buy such bonds to use in their system.

Our system of national finances should be so arranged that the renewed sup-plies of money seeking loans in the hands of one class of people could be ob-tained by that other class requiring the use of money. This can best be done by our government, which is over 62,000,000 of people, issuing a full volume of gold, silver and currency, which is the property of all the people, to be used by them as a representative basis of values for exchange.

A large reserve held idle in its vaults by the government is for the benefit of the people, to be sent at one time (like a reserve force of an army) to the support of this place, and then to other places. This reserve system will meet all demands for an elastic currency.

The people, through the government issuing and holding this medium of ex-change for their own use and benefit, share its profits and losses for the commun-ity as a whole.

The only remaining point is to provide a proper means by which the people may obtain the use of this money as needed.

This must be done by banking principles, either by the government or by banks.

If the government attempts this work it will require as much floor space as th banks now use, and as many and as able employees as are now engaged by all the banks.

That a profit may arise, the banks are now run on the most economical basis possible, and the government could not therefore improve on the present bank system.

FARMERS' ALLIANCE SCHEME.

This scheme has some sound points in it. Land can be safely used as a secur-ity in the national bank system as well as bonds. Allowing the title to land at a valuation of, say, its averaged assessed value for the preceeding five years, and not to exceed one-half of its cash value, to be pledged to the government under the form of a national bank incorporation, would give relief to the farming com munities.

It would substitute a national bank for a sub-treasury; a set of bank officers elected by the farmers for their banks to manage the loans for a set of sub-treas-ury agents; a responsibility to the government for large aggregate sums under the bank laws, instead of the inspection of thousands of small changing loans. The supervision of the Bank Examiners under present laws as to the solvency of the bank would be all that was required, while the bank officers would supervise all detail business and loans to individuals.

Provide also for the first $100,000 drawn as above, the interest to the nation shall be 2 per cent. The rate increasing on larger sums as follows : 3 per cent, 4 per cent, 5 per cent, 6 per cent, 7 per cent, 8 per cent, 9 per cent, 10 per cent, on each additional $100,000.

The object of this is to prevent reckless drawing and using at low rates.

The lower rates will develope the legitimate industries of the country. The higher rates will check the wild, rash enterprises of speculation, and furnish means to carry on business with less profit or loss until adjustments occassion regular business routine.

This is the same principle applied the world over in finances. The Bank o England raised its rate of discount. So did other European financial institutions; The same thing was done in New York recently. It is the natural law on the subject for checking speculation without killing off legitimate business.

This plan is adopted in the recent German law establishing a system of more liberal and modern financiering.

The *London Times* says: "The whole monetary system of the United States is in a muddle. This condition is due to piece-meal legislation."

The shattered fragments of our laws from 1790 to this date should be repealed by a uniform system competent to handle our finances.

The national banks should be retained, but should be unfettered, so that they could do the most good.

POLITICAL FORECAST.

Next to personal rights, no question affects the voter more sensitively than the rights of property.

One of the most important of these is the increase in the volume of money.

The political party that offers a safe increase in currency to relieve the wants of the people, and carry on the business of the nation will be offering a premium for every vote. An increase of $20. per capita for 62,000,000 population is an increase of over $100 per voter.

The laboring classes and those borrowing money, with this as a leading issue, would vote in overwhelming majorities for such a measure in utter disregard of present party lines.

It certainly will be made an issue, unless one of the dominant parties shall pass such a law at the next Congress.

If the Democrats propose such legislation and the Republicans resist it, the next campaign and Congress will be overwhelmingly Democratic. Should the Republicans propose the law and the other party oppose it, the results will be in favor of the Republican party.

But if the present parties in Congress show the people how *"not to do it,"* by wasting the time in discussing insufficient, sham and subterfuge plans, to deceive the people, they will find the voters not in the least shaken in their firm purpose.

The most critical period in the history of present political parties that has arisen since the war will occur in the next session of Congress, and on this question of the increased volume of money.

The system of money adopted by Congress must be just to all the people of the United States. The power and authority for the money has its origin in the people, and must be so planned as to be with them a co-oporating power for the common good.

The homes and property of the masses today are in jeopardy by reason of the insufficient supply of money. The industries of the nation are seriously crippled, the further development of our productive areas are brought largely to a

standstill, the laboring classes by the hundreds of thousands are out of employment because employers can not get the money with which to pay for daily
labor.

We have a nation of 62,000,000 people, an area of 3,400,000 square miles
of the richest land in the world, a national wealth of $71,000,000,000. An
annual volume of business of $130,000,000,000. An intensely active, energetic
people; government annual expenses of over $1,000,000,000, and *only* $2,082,-
568,924 *as a circulating medium with which to conduct all this business.* This is
3 cents on the dollar for over national wealth, and 1½ cents on the dollar for
our volume of business. But if you deduct from the present volume, the bank,
the United States Treasury, state and city tax reserves, there will be left for
active business work, 1 cent on the dollar of our national wealth; ½ cent on
the dollar for our volume of business. If you still further confine the money to
gold and silver it gives for active work about ¼ cent on our national wealth,
and about ⅛ cent per dollar for our volume of business.

It lies in the power of Congress to make this the banking nation of the world.
But to do this our volume of money must be so increased that we have ample
reserves at the proper places, and a free volume of money for our use and to
spare in loans to other nations.

Today we are tributary financially to foreign nations. Over $50,000,000 per
year is paid out as interest and profit to foreigners for the use of their money, of
which over $1,500,000,000 is in use in the United States. Our own money is not
enough so long as we are compelled to get this foreign aid. The financiers of
other nations are calling in all the gold they can get. France, Germany, Russia,
Austria-Hungary, England, the South American nations and others are striving
each to increase its volume of gold reserves.

England is critically suffering in the contest and our own financiers forecast a
heavy drain on our gold to meet the balance of trade this year. It is in view of
such facts as I have cited in this address that Secretary Windom said in his last
speech of an increase in our money these warning words, "Could such a medium
be secured, the grave commercial disaster which threatens our future might be
averted, had it not been for the peculiar conditions which enabled the United
States Treasury to disburse over $75,000,000 in two and a half months last fall
the stringency would have resulted in wide-spread financial ruin."

Senator Sherman said in his recent speech, "I believe a majority of the Senate
desire, first, to provide an increase of money to meet the increasing wants of
our rapidly growing country and population, and to supply the reduction in our
circulation caused by the retiring of national bank notes."

Senator Sherman said recently in a letter to me on this subject, "I will do all
in my power to secure the very best possible financial legislation by Congress."

CONSTITUTIONAL DANGER.

One of the greatest dangers in our present law is the doubt as to the constitutional power of Congress to make paper money a legal tender. The United
States Supreme Court first decided by five Justices to three that Congress had
no power to make paper money a legal tender, Chief Justice Chase rendering
the opinion.

One of the five resigned, Congress increased the number of Justices from
eight to nine; the two vacancies were filled by men who joining the opinion of
the minority held that *as a war measure* Congress had power to make paper
money a legal tender.

This decision stood five Justices to four. Three more of the four have died, and their places have been filled by those who believe in this power, and in its latest decision our United States Supreme Court holds by eight to one that Congress can make any thing, *in any quantity*, a legal tender. In other words, the doors are thrown wide open to inflation of the worst form. Even now, are proposed measures that have no limit to currency issue. A future administration and Supreme Court could over rule the above decision and hold that the whole currency issued was unconstitutional and void, and was not even a claim against the nation.

Three dangers are at the very root of our financial laws, *ruinous inflation, constitutional repudiation and a threatened change of the gold dollar as the measure of values*.

A safe monetary system is one of the essential elements of the prosperity of this nation. It must stand before the people of this and other nations, founded upon, and guarded by constitutional power, protecting it from the dangers of inflation, contraction, repudiation, or change of the standard of values, and pledging the faith, and resources of the nation as the power and will of the nation to exchange gold, silver and currency at par on demand.

With such a circulating medium sufficient in volume to meet the present and growing wants of the nation, wisely administered by act of Congress, for the benefit of the people, we would enter upon a period of prosperity, development and safety never heretofore attained, one in which financial storms would seldom occur and which could be safely handled from the great reserve that should lie idle in the United States Treasury to meet local demands, here at one time, there at another.

This legislation is possible and probable.

Congress and the people are discussing and investigating and seeking for the best method. Notwithstanding all that is said to the contrary, honesty in the minds of our Congressmen on this subject is the uppermost thought. But they look to the bankers and financiers for facts and suggestions and knowledge. If they shall receive it, they will act upon it.

With these facts and views before me I present the resolution on this subject, as expressive of the views of the Bankers of this Convention on the subject. As such it will meet with a warm and welcome reception from our legislators in Congress, and will be carefully considered by them in molding the financial laws of the nation.

Upon motion of W. D. Woolwine, of San Diego, a recess was taken until 1 P. M.

AFTERNOON SESSION.

The Convention was called to order by the chairman and the secretary read a paper by A. L. Seligman of San Francisco, entitled :

PROTECTION AFFORDED BY CO-OPERATION.

This subject opens up a field of thought that promises an abundant yield of beneficial results, if carefully considered and cultivated.

Unlike any other line of business, that of banking affords greater opportunities for the perpetration of fraud than can be found in other channels, and as a result we are called upon constantly to exercise the greatest care and discrimination in the daily routine of our business, in spite of all which, however, we continue to be, to a greater or lesser extent, the victims of well laid swindles.

It is an undeniable and unfortunate fact that if we are not victimized to a greater extent than we are, it is because the average rogue is not familiar with the inside workings of our institutions. For obvious reasons I do not propose on this semi-public occasion to go into the details generally followed by banks in the usual course of business, but shall content myself with merely pointing out what I believe to be a most dangerous practice, and yet one which I believe to be, with few exceptions, the prevailing custom in the United States. I refer to the loose and careless manner in which depositors checks are handled, more particularly in connection with the surrender of such vouchers (as a rule) with out proper receipts or acknowledgments.

Whenever a depositor makes a deposit he obtains the bank's receipt for such deposit by an entry made in his pass-book. Against the fund thus deposited, and frequently in excess of such deposits, he draws his checks which in turn become the bank's only receipt or voucher for the funds thus disbursed. The practice now is, with few exceptions, to write up once a month the pass-book by listing therein the several checks paid during month, and to return to such depositor not only his pass-book, but the actual vouchers or paid checks as well, thus leaving the bank with nothing but a group of figures which cannot be identified with any particular check or transaction and without any actual evidence whereby it may maintain its position in case of question arising as to the payment of any particular check.

It is hardly necessary for me to point out the numerous opportunities thus afforded for fraud, and it has come within my personal experience, and I dare say within the experience of many of those present, that grave questions, and in some cases serious losses have arisen out of this most unbusinesslike method.

In the conduct of our business we are necessarily dependent, in fact almost entirely so, upon our trusted employees, and I submit that in the delicate ques_ tion of personal honor, we should not deprive such employees of the only means whereby, in case of question, they may maintain the correctness of their position and their personal honor, to say nothing of the important question of loss by the bank by reason of its inability to absolutely prove its case.

Having thus placed the subject before you, permit me to suggest a means whereby we may effectually overcome the dangers I have pointed out and rest secure in the positive evidence of our integrity and correctness.

The plan I have in mind is very simple, and yet so entirely opposed to established custom that I fully anticipate objections to it, but which objections I feel prepared to meet, and I may say right here that I shall be more than pleased if you gentlemen will one and all give me the benefit of your wide experience and mature judgement on this interesting question, as I do not by any means wish to convey the impression that I consider my proposition irrefutable.

To come to the point then, I would propose to discontinue the practice of surrendering paid checks, but to retain same in the bank's possession, subject at all times to the inspection of the maker and, in order that the depositor may distinguish checks paid one from another when checking his pass-book, I would suggest listing each check by its number.

The percentage of cases wherein it might be necessary for a depositor to actually produce a particular check would, I think, be found to be very small, perhaps one or two per cent, while the advantages to the bank under this system, may be readily realized.

The present system followed by the "Anglo" goes, as far as possible without co-operation, to protect itself. We take a receipt from every one to whom we deliver cancelled vouchers, certifying only to the *number* of vouchers received and at same time enclose with pass-book a blank certificate as to correctness of account which certificate we cause to be returned to us within ten days from delivery of pass-book. We keep a careful record of such acknowledgments and thus from time to time are enabled to know positively that our deposit accounts are absolutely correct.

I believe there are one or two others of our city banks who pursue a somewhat similar course, but in the majority of cases I think banks take no acknowledgment or receipts whatever.

This brings us to the point where "protection afforded by co-operation comes into play" for no one bank can of itself set at defiance well defined customs and it is only by united action that we can hope to effect radical changes, yet how easily we can, as a whole, institute such a change, is at once apparent.

Having thus drawn your attention to a matter in which we are mutually interested, I leave the subject in your hands for consideration, feeling fully assured that any action you may or may not take, will be productive of the greatest good to the greatest number.

I thank you for your attention and avail myself of the opportunity to congratulate this Convention upon its auspicious birth, which I trust may lead to a long and prosperous life.

J. B. Lankershim, of Los Angeles, read a paper entitled:

SAVINGS BANKS AND THEIR MISSION.

The savings bank is comparatively a modern institution. It has only existed since the beginning of the present century and its remarkable growth has been during the last fifty years. Though originating in Europe, they have been so improved upon in the United States that we shall confine our observations to the banks here, more especially as foreign banks generally embrace within their business all the features of banking, paying interest on deposits, loaning on real estate, as well as doing a commercial business. With us the saving banks have developed their remarkable influence because their policy has been so clearly defined and their business entirely separated from commercial banks.

When we see the progress our California banks have made, more especially those in San Francisco, it hardly seems possible that they are the result of the few simple principles of saving banks, viz: the requiring of notice from depositors; the limiting of the amount deposited by individuals and confining loans almost entirely to real estate. Our state laws, which are very strict, I regard as

B C -- 4

model ones in this respect. These facts are so familiar to all that I merely refer to them.

The idea to which I wish to call your attention is the bank as a financial educator. We are all familiar with the old story of the bank that don't make mistakes, yet while this is hardly possible, a high standard should be the motto of every bank both for its own sake and for its customers, for the business man regards his bank book as his chart to guide him through all financial storms. Especially is the savings bank the educator of the people. Our mission is to teach the great mass of the people that the foundation of wealth and independence is the saving of small sums. None so poor but he can have a bank account. Once let a young man begin to save money and you notice an improvement. One by one his bad habits disappear, he no longer takes an occasional drink, his step is firmer and his appearance better. At first he is satisfied with saving from wages, then the thought comes to him, can I not with my labor and my earnings, begin life for myself? Am not I able as the hundreds around me? Soon he launches out as a business man, and generally a successful one; so that the best customers of the savings bank becomes finally the best customers of the commercial banks. There is no doubt that this principle is recognized in the authority given to banks of over $300,000 paid up capital to do a general banking business. It being supposed that by the time they have acquired that amount of capital they will have sufficient experience to do a commercial business.

The good effects of saving banks extend beyond the individual assisting in business and in building up the community. Look at the Eastern manufacturing towns. Their prosperity and saving banks seem to go hand in hand; so much is this the case that for a long time it was supposed that saving banks could not exist outside of manufacturing towns; but now we see them prosperous in farming and many other communities. There is very little doubt that the prosperity of San Francisco is due largely to the amount of capital, nearly one hundred millions, in her saving banks, available at all times for every legitimate business. In that city the deposits of comparatively poor people has reduced the rate of money and made it comparatively plentiful in the whole state.

I believe that the growth of our banking institutions have been to a great extent the result of wise legislation; but would not our growth be much greater should we be more united.

The Bankers Union, such as we are now forming, has been a power in other states for years and we should avail ourselves of its benefits in a community like California.

While our banks today are considered in the front rank in the United States, yet our methods in many respects are crude and behind times. It is not enough that we lock our safe doors, put our hands in our pockets and say the banking institutions are solid. We all know that. But what of our undeveloped lands and mines? Where are the manufactories that we should have, and where are the fleets that should carry our commerce to earth's remotest bounds? These are questions that we should answer and problems that I hope our Union will aid us in solving.

Is it not possible by a union of bankers, standing shoulder to shoulder, to make the reserves we carry available for twice the business that we do now and as safely? Is there not adverse legislation that we can check, and new laws that will strengthen. I believe we stand on the threshold of a new era as bankers and in the next decade we shall see a prosperity unparalled in the history of the past.

John Milner, Cashier Farmers and Merchants Bank of Los Angeles, read a paper entitled:

TAXATION OF MORTGAGES.

Inasmuch as banking deals directly with the finances of the public, everything which pertains to or has the power to affect or modify the public finance, becomes of great importance to the banker. It is for this reason that the question of the taxation of mortgages becomes worthy of the consideration of an assemblage of bankers.

I cannot be expected to say anything new upon the subject, and I can assure you that in this regard you shall not be disappointed. The policy, or the impolicy, of subjecting the interest of the mortgagee in lands to taxation was elaborately argued in that memorable contest, which in 1879, lead to the adoption of the new constitution. It is therefore no longer a question to be argued, whether it shall be adopted or not, for the result of that contest must be accepted. For that reason I shall not approach this subject in any speculative manner, nor shall I endeavor to advance any arguments why a mortgage interest in lands should be taxed, or why, on the other hand, the mortgage should not be subjected to assessment. It is to give a further illustration of a well-known law of economics that I shall present this matter. All that we can do at present in regard to this question is to submit certain observations upon the results effected by the practical workings of the plan adopted by the new constitution. Before the adoption of the new constitution, it was a matter of argument and conjecture, the partisans of the measure asserting it would produce certain results, its opponents predicting that it would work in a different manner. Now that the system has had a trial of ten years, it is easily to be ascertained whether the results which were desired to be accomplished by the taxation of mortgages have been effected.

Taking the earlier history of California into consideration, during the days when the mining industry prevailed throughout the state, the question of taxation of solvent debts or mortgages, does not appear to have excited much consideration, either in the minds of legislators or of the people; but when it became plainly evident that the real wealth of California lay not in her gold fields, nor in her mines of ore, but in her fields and valleys; and when the pioneers of California left the search for wealth in the mountains and endeavored to accumulate that same wealth in the cities and upon the ranches, then the question of taxation of solvent credits was first agitated in the minds of the people. The result was no doubt precipitated by the action of the Supreme Court, in deciding what is well-known as the Hibernia Bank case. Shortly subsequent to the decision in this case, there came sweeping over the politics of California one of those sudden, unaccountable and almost phenomenal waves of socialism or agrarianism, which was typified by the sand-lot agitators. The cry went up throughout the land, that there was inequality of taxation, and the populace, as it always does, seeing that nothing but what was tangible was taxed, conceived the idea that that which was intangible should also be subject to paying its tax to the government. Among the incentives put forth for the adoption of a new constitution, none was more potent than the demand for the taxation of solvent credits. It permeates all the proceedings of the convention which framed our present constitution, and with that provision it was adopted by the people. The champions of the measure laid their claim to the suffrages of the people upon the propositions that by the taxation of mortgages there would be, first, a reduction in the tax, and secondly, an equalization of taxation. It was asserted, prior to the adoption of the new constitution, by those who were more conservative and who had been able to watch the course of such financial laws as were involved in the question, that the class of people for whose benefit the law was designed, would probably suffer most therefrom, and that the claim made on behalf of its partisans that the measure would reduce taxation, as well as equalize the same, would never in reality be effected. I deem it unneccessary to refer to the experience of each one of you as to which of the two parties has been correct in the forecast of the workings of the law. It was the desire of the framers of that part of the constitution to compel the mortgagee to pay his proportion of the tax. They endeavored to frame the measure in such a manner that it would be impossible for any mortgagee to make a contract with his borrower by means of which the mortagagor should pay the tax; and they left ample protection in the hands of the mortagagor to protect himself in case of the failure of the mortgagee to pay the same. It was an endeavor upon their part, to make lighter the lot of the laborers and the working men who were borrowers, and it was for the benefit of such people, the law was enacted. They were told again and again that they could make no law which could not be evaded, and that the result of their passage of such a measure would simply be the imposition of the burden of taxation upon the borrower, and the result has conclusively borne out the theory of the latter.

It is a fundamental maxim that the ratio between supply and demand will regulate the value of an article, and the value of the use of money, is no exception to this rule. Let the supply of money be greater than the demand and the price for its use will be low. On the other hand, let circumstances so effect the supply that it is much less than the demand, and the rate of interest, which is equivalent to the price for its use, will be high.

It is one of the purposes of this article to call attention to the futility of any law passed by any legislature to seriously alter, change or affect this fundamental law of political economy. You cannot legislate value into anything, nor can you by simply enrolling a statute upon the statute books of our country, overcome the established laws of trade and finance. This is abundantly testified to by the operation of the law in question, for men will lend money with reference to the amount of interest which they will obtain therefor, and if the legislature adds any penalty, the lender simply protects himself against it by throwing the imposition of the penalty upon the borrower. So customary has this became that now no borrower in this state negotiates for money without ascertaining what the amount of interest will be *gross* and what it will be *net*. It has crystalized into custom. Each borrower, upon making his application, does so with the clear understanding that the rate of interest specified in his note is a varying per cent higher than it otherwise would have been, had it not been for the taxation of the mortgagee's interest in his land. And every lender, before parting with his money has made a calculation of the amount of taxes that will probably be levied against the property, for the ensuing year, or during the time within which the mortagage is to run, and has added that amount of taxation to the rate of interest he otherwise would have been satisfied with. Nor am I here to admit that in so doing, even if it be considered that there is a technical violation of the law, that the act involves any immoral turpitude. The lender has the right to designate upon what terms he will part with the use of his money; it is for the borrower to say whether he will accept the same or not. And the custom which has been established, has in reality the sanction of public usage, because it is founded upon a principle which is really violated by the statute law, a right that a man may do whatever he may see fit, with that which is his own, provided he does not, by so doing, injure his neighbor.

As I have before stated, the very object of the demand for a new constitution was the passing of this measure, and it was strongly maintained on behalf of its champions that it was passed for the very benefit of the borrowers, the laborers and the farmers. In the ten years which have elapsed since the adoption of that constitution, the futility of the provision to accomplish the end sought for has been manifested each succeeding year, the act has not benefited any of the persons for whom it was designed; on the contrary, it has been a disadvantage to them: First, it subjects the borrower to a higher rate of interest than he otherwise would be compelled to pay. This is accomplished in this way; the amount which the lender always considers may be collected in the way of taxation, is arbitrarily ascertained by himself, and always fixed at such a per cent. that it will more than include the ordinary rate of taxation. This he must do for his own protection. As a consequence, the difference between the actual rate of taxation and the amount provided for in the mortgage, differs against the borrower. On large sums of money this difference often amounts to a considerable sum; the aggregate gain of course is for the benefit of the lender. Secondly; another disadvantage to the borrower is, that in many cases, his assessment is increased, and in no case, to our knowledge at least, has there been a diminution of his assessment by reason of a mortgage existing upon the property, that is to say, it has been the customary rule of the assessors throughout the state, never to assess property much higher than thirty per cent of its real actual cash value. Since the assessment of mortgages, the valuation has been at all events equal to the amount of the mortgage, and in many cases the valuation is a trifle higher in order to leave *something to be assessed* against the value of the land; and as we have seen, the borrower always pays the tax, he has been compelled to pay upon a higher valuation than if there had been no assessment upon the mortgage. At all events, it can with safety be said that there has not been any diminution of the borrower's assessment by reason of the existence of a mortgage upon the property. Third: another disadvantage, and although a matter of detail (never theless, what are are apparently minute details are often of great importance) is that the assessment of the mortgage complicates the assessment. The listing of property, its assessment, the payment of taxes, the equalization of assessments the collection of taxes, the sale of property for delinquent taxes, and the clouds which are created upon titles thereby, are all matters of great complexity. In a newly settled country like California, the facility of transfers of real property becomes of paramount importance. Whatever tends to check or hinder the facility of such sales becomes a detriment to the country. Now, if you will consider that the title to every man's property is affected once a year by taxation (and if situated within the city, you may consider that it is affected twice during each year; first by the taxation of the city, and second by the taxatton for the state and county purposes), you will see that it should be the policy of the law to render the imposition and collection of taxes as simple and easy a matter as possible, so that owners of property may, by a plain course of procedure, remove any chance for their titles to be affected by reason of the levy of the tax. Whatever complicates this question of assessment and collection, by so much is there a chance of the title to a man's property to be affected; and by so much will clouds cast upon his title by failure to observe the complicated regulations of the collection of the revenue hinder and deter transfers of real property. Now it is within the common observation of all who have had anything to do with this matter, that too often the borrower looks to the lender to hand in his mortgage interest in the property for taxation, and in many cases the lender assumes that it is the privilege of the borrower to inform the assessor of the existence of a mortgage upon the property, and then claim his reduction, between the two, the mortgage may not be assessed, and then it frequently follows that the borrower anticipating that the lender will pay all the taxes upon the property, fails to attempt to pay his taxes, and the lender, serenely regardless as to whether the mortgage is assessed or not, likewise fails to give any attention to the matter, and the property is sold for delinquent taxes.

Likewise, even if the reduction has been specified by one party or the other-there are *two* opportunities for men to fail to pay their taxes where there was *one* before, and this multiplies the chances of delinquency. Again, it frequently happens that the mortgage falls due between the date of assessment and the date of collection, and the borrower, ignorant of his right to deduct the amount of the tax collected upon last year's rate, pays off his mortgage, the mortgage is satisfied, and then, both parties considering that there is no mortgage interest whatever upon the property, no attention is paid to its assessment, and again the interest of the mortgagee may be sold for delinquent taxes. More over, at present, in the City of Los Angeles, by virtue of a local ordinance, the city taxes are payable one-half in November and one-half in May, giving two opportunities each year for the payment of taxes, and an effort is being made to engraft the proposition upon the collection of state and county taxes. This is in the main, no doubt, a most beneficial provision to tax-payers, but it will also increase this complexity attending the respective duties of the mortgagor and mortgagee in paying their taxes. There seems to be a certain percentage of heedlessness and carelessness in the members constituting the body politic, and the greater number of chances that are given for the display of this carelessness by just *so* much will it be displayed. The number of letters which reach the dead-letter office maintains an even per cent with the population year by year. The number of people who fail to pay their taxes maintains a like proportion, and the greater number of opportunities that are given for the collection of taxes and for the display of this carelessness, by just so much will it be displayed.

Another means by which this provision of the constitution works to the disadvantage of the borrower is the prevention that it puts upon the *introduction of foreign capital*. There can be no doubt but that legislation of this character wears the badge of what is termed *agrarian* legislation. Such a provision has never been enacted by any legislature except one that has been swayed by great popular excitement when the people seemed to have lost their balance. In all states where legislation of this character has been enacted it has been repealed, when the effects have had ample time to operate. This is so well-known to capitalists that many do not desire to introduce their capital into this state whose legislation is shown to be dominated by a sentiment antagonistic to capital. Of course it goes without saying that an abundance of capital is one of the greatest means of advancing the prosperity of especially new countries, and whatever tends to hinder or impede the easy and natural flow of capital into a country is a detriment to it.

The foregoing is a brief outline of some of the many objections which can be urged against the law;but as I have said before,they are not here urged as objections because the matter is no longer open for argument. They are enumerated. They are enumerated as examples of the practical workings of the law. It may be said that inasmuch as the capitalists suffer no direct disadvantage from the imposition but the borrower himself pays the tax, why should the capitalist care whether the law stands upon the statute books or not? For the reason that although it may not directly effect capitalists, and although they are not in any great degree sufferers from the enactment, nevertheless, in a broader sense, they should endeavor to obtain its repeal. I take the broad ground that no one is more directly interested in the prosperity of a country than the capitalists; although they are often charged with being selfish in their interests, and although it is constantly the shout of the damagogue that the interests of capital and labor are antagonistic, nevertheless, we all know that they are mutual hand-maidens to each other, and that where one succeeds best the prosperity of the other follows. There is no war between capital and labor, and by labor here we typify the community out side of the capitalists. There never should be war between capital and labor. The interests of both are bound up one with the other. And it is for the reason that I believe the present enactment interferes with the natural and simple operation of the laws which govern finance that I consider the enactment detrimental to all.

Capital will thrive best where there is unanimity of opinion, and identity of interest between both the capitalist and the borrower. And, as I before remarked, the fact that the borrower is compelled to pay the tax upon the mortgage interest proves a constant source of irritation between both parties. The constant attempt of both parties to put the payment of the tax upon the other, and the constant neglect of both occassions. as we have heretofore shown, a failure by both parties to pay the tax, which results in criminations and recriminations, and adds to the intensity of a sentiment existant in California antagonistic to capitalists. This is a sentiment which exists throughout the United States, in a greater or less degree, in certain localities at all times. It is a sentiment which is akin to socialism and communism, and it is a sentiment which appears with greater intensity at certain periods in our history, and then for a time lies dormant. But it is a sentiment which we are justified in saying, is never absent and which but needs the occasion to fan it into life. It is sentiment which is much to be deprecated because it is inimical to the interests of the whole country; for, as I have said before, the absence of capital from any country means a death to its prosperity, and wherever sentiment tends to drive capital out of the country, by so much does it cripple the very people who need it most. This sentiment it should be the object of all true lovers of country to remove.

The payment by the mortgagor of the tax in question is directly called to his mind upon every loan he makes; it is again recalled every time he pays the tax; and it is further made a source of vexation upon every failure of either party to pay the tax; and little by little this vexation is adding its mite to the sustenance of the sentiment always prevailing against capital.

Another bad feature connected with this subject is that it involves the habitual violation of a law that is written upon the statute books. The law demands that the mortgagee shall pay the tax, whereas, as a fact, it is paid by the mortgagor. It is not a beneficial thing to any country to have its laws habitually violated ; a disrespect for law is thus engendered, and when once we let go the sheet-anchor of the law we are drifting upon a stormy sea.

General Grant once said the way to repeal an obnoxious law was to enforce it; and it might be that the strict carrying out of the practical effects of this measure would be the means of inducing the people to recall what was so hastily done. It is an interesting thing in history to watch the tenacity with which people cling to an exploded principle. The popular will is very obstinate. It seems that ten years of operation under this measure has not yet been sufficient to obtain its repeal; nevertheless, the indications are all that the forces necessary to obtain its repeal are at work. Preliminary to the assemblage of the present legislature, the newspapers of the state contained many interviews with prominent citizens, requesting the views of the person approached as to what he would consider the most beneficial measure that could be passed by the present legislature, and the consensus of opinion was that the repeal of the measure under consideration, would be most beneficial to the state. It is true that a measure was introduced in the Senate looking toward the accomplishment of this end, but it was defeated. Yet I would not, for that reason, feel discouraged, or have you feel discouraged, because it is very certain that California will follow the lead of such other states as have tried this provision, and will in time effect its repeal. And, moreover, this repeal will be brought about, as I predict, not through any efforts made by capitalists themselves, but simply because the people, upon sober consideration, will come to the conclusion after a test of the matter that the objects endeavored to be obtained by said measure *cannot* be accomplished by *legislation*. There are laws regulating the economics of a nation which are as fixed and unalterable in their operation as are the laws of gravitation. It has been demonstrated over and over again, in the history of all civilized communities, that any attempt made to pass a measure in opposition to these laws is as impracticable to accomplish that result as would be an enactment by the legislature of the State of California to suspend the laws that govern electricity. You cannot legislate to make an inferior metal more valuable than a superior. You cannot legislate prosperity into a country, if you pass enactments contrary to the laws of finance, which govern the proper relation between capital and labor. You cannot pass an arbitrary enactment which will be a guage of the demands and necessities of men in times to come.

Legislatures have again and again passed usury laws, all of which have been more easily evaded than they were passed, and the experience under the provision of the new constitution which calls for the taxation of mortgages, and by means of which it was endeavored to compel the mortgagee to pay the tax, was in a direct violation of one of these laws of finance and is, as we have all known, completely overcome, and although by its evasion a technical law of the statute is broken, nevertheless a higher law of finance is followed which is so plainly understood to be right that the evasion of the statute broken has the sanction of public opinion. In endeavoring to bring about the repeal of this measure it is our duty to use only such arguments as show the disinterestedness of the matter from the standpoint of a capitalist, being careful not to arouse that latent sentiment in a community which, upon every possible occasion, declares itself inimical to capitalists, but by conservative and moderate statements to show the real sufferer under the law that he has been mistaken in his realization of the benefits anticipated.

Wm. F. Bosbyshell Vice-President of the Southern California National Bank, Los Angeles, then read the following paper:

INTEREST ON DEPOSITS.

To the Bankers assembled in Convention in Los Angeles, California. March 13th, 1891.

Some one has said that "Bankers are silent workmen, in our wonderful development. If they were a little more noisy the public might be brought to appreciate the benefit banks are to the country."

In regard to commercial banks paying interest on deposits circumstances alter cases, but let us consider the circumstances as they exist with us.

I think but few thorough, fair minded men will ask a commercial bank to pay interest on even what are called time deposits. If a man stops to think of what the bank does for him, he will surely find it a convenience worth paying something for.

His bank furnishes him a safe place for his money, secure against fire and burglars; acts as his cashier in paying his bills, etc., making change, furnishing receipts (in way of order checks), and at times at the risk of having the wrong indorsement, all at no cost to him. A trade is made, one man gives his check, the other goes to the bank and gets his money, should there be an error in the counting it out to him of $10, $20 or $100, the man who gave the check loses nothing.

What would any business community be without its bank?

Think of a man carrying about with him the money needed for all his business transactions. With many people the bank pass and check books are all the books they keep.

Does not the business man owe the bank something for actually saving him money in way of avoiding express charges in transmitting his money from place to place, furnishing and cashing his exchanges? And in this section all these are done for nothing. It also adds, as it were, to his cash capital in many cases 60 to 90 per cent.

The shipper buys his carload of potatoes, oranges, barley, or what not, goes to his bank and draws on the consignee, attaches his bill of lading, and gets 60 to 90 per cent of his selling price, which possibly is all of his money back.

With the aid of his bank he has the use of double his capital at every turn, and this in many cases at no cost whatever to him. The banker bearing the expense.

By the banks the circulating medium of the country is very much increased, a matter which the Farmer's Alliance should take note of and appreciate.

It has been shown that over 92 per cent of all the deposits made in banks of the United States consists of checks, drafts and other items of bank credits, thereby increasing the circulating medium of the country over nine fold.

In this country the orange grower sells his crop and puts the money into the bank for safe keeping and draws it as he wants.

The barley grower has spent all of his money putting in his crop and wants more to pay for the harvesting. He goes to the bank and borrows some of the orange growers money. The bank gets the interest for the care and risk taken, and so it goes both have been accommodated. But, some of you may say these commercial accounts are not the ones that ask for interest. Pay interest only on time deposits. There is little doubt but the party who wishes to make the so-called time deposits is one who has taken advantage of all privileges granted commercial customers, and he ought to recognize the fact that he owes his bank something.

But what are these so-called time deposits? Time deposits of a commercial bank differ from those of a savings bank, those in the savings bank, both by custom and law are not payable until maturity, as positively stated in the certificate of deposit. While the so-called time deposit in the commercial bank almost invariably is a certificate of deposit drawing 3 per cent interest if left three months, or 5 per cent if left six months.

Sometimes both ifs on the same certificate.

They are so full of "ifs" that I shall call them "If" certificates or "If" deposits.

What can a banker count on or look for on that kind of a deposit? He does not know but he may have it to pay in thirty days, or it may be costing him 5 per cent interest.

He knows not which. That then, is practically interest on demand deposits, if not demanded. And that is surely the most deceptive kind of deposits. He rather expects the "If" certificate will run its full time, and possibly be renewed, and as he is paying 5 per cent he cannot afford to carry much of that money on hand or have it idle.

Consequently he loans more, takes more chances on his loans and if loans are scarce possibly buys bonds and stock for he must have that money earn its interest, expenses and a profit.

Then he is disappointed if the depositor calls for his cash before the if runs out.

And if any evil rumor or crisis comes with 80 or 90 per cent of these if deposits, loaned, as the savings bank his competitor has, he is sure to wish he had done less business and been safer. As the If depositors are as sure to call for their cash and all of it, as the commercial depositors, and most always in larger amounts each.

But some of you may say, that it is the custom for Eastern banks to issue If certificates, but, circumstances alter cases; in the farther East, and in the larger cities demand loans can be made on collaterals, that can be realized upon usually, at once. But even they sometimes get caught, as many were last November and December, when many of the old and so called strong banks were shaken to their very foundations, and some wholly wrecked, simply because they thought they would not be called upon for money faster than they could realize on securities, and therefore had not limited their own credit, but had taken all the business they could catch, and when the crisis came they were caught short of cash.

If that is the result under the most favorable circumstances, what can bankers in California, (except possibly San Francisco), look for who have no securities offered that justify demand loans, and if we had and were obliged to realize at once we would have no market for them. And what is worse, we are out of reach of help, as no great money centers are near us from which we could expect help in time of trouble.

Consequently every bank must stand as it were on its own cash.

In looking over the itemized statements of twenty-four National Banks of Chicago, I find but four list any time deposits, and two of these have a total deposit of less than one half million each. So the If certificates are not very popular there nor are the banks which issue them. In looking up the statements of banks in other cities, I find very few which show any, and many banks, to which I wrote in different places east of the Mississippi River, say they pay no interest.

In Racine, Wis., they issue the If certificates with interest clause two per cent., if left six months, and three per cent., if left twelve months. A very low rate of interest.

But in Omaha most all show the If certificates. The same in Lincoln, Neb., and Sioux City, Iowa. And notice these same cities have fully as many Savings Banks in proportion to Commercial Banks, as has Los Angeles.

Omaha has twelve Commercial Banks and nine Savings Banks. Lincoln has twelve Commercial Banks and four Savings Banks. Sioux City has thirteen Commercial Banks and five Savings Banks, making a total of thirty-seven Commercial Banks and eighteen Savings Banks—one Savings Bank to two Commercial Banks.

Now what are some of the figures where they are in the habit of issuing the If certificates. I find three of the larger banks in Omaha have total individual deposit of $5,386,000 of which $1,766,000 are the If certificates or about one-third of their individual deposits.

The cashier of a leading bank in Lincoln, Neb., writes me: "Our deposits are as follows: Interest bearing certificates 33 per cent. Bank accounts bearing interest 19 per cent. Individual accounts bearing interest 22 per cent. Individual accounts no interest 26 per cent." The certificates cost us an average of 4½ per cent; bank accounts, 3 per cent; Individuals, 4 per cent. (The latter are official.)

And he adds, 'the situation here is about this: every time a new bank starts, the interest allowed depositors is raised, and the rate of discount is lowered." How would that kind of banking suit you California bankers? Pay interest on 74 per cent. of your deposits, and that at an average rate of 4 per cent, and still plenty of Savings Banks. What are the results of this kind of banking? The per cent. of failure of banks is larger in the states bordering on the Mississippi and Missouri Rivers, (where the If certificates flourish) than in any other section of the United States. California bankers may well be proud of their record.

According to the State Bank Commissioner's report for the year ending July first, 1890, there had been but two bank failures out of 232 banks. And those in the most trying year of the depression after the boom.

Taking Los Angeles as the criterion for Southern California, I find that for the two years and a half from July, 1885, to January, 1888, bank deposits increased over 400 per cent, and in the next year and a half decreased 25 per cent. Many visiting bankers from the East have wondered at the fact that, with such a sudden and great inflation and reaction in Southern California, there has been but one bank failure, and that a small private bank, which will pay depositors in full, and that the only one in ten years.

I challenge any state in the Union to show in its history a record of eight or ten years, with such a per cent of growth as California has had and so few bank failures. I think that this good showing is mainly due to the fact that our banks paid no interests on deposits, therefore were not obliged to lend them to meet the promised interest.

There is no question but this country would have seen many more failures in in the last three years if the If certificate had been in fashion.

Let us now figure a little for the profit in the If certificates. I have shown that where they are in general use over 33 per cent of the individual deposits are bearing interest.

Suppose a bank carries $400,000 of deposits without interest, and by issuing the If certificates should gain $100,000, (and that could hardly be expected, if all the competing banks did the same,) making $500,000 deposits, 33 per cent of which bears an average rate of 3 per cent interest, that I think would be low, allowing for the forfeited interest.

If it lend 60 per cent, or $300,000 at 8 per cent, it gets $24,000.00 interest. It pays interest on 33 per cent, or $165,000 at 3 per cent. $4,950.00.

Say one-fourth of one per cent for losses, $750.00. $5,700.00 off. It has a net amount of $18,300.00 interest

Take $400,000 deposits, no interest, lend 60 per cent or $240,000 at 8 per cent. $19,200.00. One-fourth of one per cent for losses, $600.00. Net amount of interest, $18,600.00.

On that basis a loss to the "If" certificate banker of $300, besides the extra cost of handling more business and more risk and worry. If he thinks he can safely lend more than 60 per cent of his "If" deposits, he must expect a larger per cent of them will run to maturity, and therefore raise the average rate of interest. If you allow him to lend 70 per cent of the "If" deposits and pay 3½ per cent, he is only $150.00 ahead, and that will not pay. If there are any errors in this statement they are in favor of the "If" certificate banker.

I am satisfied if all the commercial banks in this City or State, issued the If certificates, they would not increase their deposits 25 per cent still I believe fully as large a per cent of the now non-bearing interest deposits would be made to bear interest. But some of you say, are you going to sit still and let the savings banks take all your steady deposits? I say yes, if we cannot hold them without issuing If certificates, and when we cannot get enough to pay to run the bank on a safe and profitable basis, then we had better quit banking and take to rolling pumpkins.

To sum it all up. I would say in *justice* to the banks, the great majority of the If certificate depositors should not ask interest. The issuing of the If certificate by commercial banks does not exclude savings banks, nor diminish their number. And as figures have shown, there is no profit in the practice of issuing the If certificates.

So I would say, let us not be led into temptation, but deliver us from the evils of the If certificates.

J. B. Lankershim of Los Angeles here introduced the following resolution:

Resolved, That the California Bankers Association heartily approves of the Bank Commission of the State of California, and that we believe that their work in instructing new Banks, in reforming errors in the banking system, and in guarding alike the interests of the depositors, stockholders and officers of banks, most commendable. Carried.

R. M. Widney, of Los Angeles, then offered the Resolution as per his notification of yesterday, and asks for its adoption. Carried.

On motion, resolved that the delegates in the various counties send in the name of one Vice-President, for their county, to the Secretary within thirty days.

C. E. Palmer, of Oakland, moved that the thanks of the Convention be extended to the President, E. F. Spence, and the Secretary, Geo. H. Stewart, and also to the Los Angeles Clearing House, for their good work, their attention to business, and for the hearty reception given the delegates in this city.

Carried, and ordered spread upon the minutes.

The Committee on Credentials here filed their completed report and upon motion, same was adopted.

Upon motion the Convention adjourned *sine die*.

The delegates on Thursday evening, accepting the invitation of the Los Angeles Clearing House, visited the State Citrus Fair at Hazard's Pavilion.

After final adjournment, the delegates, with other invited guests, were taken by special train to Redondo Beach, where a banquet was tendered them by the bankers of Los Angeles, at the Redondo Beach Hotel.

CONSTITUTION

OF THE

California Bankers Association.

DECLARATION.

In order to promote the general welfare and usefulness of banks and banking institutions, and to secure uniformity of action, together with the practical benefits to be derived from personal acquaintance and from the discussion of subjects of importance to the banking and commercial interests of this State, especially in order to secure the proper consideration of questions regarding the financial usages, customs and laws which affect the banking interests of the entire state and for protection against loss by crime, we have to submit the following Constitution and By-Laws for THE CALIFORNIA BANKERS ASSOCIATION.

CONSTITUTION.

ARTICLE I.

This Association shall be called THE CALIFORNIA BANKERS ASSOCIATION.

ARTICLE II.

SECTION 1. Any National or State Bank, Trust Company, Savings Bank, Banking Firm, or individual doing a banking business within the State of California, may become a member of this association upon the payment of such annual dues as shall be provided by the By-Laws, subject to the approval of a majority of the Executive Council, and may send one delegate to the annual meeting of the Association; and any member may be expelled from the Association upon a vote of two-thirds of those present at any regular meeting.

Sec. 2. Delegates shall be an officer or director, or trustee of the institution they represent, or a member of a banking firm, or an individual doing business as a bank.

Sec. 3. Delegates shall vote in person; no voting by proxy shall be allowed.

Sec. 4. All votes shall be viva voce, unless otherwise ordered ; any delegate may demand a division of the house.

ARTICLE III.

Section 1. The administration of the affairs of the Association, not otherwise delegated, shall be vested in the President, First Vice-President, Secretary, Treasurer, one Vice-President for each County which may be represented in this Association, and in an Executive Council, who shall be elected at the annual meeting, and who shall serve until their successors are chosen or appointed. The Executive Council shall be composed of nine members divided into three classes, one-third of whom shall be elected annually.

Sec. 2. Immediately after the first adjournment that occurs in the session of the annual Convention the delegation from each County shall meet and make nominations for Vice-Presidents of the Association.

Sec. 3. The Vice-Presidents shall have the supervision of the business of the Association in the counties where they reside. The banks in each county may organize under the Vice-President of the county and form a committee for local matters. But such committee shall have no power to in any manner bind or effect the interests of the organization. Such local committee may fill any vacancy occuring in the Vice-Presidency during the year.

Sec. 4. A majority of the Executive Council shall constitute a quorum for the transaction of business.

Sec. 5. Special meetings of the Executive Council may be called by request of three of its members, giving two weeks notice to the Secretary desiring him to call such special meeting. The Executive Council shall have power to fill vacancies that may occur in their own body.

Sec. 6. The Executive Council shall provide:

First. For keeping the records of the proceedings of their own meetings, as well as that of the Association annual or special meetings.

Second. They shall submit to each annual meeting a report, covering their own official acts, as well as a statement of any new or unfinished business requiring attention.

Third. They shall make full statements of the financial condition of the Association.

Fourth. Submit an estimate of the amount required to carry on the affairs of the Association according to their judgment of the business to be done, and recommend means for raising money to carry out such plans as may be resolved upon by the Association.

Sec. 7. The Secretary shall make and have charge of the records of the Association, as well as those of the Council, and of the correspondence of the Executive Council and Standing Protective Committee, and shall promptly send to each member of the Association a synopsis of reports received by him of attempted or accomplished crime against any member of the Association. Such records shall be the property of the Association, and be held subject at all times to the order of the Executive Council.

SEC. 8. The Treasurer shall receive and account for all moneys belonging to the Association, but shall pay out moneys only upon vouchers approved by the President of the Association and counter-signed by the Secretary.

ARTICLE IV.

SECTION 1. The Executive Council shall appoint aStanding Protective Committee of three persons, whose names shall not be made public. The said committee shall control all action looking to the detection, prosecution and punishment of persons attempting to cause, or causing, loss by crime to any member of the Association.

SEC. 2. The said committee when called upon for aid by any member of the Association, through the secretary, shall forthwith take such steps as it shall deem proper to arrest and prosecute the party charged with crime. Provided, however, that no expense or liability shall be incurred beyond the amount of funds in the treasury especially appropriated for that purpose.

SEC. 3. The said committee is prohibited from compromising or compounding with parties charged with crime or with their agents or attorneys.

SEC. 4. All detectives and legal expenses and costs will be paid by the Association out of any money in the treasury especially appropriated by the Executive Council for that purpose, subject, however, to the approval of a quorum of the Executive Council.

SEC. 5. All members of the Assciation, when called upon by the Secretary in behalf of the Protective Committee for information or aid, shall promply respond by giving all assistance in their power; and all members shall, at all times, notify the Secretary, who shall promptly notify the Committee of any attempted or accomplished crime reported to him as likely to affect other members of the Association.

ARTICLE V.

SECTION 1. Annual meetings of the Association shall be held at such times and places as shall be determined by the Executive Council. Special meetings may be called by the said Council if, in their opinions, circumstances require them, giving two weeks notice of time and place of meeting, together with the subject matter of business to come before such special meeting. The Executive Council shall meet to arrange the order of business on the day preceeding any general meeting of the Association.

ARTICLE VI.

SECTION 1. The expenses of the Executive Council in carrying out the business of the Association to be done by them, shall be provided for by the annual dues of the members of the Association; provided, however that the Executive Council shall have no authority to incur or contract on behalf of this Association any liability whatever beyond the annual dues hereby authorized, and only that for the purposes hereby designated.

ARTICLE VII.

SECTION 1. Resolutions and subjects for discussion (except those referring to points of order or matter of courtesy) must be submitted in writing to the Secretary, for reference to the Executive Council, at least ten days before any general meeting of the Association; but any person desiring to submit any resolution of business in open convention can do so upon a two-thirds vote of the delegates present.

ARTICLE VIII.

SECTION 1. Any one failing to pay within three months the annual dues for carrying on the business of the Association, shall be considered as having withdrawn from membership, but may be reinstated upon application to the Secretary, and paying all dues in arrears, with consent of the President.

ARTICLE IX.

SECTION 1. This constitution may be altered or amended at any annual meeting by a vote of two-thirds of the members present, notice of the proposed amendment having been first submitted to the Secretary at least ten days before the annual meeting, to be placed by him before the Executive Council that they may arrange for bringing it before the Convention under the regular order of business.

BY-LAWS

OF THE

California Bankers Association.

SECTION 1. The annual dues of the Association shall be considered due at the beginning of the year, which year shall commence with the regular annual meeting, it being understood that absent members from such annual meeting shall not forfeit their membership nor the right to become members, provided they comply with the Constitution and By-Laws and remit the amount of the dues to the Secretary within one month after such annual meeting.

SEC. 2. The annual dues of all members shall be Ten (10) Dollars.

B C -- 5

INDEX.

MEMORANDA

MEMORANDA

PROCEEDINGS.

OF THE

FIRST ANNUAL CONVENTION

OF THE

California

Bankers Association

HELD AT

SAN FRANCISCO, OCTOBER 14th, 15th AND 16th

1891

Constitution and By-Laws
List of Officers and Members. Etc.

LOS ANGELES
TIMES-MIRROR PRINTING AND BINDING HOUSE
1891

PROCEEDINGS

OF THE

FIRST ANNUAL CONVENTION

OF THE

CALIFORNIA BANKERS ASSOCIATION

HELD AT

SAN FRANCISCO, OCTOBER 14TH, 15TH AND 16TH

1891

CONSTITUTION AND BY-LAWS
LIST OF OFFICERS AND MEMBERS, ETC.

LOS ANGELES
TIMES-MIRROR PRINTING AND BINDING HOUSE
1891

FULL INDEX AT BACK OF PAMPHLET.

California Bankers Association.

OFFICERS 1891-2

President,
THOMAS BROWN   Bank of California, San Francisco,

First Vice-President,
ISAIAS W. HELLMAN   Nevada Bank, San Francisco

Secretary,
GEO. H. STEWART   Los Angeles County Bank, Los Angeles

Treasurer,
G. W. KLINE   First National Bank, San Francisco

Executive Council,

Chairman, A. D. CHILDRESS.

One Year Term.

W. M. EDDY, Santa Barbara County National Bank, Santa Barbara
T. S. HAWKINS   Bank of Hollister, Hollister
W. D. WOOLWINE   First National Bank, San Diego

Two Year Term.

A. D. CHILDRESS   City Bank, Los Angeles
N. D. RIDEOUT   California State Bank, Sacramento
LOVELL WHITE   San Francisco Savings Union, San Francisco

Three Year Term.

C. E. PALMER   Union National Bank, Oakland
W. W. PHILLIPS   Farmers Bank of Fresno, Fresno
A. L. SELIGMAN   Anglo-California Bank, San Francisco

MEMBERS AND COUNTY VICE-PRESIDENTS

At Date of First Annual Convention.

ALAMEDA COUNTY

J. West Martin, - - - *Vice-President*
President, Union Savings Bank, Oakland
Bank of Livermore - - - - Livermore
California Bank and Trust Co. Oakland
First National - - - "
Oakland Bank of Savings "
Union National "
Union Savings .
Bank of Haywards Haywards
Bank of Alameda . Alameda

BUTTE COUNTY

Chas. Faulkner - - - *Vice-President*
Cashier, Bank of Butte County, Chico
Bank of G. K. Smith - - - Biggs
Bank of Butte County - - - Chico
Bank of Chico - - - - "
Rideout Bank - - - - Gridley
Bank of Rideout, Smith & Co. Oroville

COLUSA COUNTY

W. P. Harrington - - - *Vice-President*
Cashier, Colusa County Bank
Colusa County Bank - - - Colusa
Bank of Orland - - - Orland
Bank of Willows - - Willows

CONTRA COSTA COUNTY

L. C. Wittenmeyer - - - *Vice-President*
President, Bank of Martinez, Martinez
Bank of Martinez - - - - Martinez

FRESNO COUNTY

Louis Einstein - - - *Vice-President*
President, Bank of Central California, Fresno
Bank of Central California - - Fresno
Farmers' Bank of Fresno - "
First National "
Fresno National "
Fresno Loan and Savings Bank "
People's Savings Bank - "
Bank of Madera - - Madera
Bank of Sanger Sanger
Bank of Selma - Selma

HUMBOLDT COUNTY

J. W. Henderson - - *Vice-President*
President, Humboldt County Bank, Eureka
Bank of Arcata - - - - Arcata
A. W. Randall - - Eureka
Bank of Eureka - "
Humboldt County Bank "

KERN COUNTY

S. W. Wible - - - - *Vice-President*
President, Bank of Bakersfield
Bank of Bakersfield - - Bakersfield
Kern Valley Bank - - "

LAKE COUNTY

H. C. Boggs - - - *Vice-President*
President, Farmers Savings Bank, Lakeport
Farmers Savings Bank - - - Lakeport

LOS ANGELES COUNTY

E. F. Spence - - - *Vice-President*
President, First National Bank, Los Angeles
Alhambra Bank - - - Alhambra
California Bank - - Los Angeles
Citizens Bank of Los Angeles "
City Bank - - "
East Side Bank - - - "
Farmers and Merchants Bank "
First National "
German-American Savings Bank "
Los Angeles County Bank - "
Los Angeles National Bank - "
Los Angeles Savings Bank "
Main St. Savings Bank and Trust Co. "
National Bank of California - "
Savings Bank of Southern California "
Security Savings Bank and Trust Co. "
Southern California National Bank "
State Loan and Trust Co. "
University Bank - - - "
First National Bank of Pasadena Pasadena
San Gabriel Valley Bank "
Pasadena National Bank - "
First National Bank - Pomona
People's Bank - - "
First National - Santa Monica

MERCED COUNTY

C. Landrum - - - - *Vice-President*
Vice-President, Merced Bank, Merced
Merced Bank - - - Merced
Merced Security Savings Bank "

MONTEREY COUNTY

J. D. Carr - - - *Vice-President*
President, Salinas City Bank
Salinas City Bank - - Salinas City
Monterey County Bank . " "

NAPA COUNTY

G. E. Goodman, Sr. - - - *Vice-President*
President, J. H. Goodman & Co. Bank, Napa
Jas. H. Goodman & Co. Bank - - Napa
Bank of Napa - - - - "
Carver National Bank - - St. Helena

****

ORANGE COUNTY

W. H. Spurgeon - - - - *Vice-President*
President, First National Bank of Santa Ana
Bank of Anaheim - - - Anaheim
Bank of Orange - - - Orange
First National - - Santa Ana
Commercial Bank - - "
Orange Co. Savings, Loan and Trust Co. "
Bank of Tustin - - - - Tustin

****

PLACER COUNTY

T. J. Nichols - - - - *Vice-President*
Cashier, Placer County Bank, Auburn
Placer County Bank - - - Auburn

****

SACRAMENTO COUNTY

W. E. Chamberlain - - *Vice-President*
Of the National Bank of D. O. Mills & Co.
California State Bank - - Sacramento
Farmers and Mechanics Sav. Bank "
National Bank of D. O. Mills & Co. "
People's Savings Bank - - "
Sacramento Bank - - , - "
J. H. Burnham - - - Folsom

****

SAN BENITO COUNTY

T. W. Hawkins - - - *Vice President*
Cashier, Bank of Hollister
Bank of Hollister - - - - Hollister

****

SAN BERNARDINO COUNTY

John W. Davis - - - *Vice-President*
President, First National Bank of Colton
First National - - - - Colton
Ontario State Bank - - - Ontario
First National - - Redlands
Union Bank of Redlands - "
First National - - Riverside
Riverside Banking Company - "
Bank of San Bernardino - - San Bernardino
Farmers Exchange Bank - "
San Bernardino National - "
First National - - - "
Riverside National - - Riverside

****

SAN DIEGO COUNTY

Jerry Toles - - - - *Vice-President*
Vice-President, First Nat. Bank, San Diego
Bank of National City - - National City
Bank of Oceanside - - Oceanside
Perris Valley Bank - - Perris
California National - San Diego
First National - "
Bank of Commerce - "
Consolidated National - "
San Diego Savings Bank "
State Bank - - - San Jacinto

SAN FRANCISCO CITY AND COUNTY

H. Wadsworth - - - *Vice-President*
Cashier, Wells, Fargo & Co. Bank
American Bank and Trust Co.
Anglo-California Bank, Ld.
Bank of California
California Safe Deposit and Trust Co.
Crocker-Woolworth National
First National
German Savings and Loan Society
Hibernia Savings and Loan Society
London, Paris and American Bank
London and San Francisco Bank
Mutual Savings Bank
Nevada Bank of San Francisco
Pacific Bank
San Francisco Savings Union
Sather Banking Co.
Savings and Loan Society
Security Savings Bank
Tallant Banking Co.
Wells, Fargo & Co's Bank

****

SAN JOAQUIN COUNTY

Name of Vice-President not yet received.
Bank of Lodi . . . . . Lodi
Farmers and Merchants Bank - Stockton
Stockton Savings Bank . . "
Stockton Savings and Loan Society - "
First National . . . "

****

SAN LUIS OBISPO COUNTY

McD. R. Venable . . . *Vice-President*
President, Commercial Bank of San Luis Obispo
Bank of Paso Robles , . Paso Robles
Commercial Bank . . San Luis Obispo

****

SANTA BARBARA COUNTY

A. L. Lincoln . . . *Vice-President*
Cashier, First National Bank of Santa Barbara
Commercial Bank . . Santa Barbara
First National . . . "
Santa Barbara County National "
Santa Barbara S. & L. Bank . "
Bank of Santa Maria Santa Maria
Bank of Lompoc . . Lompoc

****

SANTA CLARA COUNTY

B. D. Murphy . . . *Vice-President*
Pres., Commercial and Savings Bank, San Jose
Bank of Gilroy . . Gilroy
Bank of Los Gatos . Los Gatos
Commercial Bank of Los Gatos Los Gatos
Commercial and Savings Bank San Jose
First National . "
Union Savings "
Security Savings "
Garden City National . "

****

SANTA CRUZ COUNTY

J. J. Morey . . . *Vice-President*
Cashier, Pajaro Valley Bank, Santa Cruz
Bank of Santa Cruz County . Santa Cruz
Pajaro Valley Bank . . Watsonville

BANKS REPRESENTED AT THE CONVENTION

LOCATION	NAME	REPRESENTED BY
Alhambra,	Alhambra Bank,	J. A. Green.
Arcata,	Bank of Arcata,	J. W. Henderson.
Auburn,	Placer County Bank,	N. D. Rideout.
Biggs,	Bank of G. K. Smith,	G. K. Smith.
Chico,	Bank of Butte County,	Charles Faulkner.
Chico,	Bank of Chico,	A. H. Crew.
Colusa,	Colusa County Bank,	W. P. Harrington.
Eureka,	A. W. Randall,	J. W. Henderson.
Eureka,	Bank of Eureka,	J. W. Henderson.
Eureka,	Humboldt County Bank,	J. W. Henderson.
Fort Jones,	A. B. Carlock,	M. C. Boem.
Fresno,	Bank of Central California,	Louis Einstein.
Fresno,	Farmers Bank of Fresno,	W. W. Phillips.
Fresno,	First National Bank,	O. J. Woodward.
Fresno,	Peoples Savings Bank,	Chester Rowell.
Gilroy,	Bank of Gilroy,	L. A. Whitehurst.
Gridley,	The Rideout Bank,	Norman Rideout.
Haywards,	Bank of Haywards,	J. E. Crooks.
Hollister,	Bank of Hollister,	N. C. Briggs, T. S. Hawkins.
Livermore,	Bank of Livermore,	H. H. Pitcher.
Lodi,	Bank of Lodi,	F. Cogswell.
Los Angeles,	California Bank,	James C. Kays, E. W. Jones.
Los Angeles,	Citizens Bank,	T. S. Lowe.
Los Angeles,	City Bank,	A. D. Childress.
Los Angeles,	Farmers and Merchants Bank,	Isaiah W. Hellman.
Los Angeles,	First National Bank,	E. F. Spence, D. J. Cooper.
Los Angeles,	German-American Savings Bank,	F. S. Rowley, W. M. Sheldon.
Los Angeles,	Los Angeles County Bank,	Geo. H. Stewart.
Los Angeles,	Los Angeles National Bank,	Geo. H. Bonebrake.
Los Angeles,	Main Street Savings Bank and Trust Co.,	J. B. Lankershim.
Los Angeles,	National Bank of California,	John M. C. Marble.
Los Angeles,	Southern California National Bank,	Wm. F. Bosbyshell.
Los Angeles,	State Loan and Trust Co.,	John Bryson, Sr.
Los Angeles,	University Bank,	R. M. Widney.
Los Gatos,	Bank of Los Gatos,	B. L. Turner.
Los Gatos,	Commercial Bank,	J. R. Ryland.
Marysville,	Northern California Bank of Savings,	G. R. Eckart.
Marysville,	The Rideout Bank,	Norman Rideout.
Marysville,	Decker, Jewett & Co.,	A. C. Bingham.
Merced,	Merced Security Savings Bank,	W. W. Westbay.
Modesto,	First National Bank,	O. McHenry.
Napa,	James H. Goodman & Co. Bank,	H. P. Goodman, G. E. Goodman.
Napa,	Bank of Napa,	C. R. Gritman.
National City,	Bank of National City,	W. C. Kimball, C. B. Whittelsey.
Oakland,	California Bank and Trust Co.,	A. C. Henry.
Oakland,	First National Bank,	A. D. Thompson.
Oakland,	Oakland Bank of Savings,	W. W. Garthwaite, E. C. Sessions.
Oakland,	Union National Bank,	Thos. Prather, C. E. Palmer.
Oakland,	Union Savings Bank,	J. West Martin.
Orland,	Bank of Orland,	L. Scearce, R. B. Murdoch.
Oroville,	Bank of Rideout, Smith & Co.,	E. W. Fogg.
Pasadena,	First National Bank of Pasadena,	W. E. Arshur, P. M. Green.
Pasadena,	San Gabriel Valley Bank,	H. W. Magee.
Pasadena,	Pasadena National Bank,	T. P. Lukens.
Perris,	Perris Valley Bank,	Jas. Patterson, Jr.
Red Bluff,	Bank of Tehama County,	Charles Cadwalader.
Redding,	Bank of Shasta County,	C. C. Bush.
Sacramento,	California State Bank,	N. D. Rideout.

LOCATION	NAME	REPRESENTED BY
Sacramento,	Farmers and Mechanics Savings Bank,	B. U. Steinman.
Sacramento,	National Bank of D. O. Mills & Co.,	Frank Miller.
Sacramento,	Peoples Savings Bank,	Wm. Beckman.
Sacramento,	Sacramento Bank,	Ed. R. Hamilton.
Salinas City,	Monterey County Bank,	A. B. Jackson.
Salinas City,	Salinas City Bank,	A. B. Jackson,
San Bernardino,	Riverside Banking Company,	O. T. Dyer.
San Bernardino,	Riverside National,	S. C. Evans.
San Bernardino,	San Bernardino National Bank,	W. S. Hooper.
San Diego,	First National Bank,	W. D. Woolwine.
San Diego,	Consolidated National Bank,	Bryant Howard.
San Diego,	San Diego Savings Bank,	M. T. Gilmore.
San Francisco—City and County	Anglo-California Bank, Ld.,	A. L. Seligman.
..	Bank of California,	Thos. Brown.
	California Safe Deposit and Trust Co.,	S. P. Young.
	First National Bank,	E. D. Morgan, G. W. Kline.
	German Savings and Loan Society,	A. H. R.,Schmidt.
	London, Paris and American Bank,	Eugene Meyer.
	Mutual Savings Bank,	James A. Thompson.
	Nevada Bank,	Isaias W. Hellman.
	Pacific Bank,	Frank V. McDonald.
	San Francisco Savings Union,	Lovell White.
	Sather Banking Co.,	Jas. K. Wilson, J. S. Hutchinson.
	Savings and Loan Society,	S. C. Bigelow.
	Tallant Banking Co.,	John McKee.
	American Bank and Trust Co.,	Jas. J Fagan.
	Hibernia Savings and Loan Society,	Robert J. Tobin.
	London and San Francisco Bank,	Arthur Scrivener.
	Crocker Woolworth National Bank,	R. C. Woolworth.
	Wells, Fargo & Co.'s Bank,	H. Wadsworth.
	Security Savings Bank,	S. L. Abbott, Jr.
Sanger,	Bank of Sanger,	A. Kutner.
San Jacinto,	State Bank,	J. A. Green.
San Jose,	First National Bank,	J. A. Clayton, W. D. Tisdale.
San Jose,	Union Savings Bank,	H. W. Wright.
San Jose,	Security Savings Bank,	J. A. Clayton, W. D. Tisdale.
San Jose,	Garden City National Bank,	C. W. Breyfogle.
Santa Barbara,	Commercial Bank,	E. B. Hall, Geo. S. Edwards.
Santa Barbara,	First National Bank,	J. W. Calkins.
Santa Barbara,	Santa Barbara County National Bank,	W. M. Eddy.
Santa Barbara,	Santa Barbara Savings and Loan Bank,	Geo. S. Edwards.
Santa Cruz,	Bank of Santa Cruz County,	J. H. Logan.
Santa Monica,	First National Bank,	W. S. Vawter, E. J. Vawter.
Santa Paula,	First National Bank,	J. R. Haugh.
St. Helena,	Carver National Bank,	A. L. Williams.
Stockton,	First National Bank,	H. H. Hewlett.
Stockton,	Farmers and Merchants Bank,	D. S. Rosenbaum, P. B. Fraser.
Stockton,	Stockton Savings Bank,	Sidney Newell.
Stockton,	Stockton Savings and Loan Society,	L. U. Shippee.
Tulare,	Bank of Tulare,	J. A. Goble.
Tustin,	Bank of Tustin,	W. S. Bartlett.
Ventura,	Bank of Ventura,	A. Bernheim.
Ventura,	William Collins & Sons,	J. C. Morrison, D. Edward Collins
Visalia,	Harrell & Son,	A. J. Harrell.
Watsonville,	Pajaro Valley Bank,	John T. Porter.
Willows,	Bank of Willows,	W. P. Harrington.
Winters,	Bank of Winters,	E. E. Kahn.
Woodland,	Bank of Yolo,	A. L. Porter, C. W. Bush.
Yreka,	Siskiyou County Bank,	E. E. Wadsworth.
Yuba City,	Farmers Co-operative Union,	George Ohlever.

PROCEEDINGS OF THE FIRST ANNUAL CONVENTION

OF THE

CALIFORNIA BANKERS ASSOCIATION

HELD IN THE

CHAMBER OF COMMERCE ROOMS, SAN FRANCISCO.

FIRST DAY.

WEDNESDAY, OCTOBER 14TH, 1891.

The Convention was called to order at 10:30 by Thomas Brown, President of the Association.

The Chairman: Gentlemen, I take pleasure in introducing to you Mr. John McKee, President of the San Francisco Clearing House, who will deliver the Address of Welcome.

Mr. McKee spoke as follows:

Gentlemen of the California Bankers Association:

Our worthy President has assigned to me the pleasant duty of extending to you, on behalf of the San Francisco members of this Association, a cordial welcome to this city, and to tender their congratulations that so many of the representative bankers of this State, in response to the call of its officers, are here assembled as members at this first annual convention. Some of you in availing of this opportunity will doubtless find pleasure in the renewal of former acquaintance, and all may enjoy a personal conference with their bank correspondents, with whom, in course of business, there is almost daily communication by mail and wire. We trust these pleasant social anticipations may be fully realized and that your sojourn in this city will prove agreeable to you all in every respect.

We understand, however, Mr. President, that while there are pleasures to be had in the exchange for a season of the restful comforts of home for the excitements of travel, and that there is virtue in the allurements of change of air and scene, and that social enjoyments of high order accompany the renewals of friendly personal intercourse and the manifestations of good fellowship, yet these gentlemen are not to be enrolled as a convention of visitors, merely seeking pleasure!

If we are not greatly mistaken, these bankers are not here assembled in quest of personal enjoyment only! They, sir, as we take it, are accustomed to the restraining influences of conservative processes, which necessarily give tone to thought and life. And, sir, I think it may be safely assumed that they are here assembled, chiefly, for conference as to some important matters which have been under special study, and which if energized into controlling forces might prove beneficial to our commercial community; and further, that they are here, also, largely influenced by the ever present desire to learn more perfectly, by and through a free interchange of experiences with other bankers, how the important trusts committed to their charge can continue to be, under all circumstances, safely and satisfactorily administered.

We welcome you, then, socially as friends and acquaintances, and as bankers to the more serious matters to which we may be invited.

Gentlemen, you need not be reminded that the affairs of a well managed, prosperous bank are not centered wholly upon the immediate gain or profit in a monetary way that may result to that bank alone. Such institutions are educating forces.

From such financial centers, influences radiate of great power, tending to promote the commercial virtues of honesty, thrift, regularity and that "content which from employment springs." So that, while ever mindful of that which may insure the safety and prosperity of their own particular bank, the officers are also assisting in the development of a strong, virtuous constituency, which is the only sure foundation for the free advancement of a great State.

While thus directing the business of your own several banks and in a measure encouraging and directing the use of brawn and brain into sure employment, there are several questions of great importance and of wider range to which your attention has doubtless been more or less directed in your libraries: such as the relation of capital and labor, and of profit sharing; the assumption by the Federal Government of banking functions; the free coinage of the precious metals; and also, other and more abstruse questions in regard to money as the current medium of exchange, as the measure of values, as the standard for future obligations; the necessity for a national bankrupt law; and the need of a uniform, simple, but comprehensive bill of lading.

As to the merits or demerits of these or kindred questions, Mr. President, I am not concerned at present; my object is solely to point out that we are welcoming to our city and to our hospitalities gentlemen to whom these and related matters of inquiry are familiar subjects of consideration, and that, with pleasurable anticipation, we may expect to learn from our visiting friends something of the results of their studies in regard to some important themes.

But what as to the practical results? The expediency of accepting as conclusive the views of such men on such matters may be disputed on the ground that the opinions of conservative men must necessarily be formed from conservative stand-points; that they are opposed to innovation; that a class of men well-to-do in the established order of things do not, as a rule, advocate or desire change in such settled order of things; that bankers, generally, do not advocate reforms in political or financial affairs, because they are without need and consequent desire for radical change in the established order of business or state affairs, and therefore they as a class are not progressive guides, equal to the requirements of a rapidly increasing population and of enlarged commercial necessities.

But to these specious objections it may be at once and always replied that, in the conduct of the business of financial matters, there are a few foundation principles, well approved, which experience has clearly shown cannot in the long run be ignored with safety; and that reforms in well established financial methods, if any, must be wrought out along such well approved lines.

That ship is sea-worthy which is equipped so as to withstand the ravages of the storm surely to be encountered. History is not lacking in its registry of fair weather systems of finance and of their failure to withstand the stress occasioned by maturing obligations. These inevitable results of irregular schemes should be set forth continuously as warning beacons in the financial horizon. Communities, states and nations have been financially wrecked by seeking relief from monetary necessities through devious methods, or by venturing into the whirl of so-called progressive enterprise without regard to well approved foundation principles and without the ballast of a sufficient medium of exchange, of inherent and well defined value, current the world over. Your conservative views, therefore, should have place, and nowhere are they more entitled to be heard than in a California bankers convention.

With your further indulgence, allusion may be made for a moment to the banker's line of limitation. Is there a guide board set for his prudential guidance, proclaiming "Thus far shalt thou go and no farther," on occasions even when safety is not involved? You are all aware that in this fair State of California, Nature is ever ready to yield bountiful returns when the elements have been fitly joined in harmonious work, and that under such conditions there are possibilities of success to be attained by the laborer in any field, surpassing those of other lands. This necessarily involves corresponding possibilities of failure under other conditions.

Is there an analagous law in the commercial world? Does success in business ventures depend in great measure, if not wholly, upon the harmonious observance of certain elementary principles which may not be safely disregarded?

Are bankers concerned in the progressive prosperity of their constituents, and are they bound to study their own limitations as well as those of their clients so as to be better fitted to serve their business friends, at times, by withholding aid from, rather than by furthering, specious enterprises which lack the harmonious blending of well settled business principles in their attempted accomplishment?

If it is conceded that these are important queries and that they may be answered affirmatively, then, Mr. President, we may say, with emphasis, that in welcoming this Association to this commercial center, we have not in view an assembly of men with limited appreciation of their business responsibilities, nor a class of men actuated by a supreme law of selfishness, without regard to the correlative law of service.

On the contrary, we may claim in advance for this convention that it is composed of business men trained in the study of what may make most for the best interests of their immediate constituencies, widening out in the scope of their regard, as opportunity serves, so as to include the welfare of the State at large.

Gentlemen, we welcome the occasion which enables us to make your personal acquaintance; we receive with pleasure the men who come freighted with suggestive thoughts upon important themes affecting the interests of our State; and we rejoice in the opportunity that brings into personal communication the representatives of a class of business men who are notably interested in those things which best induce permanent peace and prosperity, who having independent opinions can give reasons for their faith, and who in their advocacy will manifest the courage of their convictions.

The Chairman: Gentlemen, I take pleasure in introducing to you Hon. E. F. Spence, of Los Angeles, who will respond to the address of welcome.

E. F. SPENCE :

Mr. President and Gentlemen of the Association :

It is indeed a great pleasure to me to be assigned the duty of responding in part to the words of welcome so cogently, so elegantly delivered by the Chairman of the San Francisco Clearing House Association, and I can assure you, sir, that I voice the sentiment of all the visiting bankers present that we accept the welcome in the same broad and kindly spirit in which it is given ; and if we do not enjoy and profit by the present occasion, I am sure the fault will not be laid at the door of the bankers of San Francisco.

I fully appreciate the lofty line of thought that pervades the whole address, and more particularly the impressive manner in which the idea is advanced that bankers must be in full sympathy with their own constituencies and make their impress upon their own communities for good, whereby the poor will be benefited as well as the rich.

I always deprecate the idea so often promulgated by thoughtless men that banks and bankers are only money bags, skinflints, shylocks and extortioners.

I believe, sir, that the bankers of America should be American in the strongest and strictest sense of the term. By the term American I mean the action of the man, not the accident of birthplace : and being thus thoroughly American the banker is *for* the people and *of* the people.

The social as well as the financial influence of the banker in his community is very great, and I would almost condemn the one whose wife's or whose daughter's dresses or trousseaus are made on foreign soil by foreign modistes, or whose overcoats are lined with any silk other than American silk.

Mr. President, at our preliminary convention in Los Angeles in March last, I took the liberty of asking a question, and now in a larger association I take the liberty of repeating it.

Is it not possible for some plan to be devised whereby the gold in the mountains can be extracted (without injury to the citizen), thereby enriching the world and benefiting millions of people ?

And if, perchance, some honest farmer in the vicinity of " Yuba dam" or the fertile banks of the "Feather" or the rich bottoms of "Sacramento's" sacred stream, should be injured and his property rendered unfit for future occupancy, would it not be well for the nation to make restitution by dredging and keeping clear the navigable rivers of the State, or give him a home of equal value down in the Southland where the orange and the banana grow, or some other good place where the *hydraulic slickens* cannot find a lodgment?

During the summer just past a change in public opinion is noticed in reference to the rights and the wrongs of the California Miner.

Newspapers and citizens of certain districts that formerly denounced the hydraulic miners are now disposed to treat them fairly, and it is to be hoped that ere long thousands of stalwart white men will have employment and every year California will yield millions and millions of gold to our National currency.

No portion of California is so vitally interested in this question as San Francisco.

When the mines of the eastern and western slopes of the Sierra Nevadas gave forth their gold and their silver by the ton, San Francisco saw her palmiest and liveliest times.

San Francisco stands today peerless amongst the cities of the Western Coast, and we of the Interior are proud of her advancement and progress.

Yet, were I as a guest not afraid of appearing rude by criticising or commenting upon the merits or demerits of my host, I would urge the bankers of San Francisco to urge the people of San Francisco (the constituency of the bankers) to keep this, the Queen City of the Pacific, not only abreast but *ahead* of the times in all things that tend to beautify and adorn and make attractive and captivate the strangers who come within her Golden Gates. I simply make this delicate allusion without elaboration.

Mr. Chairman, on behalf of our friends from the Southern portion of the State, we accept the words of kindly welcome with kindness and good feeling, and trust that our meeting will be profitable to all; and it gives me great pleasure to know that, on behalf of the friends from the Northern part of the State, we will have a response from Senator Preston of the Citizens Bank of Nevada, a gentleman whom I have known from boyhood, and who is every inch a banker and believes in the development of every part of the State, Northern, Central and Southern.

The Chairman: The next on the program is response to the address of welcome, by Mr. E. M. Preston of Nevada City. Mr. Preston will come forward.

Mr. Preston spoke as follows:

Mr. President and Gentlemen of the Convention:

On behalf of the bankers of the Northern part of the State, I wish to assure you that we appreciate very highly the words of welcome that have been extended to us upon this occasion, and we appreciate very highly the privileges which we enjoy in coming here for mutual consultation in regard to those topics which bear directly upon the business in which we are engaged. We realize that the banks themselves are the index of the financial pulse of the country; that the bankers are the first to feel depression; that the bankers are the first to feel a rise in prosperity; and, as one who comes from the North, I feel that we cannot too highly esteem the privileges we enjoy here to-day and which have been extended to us by this address of welcome, and which we are to still further enjoy in listening to the prepared addresses which are to succeed in the order of business. It pleases us particularly to know that the olive branch of peace has been extended to us from the balmy groves of the South, and that to the orange groves of Los Angeles the golden treasures of the mountains are still precious.

Gentlemen of the Convention, in the address of welcome we are told that there are three classes of topics that we are to consider: the first, those that are general in their nature, and relating to the general prosperity of California; second, those that are general in their nature as relating to banks and the banking business; and, third, we are told that we are to listen to those local topics which have a direct bearing upon the business that is before this Convention.

And, gentlemen, I know of no topic that is more interesting to us, none that is of more vital importance, than the question of the production and the supply of a circulating medium of the country. There was a time in the history of this nation when the National Government realized the importance of the gold production of California, and when the National Government put its hands into the Treasury to extend to us the means of communication, by which we could not only develop these resources, but by which they could be made readily available at a time when the nation needed our gold the most. And, fellow bankers, I believe that you will concur with me in the belief that the gold of California had much to do in preserving the financial integrity of the nation; and, while it is my earnest belief and hope that no such exigency will ever again arise (in the history of this Government) when the Government itself shall be compelled, for its very national existence, to delve in the mountains for the gold, yet there is an exigency that is likely to arise when the gold will become a commercial necessity. We hear much about the coinage of silver and the necessity of having more silver in circulation; we hear much about the free coinage of silver, and we doubtless differ in our opinions as to the policy of having the Government continue the coinage of silver as at present; but, in my experience, in my early struggles to win a dollar, in my early experience in managing the dollars of others, it has seemed to me that it is just as difficult for me to get a dollar in silver from the Government as it is to get a dollar in gold or a dollar in paper money.

In replying to the particular line of thought which has been assigned to me in this address—and I may say I highly appreciate the compliment that is paid me by Mr. Spence of Los Angeles—I am aware, Mr. President and gentlemen of the Convention, that there are present in this Association gentlemen who differ honestly from me in the position which I am to assume; gentlemen who believe that they are upon the right, gentlemen who believe that they have taken no advantage but what is right; but, inasmuch as we are to discuss both general and local topics, and inasmuch as the production of gold is a local topic in which the people in the section of the State where I reside are most interested, I am sure that I may properly express my views on that subject at this time.

The class of mining that is referred to is hydraulic mining. It has been interdicted by court; it has been suppressed by decree of the courts. There is no doubt that, as mining was first and originally conducted, much injury was done to the lands and to the streams that were affected by it. There is no doubt that many of the decisions that were rendered were rendered in accordance with equity and in accordance with the necessities that gave rise to those decisions. There is no disposition on the part of those who have been injured by those decisions to rebel against the constituted authorities or rail at that which is manifestly just and right. Yet we do feel that this matter has been carried to too great an extreme; that the zeal of those who would protect the lands and navigation of the rivers from injury from the mines, has gone to such an extent as to suppress a large class of mines that could be operated without material injury even to the alluvial lands or to the navigable streams of the Coast. I say this advisedly, because I believe that I know whereof I speak: that there are many mines that could be operated, operated profitably, and place millions of gold in circulation, that are now under the ban of the court.

We are pleased to know that in this Bankers Convention, and from the Southern portion of the State, should come such welcoming words of encouragement, that indicate that the time is not far distant when the law will discriminate between those that are injurious and those that are beneficial; when the law will say to this one, "Go, operate your mines, so long as there is no injury;" to this one, "You cannot operate your mine without injury." We believe that the time is coming when this concession will be granted; and, gentlemen, looking upon the condition of finances, and listening to the appeal for greater circulation, I am not sure in my own mind but the time is coming in the financial history of this State, of this city, and possibly of this Government, when the demand will arise that the millions of gold that are now locked up in the mountains shall be liberated; and when the demand is made, the ways and means will be devised for taking that gold out of the mountains without serious injury to any other interest in the State.

And, gentlemen, while we are not here to legislate upon the means, while we are not here to listen to the complaints of any one district, we are here to listen to suggestions and ideas that interest all. Now, it is undoubtedly a business truth, that you cannot destroy the business in one portion of the State without affecting the business at the center of the State, and remotely affecting the business of any portion of the State; and it is a fact that there are a number of counties along the Eastern line of this State where business has been practically suspended, millions of dollars that have been invested have been rendered practically without value, and millions of other dollars are still locked in the ground, because of the indiscriminating decisions of the courts. And, while we are not here to appeal to you for redress, while we are not here to complain of the injuries that we may have suffered in the past, we are here in the firm belief that, with the wisdom that is here assembled, with the conservative spirit that here prevails, and with the knowledge that you have of the financial necessities of this State, a sentiment will be sent abroad throughout this State that wherever this industry can be pursued without injury it should be allowed to proceed; and that whenever any means can be adopted by which the mines can be opened and these millions of dollars thrown into circulation, you will be the first to voice the sentiments, "Let it be done, so long as it can be done without injury."

Gentlemen, I thank you for the attention which you have given to these crude thoughts which I have presented upon this occasion, and I ask you, as fair-minded business men, as men who are interested in the financial prosperity of this State and of this city, as well as the prosperity of that section of the State which I represent, that you give this question a fair and candid consideration. |Applause.|

PRESIDENT'S ADDRESS.

Gentlemen of the Convention:

We are here to participate in the proceedings of the first annual meeting of the California Bankers Association organized at Los Angeles last March.

San Francisco extends its usual courteous and hospitable welcome to all who have come from the various sections of our State to consult and co-operate with the bankers of the metropolis.

Associations of the character represented here are now found in fourteen of the States of the Union, and the time is believed not to be distant when all other States will fall into line.

The general organization known as the American Bankers Association has been largely the moving cause in the formation of State Associations. Los Angeles is entitled to the credit of taking the imitative in starting the Association in whose interests we have assembled.

It is well that a beginning has been made. It perhaps ought to have been made years ago.

No State in the Union has greater need for an association of this kind ; our isolated position at the extreme westerly side of the country is a strong incentive for the bankers of California to come frequently together to consult with each other ; our system of banking has its California characteristics, and therefore the need of harmony and co-operation.

In many ways we can be of help to each other and to the State we so proudly call our own. The relation of the bank to the general interest is all-important. As bankers we stand between the debtor and creditor classes for the protection and benefit of both. We can not afford to antagonize either the borrower or lender ; we prosper best when those whom we serve are the most successful. We have a vital interest in all that goes to make up the welfare of the commonwealth.

It is to our advantage that all branches of industry shall be carried forward on a safe basis, and yet in a way that will admit of the utmost expansion consistent with safety and the needs of the increasing population.

We have an equal interest in the agriculturist, the miner, the manufacturer and the tradesman. A well informed banker ought to know as much as either one of these classes ; in fact he ought to have the combined knowledge of all of them. Our business demands that we shall be familiar with the staple crops of the world as furnished by the fields, the mines and the factories, and all about the freight and selling agencies for the materials produced and consumed. All these have a near or remote bearing on the credit of those with whom we deal, and in the value of the collaterals we hold as investments or securities for loans.

We have no foes to punish, no friends to reward. The path of the true banker does not lie in either of these directions. The banker is not at war with the public. He is not a monopolist. Banks help the poor quite as much as they help the wealthy, by supplying the life current to the arteries of trade and industry and thus quickening the business pulse.

Banking is not a sentiment, nor are banks charitable institutions to help the impecunious and indolent. Honestly-conducted and well managed banks are the conservators of all that is good in business, in politics and in morals.

Banks are concerned that the condition of business shall be well guarded, well developed and prosperous. They have much at stake in maintaining good government in the State and Nation from the highest to the lowest branch in the public service. Though far removed from all ecclesiastical influences, they are not indifferent to the maintenance of a high standard of morals in the community, on the ground that bad morals are apt to impair commercial integrity.

Bankers are the guardians of the honor of the business world. They have in their control and keeping the most sensitive of all plants, which is credit. We all know how the faintest whisper of suspicion affects credit, and how necessary is confidence in the achievement of success.

By standing together bankers have averted what otherwise would have been panics of great dimensions and attended with heavy losses to innocent parties.

It is difficult to conceive how the colossal commerce of the world could be carried on apart from the wonderful and far reaching system incident to bank organizations. Bankers have made it possible to do business with very little money, thus minimizing the dangers of handling it.

A man can travel the world over with very little real money in his possession at any point on his journey. He can buy a cargo of coffee in Brazil, a cargo of tea in China, a cargo of sugar in the Phillipine Islands or a cargo of wheat in California, without the payment of a single dollar in actual money. A large percentage of the world's business is on a credit basis. The bank is the foundation of that credit, and confidence is the corner stone: until some better system is devised for meeting the wants of the business world, the bank will continue to hold this pivotal position in the affairs of life.

California is to be congratulated on the soundness and extent of its banking system. No other State of like population and age has made fewer mistakes along this line. This freedom from error in the banking line is all the more remarkable from the fact of the general inexperience at first of the men engaged in the business and the great temptations incident to a newly settled portion of the country.

The fact that the banking business of the State has always rested on a solid coin foundation has no doubt been a contributory cause to the general healthfulness of our system. We have known the worth of the dollars handled, and we have been careful in the extension of credits. As a result, there have been but few bank failures in this State, and none attended with any serious loss for a long time.

B 2

The growth of banking in the State in the last decade has been remarkable. On the 1st of July, 1880, the whole number of State incorporated banks in the State was 78, while on the 1st of July, 1891, the number is 189, showing an increase of over 140 per cent. Some of this was due to the incorporation of private banks, but most of the increase is due to new organizations, many of which have come into existence in places where previously there were no institutions of this kind. Eleven years ago the 78 State incorporated banks reported a paid up capital of $25,127,140, and $79,278,280 due depositors, their aggregate resources being $119,575,520. At the beginning of the last fiscal year the 189 State incorporated banks reported a paid up capital of $49,670,414, and $165,776,311 due depositors, their aggregate resources footing up $244,547,141. These comparisons show that the banks have more than doubled their resources and deposits, while the amount of paid up capital employed in the business has been increased a hundred per cent. The figures suggest grand possibilities in the next decade, and the need for the exercise of the wisdom accumulated in years of experience by all the bankers of the State. We might apply these comparisons for the State at large to various localities with ever more astonishing results. In every considerable town or city in the State the number of banks has been increased in the past decade, while new points have been occupied. Eleven years ago San Francisco had 18 State incorporated banks, which reported a paid up capital of $16,596,- 990, deposits $65,274,111, and resources of $93,776,316. On the 1st of July last there were 21 of these banks in existence here, with a paid up capital of $30,373,- 611, deposits of $120,013,745, and resources of $169,403,770. Los Angeles presents a still more striking contrast. On the 1st of July, 1880, there was not a savings bank in that city and only three State commercial banks with a paid up capital of $177,000, deposits $931,805, and resources $1,950,903. On the 1st of July, 1891, Los Angeles had 14 State banks with a paid up capital of $2,290,600, deposits $6,732,432, and resources $10,023,190. Other interior cities, especially in the Southern part of the State, present corresponding contrasts in the banking line.

The progress and prosperity already achieved furnish encouragement and inspiration for the future. But we must not attempt to rest on the record made. Eternal vigilance is the price of success in the future as it has been in the past.

The experiences acquired will be of help to us all. Further help may come by gatherings like the present. These annual meetings will make us better acquainted with each other, and that alone will create a bond of sympathy and co-operation that has not heretofore existed to the same degree. The free interchange of thought and experience will crystalize into a better understanding of each other, and will serve to perfect the banking system of the State in all its various phases.

What the future has in store for California bankers no one knows. We all know that questions may arise to demand prompt and decisive action. With a large and live organization such as is hoped the California Bankers Association may become, we shall be in a condition to act intelligently on any proposition that may be presented, and our united opinion and action will carry with it an influence such as we could not wield as individual bankers.

Chairman: I now call the Convention to order. The Convention is ready for business. I introduce to you, gentlemen of the Convention, Mr. James A. Thompson, of the Mutual Savings Bank of San Francisco, Chairman of the Committee on Entertainment. He will state what the entertainment program is.

James A. Thompson : *Mr. Chairman and Gentlemen* — I desire to call your attention at the earliest possible moment to the excursion to Palo Alto, which is to take place on Saturday. We are invited to visit the Leland Stanford, Jr., University, by its founder, and Senator Stanford has arranged the program. Those of the visiting members of the Convention, and their respective wives, will please take the train at the Southern Pacific Railroad depot, Third and Townsend Streets, at 8:30 a. m., where a guide will meet and convey them, by the courtesy of Senator Stanford, to Palo Alto University and the stables. We also take pleasure in announcing that we are invited to lunch with Senator Stanford. A banquet has been arranged for the visitors, as well as the local bankers, but we are not to invite the ladies to the banquet. The proceedings there will be entirely informal. It will be presided over by Mr. Brown, and Mr. Gerberding will be toast-master.

The Secretary then called the roll, announcing at the conclusion that since making up his report three banks had registered as members :

Alameda Bank, representative present.

Monterey County Bank, representative present.

Bank of Rideout, Smith & Co., Oroville, representative present.

C. E. Palmer, of Oakland: Mr. Chairman, owing to our extensive program and the number of members to speak and papers to be read, I would ask leave to offer the following resolution: That the remarks of each speaker on the adoption of reports and points of order be limited to five minutes. We will have to make some such rule as that in order to get through with this long program.

Second by Lovell White of San Francisco, and carried.

Chairman: We will now hear the Secretary's Report.

REPORT OF SECRETARY.

Mr. President and Members of the California Bankers Association :

GENTLEMEN—Following an invitation sent out last January by the Los Angeles Clearing House, a delegation of California bankers, including many of those here present and representing seventy banks, assembled at Los Angeles on March 11th, 12th and 13th last, for the purpose of forming a State Bankers Association.

Provision was made for organization and membership by the adoption of a Constitution and the election of officers. The first membership fee was received by the Secretary from the Santa Barbara County National Bank on the 24th of March.

Since that time the Secretary has endeavored to keep the existence of the Association before the bankers of the State; the efforts put forth meeting with quick response from the various sections of California.

There are fifty-three counties in the State, in all of which the people are provided with banking facilities except eleven, viz: Alpine, Amador, Calaveras, Del Norte, Inyo, Lassen, Mariposa, Mono, Plumas, Trinity and Tuolumne. In seven more, viz: Sierra, San Mateo, Nevada, Modoc, Mendocino, Marin and Eldorado, none of the banks have the honor as yet of membership in this Association, but in thirty-five counties the members are distributed in very large proportion to the total number of banks, and comprise all the banks and banking institutions in Colusa, Contra Costa, Fresno, Kern, Orange, Sacramento, San Benito, Sutter and Ventura counties, and, in the counties containing ten banks or over, the following proportions obtain: Los Angeles, containing 30 banks, 24 members; San Francisco, containing 29 banks, 19 members; San Bernardino, containing 15 banks, 10 members; San Diego, containing 15 banks, 9 members; Santa Clara, containing 11 banks, 6 members; Sonoma, containing 12 banks, 1 member. A large portion of the 95 banks not on the membership list are either savings institutions, adjuncts of some commercial or national bank in the same town, or foreign corporations, doing little or no deposit business, or private bankers distant from the larger financial centers.

April 25th the membership list reached 100; July 1st, out of 216 banks and bankers, the Association claimed 136 as members, and to-day the list foots up 151; a most gratifying showing at the assembling of our FIRST ANNUAL CONVENTION.

The Constitution provides for a uniform Annual Membership Fee and Dues of ten dollars for each bank or banker. In consequence, by a process of lightning calculation, the sum of $1,510 has been received, which has been duly remitted to the Treasurer. Receipt has been given, in the case of 141 members, covering dues to date of this meeting, but the 10 banks acquiring membership since meeting of the Executive Council (July 24th) have received credit until the Annual Meeting in 1892; being practically as joining of this date.

Twenty-seven (27) warrants have been drawn on the Treasurer, aggregating $768.55, and, in the absence of information to the contrary, are doubtless duly paid.

One meeting of the Executive Council has been held, on July 24th, which is fully set forth in their report.

The detail work of this office has been of necessity somewhat heavy. The newness of the movement, the general lack of personal acquaintance among our bankers, and the difficulty of making matters clear by correspondence, have presented many difficulties. Each year added to the Association's existence will minimize these and render easier and more effective the labor put forth.

The printed report of the Proceedings of the March Convention (delivered to us with the compliments of the Los Angeles Clearing House) has been distributed to all the banks of California, the various Clearing Houses in the United States, the other State Bankers Associations, and to those requesting same. While not free from defects, the pamphlet compares favorably with those issued by other State organizations. Fifteen of these, besides our own, are now in running order, and others in process of formation. As the "Examiner" states, the *fad* seems to be catching. All have been corresponded with and assured that a representative from them would meet with a hearty welcome here. Responses are in from a number, regretting that geographical reasons alone prevent acceptance.

I desire to thank the officers and Council for their interest and confidence, the members at large for courtesy and kind expressions of encouragement, and the Board of Bank Commissioners, who are in a position to judge of the scope and utility of a State Bankers Association, for their hearty, effective co-operation and use of their office facilities during the present week.

Do not think for a moment that responsibility for the success and usefulness of this Association rests alone on your officers. If each banker will realize and act upon the truth in the children's hymn—"So, let us shine; you in your corner, and I in mine," there will be little chance for misstep, and the blending of all rays will so perfectly tone the high lights and deep shadows of our official pathway that, even with our broad guage and heavy rolling stock, quick time can be made with entire safety.

Geo. H. Stewart, Secretary.

Lovell White moved that it be accepted and placed on file; motion seconded and carried

Chairman: Report of Treasurer is next in order.

REPORT OF TREASURER.

To the California Bankers Association:

Gentlemen—I have the honor to submit the following report:

RECEIPTS.

Membership dues from 151 Banks, @ $10.00 each..... $1,510 00

DISBURSEMENTS.

Vouchers Nos. 1 to 27 inclusive, herewith............. 768 55

Balance cash on hand.......................... $ 741 45

Respectfully submitted,
G. W. Kline, Treasurer.

On motion, accepted and placed on file.

Chairman: Report of the Executive Council will be read by its Chairman, A. D. Childress, of Los Angeles.

REPORT OF THE EXECUTIVE COUNCIL.

Mr. President and Members of the California Bankers Association:

Gentlemen—In pursuance with and as required by the Constitution, your Executive Council beg leave to submit the following report, towit:

Immediately after the session of the Convention held at Los Angeles on March 11th, 12th and 13th ultimo for the purpose of organizing a State Bankers Association, the Council, with a unanimous voice, selected San Francisco, the metropolis of our great State, as the appropriate place to hold our first annual meeting, and named October 13th, 14th and 15th as the time. Since then, and very recently in fact, the dates have been changed to the 14th, 15th and 16th for very good and sufficient reasons.

But one special meeting of the Council was called, the following report of which, together with what has just preceded, practically covers the official acts of the Council since the Convention.

Minutes:

Meeting of the Executive Council held at the San Francisco Savings Union, San Francisco, July 24th, 1891, 10:30 a. m.

Present: A. D. Childress, Chairman, Presiding; W. M. Eddy, T. S. Hawkins, Lovell White, C. E. Palmer, W. W. Phillips, A. L. Seligman.

Present by request: Thomas Brown, President of the Association; I. W. Hellman, Vice President of the Association; Geo. H. Stewart, Secretary of the Association.

Absent: N. D. Rideout, in Europe; W. D. Woolwine "attendance impossible."

The Secretary of the Association was called upon and made a statement showing the present membership of 141; being a larger proportion of total Banks in the State than is the case with other State Associations, and including in the main the leading Banks and Bankers of California; also reporting a very general feeling of interest in the Association and its work and disposition to further it.

A request was presented from R. M. Widney, of the University Bank, Los Angeles, for opportunity to be heard on his "National Currency" plan at the October Convention.

A resolution by Lovell White and amendment by William Eddy were withdrawn and action deferred until two o'clock p. m.

On motion, Mr. Thomas Brown and Mr. A. L. Seligman were appointed a committee to provide rooms and make all the material arrangements for the Convention in San Francisco, October 13th, 14th and 15th, 1891, and A. D. Childress and the Secretary a committee to correspond in reference to the literary part and arrange the programme, subject to approval of the Council.

On motion of Mr. Thomas Brown, the salary of the Secretary was fixed at $50 per month from April 1st, 1891, and warrants ordered drawn for the actual expenses of members of the Council and Secretary in attending the meeting.

Adjourned until 2 p. m.

Afternoon Session, 2 p. m.:

Present: A. D. Childress, T. S. Hawkins, W. M. Eddy, Lovell White, C. E. Palmer, W. W. Phillips; Geo. H. Stewart, Secretary.

The following resolution, presented by Lovell White and seconded by W. W. Phillips, was carried unanimously:

Resolved—That the request of Judge R. M. Widney to be heard on the subject of a National Currency at the meeting of the Bankers Association of California, to be held 13th, 14th and 15th of October, 1891, is denied on grounds as follows:

1st. The views of the Judge are familiar to the members of this Council, having been set forth before the meeting of the Bankers Convention held at Los Angeles in March last and also at a meeting of the Commercial Congress of Kansas City, held April 16th, 1891, his remarks at both meetings having been published in extenso and widely circulated.

2nd. That this Council are not in sympathy with the views of the Judge, but disapprove them.

3rd. That in the belief of this Council, there was no intention on the part of the members of the Convention held as above at Los Angeles to indorse the position of the Judge.

4th. That in the opinion of the members of this Council there are local matters to be considered at the meeting of the Convention to be held in October, quite sufficient to occupy all the available time, and it is inexpedient to attempt the consideration of foreign and extraneous subjects.

5th. That in the opinion of the members of this Council, the Bankers Association of California was organized to secure the well-ordering and to facilitate the transaction of local banking business upon the most approved methods, and that it is not the duty nor the privilege of members to seek to reform the world, or to revolutionize methods throughout the United States.

The sense of those present was that the October meeting would be nominated the " First Annual " one and that the fee of any Bank or Banker joining between this date and the meeting in October would cover dues until the meeting in 1892. Adjourned.

It is a matter of congratulation that this Association, like everything in the Vegetable Kingdom in the " Glorious Climate " of California, has grown from infancy to maturity in a remarkably short duration of time.

True, 'twas a sturdy infant at birth, but nourished by the assiduous care of our genial Secretary it has grown into robust proportions and already compares most favorably, if not outranking, similar organizations beyond the " Rockies " and in other States in both numerical and financial strength. Of the 246 Banks in California, 151 are enrolled as members of the California Bankers Association, and of the 95 remaining outside the fold eleven are branches of institutions on our roster.

The financial condition of the Association is very satisfactory.

The sum of $1510 has been received from annual dues, which constitute our only income or revenue, while the total expenses have been only $768.55, leaving a balance of $741.45 on hand as per report of both Secretary and Treasurer.

While the Council can not submit an accurate estimate of the amount required to carry on the affairs of the Association during the ensuing year, it feels reasonably sure that the annual dues together with the balance now in the Treasury will be more than sufficient to defray all expenses, and therefore has no recommendations to make for raising money in any other way.

It is a matter of congratulation that the hand of death has not as yet fallen upon any member of this Association, official or otherwise, and that no vacancies in office have been declared for that or other reasons.

As yet there has been no arrest or prosecution of any party charged with crime by any member of the Association, as the Constitution provides.

In view of the fact that but seven months of the year have elapsed since the election of the present officers of the Association, and moreover that their tenure of office has been merely a period of organization, the Council suggest and reccommend that their election be simply confirmed and that they be retained in office another year or until the next general meeting of the Association.

Respectfully submitted, etc.,

A. D. CHILDRESS, Chairman.

The Chairman: You have heard the report of the Executive Council. What is your pleasure?

Wm. Beckman, of Sacramento: I move the adoption of the report. Motion seconded.

R. M. Widney. of Los Angeles: Mr. Chairman. while the motion is before the house, I wish to speak on it. Mr. Chairman and Gentlemen of the Convention: In that report is a resolution, in response to a request on my behalf to make an address before this Convention relating to the money system of the United States or an increased volume of money. I admit that the Executive Council have the absolute right to reject the petition, but I don't think that they have the right to undertake to put in the minutes of the proceedings of this body a resolution unqualifiedly condemning a thing that has not been presented to them. You can't, to-day, state whether my views are correct or incorrect on the question that I ask to address you. I have been placed in a false position before this Convention. I made an address before the Bankers Convention in Los Angeles, as any man had a right to do, having obtained the privilege. No bankers convention nor any man in it is responsible for any address made by any member of that association. That is well known everywhere. I knew very well that the views I presented could not possibly be considered by those present so they would really understand them. I therefore never asked the Convention to indorse a single idea that I put forth at that time; I never asked them to indorse the bill or the constitutional amendment that I had prepared, because I presented neither one of those to that Convention. Now, I did present a resolution, and I will read that resolution to you, and if any member of this Convention can find a single word in that resolution through which they would run a pen as being unsound in finances, then I have no objection to their taking that conduct. I shall not occupy much time and shall confine myself to the resolution. In order that no one should be taken by surprise, I introduced this resolution at the very beginning of the Convention, stating that I would call it up for vote at the conclusion of the Convention; and along toward the last, after the address, and when it was fairly brought before the Convention, they unanimously voted in favor of that resolution. Now, here is the resolution. As I read it, slowly, tell me what you would strike out of it: "Resolved: That this Convention respectfully request Congress at its next session to devise a uniform money system for the people of the United States." Has any one any objection to a uniform money system for the people of the United States? If there is any one that objects to a uniform money system for the people of the United States, I would like to have him hold his hand up. Are we to have a chaotic system, a patch-work, in preference to a uniform system? I find no one that objects to it. "With the gold dollar as the standard unit of value." Isn't that the doctrine from the Atlantic to the Pacific? Is there any one here who wants to vote for a money system with any other than the gold dollar as the unit of value? "Using gold, silver and currency for a circulating medium." That is what we are using throughout the United States to-day. It is what you are using in California to-day; and is the Convention opposed to the proper use of gold, silver and currency? It is to be devised as the best wisdom of the people who shall formulate the law may dictate. "In sufficient volume to fully meet and keep pace with the growing wants of the business of the country." No volume is fixed there. No men can fix it. It will be the result of discussion through the whole Convention; but, are we to go before the world and say that we don't want a sufficient volume to transact the business of the country? I don't think that we are. "Founding the issue of currency upon the wealth of the whole nation." This proposition to found the issue of currency upon the whole wealth of the nation is just as it is done to-day. Greenbacks, the national banknotes, have underlying them the money wealth of the United States. "Making gold, silver and currency a legal tender." They are a legal tender to-day. "And exchangeable at par on demand." Now, I don't know of any banker that ever advocated the doctrine that gold, silver and paper should be circulated as a medium and that one should not be as good as another; that they should not be circulated at par whenever required. "Fixing by a constitutional amendment the legality of such a circulating medium." The Supreme Court of the United States first decided that Congress had no power whatever to put out paper money. The decision was made by Chief Justice Chase; it was signed by four out of eight of the justices, and would have remained as the decision of the United States Supreme Court, but a petition was made for a rehearing; Congress passed a bill adding one more to the Supreme Court, making it nine, and one who signed the decision resigned, and a Republican administration appointed two men as justices who believed in the doctrine of the power of Congress to put out paper money, so that they had five that held that Congress did have the power, and four that Congress did not have it; and they have stood on that from that day down to the present, except as new members have been put on the Supreme Court. Now it is an open question. Those justices can hold, if they see fit, that Congress has no power whatever to issue paper money; and I found throughout the East, in talking with Eastern bankers, that they object to currency on the ground that it was a question whether Congress had the power to issue the money. This simply presupposes that, if Congress puts forth paper money, they shall make a constitutional amendment to prevent the change in the standard of value. [Chairman raps.] Now, I will close in a moment. The latter part of this is: "and preventing the dangers of inflation, contraction, repudiation, or change in the standard of value." We don't want any inflation. No man that understands finances wants inflation. You don't want Congress to have the power to so contract the circulating medium of this country as to affect the values of commodities, nor the power to flood this country with absolutely worthless money; you don't want to have it so that a decision of the Supreme Court of the United States may hold that the entire money issue is absolutely void, which is repudiation. Among the financiers that I have talked with, I have never met one yet in banking circles who has advanced a proposition that is not in accord with the propositions advanced in that resolution.

B 3

Now, I don't know that this Convention in Los Angeles did anything but what the soundest financiering would stand. I didn't ask you to pass upon that at that time, for I said to the members this: "I will not ask that; in this Convention they have not the time to study it, they have not the time to understand it."

Now, my objection to the resolution contained in that report is, that it is a direct blow at my arguments, at my views, without giving this Convention an opportunity to hear me argue. I am prepared to argue that before this Convention. I am prepared to argue these views with any member of the Executive Council or others.

The Chairman (rapping): Time.

R. M. Widney: Just a moment. I simply ask that that report be amended so that that resolution is left out; that they reject the application, simply, which I think they have a right to do. I think, as a member of this Convention, I am entitled to that.

Lovell White, of San Francisco: In regard to the adoption of that resolution of Mr. Widney's, if it was adopted, and there seems to be no doubt of it, I understand it was voted upon at the very last moment. When the Convention was about to adjourn, I was astonished to find that that had been adopted; and I talked with quite a number of our people, and very few seemed to be aware of the existence of it. It went through at the close of business, without understanding and without thought. I make that assertion on what I saw. That the resolution was passed is beyond question, but it was passed without thought as to its effect at the time. I think this statement will be corroborated by any number of gentlemen here now. Concerning the resolution itself, it was preceded by a long and eloquent oration or speech by Judge Widney, a very able speech, mostly explaining the meaning of the resolution, and how it appeared very harmless; but, so far as members who were present in the Convention were concerned, they associated the matters of the speech with the matters of the resolution, and that resolution, they believed, was in support of the views advanced in the speech. Now, that being so, the apparent harmlessness of the resolution disappears. The resolution indorses the speech, if it means anything in the way it is put before the public. If you approve this resolution, if you adopt this resolution, then you adopt views which support the resolution. Now, that is the way it presents itself to the average mind or any mind: that the resolution was preceded by the speech, and that the speech set forth the views of Judge Widney, and that the resolution was, if it meant anything, to sustain those views. So much for that part of it.

Now, the Judge says he has not had a chance to be heard. We all have a very great interest in his remarks, made at Kansas City. It is understood to be the gospel that Judge Widney preaches. He set it forth, and we have all read it. The only question is: Has he had a new revelation? Has he got any more gospel? If there is more gospel, we might hear it, but if that is the gospel, we have heard it. So much for that.

Now, what I have said is in the nature of an extempore speech. I have some views here, as I think we should entertain them, and will read:

The California Bankers Association is supposed to have been organized for definite purposes : those purposes being conservative, not revolutionary—preservative, not subversive—to maintain, not to destroy.

Objects of the Association may be said to be: To make parties acquainted whose concurrent action in different parts of the State are necessary for the transaction of business. To simplify and make uniform the methods of conducting affairs. To instruct the inexperienced, and to make common to all the improvements that may have been tested by any and found satisfactory.

We are not here for speculative purposes, nor as reformers.

There are now, and always have been, and always will be, questions before the public with which the Association, as a body, has nothing to do.

It may be that the financial system of the United States is faulty; but if so, we do not propose to suggest a remedy—we have no missionary work to do.

It may be that the banking fraternity is an evil in the community; but if so, it is not our place to take steps to do away with that evil.

The members of this Convention are here as the representatives, with very limited powers, of sundry banks.

Were the directors of those various banks here themselves, it would not be their province to attack, in any form, the system of banking that now obtains.

The directors of any bank may conduct its business, but cannot dispose of it —cannot sell plant, assets and good will—without consent of stock holders, and it is treachery to stock holders to consent to or to connive at the destruction of the business of a bank or the business of banking.

If views now presented for approval of the public in various parts of the country should obtain, and the schemes should be found to work on trial, the business of banking would soon become a thing of the past.

Commercial banks might hang on the ragged edge of despair for a time, but the mission of savings banks would be ended.

These things are not mentioned seriously from any fear that our present financial systems will be revolutionized in our day; but they illustrate the principle that we are here in the interest of the bankers of this State, and we believe incidentally in the interest of the people at large.

If speculative matters are to occupy the time of this Convention, there are many questions that may well demand attention; but we do not wish to engage in "Looking Back" with Bellamy nor in looking forward into the dim vistas of the future.

We propose to deal with the present; and dealing with the present, to ignore all matters not connected with the subject of banking in California.

For the time being we are indifferent as to religion and politics.

We have no choice between prohibition and high license ; it matters not to us whether the present Grand Jury of this city is legally impanelled ; and it is not a question which is entitled to most consideration, Baby McKee in the White House or Baby Cleveland in New York.

There are plenty of matters pertinent to the occasion to occupy the time of this Convention. [Applause.]

R. M Widney: Just one word, in reply. It is simply this: The gentleman refers to an apparent pushing of that resolution through the Convention at Los Angeles by improper means. Now, that was not the case. If there is anything that I despise, it is a man that will do a thing of that kind. I therefore introduced that in open session the first day, notified the Convention that I would make an address, and that I would afterwards follow that resolution up. That resolution does not indorse an address that I made; it does not indorse my position. In the first place, it is a statement of a general proposition, and I believe this Association believes in every principle stated in that resolution. It was called up in regular session, in the regular order of business, and everybody was present who had any desire to be present at that time.

With reference to the general proposition of an attack on the banking systems, the gentleman misunderstands my position if he says that I have ever uttered a word against the banking system of the United States. I say that the business of the United States and of the world cannot be carried on unless you have got a different banking system. I am in favor of getting the very best financial system that the entire intelligence and wisdom of the people of the United States can bring forth. I am advancing no hobby. I want to see the thing discussed throughout the United States, and, if we have got the best, keep it; if we have not got the best, let us get it. That is my proposition, gentlemen. If you want to vote against that proposition, let those who are not satisfied with it, do so.

The Chairman: Any other remarks?

A Member: Question.

The Chairman: Gentlemen, the motion is on the adoption or rejection of the report of the Executive Council, and that the same be placed on file if adopted.

Motion put and report adopted and placed on file.

The Chairman: The next on the program is discussion : subject, "Should the Mortgage Tax be Abolished or Maintained?" Opened by Mr. Beckman, of Sacramento.

Wm. Beckman:

Mr. Chairman and Gentlemen of the Convention:

In Los Angeles, last March, I offered a resolution that we should discuss the mortgage tax. Now, I have got a little article written upon the subject here, and I would like to have each and all of you, if you see any fault in it, to just express it; because if my proposition won't stand upon its own foundation, let it go by the board.

The question as to the amendment of the Constitution with reference to taxation of mortgages, is one of vast importance, as well to the borrower as to the lender. By the Constitution of 1879, Section 4 of Article XIII., it was attempted to make what was conceived to be a just distribution of the burdens of taxation between capitalists who lend money and those who are compelled, from necessity, to borrow it. Experience, however, has served to demonstrate to my mind, and, I believe, to the minds of many others, that the scheme thus adopted was based upon a false theory. Exact equality in any of the burdens of government has long since been demonstrated to be chimerical and beyond the reach of human legislation. It was evidently believed by the framers of the Constitution that, by placing the tax upon that proportion of the property which is represented by the amount and value of the mortgage, upon the mortgagee, equality, as between the mortgagor and mortgagee, would be attained or more nearly approximated.

It will be observed that, by the section of the Constitution to which reference has been made, a mortgage, deed of trust, contract, or other obligation by which a debt is secured, is made to be, and treated as, an interest in the property affected thereby. This mortgage, deed of trust, etc., is assessed to the mortgagee; and the mortgagee, by heavy penalties, is prohibited from imposing upon the mortgagor, by contract or otherwise, the duty of paying the tax. Theoretically, therefore, the tax upon the mortgage, or other contract, must, at all events, be paid, primarily, by the mortgagee. No good purpose can be subserved by a mere theoretical imposition of a tax upon the capitalist, unless, in practice as well, the burden of the mortgagor is lessened and the burden of the mortgagee correspondingly increased; but it is evident to the most casual observer that such is not the practical effect of this provision of the Constitution. There is nothing in the law which compels the capitalist to loan his money, or prohibits him from fixing such a rate of interest upon his loan as would at once relieve him from the burden and practically impose the payment of the tax upon the person to whom the loan is made. In the determination of the amount of interest to be charged, it is not only possible but it is practically true that capitalists have uniformly taken into consideration the probable amount of the mortgage tax in fixing the rate of interest to be paid for their money. It is true that competition, to a greater or less extent, regulates the compensation of the capitalist for the use of his money; but this would be true whether the mortgage, as such, was taxed or not: the value of the money being calculated in the net, and the amount of expenditure in the payment of taxes, etc., being taken into account in the calculation by which the net product is ascertained. In other words, in determining the amount of interest to be charged, the capitalist adds to the value of his money an amount which he knows will be sufficient to pay him for the use of his money, and also to pay the mortgage tax. The amount thus added is the result of approximation, and is made large enough to cover every possible tax imposed; and, in many instances, as the result of this necessity for approximation, is made larger than the tax afterward actually levied. The burden of the tax upon the mortgagor is, therefore, increased instead of diminished; and the purpose of this provision of the Constitution is, therefore, practically frustrated. No provision like the one under consideration can ever prove of real value to the borrower unless, by legislation, some limit is placed upon the value of the use of money and the amount of interest which may be charged. The capitalist cannot be compelled to loan his money unless he so desires, and, under the just provisions of our law, he is independent of any effort to limit the rate of interest which he may charge.

Besides, there are instances in which the borrower desires to pay off his debt, or sell his land, before the expiration of a year; in which case he is invariably required to pay a sufficient amount of interest to meet the year's taxes before the lender will accept the money. The disadvantage to the lender is readily seen when it is remembered that he finds it necessary to attend to the payment of the mortgage tax in all communities and counties in which his securities lie; and, in case of second and third mortgages upon the same property, he is compelled to see to the payment of the tax upon them also. Loans are sometimes satisfied before the taxes are due without taking into consideration the amount of the mortgage tax. In such a case, if the lender should refuse to pay the amount of the tax, or should leave the country, the party who owned the property would have to pay the tax, as such, besides paying it in the form of interest ; and there may be instances where, the lender having neglected to pay the mortgage tax, the property is sold; in which case the borrower is compelled to pay the expenses of redeeming it.

This section of the Constitution is also a great hardship on the savings banks of this State. It requires them to look after their mortgage taxes in whatever county the property may be situated. Interest is usually made payable in installments, while the tax must be paid as a whole. There is another, and I think, stronger reason than any of the foregoing why this tax should not be imposed upon the borrower. As I have said before, by adding the amount of the property tax to the value of the use of the money in ascertaining the gross amount of interest to be charged, the rate of interest in this State is correspondingly increased. Evidently, this increase of interest must interfere with the settlement and material progress of the State. To the stranger who comes from abroad with a view of investing in our lands: to the farmer who is looking for a home from which he can derive a livelihood; and particularly, to the small farmers who cultivate our soil and whose industry adds most to our material wealth, the higher rate of interest, consequent upon the imposition of this mortgage tax, does not serve as a commendation; but it rather operates to deter him from purchasing our property, or taking up his residence in our midst Unquestionably, a high rate of interest, to those who must borrow in order that they may be enabled to carry on their industries, is not conducive to the welfare and prosperity of those whose strong arms are required to develop the resources of the State. The ordinary farmer or laborer does not look behind the rate of interest, stated in the gross, to find the elements which compose it. A stranger coming from the Eastern states, desiring to purchase property, negotiates with the land owner and determines its price, and then, perhaps, desires to borrow one-half of the purchase money from a bank. When he is given the higher rate of interest, including the mortgage tax, he at once compares that rate with the rate prevailing in his own State where no such mortgage tax exists. In the State from which he comes perhaps he can borrow money for five or six per cent.; but he is told by the banker here that his interest will be from eight to ten per cent. Is it not a natural result that he will not purchase, the high rate of interest deterring him? Nothing could be more conducive, in my judgment, to our prosperity and welfare than the destruction of this mortgage tax: in order that interest, as such, should stand alone and should be reduced upon its face to the actual value of the use of money.

The question is too broad, the reasons are too numerous why this system of taxation should be abolished, to be considered at a single meeting of this Association. It seems to me, however, that the considerations already submitted ought to be sufficient to convince all persons, interested in financial matters, of the propriety of the resolution submitted at the last meeting. The resolution, however, should be amended: for, as the tax was created by the provisions of the Constitution, it must be destroyed, if destroyed at all, by an amendment of that instrument submitted to the votes of the people.

Now, Gentlemen, all I have to say in regard to this thing is that it should stand upon its own bottom, and I think that our grangers, our farmers, and all of us, should discuss this thoroughly whenever it comes up.

The Chairman: Any other remarks on this subject?

W. F. Bosbyshell, of Los Angeles: Mr. Chairman, I would like to say a few words on this subject.

The Chairman: Will you come forward to the platform?

Mr. Bosbyshell: I want to say only a few words at this time. It seems to me this matter has been discussed somewhat in our section of the State, in favor of the repeal of this mortgage tax law. It should be done. I took some little interest in corresponding and talking with members of our State Legislature, two years ago last winter and at other times; in talking with our State Senator and members of the Legislature last winter, to see if something could not be done about it; and it was reported to me that the bankers and many of the lenders of money in San Francisco, to some extent, were opposed to it. I don't know how true that is. Now, if the bankers in this section are opposed to the present tax law, cannot it be repealed? We, as bankers, and in convention, are supposed to do some active good for a purpose; and can't we take some active steps, so that before the members of the next Legislature are elected they can be pledged to repeal that law? It does seem that we ought to do something more than talk or read papers on these subjects, and if these bankers, all over this State, from the South and North and Center, are actually in earnest, and opposed to this law, and take some united action in the matter, that the law could be repealed at any meeting of the legislature.

W. W. Phillips, of Fresno: *Mr. Chairman and Gentlemen—*It is a question in my mind whether it would be a good policy to negotiate with the bankers throughout this State and go upon the record as opposed to the mortgage tax—that is, if we wish to repeal that law. We all know that the average farmer, who is generally a money borrower, looks with suspicion upon anything that appears to come in contact with his interests, and if he fixes upon the idea that we are going to annul or repeal this law, by a constitutional amendment, the chances are he will be opposed to its repeal. Whether or not it will be the best policy for us to put ourselves upon record here today as opposed to this law, I don't know; it is not for me to say; I simply have my own opinion about it; but Mr. Bosbyshell has well remarked that we can at least use our influences among members of the Legislature, or members to be elected to the next session, and that is where we have got to do our work; in getting the proper men sent to the Legislature to do away with this obnoxious law. As for myself, I agree fully with the gentleman from Sacramento. I think that law was passed when the saddle-rock element was in control of this State. I believe all of you, too, think that the men of this State should see that this law is repealed. And one feature of it strikes my mind particularly so, and that is this: that we shut out from this State the cheaper capital of the Eastern states, and that is what the farmer don't understand. He don't think for a moment that he is virtually shutting out the Eastern money market from California in all its investments. No Eastern capital is going to come here and submit to the mortgage tax in this State. I don't think there is any question about that. It will never come here, either, to go into lending or into mortgage loans. We have simply got to depend upon the capital of our own State, when it comes to that class of business. I should like to have the sense of the Convention upon this proposition: whether it is better to put ourselves on record as favoring the repeal of the mortgage tax law, or whether we should not do it. I submit it to the Convention and would like to have it further discussed.

Wm. Beckman: One moment, Mr. Chairman. I want to make this remark: I don't think it would be policy to pass a resolution here that we are in favor of abolishing this mortgage tax. It has been well said here that the people would then oppose it. Our little bank has probably six hundred or a thousand loans, all on farming lands; and when these men come in and pay their interest, I try to talk to them, as to whether the mortgage tax is an injury instead of a benefit to them, and let them discuss it in their farmer alliance associations and let them pass this law, instead of the Bankers Association. That is the view that I take. Mr. Chairman, I know that two years ago, and since, several of those large institutions had representatives here, and that they told me—I think probably told others—that California could easily have from a hundred to a hundred and fifty millions of Eastern money, if we did not have the mortgage tax. I suppose it is generally understood by members of this Convention that the Legislature can take no decisive action in this matter; all that they can do is to recommend that this subject matter be submitted; as I understand it, to a public vote, and that the voters determine as to whether the Constitution should be amended in this particular or not. That will not depend upon the votes of the Legislature. All that they can do is to merely recommend that this matter be submitted to public vote. And it would seem to me that there should be an expression of the sentiments of the bankers, in order to determine as to whether such a vote would be in favor of the repeal or amendment of the Constitution in that particular. I remember, when some previous action was taken in regard to the mortgage tax, that petitions were very numerously signed, all throughout the State, before the matter was presented to the Legislature for action, and it would seem to me that some such course as that should be pursued before any attempt is made to present the matter to the Legislature and to the people at large. As to the policy, I don't know what the sentiment of the people would be. As bankers, we can see how this thing operates; but the people don't see it and don't appreciate the matter from the same stand-point that we do or look at it in the same light, and in many respects don't understand how it affects them. I don't know, either, how the matter can be presented to them so that they will understand it, but it would seem to me that the agitation of the question in the Legislature, prior to an expression of popular sentiment, would not be likely to be favorable.

C. C. Bush, of Redding: There are two things I might particularize as effective arguments on this question: the securing of low rates of interest, and land and the high prices of it. If we can present to the voter a proposition for low money, cheap money on the one side, and if you can present to him cheap land on the other side, that I think is the strongest point we could make.

E. F. Spence, of Los Angeles: Mr. Chairman, I wish to make a suggestion: that each gentleman addressing the Convention will rise and step forward, so we will know who is talking to us.

The Chairman: I think that is a very good suggestion.

Geo. H Stewart, of Los Angeles: I move that Mr. Spence take the initiative, Mr. Chairman.

E. F. Spence: I don't wish to get up three times in one afternoon.

W. F. Bosbyshell: If that motion is put, I am certainly opposed to it. A good many of the members are not public speakers, and if we have to get up on the rostrum we will sit still and say nothing. I have no special objection that the gentlemen should be required to give their names and what bank they represent. I want to say a word on the subject under discussion. Is this motion before the house?

The Chairman: No, there is no motion before the house.

W. F. Bosbyshell: Then I want to say a word in regard to the subject on which we were talking. I realize what this gentleman has said: that it is to go before the people to be voted on, but it will never get there unless the State Legislature will put it before the people. As I understand it, we have got to get them to take the initiative step in that matter. If we are all in earnest and take some steps in the matter, we can get it through. I don't know how; whether through a legislative committee or not. It seems to me there ought to be a committee to look after this and other matters which we may want to present to the legislature.

The Chairman: Any other remarks?

On motion, Convention adjourned to ten o'clock a. m., Thursday, October 15th.

B 4

SECOND DAY.

Thursday, October 15th, 1891.

The Convention was called to order at 10 a. m., by the Chairman, Thomas Brown.

The Secretary read the minutes of the previous day's proceedings. Minutes approved as read.

The Chairman: The next in order is miscellaneous business. We will hear from the Executive Council on that head.

A. D. Childress, of Los Angeles: *Mr. Chairman, Members of the Association, Gentlemen*—While the action of the Executive Council, at their meeting July 24th, contemplated that the addresses by members would be confined to local matters, it was more for the purpose of giving preference and precedence to subjects the discussion of which would inure to our immediate benefit, rather than permitting free and unbridled license in the contemplation of foreign and extraneous subjects, which would consume the time of the Convention without visible results.

It is far from the desire of the Council to narrow the scope of the Association to such prescribed limits that its objects and aims will be thwarted, yet it has in view the placing of the proper safeguards around the Association to restrain its being committed to the views of any member without the proper consideration of the question presented.

Therefore, it has ruled that the presentation of papers by any member on such subjects as the national currency, etc., etc., must not be accompanied by motion to adopt his views or plans. One cogent reason of the Council for this ruling is, that the acquiescent vote of all public bodies is dangerous, in that it is too likely to commit the organization to the adoption of a policy without proper deliberation.

We beg leave to report that the following papers have been referred to us and will be heard with the restriction named, viz.:

Address by C. P. Soule, Cashier Bank of Eureka; subject, "The Development of Home Resources."

Address by Lovell White, Cashier San Francisco Savings Union; subject, "Ought Savings Banks to Enforce the Prompt Payment of Interest?"

Address by Frank Miller, Cashier National Bank of D. O. Mills & Co.; subject, "Improved Methods."

Address by Judge C. C. Bush, Vice-President Bank of Shasta County; subject, "Importance of Trained Assistants."

Address by A. Gerberding, Bank Commissioner; subject, "A Few Suggestions."

Address by S. P. Young, Manager California Safe Deposit & Trust Co.; subject, "The Trust Company Question."

Address by J. Reichmann, Cashier Farmers Bank, Fresno; subject, "Co-operation Between Banks."

Address by Geo. H. Bonebrake, President Los Angeles National Bank; subject, "An Adequate Supply of Currency."

Address by John M. C. Marble, President National Bank of California, Los Angeles; subject "Money."

The Chairman: Unless there is other miscellaneous business to come before the Convention at this time, I will call for the paper by Mr. C. P. Soule, of the Bank of Eureka, on "Development of Home Resources."

Secretary Geo. H. Stewart, of Los Angeles: Mr. Chairman and Gentlemen: Mr Soule, at the last moment, sent down his paper, with no remarks except that he would not be here. He designated no one to read it, and therefore the Secretary assumes that responsibility:—

THE DEVELOPMENT OF HOME RESOURCES.

It goes without saying that all should assist in developing the resources of the section in which we are located. There is no such thing as "holding your own;" you must either forge ahead, or fall behind. In this respect bankers do not differ from any other class of business men. The question is not "Should banks encourage the development of home resources?" but rather "How far should they go?" As there appears to be no criterion to follow, each particular case must be decided upon its merits.

Perhaps no class of business men have as good opportunities for judging of the needs of a community as do bankers. Their business brings them in contact with all classes; they of necessity absorb more or less knowledge of the general condition of affairs; they are appealed to, learned of, or are interested in—directly or indirectly—nearly everything of moment that transpires in a community; and consequently, if men of only moderate intelligence and observation, must surely acquire a knowledge of affairs that is well nigh impossible in many other kinds of business.

The very nature of the business compels those interested in the management of banks to be watchful and observing. In a sense they are the auditors of the community: they cast up the "grand recapitulation" of matters financial; in effect a bank is the financial pulse of a community.

To carry on the business successfully there is almost as much need for one to use good judgment and not become over cautious, as there is for avoiding the other extreme. It is very easy to drive away good customers by not looking ahead, and it is very frequently the case by so doing you assist very materially in *not* developing the resources of the country.

The question of "how far banks should go" is hard to answer, and few will have the temerity to undertake it. Many a man has failed of success because of the lack of aid just at the time he needed it. The time has passed when the banker can sit back and wait for business to come to him; customers are just as necessary to him as he is to them. It is a mutual affair: therefore it behooves the banker to aid, in every legitimate way, all he can in improving his section of the country.

This he frequently can do without taking undue risk, by assisting those who require aid in their efforts to create or build up a new industry. The effect of a liberal policy on the part of a bank in dealing with its customers, can be plainly discerned. It readily shows itself in the volume of its business, in its growth and keeping pace with the times.

One conspicuous example might be cited of the wisdom of this policy, of an institution which has always lent its aid toward the material development of this Coast, has been foremost in its efforts to build up our Western Empire: and to-day its name is known in every household, it stands preëminent in the ranks of financial institutions.

The Chairman: Is there any discussion on the paper just read? If not, we will proceed to the next. We will hear from Mr. Lovell White, of San Francisco.

Lovell White then addressed the Convention:—

OUGHT SAVINGS BANKS TO ENFORCE PROMPT PAYMENT OF INTEREST?

As a matter of abstract principle, mortgage debtors are not averse to payment of interest; but, in practice, many, if not a majority, delay that duty to the last possible moment.

The temptation to delay approaches them in a variety of forms, that of land hunger taking the lead with country debtors.

The average farmer wants an adjoining or additional tract of land: and to its purchase he will, if permitted, devote the ready money that should be used for other purposes, and will incumber himself with debt beyond the limits of prudence.

Others move too fast in the line of development and improvement, while some are extravagant in personal or family expenses.

So soon as payment of interest is neglected there begins to be peril of fore-closure, with probable loss of estate to the debtor, and an undesired acquisition of real estate by the savings bank, if such be the creditor.

The money lenders of any community are responsible for the habits of debtors so far as relates to payment of interest.

In communities where values are sharply defined and relatively permanent, mortgagees neither expect nor desire to acquire real estate by foreclosure, and therefore refuse to exercise forbearance: the result being that borrowers become educated to the prompt payment of interest.

In California the reverse has been the case.

In early days the inducement for wealthy individuals to make loans was not the interest, large as was the rate, but the hope of acquiring the estate of the debtor through ultimate foreclosure.

How often this hope was realized tradition tells us, and the records of the counties show.

Where there is a willingness to acquire the landed security, the creditor does not enforce, and usually does not even demand, payment of interest.

Two prominent money lenders of the State, who have grown rich through fore-closures, have been heard, within a few months, to declare that they never de-mand interest so long as they consider their security ample.

The meaning of the remark is obvious: the clemency of the creditor is the ruin of the debtor.

Lulled by hopes of good times coming, the borrower drifts on, careless of expenses, making extravagant improvements and rash investments, until the debt becomes so large as to be unmanageable; then follows desperate efforts to borrow money elsewhere, a little weary waiting for something to turn up, and the agony is over: the title to the lands vests in the mortgagee.

It is quite conceivable that savings banks may make large profits by following the methods pursued by individuals, taking in real estate under foreclosure and reselling as opportunities offer; but prosperity of the kind is delusive: the bank that loads up with real estate loses prestige with depositors, and the one that forecloses many mortgages will not be in favor with borrowers.

That, from the standpoint of the savings banks themselves, it is desirable to collect interest when due, scarcely admits of question.

The depositors of any given half year are entitled to their due share and proportion of the earnings of that half year, and no more; and to arrive at those earnings of the term, the interest earned therein must be computed, and when computed some record must necessarily be made of the amount.

Any dividend calculations not based on ascertained earnings of the term for which the dividends are to be declared, will do injustice to the depositors of that term, or of a term to follow later.

The law of the State, as interpreted by the Supreme Court, forbids the use of the uncollected interest in the payment of dividends.

It follows that where collections of interest are meagre there must be an ignoring of the proper basis for dividend calculations, or some evasion of the law: in either event book keeping is complicated.

Banks with large amounts in their contingent funds, or with other reserves at command of the directors, cannot, perhaps, be said to evade the law, but they are compelled to make a multiplicity of book entries to arrive at desired results.

With the closest possible collections of interest the difficulties are not entirely removed, but they are reduced to a minimum.

While debtors seize upon slight excuses to ask extension of time for payment of interest, and, if their requests are granted, are profuse in expressions of gratitude, their later and ultimate thanks are for those who keep them up to their work by demanding strict compliance with stipulations.

Every experienced officer of a savings bank will call to mind instances where his institution has been, in view of results, reproached for its clemency, and others where debtors have been grateful for what they considered in the first place undue severity.

The prosperity of savings banks is just as inseparably connected with the prosperity of the borrowers as with that of the depositors; for without solvent borrowers no loans can be made, and plethora of idle money has a rapid wasting effect on dividends.

That which tends to the prosperity of the borrower is in the interest of the bank, and the very first lesson in prosperity is regard for engagements and performance of contracts.

In this respect borrowers are to be educated, and the duty of teaching devolves on the banks.

Of course there are, and will be, instances where forbearance can be exercised with safety to the lender and real advantage to the borrower. Such may be the case where there is complete and unusual failure of crops, or loss of improvements by fire; but all requests for extensions should be closely scrutinized, and it should be the rule and not the exception to enforce prompt payment of interest, the alternative being collection of principal by foreclosure if necessary.

The Chairman: Gentlemen, you have heard the remarks of Mr. White. Any discussion by the members of the Convention? If not, we will proceed by calling for the address of Mr. Frank Miller, Cashier of the National Bank of D. O. Mills & Co., Sacramento; subject, "Improved Methods."

Frank Miller spoke as follows:

IMPROVED METHODS.

In the morning, before working hours commence, a banker's life seems easy. He leisurely opens his vault and his mail and then his bank doors, and may have a quiet day: yet he can never tell what is in store for him. Usually he has many calls from clients on varied and important matters, some of which may not be on banking business. His advice is sought on many things, and he must be as wise as a serpent yet as harmlesss as a dove.

The least difficult of his labors will be the receiving and paying of money and checks. The volume of checks seems to be increasing daily as to numbers, while the average value of each check is diminishing. The banker must do an immense amount of labor for no compensation in order to keep a large stream of business flowing under his hands, in the hope that in that stream he will find good fishing.

His greatest care will be in the loaning of his spare cash. He must lend some of his deposits or give up the banking business; his own capital can be turned without a clerk, but to handle other peoples money requires a staff of servants and some losses too. He must lend to the good and refuse the bad; and he will often find that he has done just the reverse: The bad man has the bank's money and the good has been driven away by an unwise refusal of his request. In spite of betrayals of confidence and errors of judgment on past loans, he must keep lending, and usually without security. If all borrowers gave security, then would his lot be a happy one; and if his depositors did not have the right to withdraw all their funds in one day, then his lot would be *very* happy.

The commercial banker, whom we have been describing, often envies his brother who is in a savings bank. The latter can be a well fed and good tempered Christian, never guilty of profanity; while the commercial banker is frequently just the opposite.

The reason of this difference is found in the two words, "human nature." The commercial banker trades on human nature and the savings banker trades on real estate.

Can the situation of the former be improved? Can he make more money without increasing risk and worry?

Suggestion Number One—There is a clause in the National Bank Act which provides that no National Bank shall be attached before final judgment; and this undoubtedly gives a fighting chance, in case of distress, to call up distant reserves. If no attachment could be issued against a State Bank before final judgment, then sudden panics and accidents would not be so terrible.

Suggestion Number Two—The handling of credits seems to be done on a different basis in California as compared with some other states. Elsewhere book accounts cannot be easily collected, so notes prevail.

Here a well kept book account is legally a demand loan.

Our bankers and merchants got in the way of doing much business on running accounts, because the profits were large and the number of accounts was small. Times have changed. Now the number of accounts must be large and the profits small.

The old method must give way to Eastern forms; but if a good rule is adopted as to overdrafts it will gradually be ignored under the powerful competition for good business.

It is proper, therefore, to urge that some legislation should be had so that all may start fair. It has been said that book accounts should outlaw in six months; but we think that the abolition of interest on all unsecured loans, as hereinafter stated, is a better plan.

Let it be enacted that, excluding public corporations, no one shall be compelled at law to pay interest except out of securities pledged to the lender.

If such a law cannot be passed, then let bankers make a public agreement that they will collect no interest except on loans covered by securities and then only to the limit of the securities in hand. This idea will require a little explanation.

If it were carried into effect bankers would take no unsecured loans except in the form of time notes (non-interest-bearing); and deduct the discount. At maturity they would collect or re-write. When some delay occurred as to payment they would carry the loan without interest only so long as might seem wise at the moment.

It is respectfully submitted that the present custom of collecting interest is dangerous, as it often begets a shiftless and soporific habit of letting things stand without renovation.

It may be said, and truly too, that business should not be hampered and entangled with too many rules and laws; but a moment's reflection will show that we propose to abolish customs and laws which have stood so long that men fail to consider their artificial origin.

Interest is not like any law of nature, and its growth exceeds any increase under God's laws. Time and again have nations risen in revolution against the titled holders of vested interests and killed their creditors, and thus cancelled oppressive obligations.

Suggestion Number Three—Upon the hypothesis that over-drafts and past-due notes can thus be got rid of, and that competition cannot break the equal start thus secured, then we may imagine some further benefits that could follow without causing too much labor to fall on the many bankers who are already overwhelmed with a multitude of small cares.

A banker could require all checks to be marked or certified before payment, and thus could take on new accounts without limit, even if they were of small size.

The average balance of loanable money obtained from a great number of small accounts is more reliable than the balance from a few large accounts. The former is well worth the increased expense of clerkhire, and the existing element of risk would be removed by this proposed plan. The objection, even in a large city, may not be great as to a plan of this kind. Many checks come in through the clearing house and time is had for examination before payment. Where depositors put in their bank, checks on that same bank, a printed stipulation could be put in the pass books that such items cannot be finally passed until a certain hour of the same day. The only checks therefore to be certified would be those presented to the paying teller. The English banks are larger and more profitable than ours, and their custom in this respect must be different from ours. It would be interesting if some member of this Convention would describe their methods, and we would probably be benefited by adopting some of their time-tested rules.

Suggestion Number Four—Time checks might be found useful and easy to handle. People could be encouraged to issue time checks—or notes that could be collected at a bank on a definite day and for a definite sum—free of any interest-bearing phrases.

Such paper, after several endorsements, would drift into the bankers hands at a fair rate of discount and give him very good business; but he would have to keep his eyes open for "accomodation paper."

Finally, it seems as if commercial banks were too much prone to favor only a few large firms who are allowed to draw at will, and use their own and their bankers' means to continue a system of standing book accounts, based on the hope of the continuance of the large profits of early days. New merchants can get, and hold, no trade until they have capital or credit enough to carry each customer in the same fashion.

Meanwhile the Eastern traders are underselling in this market and taking negotiable paper; for the ordinary man will always give cash or short paper to the lowest seller and make his other creditors carry him.

It would seem as if a reform must occur, and it behooves us to drop all slow and limited methods and adopt the approved systems of larger banks.

Instead of lending on the reputed wealth of a borrower's big ledger, we must tell him to bring in his customers' paper for discounts.

The Chairman: Are there any remarks to be made on the paper read by Mr. Miller? If not, we will hear from Judge C. C. Bush, Vice-President of the Bank of Shasta.

Frank V. McDonald, of San Francisco: Mr. Chairman, would it be out of order to make any remarks on the papers we have passed? I would like to make some remarks on Mr. White's paper.

Motion that Mr. McDonald be heard was made and carried.

The Chairman: We will hear from Mr. McDonald.

Frank V. McDonald: *Mr. Chairman and Gentlemen*—I think that the paper of Mr. White is worthy of a great deal of careful attention on our part. If a large savings bank such as the Savings Union finds it desirable to enforce the prompt payment of interest due on mortgages, it certainly ought to be evidence sufficient to all of us that the system is a good one, because, with their large reserve and with their easy means of making up for a deficit of interest at any given time, their experience has still shown them the necessity of this. I say it is something that ought to have strong weight with us; and it is all the more gratifying for me to hear him ex press these ideas, because, in our connection with the smaller savings banks, we frequently have thrown up to us the proposition that larger savings banks of the city do not pursue this course. We have endeavored to collect our interest with the utmost speed. We have lost a number of customers by so doing, but we have always thought that it was the duty of savings banks to collect interest promptly; that their money was pay-able twice yearly, and therefore it was not only due but it was a practical necessity that their interest should be promptly collected. Now, as Mr. White has stated, there are a number of institutions in this city, and large private capitalists in this city, that make a business of lending their money for any time that the borrower wishes, and the savings banks are brought into direct competition with these large capitalists; and, as we all know, in this community, there is a very large amount of loanable cap-ital in the hands of wealthy citizens; therefore the banks are all the time more or less in conflict with these capitalists. Now, if the savings banks will only make a rule, enforcible as far as interest on mortgages is con cerned, that it shall be paid promptly. it will make the burden of all of us a great deal easier. This is a subject more important than some of us realize, and has frequently been slighted; and I know that is particularly so, not only in San Francisco, but also some other cities of this State. We have cor-respondence often, in our limited business, saying such and such loaning people have done so and so; and where they have removed from us, they have gone to those people and secured extensions. I think if the Con-vention will take hold and try to carry out this idea, it will greatly facili-tate the carrying of the burdens of the savings banks, and the benefits from which will be found to be just as Mr. White suggests.

The Chairman: If there are no further remarks, we will hear from Judge Bush.

J. B. Lankershim, of Los Angeles: Mr. Chairman, will you allow me a few words? I was very much pleased with the remarks of Mr. White in regard to the collection of interest I have been in the business of a savings banker about three years, in Los Angeles. In that time our bank has made considerable growth. While I have had not much experience in the banking business, I have endeavored to study up the subject, endeavored to make the acquaintance of gentlemen in the business of savings banking, so as to learn the rules as far as possible. I will state that the first rule we made in our bank was positive collection of interest on the day it was due. Of course, on the start it met with some difficulties. Parties would come in and claim that the loan was perfectly good, and want it extended. But I considered it strictly as a business relation, and we have collected very promptly, and the result has been that we now have them paying up every three months, paying the entire amount of their interest, and in case they fail to do that, we collect the principal and interest, and it has been most satisfactory; and as a savings bank man, I should suggest that practice every time.

The Chairman: Any other remarks? We will now hear from Judge Bush.

C. C. Bush, of Redding:

IMPORTANCE OF TRAINED ASSISTANTS.

Mr. Chairman and Gentlemen of the Convention.

The subject submitted by your Committee admits of so broad a construction that anything I might say, I fear, will fall far short of importance, in an assemblage of able financiers. And the subject, as suggested, seems indefinite: does it apply to directors as assistants? managers as assistants? cashiers as assistants—or assistant cashiers? city banking or country banking?

With all deference to the Committee, I suggest the better question would have been: "Where and how can assistants be trained to serve the best interests of the bank"; and shall take the liberty to treat it from that standpoint.

All will admit the importance, but we may differ as to the training. To be an assistant, in its full sense, in a large city bank, the training or education should be much broader and more comprehensive than in a country bank.

Having had no experience in city banking, and but limited in country, I shall treat the subject more from the standpoint of a business man, and shall speak more particularly of cashiers and their assistants.

The first question is: "What kind of training will make the assistant most valuable to the bank?" The first requisite should be a love for the business. Some of you may consider the word "love" a strong one, or even absurd, in connection with so cold and calculating a subject. But we of the grey locks know from experience the difference with which we performed our duties in our younger days, for the *pay* that was in it or because we had agreed to, and the manner in which we now follow our calling, from love of the labor and the intense satisfaction that work well done brings to us; or in other words, as a distinguished writer expresses it, "the happiness of love is in action."

Next, a good business education. Not necessarily a graduate of Harvard or Yale: while a diploma from either of those distinguished and worthy educational institutions may be necessary for a first-class ball pitcher, catcher or first baseman, a valuable assistant for a bank can be made without.

In this cosmopolitan State the more languages one can speak and write the better; although I have known some most excellent assistants—aye, among the best—that could only use the language most generally understood in America, and that not above criticism.

A good and rapid penman; quick and correct calculator; strict integrity; undoubted veracity and good moral character: with these qualifications, for a foundation, the assistant is well equipped to receive a training that will make him valuable to the bank.

The first training should be an assurance, from the bank, that as long as he performed his duties he should be secure in his situation. This is not only just to the assistant, but equally just to the stockholders. No relationship or friendship should control in the matter, only the interests of the bank ; and on the other hand he should understand that a failure to perform his duties will surely result in dismissal: ties of blood or others should not arrest the decree. Having this assurance, his training may be said to have fully commenced: and in this training the public has much to do.

The assistant soon discovers that it is the feeling of the general public that the bank is the particular bird all are justified in plucking: and, with too many, by fair means or foul ; he learns that nearly every case needs a different treatment ; that the iron clad rules that are supposed to exist in all banks must, at times, be bent to suit the emergency for the best interests of the bank, and make it popular with the public—which should ever be his aim in this day of sharp and active competition: not to attempt to compel the public to do business with the bank from sheer necessity, but because it meets with honest, polite and courteous treatment from its assistants. The old political saying that "molasses catches flies" is just as true in banking as in politics. It is as easy, and much more popular, to refuse a loan pleasantly and with a few explanations, as to do so in an abrupt and offensive manner. Collections can be made with discretion and courtesy instead of with an air of superiority and power.

A case in point may not be out of place as happening in this city: Patrons of a certain bank had been doing business with it for many years ; at the time of this incident a new party came into the firm, and, together with one of the old, called to be introduced to the bank president and ascertain if the old accommodations would be accorded the new firm. The accommodations to be extended were satisfactory ; nevertheless the firm changed its business to another bank, and the only reason was the abrupt and unpleasant manner in which the president acceded to the request. When the president learned of the change he endeavored to regain the lost business, but it was too late. His training in another calling, during flush times of California, was not suited to the banking business at a later period.

The management of a bank successfully is a training to an assistant that is welcome and appreciated; but the mistakes are more impressive and more lasting—I might say everlasting. As illustrating this latter idea, I claim your forbearance to cite an instance; not, however, connected with banking, but just as applicable.

At the time stages carried mail, express and passengers from the terminus of the railroad at Redding to the terminus at Roseburg, a driver, on his trip north, halted his team on top of Pit river hill to repair the brake ; while on the ground the horses started down the steep grade, running at high speed ; the wagon was overturned, a lady passenger (a particular friend of the superintendent of the stage company) seriously injured, the stage wrecked and a horse or two killed. At that time there were several old and experienced drivers at either terminus, waiting for a job; as soon as the accident was known they hastened to apply for the situation ; the superintendent replied that there was no vacancy. "Why," the applicants asked, "are you not going to discharge so and so for letting his team run off and nearly killing your friend?" "O, no," replied the superintendent ; "he will never do that again: he knows better now." Nor he never did, although he drove for years afterward.

And so it is with the mistakes in a bank ; it is part of the training that is most effective. And I venture the assertion, without fear of contradiction, that all make mistakes: directors, managers, cashiers and assistant cashiers, the millionaire banker as well as the smaller.

The assistant is not only trained by the mistakes of his own bank, but by the mistakes of other banks; and in like manner is he trained by the business methods of others. If he receives prompt returns and prompt correspondence from others, to use a homely phrase, "it is catching;" and he endeavors to reply in kind. If he learns that other banks are traducing the reputation of his own, he not only feels like returning the injustice with interest, but is very apt to do so; and this kind of training is hurtful to all interests concerned.

If the directors or manager are severely censorious of the assistant's errors of judgment, and fail to, or but grudgingly, approve of his good work, he is trained to labor for his salary and not for beneficial results.

If the directors or manager withhold their confidence to an unreasonable extent from the cashier, they train him to do likewise; and as the cashier is so situated as to know the innermost workings of the bank, its best interests are not always served on account of such faulty training.

The cashier or assistant in a bank is under training from the moment the bank opens until it closes, and that of the severest kind. He meets the shrewdest of honest financiers and the deepest dyed scoundrels, both intent on the same object—that of getting the best of the bargain. He comes in contact with the highest culture and the grossest ignorance. The first often endeavors to instruct him as to his duties, the other he must instruct in order to do business with. He is not only the custodian of the bank's funds and secrets, but, in a country bank, the custodian of the funds and confidence of the greater part of the community—referee as to values and character, and valuable to the bank for the training this gives him, and that he could not receive in any other situation.

By close reading and study of the valuable printed matter that all well conducted banks are provided with, the assistant acquires much valuable banking knowledge, his ideas are broadened and he becomes less a local operator.

No Harvard, no Yale, no university nor other business situation can thus train him. They may lay the foundation, and lay it well, upon which this superstructure can be erected: but they cannot train the assistant so that he is a necessity to the bank, and prepared to assume what is termed higher duties when called upon.

Therefore, I submit that the best training is received by service in a bank; and the responsibility of properly trained assistants depends greatly upon the importance the management attaches to having the interests of the stockholders faithfully served.

I am aware that some of my remarks are not applicable to the question, nor keep closely to the text, and recognize that an apology is due for imposing them on an assemblage of distinguished gentlemen, even by request, and make it in these words: If the California Bankers Association is worthy of sustaining and up-building, it is obligatory upon its members to do something when called upon by the proper officers; if it is not the best that can be done, it may call out the best from others in friendly criticism.

The Chairman: Gentlemen, you have heard the remarks of Judge Bush. Any remarks to be made by the members of the Convention? Is there anything under the head of "New Business" you desire to offer?

Lovell White, of San Francisco: *Mr. Chairman and Gentlemen* — With your permission, I will offer a resolution:

Resolved—That the members of this Convention, as citizens of the State, and in their capacity of individuals, would be pleased to listen to remarks from Judge R. M. Widney, at any hour he may appoint when the Convention is not in session.

R. M. Widney, of Los Angeles: Mr. Chairman, I was not aware that that resolution was to be introduced. I should be pleased to address, not this Convention, but the individuals who are here, and any who may wish to be present to listen, at any hour of the day or evening when the Convention is not in session. Friday evening would suit me as well as any other time or any other hour. I can assure the Convention that never at any time in the past have I endeavored to compromise this Convention or drag it into the support of any ideas that I might entertain on finances. That is not my way of doing business. I appreciate this resolution, and would be glad to respond to it at any time that the Convention will fix. I would suggest Friday evening, at any hour that is satisfactory, or any afternoon.

E. F. Spence, of Los Angeles: I second the resolution offered by Mr. White.

On vote being had, Mr. White's resolution was carried.

The Chairman: At the request of Judge Widney, we will name Friday evening. At what hour, Judge, will suit you best?

R. M. Widney: At what is the customary hour of the people of San Francisco?

The Chairman: Eight o'clock?

R. M. Widney: Eight o'clock; yes, sir. I wish to express my thanks to the Convention for the resolution.

The Chairman: I announce to the Convention, then, that Judge Widney will address the citizens and members of the Convention, as individuals, on Friday evening, at eight o'clock, in this room. If there is any thing else under the head of "New Business" we would like to hear from you, gentlemen, now.

George Ohleyer, of Yuba City: Mr. Chairman, I have a short address.

The Chairman: Step forward to the platform, please. Gentlemen of the Convention, George Ohleyer, of Sutter County.

George Ohleyer: *Mr. President and Members of the Convention*—We regret exceedingly the introduction of the hydraulic mining question into the deliberations of this body, even in the form of an address, or response to an address of welcome. It must be apparent to every delegate on this floor that such themes are foreign to the objects and purposes of a bankers convention. As well might this body discuss the supply of wheat, and the manner of its production, or that of wine, wool, or agricultural productions generally. All our representatives of wealth are equally as necessary as gold. We do not agree with the sentiment advanced yesterday that there has been an indiscriminate suppression of mining by the courts; the line only having been drawn against hydraulic mining, and only such as has ever produced an insufferable nuisance. The assertion made and published to the world amounts to an unjust reflection on the courts and the men who have been struggling for ten years to preserve their homes and property from the onflow of hydraulic mud. It goes further: the sentiment seeks to combine the legitimate with the illegitimate modes of mining, thus telling the world that all methods of mining are under the ban of decrees from which they must be rescued by appealing to public sentiment. That the hydraulic monitor may complete the ruin of the Sacramento river and the great valleys, the proposition is made that the Government furnish the settlers with homes in lieu of those to be abandoned. It is sufficient to say that such a proposition is untenable from any standpoint, and one we feel sure will not be entertained by this Convention. When the State was taxed, some years ago, to build restraining dams for the benefit of the hydraulic miner, the greatest opposition to such tax came from the Southern Citrus Belt. It should be understood that the delegates who spoke yesterday in the interest of the "Little Giant" are intimately related to the industry that has created such havoc on the farms and rivers of the valleys, and that they are not the expressions of disinterested citizens.

The Chairman: I think the remarks are a little out of order, because the gentleman did not submit his address to the Executive Council: but I suppose it is permissible to let the matter go before the Convention.

E. F. Spence, of Los Angeles: Mr. Chairman, might I have a single word in reply to our friend? He misunderstood my proposition. There was no plan proposed. I merely asked the question: "Could some plan not be devised whereby more gold could be obtained?" That was about all I said. Anything further than that, was in the way of pleasantry; no intention to injure anybody; merely asking, as sensible men, could not some plan be devised? Now, it was only that and nothing more. No intention in the world to oppose any one's interest. I don't think it is wrong, I don't think it is a fire-brand even, to ask the question; and cannot sensible men meet together, talk matters over, discuss matters about which we differ, without taking that view of it: that there is an intention to injure? Farthest was it from my thought to injure anybody, to even suggest a plan by which anybody could be injured. I only suggested the plan: cannot some plan be suggested? That is all. If I hurt the feelings of any gentleman present, or any interested farmer in the State, I regret it.

George Ohleyer: I don't wish to take up the time of this Convention in discussing this question, but it is a question of very great interest; it is a question that affects the people of the Sacramento Valley more than any other, and any proposition, even this harmless question "Cannot something be done to revive this industry?" is a question of very great moment with us. You all know, every gentleman on this floor knows, that we have been seeking for a solution, on terms that will satisfy everyone, all of ten or twelve years. Now, they have come into this Convention and brought up the question, "Cannot something be done?" Why, we don't care; let them invent something; let them invent some way. It is only the nuisance that we complain of. I don't believe I did misunderstand the gentleman. I don't undertake to misrepresent him, I don't wish to misrepresent him. But if the question is to be discussed here at length, why of course we will be heard later. Perhaps there has been enough said now,

E. F. Spence: Of course, Mr. Chairman, this Association is not asked to endorse anything. These are merely questions for the people to study. We don't decide anything. We are not asked to endorse anything at all. We are not committing ourselves to anything. I don't think it does any harm here at all.

A. C. Bingham, of Marysville: I think the feeling which manifests itself amongst these gentlemen here representing the Sacramento Valley and the Center of California, on this matter, arises from the somewhat peculiar method in which this question has been brought before this Convention. The gentleman from Los Angeles, as a representative of Southern California, responds to a very pleasant address of welcome from the Chairman of the Chamber of Commerce of San Francisco: and in those words of thanks for the courtesies extended, he takes the opportunity to bring forward the hydraulic mining question; then Mr. Preston, of Nevada City, responds also for Northern California's very large territory, and brings forward the same question. I assure the gentlemen of the Convention, as a banker of one of the smaller towns of Northern California, we were not prepared for the introduction of the question here, as we did not deem that this would be the proper body before which to discuss it; and the objection will be raised to its being introduced in this way, that this question was suggested in a very similar form by the gentleman from Los Angeles at your first Convention, which I did not have the privilege to attend; afterwards expressed that the Bankers Convention had approved a plan suggested, or a matter brought forward in that Convention was published throughout the mining press of Northern California. The question is a very great one; and, if it should be discussed at all, upon the basis of devising the means of continuing the hydraulic mining, it should be taken before a body of men prepared to give the time that that discussion requires, and both sides to this controversy should have ample time to prepare themselves and present to such convention the full statement of their side of the question, each for itself. As far as devising means is concerned, there is simply one thing I would like to suggest to this Convention and to the gentleman from Los Angeles: First, here is the theory that miners have generally, that the cities of Northern California are inherently opposed to mining; second, that there is an enmity exists between the valleys and the mountains. That is entirely a mistake. The mining interest is a great interest, a support of the valleys and, for a long time, the people owning the land not fully brought under cultivation. It was only when they were forced, by necessity: when they saw thousands of acres being swept out, farmers driven away, valleys and rivers filled up so as to be of no value, navigation obstructed, the Sacramento even being filled with millions and millions of cubic yards that were coming down into the upper beds: that this work was undertaken—then, at the request of the mining gentlemen in one branch of the State Legislature, the Government of the United States appointed the very ablest engineers (and three different experts) ever known in this State, to devise means, as engineers, whereby this work could be carried on: and, so far, without any successful conclusion. Efforts have been made to devise means, by the Government itself, by the very best ability of its engineers. Therefore, it hardly seems to me that a little simple expression before a Bankers Convention, "Is there some way of devising means by which this work can be carried on?" is in suitable form. It is something entirely out of place, and I don't wish to discuss it. I will say this, though: that we are now occupying a room in the Chamber of Commerce in San Francisco; that body feels the wonderful value of the harbor of San Francisco, and knows the difficulties of the navigation of the bar, at the head, beyond the head; that same body years ago was somewhat aroused as to the question of the danger to that bar, how the material of the mines had worked into it, threatening in fact the commerce of San Francisco with ruin, and the great harbor which is really the wealth of this State. They called upon Professor Davidson, who said to the Chamber of Commerce, this: "Your bar will never be injured by the hydraulic mining. It is built up by the sands of the ocean, but it is the scouring passage of this great reservoir of yours which keeps that bar in. If you permit mining debris or any other filling to interfere with the channel, when you reduce the resorvoir capacity of your harbor to a certain point, then the equilibrium now established will be lost, your bar will fill up." Now, no engineer could say just how far you could go on safely and fill any one of your tributary veins, and it is a question of such importance that certainly a prudent man, certainly a prudent banker, would stop on the proper side; he would leave it to the natural wash, leave the centuries and centuries it may require to impair that harbor, without permitting an unnatural flow caused by the extraction of a few million dollars of gold to go forward and ruin the commercial prosperity of San Francisco. Gentlemen, I thank you. [Applause.]

The Chairman: Any further remarks?

Frank V. McDonald, of San Francisco: Gold is obtained from but a few places of the world, and it is one of the burning questions of the whole world; therefore, it would be perfectly natural, where such a great question has been raised, that somebody should ask if our great stores of supply cannot be further developed with safety to other interests. It is not a question like the supply of fruit and wheat. They can be raised anywhere in the world. It seems that this question could be raised, without exciting every farmer that lives in the Sacramento Valley.

A. D. Childress, of Los Angeles: As Chairman of the Executive Council, I will take this opportunity of explaining the difficulties that have come before your Council in discriminating as to what matters should come before this body. As the gentleman says, the remarks of the member from Southern California, made at the last Convention, at Los Angeles, went forth to the people as an endorsement of hydraulic mining, and it was as if it was a quasi endorsement of the bankers of California. It is the same difficulty that is presented in the question of Judge Widney's address before the Bankers Convention in Los Angeles on the currency question. I want to state it here, very emphatically and very forcibly, that there is no animus in the minds of the Executive Council that excited or that produced the resolution which was read yesterday in its report; and as a matter of fact, the passage of that resolution by the Bankers Convention at Los Angeles last March was the means of giving to the country the impression, by publication in various journals, banking and otherwise, throughout the United States, that the Bankers Association of California endorsed the currency plan of Judge Widney; while, as a matter of fact, it is within the knowledge of every banker who is a member of this Association that his plan was not endorsed and that the passage of that resolution, as Judge Widney read it here yesterday, had no reference to the adoption of his plan; and the Judge will remember that he remarked, when that resolution was brought before the Convention, that the passage of it did not mean an adoption of his plan at all, but merely a resolution to get the matter before the people and before Congress. Notwithstanding that fact, this Association has been burdened with the responsibility of the endorsement of a currency plan which originated with Judge Widney. However much complimented this Association might feel by the endorsement of a plan emanating from one of its members, whatever its merits might be, it is not within my province, or the province, I might say, of the gentlemen of this Association, to adopt. At the same time, this Bankers Association did not want to go before the people of the United States seemingly endorsing any plan, without the mature consideration of that plan which should be given to such a matter; and the harm that has accrued to this Association by the published reports that were made in the banking journals, in the newspapers, in other journals and the press generally throughout the country, has led the Executive Council to be most careful and most particular in allowing any papers to come before the Convention that might commit this Association to the adoption of the views of any member. It is very well known to every man who participates in the discussion of questions before a public body that the acquiescent vote of an assemblage is a large one; that I can frame a resolution and probably pass it before a body of very intelligent men, and yet, if the vote was taken in detail, it might not find the whole endorsement of that body. But men are frequently prone to sit and listen to discussion and not raise their voices in behalf of or against the question at issue; and for that reason, and no other, the Executive Council wants to make it very plain to the Association that they have eliminated any resolution accompanying the expression of the views or plans of any individual member of this Association. We have arrived at this conclusion after very mature deliberation. We feel that it is a safeguard to this Association to prohibit a resolution to accompany any plan, or the adoption of any plan, presented by any member. The gentlemen very appropriately remarked, as I have said before, that the very few words or reference by Mr. Spence, at the Convention last March, were misconstrued through the press or through certain papers in the country as an adoption of the views of Mr. Spence; or simply his references to hydraulic mining as an endorsement by the Bankers Association. The Executive Council feel that their conception of the benefits to be derived from this Association are very broad, and that they do not want to narrow them down to the discussion of purely local issues; but they want to confine the discussion of all these questions to the discussion of them alone, and not burden the Association by the seeming endorsement of any plan or project gotten up by any member. Judge Widney very appropriately

B 6

remarked, at one of the monthly dinners of the bankers of Los Angeles, that the time he had devoted to his currency plan occupied the long period of two years; and that it was not possible for any one to properly criticize it without giving it the same mature deliberation and thought he had given it. The Judge's remarks were most appropriate. He has given the question serious consideration; and, if his theory is correct, the individual bankers of this Association would be very proud to have one of their members originate a theory, a currency plan, that would be adopted by the whole nation. But, at the same time, by his own theory —that it takes a long time to properly consider and properly weigh such an important question—the Judge, or any other member of this Association, presenting a plan for national currency, cannot hope for this Association or for any like body, in a few minutes. to adopt it as a whole. I thank you, gentlemen, for your attention. [Applause.]

R. M. Widney: I will help Mr. Childress and the Executive Council out of any dilemma, or any appearance of an intention to do a thing that was unjust. It is absolutely impossible for a speaker or a committee to control what the public press may say or what construction may be given. I don't know of any body of men in the world that undertake more carefully to be accurate than the members of the press. They have no interest whatever in misrepresenting any public matters or the facts, because it must recoil upon them; but in the hurry of condensing reported statements and then again condensing that, in connection with all the matter that goes into the public newspaper, it is absolutely impossible for them to use words that will include all that ought to be included, and exclude all that should be excluded; and therefore the intelligent public of the United States understand that the reports that go through the newspapers are as near accurate as under the circumstances they can be given. Now, as a lawyer, accustomed to addressing juries and courts, I well understand that no body or individual that was ever addressed by a speech endorsed that which a speaker says. I may argue a case before the Supreme Court of this State, and I may give twenty different reasons and points, all why it should be decided in my favor; on some one point alone the Supreme Court may decide that case in favor of my client; and the Supreme Court, in rendering their decision upon it on that point, may absolutely disagree with me on the nineteen other points in the case; if my case rested on those other nineteen points, they might reject the whole thing. So that we understand that, when an address is made, and a resolution is passed by a convention, the resolution expresses the views of the convention on the points that are stated in the resolution, and in no manner endorses the address.

Now, last March I was very careful in this matter, in going before the Convention. I said to them that they could not, in the hurried manner in which an address was presented to them, understand any financial system accurately and carefully; that I would not put it upon the Convention or ask them in any manner to endorse my views on the subject. I went still farther, and I said, "This resolution is presented for the following reasons: I have recently been East, and I have talked with a great many bankers in the East, and they attribute to the bankers of the West and to the bankers of the Pacific Coast the wildest financial ideas: that we are inflationists, in the extreme sense of the word, and we are in favor of the Sub-Treasury plan; that we are in favor of almost every wild financial scheme that comes to us, I suppose. I told the conditions and told the bankers of the City of New York, and Boston, that no such wild ideas were entertained by the bankers of California. I said, "Now, I believe that this resolution represents sound financial propositions, without regard to my scheme"; for I did not present my scheme to the Bankers Convention at Los Angeles. It is embraced in a bill prepared for Congress, and a constitutional amendment; and it was never even referred to the Bankers Association; it never was even published in your minutes; it has never been published in this Association. "Now," I said to this Association, "I believe that these resolutions will correctly place us bankers before the bankers in the East as to what we do believe on the question of the gold standard and uniform system of currency and so on." Now, it was in response to that, and to that alone, as I understood it, that the resolution was passed. Now, when the resolution was passed and my address became a matter of public property, individuals misunderstood it; they misconstrued it; they undertook to connect the two together, and claim that one was an endorsement of the other. I don't think it was. I don't think, as a convention, that we can understand and endorse any of these complicated questions. I don't think it is possible for us to do it. I have not, gentlemen, ever entertained the least feeling of hostility toward the Executive Council for their action.

The Chairman: Any other remarks? There being no further remarks, we will hear from Mr. Gerberding; subject,

A FEW SUGGESTIONS.

A. Gerberding, of San Francisco, one of the State Bank Commissioners, addressed the Convention as follows:

Mr. Chairman and Gentlemen of the California Bankers Association:

Your circular requires an address "upon some live topic of interest to bankers." I offer three live topics of interest to everybody, and take my text from the fourth chapter and second verse of the last report of the Bank Commissioners (a work which, like other good books, is not much read), where I find the following words:

"There are at present three questions of vital importance to California, and worthy the careful attention of all bankers. These are: first, the construction of the Nicaragua Canal; second, the need of proper immigration; third, the establishment of irrigation bonds upon a marketable basis; and they present themselves as a triple alliance necessary to our prosperity, appealing directly to the patriotism and the pockets of all Californians."

It is now my purpose to elaborate this brief statement to the extent of ten minutes of your patient attention; and apologies for subjects that are perhaps threadbare, or possibly dry, are unnecessary: for when you attend a bankers convention you do not expect "to soar upon the poet's wings to the furthest realms of fancy and there cull the loveliest flowers of imagination". You are not here as dreamers, but as materialists representing the most material of all things —money. The poet and the painter and those that furnish the better things of life come after you: for upon the material depends the aesthetic.

The establishment of wealth produces requirements that can be gratified only by art and science, and with these come a retinue of luxuries to satisfy the newly created capacity and occupy the time for indulgence; and as these so-called luxuries become necessities, we attain a higher state of civilization. Reducing these apparent platitudes to a very common denominator, we have: "Money makes the mare go"; and if, in your minds, the mare represents life in its best phase, including time and ability to indulge in a full development of the heart and the brain, you have my reason for addressing you upon money-making propositions.

Custodians as you are of 300 millions of dollars—the very blood that courses through the arteries of our great commonwealth—look for a moment beyond the walls of your counting houses and contemplate enterprises which, though not of today or of tomorrow even, are to accomplish untold benefits to your State; indirectly at first, but in time so directly that they will figure in your balance-sheets. And why is your attention demanded? Because, coming as you do from every corner of the State, representing as you do the vital forces of California, you wield an influence greater than all others. Without your consent not a wheel turns, not a structure rears its walls heavenward; but with it the mighty train of commerce rushes onward with accelerated speed, freighted with enterprise, industry and prosperity.

To many, the Nicaragua Canal is a vague proposition; to all it is a desirable undertaking; but only to a few is it an imperative necessity; and upon these few has thus far devolved the entire burden of building public opinion.

What American lives whose heart would not swell with pride to see the commerce of the world saluting the stars and stripes as it entered an American highway, and paying tribute to Uncle Sam as it left it? What Californian breathes who does not rejoice in the development and consequent prosperity of our own millions of square miles? What more appropriate and interesting problem for the careful consideration of a convention of California bankers? Your own State will save $6,000,000 annually on her wheat alone, and savings are but profits in disguise. But you recline in your easy chairs and say: "Yes, the Canal ought to be built." You listen attentively to the Hon. Warner Miller, and when he pictures this great American enterprise, the temperature of your blood rises enough to bring forth applause. You commend the words of John Sherman when he says: "A commercial company in India has been converted into a vast empire; the single port of Hong Kong is made to dominate a great population in China; the control of the Suez Canal and of Egypt has been purchased in the stock market; these are sufficient warnings to the American people to avail themselves of the opportunity now open to them to protect their coastwise trade and at the same time, with little cost and no risk, to contribute to the world one of the greatest achievements of mind over matter that has ever been undertaken."

But all this does not build canals; neither can they be built by passing around the hat. The undertaking is too great for individual enterprize; though this may be doubted, for it is said that there are many citizens of this Democracy whose personal possessions are more than enough to pay the entire cost. However, I take the line that it is a national work; a part of the great policy of a great nation. Let the Government build it. But will our solons in Congress assembled act in time? In view of the miscarriage of an honest, equitable proposition, prepared by six of the wisest men in the land and submitted to the last Congress, there is great danger that ere our legislators appreciate the vast importance of this move, England, or Germany, even now endeavoring to possess themselves of the coveted prize, will, with the love of gain on one hand and the spirit of conquest on the other, wrest from us the greatest boon of the age.

There is no time to be lost; and it is suggested that the 8000 banks of the United States make an appeal to the 444 members of the next Congress asking, aye demanding, the construction of the canal. Of these 8000 banks 3600 are Nationals; and to these we must apply, relying upon them to win the cooperation of all the others upon the ground of brotherhood and general welfare. But why limit ourselves to Nationals? For the reason that we propose to give them a new Government bond upon which to base bank circulation. Many bankers conventions have listened to lamentations over the redemption, and search lights are now illuminating the country in quest of a new bond. We ask no favors, we merely demand that our country add to its strength, glory and profit: and by so doing, incidentally gratify the general demand for a greater circulation, with no loss to the nation or the individual members thereof. When we remember that the Government has paid in interest nearly the face value of railroad aid bonds, thus giving about 63 millions to personal enterprise, we submit in all justice that our request is a modest one. Our own State, from her shores to her mountain peaks, from her busy marts to her peaceful valleys, cries out for cheaper transportation: and the opportunity is affored to the California Bankers Association to voice this sentiment in practical words and figures. Simply this: to ask all other bankers associations throughout the country, and through them all the banks in the United States, to join in an appeal to Congress to construct the canal upon a new issue of bonds, to be used as a basis of circulation.

Details are unnecessary here, but a general summary of the proposition may be thus presented: The canal will be constructed if Congress so determines, and Congress will so determine if public opinion demands it. An immense factor in this public opinion is the influence of the bankers; and they will aid, for the reason that out of the canal is to come a much needed element of their business, viz.: a new bond. Imagine, if you will, 8000 bankers, from Maine to Texas, from Washington to Florida, rapping at the doors of Congress and crying in one voice: "Build the canal"; and the great work would be accomplished. It is then in order for the California bankers to formulate the proposition and submit it to the fraternity throughout the country—appealing to them not alone through a patriotic sentiment, but holding forth the promise of a new supply of their stock in trade.

I would that stronger heads and braver hearts were imbued with an enthusiasm that would, in voice of thunder and words of fire, proclaim throughout the land that the union of the oceans be sanctified only beneath the stars and stripes! [Applause.]

Great as this undertaking may be, there is still more work to be done. But recently there assembled here an Immigration convention; and, while it may be said that when the transportation problem is solved the immigration question is settled, there still remains much that, by concerted action, can be accomplished. It is contended by a few that it is best to depend upon natural growth, and that a slow development, incident only to ordinary causes, is more lasting and beneficial than the forcing process of modern enterprise. But this is a fallacy; for it must be remembered that we are living in an age of "push," and that our State represents a great bazaar in which we are all partners, and of which you are the cashiers, and where we have everything to sell of the best quality and at the lowest price. It is incumbent upon us to advise the world of these facts, and to do those things that will bring customers and convince them that our goods and our methods are superior to those of our neighbors. Other organizations are doing their part of the work, but they need help: they need you in their council. You now hold $107,000,000 in mortgages upon realty, the value of which depends solely upon population ; and when these lands are seeking buyers it means depreciation, but immigration means buyers seeking these lands and that means appreciation: and then follow prosperity and dividends for all.

As you take further account of stock you find $11,000,000 of irrigation bonds, shop worn and frayed at the edges because of faulty manufacture. Should not something be done to put these in order ? You say it is not your business : but any item of this magnitude is worthy of attention, and is so interwoven in the sum total of assets that its care becomes almost a duty. There is fault somewhere. Can it be discovered, and can it be remedied?

The difference between irrigation bonds and other debentures readily saleable, seems to be that while the latter are secured by completed undertakings, the former are based upon work anticipated ; and how well this work is to be done and its value when completed are unknown quantities; but the law says the security is not the mere ditch, but the land upon which this ditch is to pour its bounteous waters. The law further says that these bonds are good; and yet the capitalist, anxious for a profitable investment, declines to purchase even at a discount. I repeat, it is the duty of someone to correct this wrong ; and I ask, could not a remedy be found by a convention of California bankers? These three propositions, viz.: first, The Nicaragua Canal ; second, Immigration; and third, Irrigation Bonds, are worthy of the thoughtful, careful considerations of this body ; and afford an opportunity to go beyond the funeral of resolutions in the graveyard of the minute book, and of contributing your share to the blessings that have already been showered upon the people of California.

The Chairman: Are there any remarks to be made on the address by Mr. Gerberding? If so, they are now in order.

A. D. Childress, of Los Angeles: Mr. Chairman, in view of the fact that the Association will have ample time tomorrow to finish its deliberations, and as all the country bankers desire to call on their correspondents to pay their respects and will not have time to do so if we have our meetings as per program, the Executive Council suggests that we adjourn at twelve o'clock until tomorrow morning at ten, unless some member has special business to bring before the Convention this afternoon.

The Chairman: Is that a motion?

A. D. Childress: Well, it is not necessary for it to come before the Convention in the form of a motion. Unless there is some special business to come before the Convention this afternoon, we will have ample time to finsh the program tomorrow.

Frank V. McDonald, of San Francisco: I move that we be allowed the privilege of calling up Mr. Gerberding's paper at some future time, if we don't discuss it now. That is a very comprehensive paper. If there are other papers to be read, we can take it up and discuss it fully some other time. I move that the house have the privilege of calling up at any time the paper of Mr. Gerberding, for discussion.

Motion seconded and carried.

A. D. Childress, of Los Angeles: I move, Mr. Chairman, that we adjourn until tomorrow morning at ten o'clock.

Motion seconded and carried.

The Convention adjourned to Friday, October 16th, at 10 a. m.

THIRD DAY.

FRIDAY, OCTOBER 16TH.

MORNING SESSION.

The Convention was called to order at 10 o'clock a. m., by Chairman, Thomas Brown.

The Secretary read the minutes of the previous session, which were approved as read.

The Chairman: Proceed with the next business.

The Secretary: I am requested to read the following program for the day:

Address by S. P. Young, Manager of the California Safe Deposit & Trust Co.; subject, "The Trust Company Question."

Address by J. Reischmann, Cashier Farmers Bank of Fresno; subject, "Co-operation Between Banks."

Address by Geo. H. Bonebrake, President Los Angeles National Bank; subject, "An Adequate Supply of Currency."

Address by John M. C. Marble, President National Bank of California, Los Angeles; subject, "Money."

Resolutions.

Miscellaneous and Unfinished Business.

A. D. Childress, of Los Angeles: Mr. Chairman, we have with us this morning Hon. H. I. Wiley, ex-State Surveyor General, who is intimately connected with the promotion of irrigation district interests, and the Convention would like to hear him. Mr. Chairman and Members of the California Bankers Association, I have pleasure in introducing Hon. H. I. Wiley.

H. I. Wiley spoke as follows: *Gentlemen of the Convention*—I very highly appreciate the honor of having an opportunity to address so distinguished a body of representative financiers of this State, and I should undertake to do so with a great deal of timidity were it not that I had discovered that there is really no one properly authorized to rise in defense of the irrigation districts of this State, organized under the Wright act. It has been my province for nearly two years to be intimately connected with the affairs of these districts and to have an opportunity to study all the phases of the act under which those districts are organized and its operation. And I respectfully submit to you that the matter is not properly understood by the public; and if my observations are to be at all depended upon, it has not been understood by the financiers and by the bankers, without whose aid and support and approval these securities issued by the districts would be absolutely valueless. The framers of that act were actuated only by the best of faith. It was their intention to frame an act which should be such an absolute security to the bond purchaser and the bond holder that the interest and principal money loaned to the districts would be paid promptly and without fail; that the securities issued by these districts might be equal in value to United States Bonds or English Consols. As I say, that was the intent and design of the framers of that act. If they have failed in all particulars and respects to create an act which is perfect, that is not a surprising thing. No organic law within the history of this world ever was created perfect. The Constitution of the United States is looked upon as a noble document, but, if I am not mistaken, there are fifteen amendments to that. Therefore, it is not a surprising thing that there should be some defects in this act providing for the organization of this quasi municipal organization for the purpose of developing the interests of this country. In the beginning of the discussion of this act of the Legislature, I, together with a number of gentlemen, were called into consultation; and we at that time recommended that they should create a State organization, to be composed of experts, attorneys and engineers, who would have general supervision over the organization of each and every district, and thereby permit the organization only of such as would be above and beyond reproach. But that would have necessitated an appropriation; and the promoters of the act were afraid that, if they handicapped that bill with an expensive commission and the necessity for a further appropriation, that it would not become a law, and they thought that the State organization would be a natural outgrowth of the district organizations themselves; in other words, after several were organized, a dozen or fifteen or twenty, the whole number would create a State organization, to have this supervision. But that was a fatal error, that lost great value that it would have been to these districts to have had this State supervision, which would have given a definite standing to the securities which they might issue as a result of their organization. For several years these districts went on organizing. They undertook to dispose of their bonds. There was the competition as between districts. The financiers of this city and of the State were appealed to to give their opinion in relation to the value of these securities. They made partial investigation, which resulted in the condemnation of these securities. It finally became evident that it would be impossible to dispose of any of the bonds here. New York wouldn't touch them. European financiers, of course, appealed to their correspondents here for information, and the best they could give was, " We don't know their value": with the result that it became absolutely impossible to place any of these bonds. A number of us who were here and recognized this finally determined that something must be done. This worthy body, the Chamber of Commerce, was appealed to. They were called in and the matter discussed. They requested the bankers of San Francisco to get together and consider this matter. They did, and we were referred to that distinguished body, the Clearing House. They announced to us that the consideration of a proposition of that kind did not come within their jurisdiction; their charter did not contemplate such a thing. Finally we appealed to representative bankers to a po nt an examining commission that would examine the land, in the event of a loan being requested or a sale made; and the best that could be done finally was that a number of public-spirited gentlemen, representing the banking interests of this city, agreed, in their individual capacity, to endorse an engineer and an attorney, if properly recommended by the irrigation districts, and that, I am happy to say, was done. That provided, then, for a machinery by which these districts might be exhibited. And, I remember once stating before in this room, all we asked was that the financiers establish a series of sieves, and we pour these districts in and run them through these sieves, and then we would like to have from the bankers a certificate with reference to the character and standing of the districts and their securities, which happened to pass through these sieves. That has been a successful provision, and today the districts, as fast as it is possible to do so, are being examined and reported upon. It would appear to me that it was a matter worthy of the consideration of this distinguished body of financiers to determine as to whether or not it would be an appropriate thing for them to give some commendation to the districts which do come up to the proper standard; to make a very emphatic and positive distinction between the districts which are determined by this process to be good and those which are still to be heard from; practically put every district in this State on the black-list, removable therefrom solely on their having passed a successful examination before these gentlemen who are endorsed by twelve of the leading financiers of this city.

I will not here concede that there are any defects in the Wright act, under which these districts are organized, although there may be. If there are, they can be remedied by the same authorities which created that act; and it would appear to me to be worthy of the province of gentlemen occupying the positions which you do in this State, either directly or through your attorneys, to give the irrigationists the benefit of your mature judgment and wisdom, and suggest to them all or any defects which you may have discovered in this act, in order that they may be able to act intelligently in undertaking to remedy them. It is not my design or desire to suggest that any one should buy irrigation district bonds. There are too many favorable opportunities for the investment of capital in this glorious Western country to make a six per cent. bond a desirable investment. It is to the older countries, which have grown wealthy by the development of this great, rich country, where the great mass of accumulators live, where the rates of interest are low—it is there that we must look for purchasers of these bonds, bearing these rates of interest.

On the 20th of this month, next Tuesday, there will assemble in Los Angeles a convention composed of representatives from each of the irrigation districts of this State, for the purpose of consulting with relation to all the matters which may be of interest to them. If it should be deemed wise by you, it certainly would be a matter of infinite encouragement to them if you would show, by a resolution or some action of this distinguished body, a friendly interest in the effort that is being made by the districts which are properly organized to secure the reclamation of arid lands of this State and rendering of them productive.

It would be silly for me to undertake to enunciate or undertake to define to you the enormous benefits certain to inure, not only to yourselves, but to all the people of this State, as the result of the successful carrying out of some processes by which these lands could be brought into cultivation. The Wright act furnishes the only opportunity for the whole community to procure cheap water. It may not be the best thing which could have been done. It might have been better for the State to have control and jurisdiction of all the waters of the State and their distribution; but this is the best thing that we have in hand at the present time, and I respectfully submit to you that, if irrigation cannot be successfully developed through the medium of that act, we are then going to be compelled to fall back upon the corporations, who will secure the control of the water and charge whatever rates they see fit for its distribution; which would be, of course, simply making the holders of these arid lands pay tribute for the balance of their natural lives in order to live on the land at all. In the convention to be called in Los Angeles, among other things, they will create what they designate as a legislative committee. Instead of their undertaking, during the few days which they will be together, to discuss all of the many questions of great importance which will come before them, they will appoint, as I say, a legislative committe, to which will be referred all important questions requiring serious deliberation. That committee will be empowered to hold sessions at such times as they may deem fit and best and in such localities as they may determine, for the purpose of hearing evidence, testimony from attorneys, capitalists, and all others who may have any objections to offer to the act or its operation, or who may have any suggestions to make with relation to subsequent legislation. That committee will be empowered to draft amendatory acts to be presented at the next session of the Legislature; both powers, withal, so general that it will become possible to so arrange as that the most superior wisdom of this State may be brought to bear to formulate any amendatory matter which may be considered necessary. And I sincerely hope that each and every gentleman here who takes any interest in this matter at all will consider himself morally bound to communicate with that committee at some time, in the event of its ever being necessary, his own suggestions in relation to this matter. I believe that, if the bankers of this State would view with a friendly spirit those of the districts which are determined to be above reproach, we would have no difficulty in disposing of these bonds and bringing into the State eventually anywhere from ten to twenty millions of dollars of outside capital to be invested in the development of our resources.

There is one great and serious question which, in conclusion, I would like to call your attention to, and that is this—and I think it furnishes a wonderfully superior opportunity for leading men of wealth to make an investment which would redound very largely to their benefit; of course, now, prior to the institution of this machinery for the examination of these districts, why it was each district for itself and devil take the hindmost, and they, of course, were constantly competing one with the other and resorting to all those tactics which competition naturally engenders. That was a very disastrous thing; but now that this machinery has been created, and practically they are poured into a funnel and forced to a narrow point through which only one can emerge at a time, that competition ceases for the time and competition will only be among those that have passed this examination, and then they will pass these on, and then there will be a competition between only two or three or four districts. I refer to the organization of an underwriting association or guarantee association which would purchase these bonds at, we will say, ninety, which you can buy them all for at the present time; as then, on the strength of the purchase of these bonds, they would issue their own bonds, bearing five per cent. interest instead of six, running for twenty years, and payable at maturity, most of these bonds being payable in installments after the tenth year; and, by a very simple arithmetical calculation, you can see that an organization created for that purpose and purchasing these bonds at that rate would have it in their power to make between three and a half and four million dollars on ten millions of dollars of bonds in twenty years, practically without ever incurring any expense further than the maintenance of their own organization. The effect of that would be to create a bond which—I am told by brokers in New York—would be first-class, and "gilt-edged," to use your vernacular, in every respect; and I respectfully submit to you, gentlemen, that it is a matter worthy of your consideration.

I had no intention of undertaking to discuss this matter at all until this morning, when I learned that there was no representative of the irrigation districts here, no one authorized to speak for them; and I simply did what I thought was to perform a conscientious duty to come before you and present, in a very crude way, these few facts; and crave from you friendly and kindly consideration for these districts, which are founded by an act which was created in absolute good faith and which is almost entirely in the interest of men who are seeking to carry out its provisions.

To conclude, and illustrate to you just how positively some men are acting in good faith in this matter, I will state that, while undertaking to dispose of some of the bonds of a district in which I am interested, I was met with the objection that there might at some future time be an attempt on the part of some of the land holders of the district to evade the payment of the interest and principal to the bond holders. I made that statement to the representative citizens of the district, and they told me that, if I would go to the attorneys of the bank which had made this objection and request them to draw up a document, in any form that they might desire, with any limitations, restrictions or provisions that they could possibly think of, binding them the more solemnly and positively to meet those obligations when they became due, no matter what the language or tenor might be, they would willingly and cheerfully, each and every one of those land holders, sign that document. And that, gentlemen, is the spirit of the majority of the people who are interested in these irrigation districts. I am very much obliged to you for your kind attention.

The Chairman : The question of Irrigation bonds is a very important one to the interests of this State. Is there any gentleman present who would like to speak on this subject? I have no doubt that bankers would be very glad to hear from any member who desires to address the Convention on this subject.

Frank V. McDonald, of San Francisco: *Mr. Chairman and Gentlemen of the Convention*—This irrigation matter was referred to the San Francisco Clearing House. We all know that it was a matter of great regret that the Clearing House could not consider it, owing to lack of jurisdiction. As we all remember, every one of the members present expressed the greatest interest in this irrigation problem, and all hoped that some way might be devised by which those bonds could be made acceptable to bankers here and to purchasers of bonds all over the world. But they also admitted, in an indirect way, that there were a great many difficulties, some of which they considered serious, in the way of recommending those bonds to purchasers, without any change of the present method of listing bonds or preparing the bonds. Now, we all know that the irrigation question is one of immense importance to this State. We also know that if those bonds could, in any manner, be made acceptable to the financial interests of the world so that any financier could cordially recommend them, that they would be a security unexceptionable in character, a security that would be sought after, a security that would not need to go begging at ninety cents, a security that would not need to go begging, but would demand a premium ; and we also know that, in this State, it would be perhaps the most acceptable way of inviting foreign capital. Now, we also know that the bankers, in this city particularly, for months have had communications from all over the world, asking our opinion, begging direct or indirect endorsement, in some way, of these bonds. We also know that every time we have referred the matter to our attorneys, or have looked into the question from a business standpoint, we have been unable to give that endorsement that we should like to give. At the same time, it is a question of great interest, and there are a great many here to speak, and I hope they will speak on the subject. I only wish to say this, for my part: that if a body, a good committee, is appointed, from the representative bankers of this Coast, and they will undertake to investigate this question, and they prepare and submit a favorable report, I, for one, will be willing to subscribe to fifty thousand dollars of those bonds, to be taken within a year. I don't see how we are going to get this thing started unless there is some definite action taken. Make a business-like report, and, if the bankers of this Coast will take a million dollars of those bonds, the future is easy. If we reach that point where we can safely do that, why there will be no more question about the placing of the bonds than there is about placing a State bond.

Geo. H. Bonebrake, of Los Angeles: Mr. Chairman, I seldom speak much, but I am just in receipt of a telegram from a friend of mine who is largely interested in irrigation bonds in the Southern part of the State: and he has requested me to present that matter to this Convention, and see if some kind of an endorsement could not be made by the Convention, or a committee appointed with reference to this matter. Now perhaps all of you don't understand the nature of these bonds. You don't need irrigation up in the mountains or Northern part of the country, where you have your cold and your debris, nor do you need it down in the Sacramento valley ; but we do need it down in Southern California, as most of you know. We have a fertile country there ; we have a soil that will produce almost anything, under proper circumstances, but it must have water. Heretofore the water has been owned by private individuals, principally, and by corporations; and many of those corporations own a much larger amount of water than they could use or was necessary for the land they cultivated. Right alongside of them was land lying thirsty for this water, but there was no way by which the owner of that land could get that water, except by purchase at exorbitant prices. The Wright law, as I understand it, comes in and allows large districts of land to form corporations and purchase these water rights and conduct the water onto the land so as to bring the larger amount of land into cultivation. To illustrate: we have land in Southern California that is not worth over twenty to forty dollars an acre, perhaps—just what it is worth to graze sheep or raise barley. Almost alongside of it, within rifle-shot, is land—I don't say it is worth it, but I say it will bring from four hundred to five hundred dollars an acre: and it is all because the water has been put upon that land and it is being made susceptible of producing, of bringing in the best results. This Wright law does that. It simply buys the water and puts it upon the land, and levies a tax upon the land-owners to pay for it. Six per cent. is the largest amount which they are to bear, and the interest is payable for eleven years: and along with it one tenth of the principal, running twenty years. By the time the principal becomes due, it is supposed the land is under full cultivation, with bearing orchards, and it will not be a hardship for the then owner to pay. This is the character of the bonds. It is a matter of great importance, particularly for our section of the country, in the South; and, more than that, it is of considerable importance directly to the entire State. It has already developed thousands of acres, and brought land worth ten dollars an acre to a point where it is sold for a hundred, two hundred and three hundred dollars an acre. If it is established that these bonds are good bonds, lenders will take them as collateral and loan money on them. I think it is a very important matter; and, although the Executive Council have decided that none of these things should come into the Bankers Association, perhaps it is limiting the scope of the Association to say that these resolutions must be passed by. But if a committee should be appointed, as suggested by Mr. McDonald, to take this matter into consideration and report at the next meeting of the Bankers Association, it seems to me it would give them the little encouragement that is necessary. I will not make any motion: I will leave that for others to do. But we would like to have a good feeling on the part of the bankers in reference to these bonds. The Supreme Court has decided in every case that they are legal in every feature. There is a case now in the Supreme Court of the United States, and if that case is settled favorably to the irrigation bonds, it will settle the last objection. Until that is done I could not advise any of the bankers to take them as collateral security, because I would not do that myself; but that will take away the last objection to them, and then we may just as well market those bonds in the East and Europe at a reduced rate of interest; and, if they are marketing them, it will be to the interest of California bankers to see that they are good, or to at least encourage them.

Louis Einstein, of Fresno: *Mr. Chairman and Gentlemen*—Although being of a rather timid disposition and not accustomed to public speaking, I cannot resist the temptation to say something on a subject that is so important. I come from a locality where a burning desert has been made fruitful and turned into vineyards through the aid of irrigation. Under my observation has come the difficulty of placing bonds; but, as Mr. Willey has plainly told you, the districts are willing to do most anything to get means to establish irrigation districts, build canals, in order to make the balance of the State that requires irrigation as fruit-ful as those localities that have had the benefit of irrigation. As I understand, a committee has been formed, voluntarily, composed of bankers of San Francisco, and able lawyers, also some engineers, to examine into the legal propositions, the value of the lands and the feasibility of the projects in the various districts. Mr. Willey says, "if the law should not be perfect." Of course, I am not sufficiently posted on law to know whether it is perfect or not. I am told there are no better bonds that could be issued, if the proceedings of law have been thoroughly regu-lar. It seems to me it is a subject of great interest to the bankers at large to give the bonds all the encouragement possible; and I think the best encouragement would be for some of our large savings banks here to examine the bonds thor-oughly, either through this committee or some committee that they might have faith in, and to buy some of the bonds. That would probably be the best en-

couragement. I, personally, urge my friends to give them a standing, realizing
the importance of placing them. While at home, I have encouraged the establishment of a few districts, and where the men are fearful purely on the ground
that that law might not be regular, I tell them that I would personally be willing to
take any chances to irrigate that soil and make it productive. As I have said before, as to the legal aspect of the bonds, I am not prepared to offer an opinion. If
this committee now existing is considered competent by the Bankers Association
to report upon the act and upon the various districts, I hope the bankers will receive their report and act upon it immediately.

The Chairman: There is no committee appointed yet.

Louis Einstein: I understand not, by the Bankers Association; but I
understand there is a committee existing now, formed at the request of the various districts, simply to give them standing. Mr. Willey so stated, and I have
that knowledge myself. It is a subject that is as important as any this Association can take up. That is, thoroughly investigate the law itself or have it investigated—the various districts, and the bonds to be issued—and encourage them in
every manner possible; not, as Major Bonebrake suggested, to report at the next
meeting, but take action as quickly as we can possibly do it: because many of
these district bonds have been going begging, and, of course, unless the bonds
go recommended from California, they will not be purchasable anywhere, or saleable anywhere. I would suggest, then, that we take immediate action, Mr.
Chairman.

The Secretary: Mr. Thompson desires to make a short statement to
the Convention.

James A. Thompson, of San Francisco: Mr. Chairman, if you will
permit me, I will make a statement with regard to the excursion that has been
arranged by the bankers of San Francisco for their visiting brethren. You are
invited, with the ladies of your party. I don't know any other expression to use
in this connection. I said something about "respective wives," a day or two
ago, but we mean by that the ladies who accompany you. You will please meet
at Fourth and Townsend Street station tomorrow morning at half past eight
o'clock sharp, where transportation to and from Palo Alto University will be provided. The program as mapped out is arranged by Senator Stanford himself,
whose guests we are on this occasion, so far as visiting the University and partak-
ing of lunch is concerned. The train will leave at half past eight, and at the
train tickets will be provided for the bankers, members of this Convention, and
their wives and daughters. We will visit Senator Stanford's stables, then the
University, and thence go to his house, which we expect to reach about half past
twelve or a quarter of one, and partake of lunch. We hope to leave Menlo Park
at half past two, reaching the city at three o'clock in the afternoon. In the evening the bankers of San Francisco invite you to a dinner at the Palace Hotel, but
we are not at liberty to invite the ladies to the banquet. Tickets for this banquet
will be supplied you here. Members of this Convention who have registered their
names will please come and receive their tickets. We will endeavor to have
tickets delivered to those members who are not present this morning, at their
addresses in this city. The banquet at the hotel will commence shortly after six
o'clock. After we get you there, we hope to take good care of you until late in the

evening. Come dressed just as you are. This is not a formal dinner and we have no prescribed dress. It is safe to say, if you come in any attire you please you will find plenty of company.

The Chairman: *Gentlemen of the Bankers Convention*—I have just received a telegram from San Jose, reading as follows:

"*Thomas Brown, President Bankers Association, Chamber of Commerce*—San Jose extends greeting to and cordially invites the Association to hold its next meeting at San Jose.
[Signed]   B. D. Murphy, H. D. Wright.

A. D. Childress, of Los Angeles: Mr. Chairman, I think it will be a simple matter of courtesy for this Convention to thank the good friends of San Jose for having extended this invitation to us. Of course it is a matter for the Convention to decide, as between San Jose, Fresno and Sacramento, in selecting a place for holding the next annual Convention; but I move that a resolution of thanks be sent to the people of San Jose for the invitation, in reply to their telegram inviting us to hold our next meeting in that city.

Geo. H. Stewart, of Los Angeles: In order that those gentlemen may not be waiting at the telegraph office for a reply without receiving a response, I second that motion, and suggest we also advise them that action will be taken in due course upon the invitation.

Mr. Childress: I accept the amendment.

On vote being had, motion carried.

The Chairman: The Secretary will respond accordingly.

Pursuant to resolution, the following telegram was forwarded:

"*To B. D. Murphy, H. D. Wright, et al., San Jose, Cal.*—A resolution has been passed by Association, thanking you for your cordial invitation. A vote will be taken for place of next meeting, as others extend invitations.   Thomas Brown, President.

A. D. Childress, of Los Angeles: *Mr. Chairman and Gentlemen*—Among the visitors here this morning is Captain William L. Merry, whose interest in the Nicaragua Canal is known not only all over the Coast but throughout the United States. The Convention would like to hear from Captain Merry on the subject of the Nicaragua Canal, as it is one of the subjects that ought to come before this Convention very prominently, as Mr. Gerberding, our Bank Commissioner, yesterday suggested. I have the pleasure, gentlemen, of introducing Captain Merry.

William L. Merry: Gentlemen, I thank you for the opportunity of saying a few words which may be of interest to you on this occasion. I desire, in the first place, to say that the canal question is, in this country, quite an old one— of recent date, of course. If you go back four hundred years, you will still hear about the canal; but, going back to 1882, to show you how near the canal bill was at that time to being passed, I will merely say that, with the efficient assistance of the late Senator Miller, and Mr. Kasson in the House, a bill was passed in the Senate, with a three per cent guarantee on seventy-five millions of dollars for seventy-five years, the Government securing itself practically by a provision for purchasing the canal at its cost at any time and having its free use for two centuries. The bill was passed by the Senate, and was introduced in the House, when we couldn't take it up, except out of order; we couldn't reach it on the calendar on account of business, and, on a call of the House, requiring a two-thirds vote, it missed passage in the House by five votes: showing that, even in 1882, we had Congress on our side for the construction of that work, with a Government guarantee, by a large majority: but the two-thirds vote was lacking by five, and the bill at that time failed.

The company at that time existing, the predecessor of the present company, had an arrangement with bankers in New York to furnish the seventy-five million dollars, at par, for the bonds. Had that bill passed, the canal would now be constructed and opened. However, the bill failed.

The present organization, succeeding to that, has made no special effort for any assistance from the Government. There was a bill introduced at the last session, by the Senate Committee upon Foreign Relations, consisting of Senator Sherman, Mr. Evarts of New York, Mr. Edmunds of Vermont, Senator Morgan and one or two others whose names I don't remember, the first men of the country and leading statesmen of the country: a bill of similar character, and similar bonds. To this bill I desire to call your attention. In that case, the Government was to have placed in escrow, in the hands of the Secretary of the Treasury, seventy million dollars of the company's capital stock; the whole capital stock being one hundred millions. They were to have the issue of bonds placed in the hands of the Secretary of the Treasury by the company; and the President was to appoint five engineers, who were to examine the work as the construction proceeded, and, upon the report of those five engineers that the work had been done, the bonds were to be issued to the company. The Government always had the right of purchasing the stock prior to the maturity of the bonds. They were twenty year, three per cent., guarantee bonds. That bill was introduced late in the Senate; it was objected to by one senator from this Coast, and, that senator representing the State which had gone on joint resolution in favor of the bill, owing to his fallacious position the bill was withdrawn, because it was seen that, if it was passed in the Senate, it could not then be passed in the House. The company made no effort to pass that bill, and it will make no effort to pass any bill in Congress; it will not go to Congress as a suppliant for support, as it would be bled by the lobby, and ultimately fail or pay very heavily for the privilege; and the company is composed of patriotic gentlemen, who will listen to anything that is in reason, and are ready to meet Congress halfway in any effort for Government construction under Government control.

Now at present this scheme is tending into the control of English private capital. Its promoters have to go wherever they can get money for construction. The first thing that arises, is this: the sale of those bonds at a discount. You may realize what that discount would be when I tell you that the Suez Canal bonds commenced at sixty per cent., and they are now earning sixteen to seventeen per cent. per annum, and the British Government owns a controlling interest in the stock. Now, a work that is to cost ninety millions of dollars may be made to cost two hundred and eighty to two hundred and ninety millions, in stock and bonds; and the State of California and the Pacific Coast will surely have to pay a remunerative tax which will pay for the investment. The amount is so large and the conditions are such that the company will have to sacrifice its securities to obtain private capital, and consequently it is in the interest of the producers of this Coast and the merchants of this Coast that this work should be controlled by the Government, with such wise and beneficent provisions as will secure a low rate of toll, by a construction based upon actual cost. That is what California needs; it is what the Pacific Coast needs.

I desire to say, further, gentlemen, that it is the key to the solution of the position that we occupy upon this Coast. Irrigation, no doubt, is a great and a beneficent work; immigration is a necessity; but let me tell you that thousands of acres of potatoes are rotting in the Sacramento Valley because it will not pay to take them away; grapes are selling at five to seven dollars a ton. It is clear to my mind that, positively, the productions of the State have no market; and what is the use of bringing more men to produce in this State, when we consume but ten per cent. of our products and have ninety per cent. more to be sold? Even now we are in a position where we shall go from bad to worse. Our orchards are producing a little more every year, and we have no market; and we shall have no market, except in a limited way, in the next four or five years, or until that work gets us the necessary relief. The railroads are incompetent to deal with the problem; they cannot, if they desired; the conditions are such that they cannot control the situation. Remember, gentlemen, that water transportation is, in cost, one to five, as compared with railroad transportation; and that is the solution of the difficulties that we labor under.

I don't know that I need to say anything further about this, except that the canal is certain to be constructed. The conditions are such that it may require two or three years longer to get the work well under way, by reason, possibly, of the difficulty in disposing of the stock of the company or its bonds, but the work never will stop; it will be constructed, either under Government control or without it : but, if under private control, California and the Pacific Coast will have to pay the toll that will pay those capitalists who buy those bonds at a discount and have fortunes out of it—millions for handling the stock of the company.

The work, gentlemen, has its political aspect. I need not say that I would be mortified to see that work, the last remaining great work of that character, go under the control of our commercial competitors. Still, if we haven't the money, if we haven't the disposition, if we haven't care enough for the future, if we haven't enough of national business capacity, to do that work and keep it as an American enterprise a portion of our coast line, certainly it will go to the people who do appreciate it; and there is not the slightest doubt that it will cost millions of dollars more if that is done. It is the key to the political and commercial situation in this Coast and of the United States.

I want to say one thing further about the position of this Coast. If you study the question of transportation and the geographical position of the Pacific Coast, one or two points will strike you with remarkable force. Just consider that we are farther from the great centers of the world than Calcutta or Bombay, because they are reached through the Suez Canal. If we want to reach China, we have to go across the widest ocean on the globe; if we want to go to Europe, we have to go sixteen thousand miles, around Cape Horn, or three thousand by rail and a three-thousand-mile steamship voyage. It is out of the question to talk of rapid development on this Coast until navigation of a cheap kind is found for moving the products of our soil. I think that the conditions are such that any-body who studies can understand them; and I tell you, gentlemen, this is the solution of the prosperity of the State. People may say it takes too long; that you have to wait for years. Well, suppose we do? If this bill had been passed in 1882, the canal would be constructed today. You may talk of competing trans-

B 5

continental railroads; but you can't get any, except possibly the Atchison, Topeka & Santa Fè, and this will take two years to three or four years, at best, before it can get here: and then, after all, the solution wouldn't be what we want; although I admit that the solution would be of value in that direction.

Consequently, anything that this Convention can do, anything that this conservative and eminently respectable body of gentlemen can do to place this enterprise upon a footing so that it will be an assured success and receive the support of the people of this Coast, will be received with great pleasure and thankfulness by the company itself and by the patriotic people, who will remember this as one of the crowning achievements in the history of American enterprise and American commerce. [Applause.]

The Chairman: Any other remarks? If not, we will proceed with the next order of business.

W. W. Phillips, of Fresno: On behalf of the citizens of Fresno and the Fresno bankers, I wish to extend a hearty invitation to this Association to assemble at the next annual meeting in the new Chicago of California, Fresno [Applause.] Fresno, if anything, is enterprising. We claim to be the queen city of the San Joaquin valley. We are known still as the great raisin seller, and if you should go down there next year we will give you all the raisins you want and show you how they are packed. We have an elegant hall, and we have plenty of good things to eat down there. I know this matter will come up before the Executive Council, but I simply wanted to extend an invitation to the Convention at large.

William Beckman, of Sacramento: We have to suggest a place for the next annual Convention; that is Sacramento. There are five banks there, and each and every one of them extends a hearty invitation to us to meet there. If you come, we will try and entertain you with our best ability.

C. W. Breyfogle, of San Jose: Mr. Chairman, I have nothing to say against the new Chicago, except if there is anything that a banker needs it is rest, and the best place to obtain that is in the Santa Clara valley. I wish, on behalf of my colleagues here present and on behalf of the people of San Jose, to emphasize the telegram which you have received this morning.

The Chairman: Are there any other suggestions to be made in regard to New Business? If not, we will proceed.

Frank Miller: Mr. Chairman, against the rules of business of this assembly, I present a resolution. Before reading, I suppose it should go to the Secretary and Chairman, to see whether it can be received. The subject is the Nicaragua Canal.

A. D. Childress: I move that Mr. Miller read it and let the Convention act on it.

Motion seconded and carried.

Frank Miller:

"*Resolved*—First, that it is the sense of the California Bankers Association that the Nicaragua Canal should be built; second, that the United States should afford the means for its construction; third, that an issue of bonds for the amount of its cost, to be issued under the National Bank act, as a basis of bank circulation, is desirable."

I am well aware that the By-laws forbid the introduction of resolutions except after ample notice, but I desire to leave this in the care of the Association for such consideration as may be had.

The Chairman: Gentlemen, you have heard the resolution as read by Mr. Miller.

W. W. Phillips, of Fresno: I move, Mr. Chairman, that the rules be suspended and that we take a vote upon the adoption of the resolution.

A. C. Henry, of Oakland: Before that resolution is passed, I should like to hear the expressions of some of the bankers of this Convention. I am strongly in favor of that great enterprise, and the United States should have control of the building of that canal. It has been well said by Captain Merry that it is of great interest to this State. Look at the condition we found this country in thirty-five or forty years ago, and look at the position of it today. Unfortunately, we are pioneers; we are on the outskirts; with all the great commercial centers we are not in direct communication except by long water routes and by expensive railroad travel. Therefore, I think it is the duty of this Convention to support that resolution. There is one clause, however, that I do not think it would be advisable for us to put in. That is the clause stating that the bonds shall be issued by the National banks for the purpose of circulation. I have no objection to the banks having it, but I don't think that we should put that question before Congress; that is a question for Congress to decide, what is to be done with the bonds. Let us go before Congress, representing the people of the State of California, asking Congress to take hold and provide this seventy million dollars, which will not be a drop in the bucket for the Government, to encourage and secure control of this work; and as Captain Merry said, not let any foreign nation come in and control the commerce between the Pacific Coast and the Atlantic. Therefore, Mr. Chairman, I move that the portion of that resolution referring to National banks be stricken out.

J. B. Lankershim, of Los Angeles: I second the motion.

Here the resolution was re-read by the Secretary.

Geo. H. Bonebrake, of Los Angeles: Is the motion before the house?

The Chairman: Yes, sir, the motion is before the house.

Geo. H. Bonebrake: In many respects, I am in favor of this resolution. I am in favor of the Government building the Nicaragua Canal itself, and owning it, without the intervention of any company. We have seen the effects of those things, and the Government might as well build it in the beginning as at the end. Yet, if that is the best thing we can do in order to obtain the Nicaragua Canal, let us do it. But in regard to the proposed amendment in reference to the section of the resolution providing for the use of those bonds for the purpose of National bank issue: Now, I am president of a National bank myself, and am always aroused when those matters are referred to. I would like to say here—and I know that my fellow National bankers will understand it, and others will too, perhaps—that the National banks don't want these bonds for circulation. There is a mistake about that in the minds of many persons. I often hear it spoken of, that it is a fine thing ior the National banks to have bonds for circulation. I wish to say that there is no money in circulation for them, and four-fifths of the banks today wouldn't take any more than the bonds which they are compelled to hold. I can see a banker in this house, the capital of whose bank is perhaps four or five hundred thousand dollars; he has that much in circulation; he is compelled to buy some bonds in order to be able to do business under the National Bank act; but he don't want more, simply because it doesn't pay. We don't want those bonds for the purpose of circulation. We are willing to give up all the bonds we have now for circulation, if the Government will only relieve us of the obligation of keeping them. If some other provision would be made by which we can act under the National Bank act and be without bonds, we are perfectly willing to surrender our circulation of them and give them up. I think that that part of the resolution should be left out.

Frank Miller: With permission, I would like to withdraw that provision. I accept the amendment.

A. D. Childress: That the third clause be stricken out?

Frank Miller: Yes, sir.

A. D. Childress: Then the resolution will read as follows:

"*Resolved*—First, that it is the sense of this Convention that the Nicaragua Canal should be built; second, that the United States should afford the means for its construction."

The Chairman: Gentlemen, you have heard the resolution. Are you ready for the question?

Vote being had, the resolution was adopted.

The Chairman: Is there any other New Business?

W. W. Phillips, of Fresno: There is a question before the American people today, and should properly come, I think, before every bankers convention throughout the United States, and especially so of California; and it is a question that has not thus far been brought up by any member of this Association. I had hoped that it would be. I desire to call the attention of the Convention to the free-coinage silver question. I think it eminently proper and fit that a California Bankers Association should put itself upon record upon this vital question of the day. The people East believe that California is for free coinage. They formed that opinion and judged from the fact that we have a great ore-producing country of silver. I am satisfied that they are in error on that proposition, at least so far as the bankers of this State are concerned; and in order to get this question properly before the Convention, I would like to at least take the sense of the Convention in a vote. I will not present a formal resolution, as that is restricted, I believe, and prohibited by our Constitution. But this is a question that is today agitating the whole American people; it is a new issue, and both of the great political parties are struggling with the problem; and I think that this Convention could in a measure present the matter to the American people so as to avoid having California misunderstood. I know that some of the bankers present are identified with the silver interest. Perhaps they would not want to put themselves on record. Of course we can have their voice in the minority, if they are in the minority; and while I believe that most of us are in favor of the gold standard—the same as Great Britain, which for centuries past has stuck absolutely to that gold standard, and which today is the financial center of the world—I mean London—yet, it is a question that ought to be discussed. There have been a great many magazine articles written upon this subject recently, and the question ought to be discussed by this Convention; and I therefore bring it up in the way I do, without having given notice.

The Chairman: If there is any member of the Association who desires to make any remarks pertinent to the question, we would like to hear from him.

A. C. Henry, of Oakland: Mr. Chairman, since the gentleman has called up the subject, I would like to hear from him on it.

W. W. Phillips: Gentlemen, without having prepared myself to speak upon a proposition of this kind, and without being in any sense a public speaker, I don't know that I could do the subject full justice. I can only say this: that in the race of competition as between the two coins, gold and silver, they have had a fair race; that gold has almost superseded silver as a standard of value; that the Latin nations who have tried the silver experiment are rapidly getting out of it or doing away with it; that while we might be called gold bugs by the Farmers Alliance or by the silver producers, I think that it is the only standard of value. And I may say that there is no comparison between the two coins when it comes to convenience. If a man comes into your bank with a check for a thousand dollars, and silver is a standard coin, you hand him a thousand dollars in silver and he would look with blank amazement at you and ask if you take him for a dray horse. A thousand dollars in gold, while it is a little inconvenient, can be carried, or held in the hand for that matter. Our Government has endeavored to help out the silver producer, and has done a great deal in that respect by the issue of silver certificates. They are sticking to silver in Washington, and while we are issuing a silver dollar that is worth only about seventy-eight cents, it is to be hoped that in the future this silver bullion will be manufactured into an honest dollar, a dollar with an equal value to a gold dollar. We understand, of course, that the Government has aimed to make the silver dollar worth a dollar and pass current as a dollar, but I believe that the profit made upon silver has been enjoyed long enough. There is made about twenty-two cents on every dollar, or at least that much is got by way of coinage by the Government. It strikes me very forcibly that this has gone on long enough: that we have got pretty near enough silver, and that the gold standard should be adhered to because it is the true standard. I only brought this question up to elicit discussion and to put the Bankers Convention on record.

W. D. Woolwine, of San Diego: I am informed that there is a gentleman here that will present a resolution on that very subject, and for that reason I would suggest that no action be taken at this time.

R. M. Widney, of Los Angeles: Mr. Chairman, I would say something on this subject, only the Executive Council would sit down on me and say that I should not discuss finances.

The Chairman: The next on the program is the address of Mr. S. P. Young. Gentlemen of the Convention, I take pleasure in introducing him to you.

S. P. Young, of San Francisco: *Mr. Chairman and Gentlemen of the Convention*—I have taken for my theme,

THE TRUST COMPANY QUESTION.

An authority upon the law of trusts has defined a trustee to be a "person in whom some estate, interest or power, in or affecting property of any description, is vested for the benefit of another."

During the last few years, in many of the Eastern and Middle states, laws have been enacted vesting artificial persons—corporations—with authority to execute various classes of trusts, which formerly had been confided only to natural persons.

Under this recent legislation the employment of corporations in the execution of trusts has rapidly grown in public favor, and the business of trust companies thereby largely increased.

In Boston, New York and Philadelphia, the trust companies transact an enormous business; and their continued prosperity in these wealthy and conservative cities, with scarcely a single failure or default, is the best evidence possible of their value to the community.

I note, from a tabulated statement in a late number of Rhodes' Journal of Banking, that the sixteen trust companies doing business in the City of New York, with a paid up capital of $15,250,000, have a deposit account of about $180,000,000 ; and that their earnings for the year, after deducting all expenses, amounted to over $4,500,000.

The Board of Bank Commissioners of Massachusetts, in their last annual report, in referring to trust companies, say: "These trust companies continue to grow in financial standing and value as state banking institutions. They also occupy a very high and important position as a medium for transacting matters incidental to banking business, and of such range, diversity and importance as to give them high rank throughout the country."

The great utility and value of trust companies, or corporations doing a trust business, has not, as yet, come to be much understood in this State: for the reason that our people are not fully educated up to the many advantages they possess.

Until about four years ago, there was no law whatever on our statute books empowering a corporation to act in a fiduciary capacity. At that time, a law was enacted authorizing corporations to act as executor, administrator, assignee, receiver, depositary or trustee ; but it was found very defective, inasmuch as it did not require the State authorities to exercise any particular supervision over them: moreover, it did not demand adequate security for the protection of trust funds which they were authorized to receive.

At the last session of the Legislature a new law was enacted which gives to the State authorities—the Board of Bank Commissioners—full and complete supervision over all the business affairs of such corporations. A corporation, to do a trust business, under the present law, must have a paid up capital of not less than $250,000; and before accepting any deposit of trust funds must deposit with the Treasurer of State, for the benefit of the creditors of the corporation, the sum of $200,000 in state bonds or mortgages; the same to be held subject to sale and transfer and the disposal of the proceeds, upon the order of a court of competent jurisdiction.

This law declares, moreover, that such corporations shall be liable, to the full amount of their capital stock, for any failure to perform any duties incumbent upon them.

Some of the other valuable provisions of the law are the following:

It authorizes any court that has appointed and has jurisdiction over an executor, administrator, assignee, receiver, depositary or trustee, upon the application of such officer or trustee, or upon the application of any person having an interest in the estate, to order such officer or trustee to deposit any moneys of the estate with such corporation, and upon making the deposit he to be discharged from further responsibility; and that the money deposited shall be paid out only upon the order of the court. It makes it lawful for any Public Administrator to deposit with such corporation the funds of any estate upon which he is administering, and relieves him from making deposit with the County Treasurer; and thus saves to the estate the one per cent. which the law requires to be paid to the County Treasurer for receiving and disbursing such moneys; and the law also authorizes the court, in its discretion, to direct the Public Administrator to deposit estate funds with such corporation.

It requires the payment of interest upon all moneys deposited, at such rate as may be agreed upon, or as shall be provided by order of the court. It limits the amount of money which any such corporation shall have on deposit, at any time, to ten times the amount of its paid up capital and surplus; and its outstanding loans shall not, at any time, exceed said amount.

It authorizes the Board of Bank Commissioners, whenever it shall appear to them, from the semi-annual report of any such corporation, that the value of the personal property and cash held and possessed by them by virtue of the provision of this law shall exceed ten times the amount of the deposit made with the Treasurer of State, said board shall require said corporation forthwith to increase its said deposit to the sum of $500,000 in bonds or mortgages.

The law requires that each corporation shall file with the Board of Bank Commissioners, semi-annually, a statement of account, showing its financial condition; also, a list and full description of all the trusts held by it. Such statement must be verified by the affidavit of one of the managing officers and two of the directors or trustees of such corporation, who must also state in such affidavit that they have examined the assets and books for the purpose of making such statement. Any false swearing in regard to such statement shall be deemed perjury and shall be subject to the punishment prescribed by law for such offense.

It makes it incumbent upon one or more of the Bank Commissioners, as designated by the Commissioners, annually, or as often as in their judgment they may deem it necessary, without previous notice, to visit and to make personal examination of the solvency of any such corporation, its ability to fulfill all its obligations, and report its condition to the Attorney General as soon as may be after such examination.

Such Commissioners are given power to administer an oath to any person whose testimony may be required on any such examination, and to compel the appearance and attendance of any such person for the purpose of examination, by summons, subpoena, or attachment, in the manner now authorized in respect to the attendance of persons as witnesses in courts of record in this State; and all books and papers which may be deemed necessary to examine by the Commissioners shall be produced, and their production may be compelled in like manner.

And the Commissioners are further empowered to revoke the certificate of authority granted on behalf of such corporation if, at any time, they shall have satisfactory evidence that any statement or other report required or authorized by this act, made or to be made by any officer of such corporation, is false. Such revocation shall be sufficient cause for the removal of such corporation from any appointment held by it under the provisions of the act.

Without further reference to the various provisions of this new law, I would state that in drafting the measure it was endeavored to place all the safeguards possible over corporations which might organize thereunder, in order that trust funds that might be deposited with them should have as near absolute protection as human foresight and experience could provide.

In this communication, I especially desire to direct attention to the superior advantages a trust company possesses over an individual in the protection of trust funds and the carrying out of trusts.

Upon the all-important proposition of the safety of the fund, there can be no question that the corporation trustee is, in the very nature of things, a far safer depositary than an individual.

A trust company has a fixed capital, and a basis of security which is known. Its standing and methods of business are open to the scrutiny of public officials, and the security required of trust companies and the liability imposed upon them by the California statute afford the most ample guaranty for the administration of trusts, and render it certain that funds intrusted to their keeping will be surely transmitted to the beneficiaries.

A trust company does not die but survives the persons who compose it, and can act as trustee continuously until the close of the trust.

Its location is fixed and well known, and its office is always open during the business hours of the day.

A trust company has officers and agents familiar with the law pertaining to trusts and the management of estates, and all matters of detail are confided to those who are fitted by long experience for the work and can do it more speedily and at less expense than those unaccustomed to such affairs.

On the other hand, of individual trustees it can truly be said that "Time and chance happeneth to them all."

The pecuniary worth of an individual is a private matter, and very erroneous estimates are oftentimes made: but if the individual trustee is ever so responsible at the time of his appointment, there is no certainty, in the vicissitudes of fortune, that he will remain so until the close of the trust; and should he suffer loss of his individual fortune, trust money invariably goes with it. The sureties of an individual trustee, having had no interest or control, feel under no moral obligation to respond for their principal, and they are almost invariably successful in evading any attempt to compel payment by them.

An individual trustee who is responsible has, generally, large business interests of his own, and cannot give the time to trust matters that they demand. In consequence, they are given over largely to employés, who have neither the capacity nor experience to manage them wisely, and no inconsiderable loss results from want of familarity with the business, or from neglect.

It is not known whether the individual trustee will live to administer and close up the trust; and, in case of his death, under the decisions of the courts of this State, a suit in equity, with its attendant expenses against the trust fund, becomes essential to the settlement of the the accounts of the trustee.

There is also involved, in the appointing of an individual trustee, the question of integrity, as to which there are many instances of sad disappointment.

Almost every morning paper contains an account of some defaulting agent who has been speculating with trust funds, and dependent people, who supposed themselves amply provided for during life, find all lost with no redress. A trust company may lose through a defaulting employè, but the loss does not affect trust funds.

In an article upon "Defalcations" Judah B. Voorhees, Esq., who for thirty-five years has been Clerk of the Surrogate's Court of Brooklyn, New York, in speaking of the employment of trust companies in the capacity of executor, trustee, guardian, etc., upon which subject he is an accepted authority, says:

"I do not believe that the general public, as yet, fully realize the value of trust companies in these various functions, and so I desire to do my part in bringing them to a knowledge which will save untold misery and ruin. You cannot tell where the best man in the world will bring up in ten years. He may be dead: he may become insolvent: he may go crazy, and throw your money out of the window, with no more sense of responsibility than a baby, before people know what ails him: or he may make some honest mistake of law or judgment that costs your estate very dear. When you leave it to a trust company you find it, be it ten years hence or twenty. It does not fail: it does not go crazy: it makes no mistake (if it should, it is amply responsible) and it takes no chances. I have seen their workings from the inside, and I can and do thoroughly commend them to any community."

F. Rudd, Esq., of New York, one of the independent thinkers and writers of that city, in an article entitled, "How not to make a will," thus expresses himself in respect to trust companies.

"A trust company, you know, of course, is a sort of legal what-is-it, made up to resemble a very rich person: which it does in almost every particular, except that it isn't mortal, and that it always stays rich. The fundamental principle of a trust company is, that everybody is to trust it, and it is to trust nobody. It never makes mistakes, never dies, and never resigns anything that there is any money in. It can be pretty much anything, except a husband, a father, or twins: the enabling statutes for these extensions not having been passed yet. It will hold your stakes if you cannot trust the other man, and *vice versa*: it can be your receiver if you fail, your committee if you go crazy, and your executor if you will appoint it and perish: and as an executor it certainly offers some important advantages. It will not run away. It will not steal. It will outlive your family. It will go safely always. Above all, it will do exactly what you tell it to do, first, last, and all the time. Is it not hard to improve on an executor like this?"

It is evident that safety and efficiency in the administration of trusts will be more certainly attained through corporation trustees than individuals: and with the security that the statute of California provides, there can be no doubt of the absolute safety of trust funds placed under the control of a trust company organized under the laws of this State.

"Into the wide field of trusts," in the language of the editor of the Surrogate of New York, whose opinion I fully indorse, "wherever exactitude, intelligence, conservation and permanency are the things needful, the trust company has come, and has come to stay. Many people will be slow to comprehend how an artificial entity can be adapted to such delicate functions, and it may take time to educate them up to it. But for ourselves, it would not surprise us to see the trust company succeed to the individual executor and trustee, as surely and steadily as the insurance company has replaced the underwriter, or the indemnity company the surety, or as the title companies are superseding the conveyancer."

The Chairman: Gentlemen, you have heard the address of Mr. Young. If there are no remarks on it, Major Bonebrake will deliver his address now. We will hear from Mr. Reichman later. Gentlemen, I introduce Major George H. Bonebrake, of Los Angeles.

George H. Bonebrake spoke as follows:

Mr. Chairman and Gentlemen of the Convention:

My subject is:

AN ADEQUATE SUPPLY OF CURRENCY.

There are few subjects more frequently discussed than that of the Currency. All believe that it should be coin, or such promises to pay as will command coin on presentation. It should also, all agree, be abundant, and adjust itself to demands of trade.

Is the realization of such a currency possible?

The discoverer of such a system should be canonized, be made a saint for Christians and a joss for Chinamen. He should at once be appointed Secretary of the Treasury, even if he was not born in Ohio. We would have no further use for alchemy, nor longer hear the refrain of the crank who is abroad in the land.

Should such a currency be ever approximated, the financial world would certainly be most happy. The bankers of our country particularly would hail with joy a system of currency, whether coin or paper, which will adjust itself to the wants of trade and always be worth one hundred cents on the dollar; not so cheap as to lead to irresponsible speculation in good times and when the collapse shall come, as it surely would, leave the whole country in desolation and bankruptcy: nor so dear that in times of great distress, and when panics threaten to destroy banks and business, that not one, even be he the possessor of Government bonds worth $1.16¾, can borrow it for twenty-four hours.

But how can we approximate such a currency?

The National bank notes came the nearest to it, and for a time answered the purpose; but such a great hue and cry was raised about the National banks that many of them refused to accept the privilege of issuing their own bills, and, only when compelled by the Government to buy bonds, took the minimum amount. There is no longer profit in it, and most National banks would be happy to be relieved of their burden if some way could be arranged to free them from the purchase of the bonds at high premiums and yet retain the censorship and guardian protection their customers desire from governmental supervision.

No association of capitalists will organize into a National bank to make additional profit over a private or State bank, unless where money loans at a less rate than five and one-half per cent.

This volume of National bank currency is constantly being contracted; and let the Government withdraw the compulsory and obnoxious requirement compelling them to purchase so large an amount of bonds at a high rate of premium, and many speakers and politicians will find their principal stock of trade exhausted—will have to write new speeches for the hustings ; for the banks themselves will surrender their issues as quickly as they can get them by express to Washington.

The National bank currency has performed its duty nobly. Never in its history, in a single instance, anywhere in the United States, has it failed to be worth one hundred cents on the dollar to the man who possessed it, either for his necessities or his pleasures.

The only advantage, however, this currency possessed over the greenbacks was the elasticity of its volume. But the premium on bonds and the short time till they are due has destroyed this only quality, and their days are numbered. Some other plan must be matured.

The volume of money, including gold and silver and currency, should not be less than say thirty dollars per capita. This may seem large in comparison to that of some European countries: and yet it is not out of proportion when we consider that ours is yet a practically undeveloped country, a country of distances; that at least twenty per cent. of the business is done through the mails, and the average time consumed in transmission and handling is several days, thus immensely curtailing that almost immediate transfer in countries like England and the Continent, where population is dense and almost the entire monetary transactions are confined to a few cities; but in our country, where not only the population but the business extends from Duluth on the north to New Orleans on the south, and from Maine on the east to California on the west, with intermediate cities which favorably compare with the first cities of the world in wealth, refinement and population, we need a much larger circulation per capita than any commercial country with which we have yet been compared to produce equal facilities of exchange.

Silver and gold should be and can be kept of equal value.

If, therefore, thirty dollars per capita—to be increased as population increases, taking the annual increase of the last ten years as the basis—should be the amount decided upon, it would be an easy task for the Government to maintain this volume of greenbacks and National bank notes at par with gold and silver of equal value; provided this currency was made a legal tender for all debts, private or public: except the duties on imports, which should be always payable in gold.

True, this might lead to what some might call an inflation. It certainly would produce an increase of values. But could not the farmer stand a small increase in the price of his wheat and his corn and his potatoes, and a cent or two per pound on the price of his hogs? And could not the laborer, without becoming demoralized, stand a little inflation in his wages? And would not every bank and banker be benefited by a slight inflation? Is it not for the interest of the capitalist as well as the laborer that the latter should receive more than remuneration wages rather than less?

The capitalist makes money only when money is in circulation; and if the worker received five dollars per day instead of two-fifty, it appears to me that he

who has superior abilities in making money can add much more rapidly to his
already abundant accumulation and should be the last one to complain of abundant money.

It certainly is a fact, although I have never heard anyone bold enough to make
such a seeming paradoxical assertion, that the rate of interest is lower in dull
times and a continuing close money market than when the wheels of activity are
heard revolving throughout the country.

Seasons of high prices and great activity are the bankers' gala day. Then the
rate of interest is high, because the borrower can afford to pay it and collections
are prompt. When "times are hard" for banks, the rate of interest is low, because the merchants, the manufacturers and such persons as the banks can with
safety loan to, do not need additional money. Their business and profits do not
justify paying a high interest. The rate therefore declines. The reverse of this
is true only in times of panics and perhaps in a few cities where money is used
chiefly for stock speculation. Thus we have the conclusion that banks can make
more money when business is active and prosperity general than, when is
usually supposed, in times of depression.

Thus we see that it is to the interest of all classes to have plenty of money,
and it is not only money that represents circulation. Confidence in values add
many millions to the volume of exchange compared to the few millions thus
actually added in paper and coin.

Thus we can have plenty of money for all business purposes, proportionately
increasing with trade and population.

Now, how shall we protect ourselves against the periodical recurrences of such
panics as sweep over the country with the force of a tornado and in a single day
destroy millions upon millions of values, leaving in its wake thousands of bankrupt manufacturers, merchants and financial institutions, and general business
distress? This condition of things is brought about by the loss of confidence; that
this afternoon or tomorrow values may be lower by reason of the scarcity of
money. Everyone is looking for it. Banks add to their reserves because at any
moment the depositor may call for his money. The merchant collects his bills
to make his discounts, the speculator offers fabulous rates to carry his stock
until the next day, and the whole country is convulsed in what is properly called
a "panic": in which the business men, including many bankers, act as reasonless
as a stampeding herd of Texas cattle. All this because no kind of security will
bring out the coin from stockings and pockets. The remedy is very simple, and
the action and success of Clearing House certificates are so recent that it seems
strange that the remedy has not been applied by the Government. It is simple.
Let the Government issue a convertible two-per-cent. bond in place of the
present four-per-cents., redeemable only at the pleasure of the holder, either in
coin or paper at the will of the United States Treasurer; adjusting the extra two
per cent. by discounting the same, say at the rate of two and one-half per cent.,
issuing therefor bonds, or pay this surplus in cash. Thus all the bond holders,
particularly the National banks, who are the largest owners, would surrender
their fours and accept the new issue.

Not even Alliance adherents can object to this plan, as it does not increase the
public debt; and any of us or them would rather have the bonds continue at that
low rate than reach into pockets and pay them in cash.

The Government could prepare and hold Treasury notes for the amount of these bonds, pledging the property and honor of our sixty-five millions of prosperous people for their redemption when issued: place them in the vault of the United States Treasury instead of the cords of silver now piled up in its bursting bins: and when such money stringency as occurred a year ago shall threaten the business interests of the country, and the rate of interest shall begin to go up point after point, then the holders of those convertible bonds drawing only two per cent. interest would march to the Treasury, not simply and alone as spies, but in battalions, to get the currency to loan at a high rate, which business for a short time might be compelled to pay: among whom would be many banks and bankers, which during an easy money market are carrying millions of practically idle money in the large reserve cities at no greater rate than two per cent. When the stringency is over and there is again a plethora of money, these capitalists slowly but with no less steady tread would march to the Treasury Departments at Washington and again exchange greenbacks for their bonds.

The picture I have drawn would, however, always remain a fanciful sketch, as with such a reserve and such facilities only a slight stringency could occur; and any panic could be averted in its incipiency on the principle that the Irishman prevented a great runaway disaster by stopping the horses before they started.

First—I have attempted to show that we should have an increase of the circulating medium, and that the National banks can no longer be depended upon for this purpose.

Second—A continuing increase in proportion to population and business.

Third—That a reserve should be provided, convertible into bonds bearing a low rate of interest and vice versa, to prevent the losses periodically occurring from frequent extreme stringency.

Fourth—That business would revive and all classes of people would be permanently benefitted. The banks would make more money, and all the people would make more money. It has been charged, and to some extent justly, that the banks are opposed to any expansion, and that *their* interests are hostile to the interests of the masses. This should not be so. They can only be prosperous as the whole country prospers. The prosperity of all is identical, and the bankers of this country should keep in touch with the people of which they are a part, and should carefully disparage any legislation that would seem to look toward the oppression of the masses, financially or otherwise; for we should not forget that this is a Government of the people, for the people, and by the people.

We have long ago learned that all single interests of the land should stand aside for the greatest good of the greatest number. That an expansion of the currency kept on a parity with silver and gold would be strictly in this direction, who shall gainsay?

In the lurid war times we saw the results of such expansion; and I do not doubt the fact that plentifulness of money led to an increase of patriotism among the people of those days. A niggardliness in the volume of currency makes the Government appear unmindful of the comfort and happiness of those who live under it; and I believe no greater impulse could be given to love of Fatherland than a reasonable and proper increase of our circulating medium. It would mean more school houses on our hillsides to fly from their towering shafts the banner of the stars. It would mean more grand and beautiful churches, lifting their spires to the sky. It would light the fires in forges now cold beside the silent anvils, and would start the whirring wheels and flying shuttles where dust now lies upon the lines of shafting and the rusting pulleys. It would mean better garments and better homes for the poor, and a general awakening of commerce to the benefit of every toiler in the land. It would drive from our financial sky the gloomy clouds of disaster which at times lower and menace as the threatening and destroying cyclone, and it would freshen the turgid streams of traffic as the rain from Heaven quickens the rivers that lead into the sea. Following in its happy train would be a people proud of their flag and their country, in prosperity, contentment and patriotism.

On motion of W. D. Woolwine, of San Diego, the Convention adjourned to 2 o'clock p. m.

October 16th., 2 o'clock.

The Chairman: The Convention will come to order. The next business in order is an address by J. Reichman, of Fresno; subject, "Co-operation Between Banks." Mr. Phillips, of Fresno, will read it.

W. W. Phillips, reads :

CO-OPERATION BETWEEN BANKS.

Mr. Chairman and Gentlemen of the Convention:

The object of our Association being: "to promote the general welfare and usefulness of banks and banking institutions and to secure uniformity of action," etc., etc., I wish to submit a few thoughts which strike me as tending, very materially, to further these objects, by bringing about such co-operation between banks as would inure, not alone to the benefit of the banks, but to the depositors and patrons of our institutions as well.

*Certificates of Deposit—*I believe it is within the province of this Convention, and in my opinion it would act wisely, to pass a resolution providing for and pledging its members to cash the certificates of deposit issued by the members, upon proper identification of the holder, without discount or exchange charges. By this method a depositor, wishing to travel to some other portion of the State, for the purpose of seeking investments, a new home, or even recreation and pleasure, would not be compelled to withdraw his deposits from his banker and invest the same in San Francisco exchange, which he may never have occasion to use and perhaps ultimately returns to be cancelled and credited back: but he would simply convert his balance into certificates of deposit, with the assurance of his banker that they could be cashed, at par, with any member of this Association. Deposits would thus not be reduced unnecessarily, and the patrons of the banks would save expense and often inconvenience.

*Collections—*There should be established by this Convention some uniform rate of charges for collections and exchanges, so that, when a paper is presented at our counters, we would know positively how little to charge for cashing the same, without incurring loss.

Exchange—San Francisco being the Clearing House for the Pacific Coast, the bulk of our drafts are drawn upon our San Francisco correspondents; these we remit to other interior banks for collections sent us, and we sell them to parties for use in other interior towns where we have no correspondents. Some rule should be established which would protect the holder from being taxed for exchange charges at both ends. I will give an illustration: A party goes into a bank at Fresno and asks for a draft on Woodland; he is informed that we do not draw on Woodland, but that we will give him an exchange on San Francisco which he can cash at Woodland; we charge him one-fifth or one-fourth per cent. for the same; but when he gets to Woodland and proposes to cash his draft he is informed that he will have to pay perhaps one-fourth per cent. for exchange; he replies that he has already paid the exchange at Fresno, and thinks it is a hardship to be taxed twice. The next time he has occasion to take funds with him to some other town he will endeavor to get the largest currency bills and carry them instead of drafts; and I don't blame him much if he does.

In my humble opinion the members of this Association should establish for themselves such rules as they may deem best for co-operation and reciprocity, as would make it to the interest of every bank and banker in the State to become members, because they would derive some tangible benefits. Thus we would enlarge and promote the general welfare and usefulness of the institutions which we have the honor to represent. JOHN REICHMAN.

The Chairman: Any remarks on the paper just read?

E. F. Spence, of Los Angeles: Mr. Chairman, I wish to ask the gentleman if the idea is that this Association should form a company to carry out those ideas of finances? If so, I shouldn't approve of any such scheme at all.

W. W. Phillips: I don't think that that is the idea suggested at all. I think he intends to convey this idea: that any member of this Association would be willing to cash its brother members' certificates of deposit without charge—cash his exchange without charge; the holder of the paper, having paid exchange at one end of the line, should not be taxed at the other, if the bank issuing the Certificate is known to be a member of this Association. Now, for instance, when these certificates or drafts are issued on our bank, and the party is going to Los Angeles, we would naturally say, "Go to a certain bank in Los Angeles," naming one belonging to the Association; then he could get it cashed without charge. In that way it would make a customer, perhaps, for this Association. And in regard to the certificates, that was simply suggested for the reason that it would perhaps keep a deposit longer than would otherwise be done. And it would work the same way with every other bank in the State; instead of drawing exchange and having your account show that you had so much less on deposit in San Francisco, why you would have it in your own vaults; and you would have a current draft with, you might say, every member of this Association.

E. F. Spence: If the gentleman's idea is that the members of this Association pledge themselves, one to the other, to carry out certain things, I don't think it is a good policy to have any such compact at all. We should keep this Association as free from pledges as possible. I think it will keep the feeling better not to make any pledges one to the other. The chances are ten to one that those pledges will be broken; if not broken, some person will think they are broken; then there will be crimination, recriminating, fault-finding, etc. If a man is traveling from Fresno to Los Angeles, why, I will speak for Los Angeles to treat him very kindly, to the best of our ability.

The Chairman: If there are no other remarks on that subject, we will hear from Mr. J. M. C. Marble, of Los Angeles; subject, " Money."

J. M. C. Marble, of Los Angeles, then read as follows:

MONEY.

The last census shows that we have in round numbers a population of sixty-three millions, and a national wealth of sixty-three billions. A century ago this country was virtually bankrupt; today it is the richest country in the world.

The laboring element earned last year not only their board and clothing, but enough more to make up all losses and waste by land and sea; and in addition, two billions to add to the wealth of the country.

The unsatisfactory feature of these prosperous conditions is that thirty-one thousand of the people, but little more than enough to make a good sized village, have secured, by usufruct or manipulation, four-sevenths or thirty-six billions of this great wealth. The remainder of our population, composed of the bone and sinew of the land (numbering 62,969,000), have, by the sweat of their brows, secured the smaller part—the remaining three sevenths or twenty-seven billions.

It bodes no good to the common wealth that the employing class is decreasing, and the employed class is rapidly increasing.

Wealth is power—intensifying avarice and luxury: the prime cause of ruin to every state that has existed. The millionaire and tramp are the complement of each other—the disturbing and dangerous factors in society.

When one two-thousandth part of our people, born naked like the balance, absorb the principal part of the net results of labor in the land, something is wrong: and there is call for careful study of economic laws, of which those relating to finance, with which this Association deals, are so important.

The old saying, "there is nothing new under the sun," applies well to theories of finance, as anyone can easily prove by turning over the pages of the past. Even the plan of Government loans—to anyone who had anything to pawn—at two per cent. per annum rose to the dignity of a pamphlet advocate in 1843, and was again revived during the war.

We only need to heed the admonitions and experiences of history to prevent confusion and great suffering and loss to the principal part of the people.

In the present age we find money divided into two kinds, principally: metallic and mixed. In any such discussion the first interrogatory that naturally presents itself is, what is money? The common answers are: anything, which freely circulates from hand to hand as a common acceptable medium of exchange, in any country, is, in such country, money. In other words, any article is determined to be money by reason of the performance by it of certain functions, without regard to its form or substance.

Another definition of money is that it is a term applied in the first place to the circulating medium, and is a general term signifying the circulating medium, or anything that represents it.

Money is only a tool: merely a contrivance to diminish the friction of exchange; one of the laws being that equivalent must be given for equivalent. That these definitions are correct is well proven by the diversity of things used as money. Among the Greeks and Romans, cattle were so used; iron, among the Lacedemonians: tin, in Syracuse; lead, in the Burman Empire; platinum, in Russia; land, under the Cæsars; leather, among the Carthaginians; in China, the middle bark of the mulberry tree, with the law of death to counterfeit or refuse to take. Britain, at time of Norman conquest, used two kinds of money: one living, the other dead—the former slaves and cattle, the latter metal; South Sea Islands, axes; Africa, cowry shells; in many places, copper; in India, cakes of tea; in China, pieces of silk; Abyssinia, salt; cod fish, in Iceland and Newfoundland; skins of wild animals, used by Russians, Indians and Illinoisans. Wampum, used among the Indians, was at one time a legal tender in Massachusetts, as also beans and bullets.

At one of the great fairs in Russia the price of tea has first to be known before the prices of other things are fixed; thus it becomes the standard.

The absence of money in early days caused taxes and church rates to be paid in kind.

The action of money is to substitute double for single barter; instead of trading the commodity you have for the commodity you want, you trade your products first for that which every one wants—money—and second, the money for what else you want. Therefore, in earlier and ruder times, people adopted as their tool of exchange that article they possessed that was desired by the greater number, or all. By bartering for such articles they could most easily secure the supplying of their wants; and were there no such thing as money all the products of the earth would be exchanged by barter.

The ideal money, approved by experience of the ages further back than written history goes, has been the precious metals. They have been used by every country and every people ever known, that could obtain them; and the lesson of our own near past confirms the verdict of the ages, that the precious metals are the most perfect money and ample for any and all times.

California maintained gold payments during the long suspension of this country, commencing in 1861. Had the whole country adhered to the principle that a fixed and reliable standard of value was better than an unredeemable daily varying one, like suspended paper money, the war would have cost many fold less: and the immense taxes then, ever since, and now made necessary by such money, been saved.

I know the plea of great necessity will be urged; it may have been a political, but it was not a financial necessity: and what California did all the States could have done, and thus have saved the great unseating of values, with its stimulation to gambling and speculation, that has resulted in transferring so much of the wealth of the people to a fortunate few.

So to the second natural interrogatory, what is the best money? The answer has been given. The precious metals form the most convenient material for money. They are subject to little fluctuation of value; they are durable, extremely divisable, and of small bulk in proportion to value. They readily take and long retain the impress of any stamp made upon them; they are not a fluctuating or uncertain standard, for if melted down or cut into pieces they will procure nearly as much of any commodity as when in the coined state.

B 10

The precious metal is intrinsically worth what is bought with it ; therefore no artificial or legal enactments are needed to keep it the true money, at a level the world over.

Coinage is not now nor ever has been necessary to cause gold to exchange for other property. Government stamping is simply for convenience in exchange. Impressing a stamp on the metal is simply to relieve from the trouble of measuring it, and so save every man from carrying about with him a bottle of acid and a pair of scales.

Intrinsic value in money is the necessary element, or else light coin would pass as readily as heavy. It is the value of the coin in the metal market which enables this tool of exchange to command equal values everywhere.

In order to render any substance available as a circulating medium, the essential quality required is that it be universally desired as such. It should be as little as possible liable to fluctuation. The precious metals best satisfy these requirements. The worst vice an article used as money can possess is unsteadiness of value ; and the debasement of the instrument of exchange, or the over-issue of its representative, is a fraud, effecting every trade and converting all credit sales into uncertainty and gambling.

Coin, metallic coin alone, is true money. Checks and bank notes are not ; dishonor them and you have nothing.

The popular clamor now is for a mixed currency, and the largest increase in the poorest part of it is demanded.

What is mixed currency?

It is a currency composed part of value and part of credit.

A mixed currency, to be reliable and beneficial to the public, must be what it proclaims itself to be—convertible into coin on demand. Therefore, a sufficient quantity of coin must be held to redeem it.

Its fluctuations will always be least when the proportion of specie to paper is greatest, and vice versa.

Historically it is found to be true, that a credit currency has never yet been kept within the natural limits of the value currency of the country in which it was established. The Continental money, the assignates of the French Republic, the bank money of England during the Napoleonic wars, the greenback of our recent rebellion, the currency of Russia, of Argentine Republic and Chili—these named are but few of the very many lessons of history, all going to prove this.

Such currency kept even England under suspension more than twenty years, and the United States nearly as long.

With a mixed currency—the more issued the more wanted—the supply does not satisfy the demand ; it excites it. Like an intoxicating stimulant taken into the human system, it creates an increased desire for more, and the more it is gratified the more insatiable are its cravings.

The issue of paper money does not make money, neither does it render money abundant. If it be issued to such an extent that its soundness is doubted, it produces an effect precisely the reverse. Panics, with their devastating effects, come at the height of expansion, when there is the most currency. In 1837 and 1857, the great panic years, there was more currency per capita in the country than ever before ; and the examination of statistics more lately will show like conditions in the more recent crises and pressures.

Were there solid coin back of every dollar of currency, speculation would largely cease, and panics lighten or disappear.

The Bank of Hamburg has existed since 1619, and has never issued a promise but what it had the coin to meet. Such banking does not induce distrust or produce panics.

A piece of fine paper, the intrinsic value of which is too small to be easily expressed, will buy anything you wish to eat, drink or wear, and possibly get intrinsically valuable gold or silver in payment. It is because the taker knows that if he presents it to the issuer, he will get the coin for it ; but were it known that it would not be redeemed as noted on its face, it would no longer have par value: even doubt would depreciate it.

If paper money is wealth, any government might become rich by simply increasing it ; this is a fallacy. The old couplet has it right, whether of money or other things :

> "The value of a thing
> Is just as much as it will bring."

A true note is simply a receipt for property held by someone else. Destroy the note or the receipt if you will: the property it represents, the real wealth, will remain the same. Were all the paper currency of the land suppressed, it would make little difference. The country would adopt the California plan—transfer property by check, or the real coin, in place of using a phantom.

In fact, currency notes, like checks for baggage, may be considered tokens entitling the holder to obtain the coin from the place of storage when he wants it.

The instant that paper money is unable to procure the value mentioned on its face, it sinks into a mere piece of paper, good only for what it may ultimately yield.

No issuer of notes can, by any possibility, add to his resources and power of lending by means of convertible notes, except to the extent that the public will keep them in circulation and not present them for payment.

The issue of notes smaller than the public could employ and keep out in circulation, means only an inconvenience really trifling. Checks and bills would be more freely used, and that would be the whole of the matter.

In the use of a mixed currency, the vital question is its proportion as to the precious metals. If we adopt the Bank of Hamburg rule no evil can ever come from its use.

If we adopt the English proportion it may be safe; and yet they have frequent times when coin is hardly to be had, and distrust and bankruptcies follow.

In the issue of our Continental money, no depreciation came on the first nine million dollars. After that its depreciation was rapid, and it soon became valueless except for wall and waste paper, and this under legal-tender acts of the strongest character both by State and General Government; even Massachusetts redeemed her legal tenders eleven for one.

Paper notes are but paper—paper tools if you will : not the property of capital itself. Interest, so important to all, does not depend on more or fewer tools of paper being used, but on wealth available for lending.

The wealth of a country consists of things tangible, such as coal, iron, tin, lead, copper, cereals, cattle, fish, wood, cotton, etc., etc.; with much of these a country is rich without a coin in it. France, of whom we hear so much financially, with her boundless stores of corn, wine and oil, is, of her own, naturally wealthy ; and money in such a country is only the medium of exchange, by which wealth is made available. Money forms but a small part of the capital of any country. The New York Clearing House accomplishes more buying and selling every week than the whole quantity of currency in the country.

An uncertain currency is only good for gamblers. Money is only an instrument used in buying. Money does not directly produce, nor create any additional power of buying which would not exist without it. It only serves to place wealth in different hands. The action of bank notes is simply to procure property from one part of the people and transfer it to another ; checks and coin do as well.

A single standard is the only just one, unless, when you have two or more, they are interchangeable : otherwise, injustice is likely to result on every transaction calling for a measure of value. Where two standards exist, the more valuable will disappear.

England changed from the double standard to gold before the opening of the eighteenth century. It was brought about by her undervaluing silver, which caused it to disappear from England, going where it was better appreciated, principally to France. In this country, Congress, in 1792, fixed the relative value of gold and silver as one to fifteen. This undervalued gold, and as a consequence gold disappeared, going to other lands where more highly esteemed : and as a consequence could not be maintained in circulation here.

In 1834 the ratio was changed to one to sixteen, while the nations generally were rating it as one to fifteen and a half. This undervaluation of silver by us resulted in such large exports of silver that in 1853 the ratio was changed to one to 14.88. More recently it has been changed to one to sixteen. The wonderful increase in the production of silver in recent years has so diminished its purchasing power that the difference in the two metals is much more than our present declared ratios. As a result of valuing gold so much under its real value as compared with silver, we saw over $77,000,000 go to Europe the past summer ; and in the struggle to boom silver we have become an importer in place of an exporter of that metal, as in the past, and this at a time when our production of that metal is very large and our storage vaults full of it. Europe is intelligent : knows the cheaper metal, and takes it.

The discovery of gold in California and Australia caused European economists to predict a great decline in its value, causing many countries to demonetize gold and make silver the only legal tender. More recently, the current opinion has changed, and the same countries have re-adopted the gold standard.

As the sum of human life is making and exchanging, the more the need of perfect money. Its convertibility should not be placed at the mercy of political parties. It sounds very well to represent that all currency should emanate from government ; its wealth, its great wealth, makes it the best source, and with the great power of the army and navy back of it no one dare say nay to its mandates: so we hear. Correct principles in finance are a stronger power than any government. The English army, with a Wellington at its head, who could conquer a Napoleon, could not make suspended Bank of England notes the equal of gold during their long suspension. The bayonets of Chili or of the Southern Confederacy had no such power : and even the immense armies of our country, headed by a Lincoln, said armies receiving depreciated paper for their pay when at times it was worth less than forty cents on the dollar, could not make legal tender greenbacks the equal of coin or of the money of the world. With all the power of government exerted, phantom currency will be phantom still.

The term dollar should either be dropped from our vocabulary, or else made to always mean the same. In fact, it is an open question if the errors of the past would have not been less if we had never permitted ourselves to use a term of doubtful meaning, but had spoken of the precious metal, whether coined or not, as so many grains of the metal.

All understand that an increase in currency results in a stimulated market, which soon becomes a tight market. So sanguine are enterprising men in an easy money market, they imagine the relaxation is greater than it is: and as a result speculate until they want more money than they can get. Rates of interest become high, which means that security and credits are bad: and as a result the crash comes.

Up to a certain point, money is a necessity; beyond that it engenders speculation and gambling, with all the demoralizing results that come from that condition. When credit is good, productive power is most efficient.

The actual portion of money in use is variously estimated—1-50 to 1-127 of the whole capital of a country—and when you make the volume more than is necessary for use, it causes a rise of prices, which is misleading: people believing it to denote an increase of wealth, when it really marks the diminished purchasing power of money. Nature's way is stronger than any law to equalize its value, and increased beyond its needs it must fall.

The question of money is older than civilization; there is nothing new in it. The rudest nations have always been found adopting some contrivance with advantage for exchange. The question for civilization is to improve it.

Let the bankers rise to a man and repudiate the thought that government fiats or laws, or constitutional amendments either, are money or can make money: and give the laboring people of the land, who create the wealth of the country, a money not subject to the manipulation of business sharps, speculators and politicians, so that the poor-paid laborer or the wealth producer may have a cash that is constant in its purchasing power. If this money is the precious metal, or a perfectly sound currency, and is issued in excess, it will adjust itself by exportation or redemption. If it is a currency of paper, doubtful of specie redemption, it will lose purchasing power, so that a day's wages will buy less of the necessities of life.

I have heretofore stated that currency is of two kinds, metalic and mixed; we may go further, and say: convertible or non-convertible. I take it none will argue for the latter.

In conclusion, were you to ask suggestions for the best currency easily attainable, I would propose:

First—That the Government retire every note it has out, not represented by coin in the treasury.

Second—That it establish free coinage of the precious metals, both gold and silver.

Third—That the standard gold dollar remain of the same weight and fineness that it is today.

Fourth—That the silver dollar be increased in weight to such an extent as to cause the metal in it to be equal to the value of the gold dollar in the markets of the world.

Fifth—That the Government receive gold and silver on deposit and issue legal tender certificates redeemable on demand, in gold or silver at holder's option.

This would mean that the Government would always be as strong as even the Bank of Hamburg, by having on hand a dollar specie for each dollar of currency out: thus relieving the nervousness that is sure to come when even the public treasury gold reserve reaches near its minimum, the $100,000,000 held to redeem the greenbacks now out; or, again, to relieve such unrest as comes when the Bank of England's gold reserve approaches the minimum.

Should Congress decide that further increase of currency was desirable, beyond what is provided for above, authorize the further issue of currency against deposits of Government bonds.

That is, let any person or corporation possessing Government bonds have the privilege of depositing them in the Treasury, and on so pledging them receive their par value in currency, redeemable at the National Treasury: the receiver of such currency to pay an annual tax thereon of one per cent., and for all plates and expenses of issue and maintenance of the currency, and further be required to keep such reserve in coin in the Treasury as may be deemed wise, for its redemption.

We find that so far as our present National currency is concerned, that the oppressive requirements of our laws have largely caused its retirement; and that, while the Government stands ready to issue its certificate at par against silver only worth about eighty cents on the dollar, it discriminates against its own credits and will not issue currency to National banks at more than ninety cents on the dollar, even when bonds are worth 115 or 120, or over, and also requires a further margin of five per cent. to be kept in the Treasury for redemption.

During the late war, when Government bonds were worth forty cents or so on the dollar in gold, a bank could get the same ninety per cent. of par value, without putting up the five per cent. in coin additional as is now required.

No currency was ever issued more satisfactory to a people than our National currency. It has been a source of great income to the Government by the large amount of taxes it has paid into the National Treasury, and has never lost a bill holder a dollar. For this, however, no credit should be claimed, as a bank has no business to break ; if it does it is simply from neglect of the most ordinary precautions—from violation of the most universally recognized rules.

Deferring, however, to the ruling of the Executive Council, I refrain from presenting a resolution I had intended offering.

The Chairman: You have heard the remarks of Mr. Marble. They are now open to discussion.

James K. Wilson, of San Francisco: I rise for the purpose of asking permission to present a resolution whereby an expression can be obtained from the Convention, if it be thought best, upon the question of free coinage of silver, or otherwise ; and, as the proper way perhaps to get that before the Convention would be to ask a suspension of the rules of that body, I will ask for a suspension of the rules for the purpose of proposing the resolution.

W. W. Phillips, of Fresno: I second the motion.

Motion put and carried.

The Secretary: The resolution as presented is as follows:

" *Resolved*—That it is the sense of this Convention that the unlimited free coinage of silver would be detrimental to the best interests of this country."

J. K. Wilson: *Mr. Chairman and Gentlemen*—If I may be permitted, I will occupy only a very few minutes of your time, in the way of some introductory remarks; and, if you please, then those who are more able to do so will present their views on the question. There are only a few lines that I will read:

Of all the attributes of sovereignty, no one carries with it a more solemn responsibility, or calls for a higher degree or wisdom, than the power of regulating the common currency. The currency of a country affects not only the health of the body politic, but it involves deeply the pecuniary interest of every member of the commonwealth.

There is a universal consensus of opinion among writers on political economy, that the value of all currencies depends upon their quantity. This is a natural law, and government can neither change nor avoid the operation of natural laws. It would be silly—worse than that—for any government, for example, to declare that after a certain period equal quantities of silver and gold should have the same value. The value of silver will always be regulated by the ease or difficulty with which it can be procured. In fact, the value of all coin depends solely upon the cost of production. If gold were as easily or as cheaply produced as silver, it would have no more value than silver. The value of 371¼ grains of pure silver, which is the amount contained in a silver dollar, is about 76 cents in gold. No amount of legislation, no amount of increase or decrease in exchanges, nothing but a change in production or *use*, will alter the value of silver, at least *as long as the great commercial countries of the world maintain gold as the standard of value.*

Free coinage of silver by the Government of the United States would certainly invite the silver products of the world to this country for coinage, as long as we have gold to give for it in exchange. Instead of giving us more money, it would give us less ; because, for every silver dollar coined, a gold dollar would go out of circulation, until finally we should be robbed of what we have.

It is not to be denied that a certain amount of silver coin is useful, if not necessary, for the business requirements of the country. Just how much silver currency can be profitably employed is not easily said, but it is safe at least to say that the 488 millions of silver dollars and subsidiary coins already coined are quite sufficient for the needs of the United States.

This is not a political question. We have Republican Senators going about the country, advocating that private individuals pass 75 cent dollars for 100 cents. You nave Senator Sherman, the leading Republican, saying (and this is taken from an extract published in the August number of the California Bankers Magazine): "No American would be such a fool as to present his gold for coinage into *sixteen dollars* when with that gold he could buy enough silver bullion and have it coined into twenty dollars"; so the Republicans are divided upon the question. You have ex-President Cleveland declaring, not only against free coinage, but against storing such heavy bulk of 410 millions of silver in the vaults of the Treasury: while you have a Democratic House of Representatives pledged to pass a free-coinage-of-silver bill ; hence the Democrats are also divided.

Coinage is a mathematical subject, like banking, and can have no place as a political question. Political parties have to decide upon it, but it is not a political question. It is a purely mathematical one, of commerce and banking. The people look to us for our judgment as bankers, and not as politicians.

The other Bankers Associations throughout the State, as also the State Conventions, are declaring themselves decidedly upon this important question; and is it not exceedingly appropriate that the Bankers Convention of California speak its views and let it go out from this Western Coast that we speak for the best interests of our common country?

A. D. Childress: Mr. Chairman, I move that the roll be called and that the Convention take a vote upon this resolution.

Motion seconded.

E. F. Spence: I am glad that the gentleman has made a speech upon the subject, and would like to hear other speeches made on the opposite side, but I question the policy of this Convention even taking a vote upon the question. It may be a fire brand and it may not be; and I believe it should be tabled and that we should not express any policy on it. Hence I move to lay the whole subject-matter on the table.

W. D. Woolwine, of San Diego: I second the motion.

A. C. Henry, of Oakland: I am opposed to laying that on the table. The first question is, what are we here for? We have come here, and this is the third day that we have listened to papers read by different bankers on different subjects, theoretically; there has been no question come up before this Convention today for a debate until this present one. Now, if this Convention of bankers has not the courage to place itself upon record, either for or against the subject, then, in God's name, what are we here for? Now, gentlemen, this subject has been discussed all over this State and all over the United States. There have been speeches made, pamphlets written—whole volumes written by men who have no more interest in banking matters than a Chinaman, men who know nothing about banking, men who have never spent two hours in a bank, men who don't know the first principles of it, but men some of whom happened to be in Congress; and self interest made them take a position in the matter, and they are taking it today upon the silver question. Now, we are here for an object. If we are not here for such objects as discussion of these great questions of the currency of the United States, then what are we here for? This question of finances has existed ever since the formation of this Government, down to the present time, and as long as the Government stands and as long as man lives the question will come up. Now, I am personally opposed to the free coinage of silver. We have a standard. Our standard is gold. That is the standard of the world. Observe the position that the Government has occupied during the last ten or fifteen years, as between silver and the Government's promise to pay. They are not sufficient to carry on the business of this Government. The last Congress passed a law which was a compromise with John Sherman. I believe there is no man in the United States who has studied this question more carefully than John Sherman—or John Knox; but Sherman in particular has made this a study for years and years. Other men think because they have studied the question for a year or two that they know more than the best financiers of the United States. Why should we want free coinage? Under the silver bill existing today, the Government is almost compelled to coin four million five hundred thousand dollars in silver per month, making fifty-four millions per year. How much did you produce in the United States in 1889, or 1890? You have produced only a little over seventy millions. Now, while coining fifty-four millions, it leaves only a balance of about sixteen millions for working mechanics and arts. The Government has said to the people, virtually, "We are willing that you coin every dollar of silver brought up by the United States." Now, do you want anything more? Do you want it to coin silver free of charge? It is worth only about seventy-six cents on the dollar, and it is taking our gold away from us. You have had the experience. We may be called "gold bugs"; I care not what they call us. Look at the history of the country in 1861, 1862 and 1863, when the Government was trying to save itself from the greatest rebellion of the civilized world! Where did she receive her supply of gold from? Didn't it come from the State of California, where they produced it? Doesn't any man whose hair is as white as mine is know that that is the fact; and know also that had it not been for the State of California and the gold she furnished, the Government would have been almost unable to meet its obligations? They may talk of us and howl "gold bugs"; but, gentlemen of this Convention, let the Government understand that here on the Pacific Coast today all we advocate is keeping gold, silver and currency equal, so that one dollar is as good as another—uniform. I want this Convention to say, "Yes, we are in favor of the gold standard as the standard of the world"; and to say that we are for or against free coinage of silver. I myself, individually, am opposed to the free coinage of silver, and I want this question brought forth before this Convention. [Applause.]

W. D. Woolwine: Question.

Frank V. McDonald, of San Francisco: *Mr. Chairman and Gentlemen* —I think it is well enough—[Mr. McDonald resumed his seat, owing to difficulty of being heard.]

A. D. Childress: Mr. Chairman, I move that Mr. McDonald be heard.

The Chairman: The question is on the motion of Mr. Spence.

A Member: Call the roll.

The Secretary: Mr. Chairman, was it ordered that the Secretary should call the roll on the question of laying on the table? I think not, sir.

The Chairman: The question is on the motion of Mr. Spence to lay the resolution on the table.

On vote being had, motion was lost.

A. C. Henry: Now, Mr. Chairman, I call for the original resolution, and I ask for the roll to be called.

The Secretary: The resolution is as follows:

"*Resolved*—That it is the sense of this Convention that the unlimited free coinage of silver would be detrimental to the best interests of this country."

E. F. Spence: I wish to ask a question. Would it be out of order to propose an amendment: that we are in favor of the present method; that the present system is favored by the Convention?

A Member: Not at all.

E. F. Spence: That we endorse the present action of the Government in coining fifty-four millions per year of silver.

A. C. Henry: Is it understood, Mr. Spence, that would be in addition to the present resolution?

E. F. Spence: Just merely in addition to that.

J. K. Wilson: I did not offer the resolution with the idea that there is anything disagreeable or any antagonism to be brought out by it. It was only, as the gentleman stated there, that we, as a body of representative bankers of this State, will not adjourn and go away without an expression upon this subject; and I would like to request, if it is not against the wishes of this Convention, that the resolution be decided, one way or the other, just as it reads there; and then subsequent action with regard to anything to be added may be properly had.

Vote by roll-call was had.

The Secretary: There have been sixty-four ayes and no nays.

R. M. Widney, of Los Angeles: I think there are members in the Convention who understood it was only the affirmative that was called for.

A. C. Henry: Well, it is usual, when a vote is taken, for each member to answer either "aye" or "no."

R. M. Widney: I understand there are gentlemen present who are in favor of free and unlimited coinage of silver. The gentleman who read the preceding article I did not hear answer "yes" or "no," and I thought he was under the impression that the noes would be called for after the ayes got through.

A. C. Henry: That would seem to be a rather singular proceeding. It is the first time in my life that I ever heard that, when the roll is called, the ayes answer first and the noes afterwards. There is no need of it at all.

J. K. Wilson: In answer to Judge Widney, I will say this: that the coinage, at their actual value, of the two metals, is very different from free coinage at seventy or eighty cents.

R. M. Widney: I offer the following resolution:

"*Resolved*—That this Convention is not opposed to the use of the silver product of the United States at its commercial value."

I understand that Mr. Spence's idea was, as he suggested it, as I put it in this resolution: "Resolved: That this Convention is not opposed to the use of the silver product of the United States, at its commercial value, for money purposes."

The Chairman: You offer that resolution?

R. M. Widney: Yes, sir.

The Chairman: Any second?

Resolution seconded

E. F. Spence: Judge Widney didn't understand my idea. Possibly it was my obtuseness in presenting it that made it unintelligible to him. Now, we have all voted on, and heartily believe in, the resolution just passed. Yet I doubt the policy of passing on the question, because masses of the people of the State think that silver should be coined free: they say it is the poor man's money; and by this action we may array our friends against us. That was in my mind when I made my remarks on the subject. Again I wish to offer this resolution:

"*Resolved*—That we endorse the present action of the Government in issuing fifty-four millions of silver annually."

I make that as a resolution: that we approve of the present action of the Government in coining four and a half millions a month.

Resolution seconded by W. D. Woolwine.

W. W. Phillips, of Fresno: Wouldn't that compel us to buy foreign silver to keep it up? I would certainly oppose it, if we had to buy foreign silver to keep it up.

A. C. Henry: That is the law today. It is the law of the land, and all we can do is to sustain it. The supposition is there that we have to buy more silver or amend that action. Congress has the right to repeal it. Therefore I say it is useless, as far as that goes; it is only acquiescent of what the law is today.

R. M. Widney: The resolution I offered was seconded, and was intended to cover the same ground as Mr. Spence's, and my point was this: parties, both among the bankers and outside, are seeking to use every handle that they can with reference to the free coinage of silver. Now, this resolution merely represents, I think, our views: that is, that we are opposed to the unlimited free coinage of silver, but that we are not in favor of the entire disuse of silver. Now, if that is all, every man knows that that covers identically the same that I have put in this resolution. It is simply to get this Convention exactly where it does stand, so no one can ever misconstrue it on one side or the other.

A. D. Childress: Mr. Chairman, it will be necessary to move a suspension of the rules.

A. C. Henry: I move, then, that the rules be suspended.

J. K. Wilson: I second the motion.

W. D. Woolwine: I move that the vote be taken viva voce.

The Chairman: The motion is seconded

Here vote on motion to suspend rules was had.

The Chairman: The ayes seem to have it.

A. D. Childress: Division of the house, Mr. Chairman.

The Chairman: The ayes will rise.

The Secretary: Twenty-six, Mr. Chairman, I make it.

The Chairman: The noes will rise.

The Secretary: Twenty-eight, Mr. Chairman, I make it.

The Chairman: The motion is lost. The next business in order is Miscellaneous and Unfinished Business.

R. M. Widney: Mr. Chairman, I was going to renew the original resolution I made. I am informed that, although they voted against the last resolution, there are others who wish to vote in favor of it as I have worded it. I renew the resolution:

"Resolved—That this Convention is not opposed to the use of the silver product of the United States, at its commercial value, for money purposes."

A. C. Bingham, of Marysville: I rise to a point of order: it is not in order, after once having passed the proposition, to again thereafter bring forward the same. The Judge makes the statement that it is the same proposition. His former proposition was the same as that. It has been before this body, and the motion is lost: consequently he cannot again bring it up.

The Chairman: The proper way would be to move a reconsideration. The point of order is well taken.

R. M. Widney: The point that is made, and on which they have asked me to renew the motion, is this: that in the one you have just voted down, a fixed amount was indicated; whereas, this simply leaves it for " the use of the silver product of the United States at its commercial value." That is the resolution.

Frank V. McDonald, of San Francisco: Mr. Chairman, upon that proposition I do not think there is any difference of opinion at all. Everybody is in favor of silver to a certain amount for circulation; we have silver mines that we want to coin silver from. But the proposition that was voted down was to coin fifty-four millions a year.

A. C. Henry: There is no question before the house. The only question is that resolution, and if we can't get through with that we had better take up something else.

J. B. Lankershim, of Los Angeles: Mr. Chairman, I think there will be no objection to this resolution of mine:

"Resolved—That the thanks of the California Bankers Association be extended to Mr. A Gerberding for his able article read before us, entitled, "A Few Suggestions"; and that we take this opportunity to express our appreciation of the interest he and his colleagues, together with the National Bank Examiner, always have taken in the welfare and success of this Association."

Resolution seconded, and on vote adopted.

R. M. Widney: My resolution was seconded, and I think we are entitled to have a vote upon it. The motion is before the body and is seconded.

The Chairman: As to renewing that motion, I don't know about the legal rule. I will declare the gentleman out of order.

A. C. Henry: Mr. Chairman—

R. M. Widney: The resolution was—(to Mr. Henry) You may take the floor.

A. C. Henry: What is it?

R. M. Widney: I say, you may take the floor; I yield the floor to you.

The Chairman: The gentleman is out of order.

R. M. Widney: Did the Chair pass upon the point of order that was made.

The Chairman: Yes, sir; I passed upon it.

R. M. Widney: Was the point of order well taken, or otherwise?

The Chairman: I think the point was well taken.

R. M. Widney: It seems to me that is not—

George H. Stewart, of Los Angeles: Mr. Chairman, I rise to a point of order. The Chair has already decided that question.

R. M. Widney: I claim that the Chair has not so ruled; and, if it has, I appeal to the House for a decision.

The Chairman: Judge Widney has appealed from the decision of the Chair. I will call upon the Convention to vote upon the proposition whether the Chair shall be sustained or not. All in favor of sustaining the Chair, will rise.

The Secretary: Thirty-three, Mr. Chairman.

The Chairman: Those of the contrary opinion, will please rise.

The Secretary: Twenty-four, Mr. Chairman.

The Chairman: The Chair is sustained.

A. C. Henry: Now, Mr. Chairman, there seems to be a little misunderstanding about the parliamentary rules. The gentleman got up here and offered that resolution, and the gentleman on the other side got up and called a point of order; and now, since some other business is transacted—you have transacted some other business—the gentleman now has a perfect right to come in, any time afterwards, and renew his motion.

R. M. Widney: I understand, then, that this resolution that I offered may be introduced?

A. C. Henry: Why, certainly. The Chair decided the point was well taken and you were out of order; that stands until other business has been transacted; when that business has been transacted, you have a perfect right to take that up again.

R. M. Widney: Then I renew the motion that I made.

Frank V. McDonald: The trouble with the motion that the Judge made is as to the unlimited amount; there is no amount mentioned at all. I move that there be added the words "in reasonable quantity," or something of that kind; otherwise we would go before the country as advocating the issue of silver in any quantity.

The Chairman: You offer an amendment?

Frank V. McDonald: Yes, sir; I offer an amendment, "in reasonable quantity," or something of that kind.

R. M. Widney: I have no objection to the amendment.

The Chairman: Judge, will you read the resolution again?

R. M. Widney: The resolution is:

"*Resolved*—That this Convention is not opposed to the use of the silver product of the United States, at its commercial value, for money purposes, to such an extent as may be needed."

I think that will do.

Lovell White, of San Francisco: Mr. Chairman, I move that that motion lie on the table.

A. C. Henry: There is no resolution before this house until, according to your rules, the rules are suspended. Now, I move, sir, that the rules be suspended.

Mr. Henry's motion to suspend rules, seconded and carried.

R. M. Widney: The resolution is:

"*Resolved*—That this Convention is not opposed to the use of the silver product of the United States, at its commercial value, for money purposes, to such an extent as may be needed."

Lovel White: I move that that resolution lie on the table.

Wm. M. Eddy, of Santa Barbara: I second the motion.

Motion put to a vote, and declared lost.

The Chairman: The next question is on the resolution as offered by Judge Widney.

E. F. Spence: I wish to ask a question of Judge Widney. Does he mean silver coin? Does he mean silver dollars? He said "silver."

The Chairman: Silver dollars, I suppose.

E. F. Spence: He don't say that.

R. M. Widney: I say, the silver product to be used for money purposes.

E. F. Spence: What does that mean?

R. M. Widney: That you coin it into half dollars, or two-bit pieces, or dollars.

Here vote was had upon the resolution of R. M. Widney, resulting in adoption of the resolution.

The Secretary: Mr. Chairman, I ask that Mr. Widney hand in that resolution in writing.

W. D. Woolwine, of San Diego: Mr. Chairman, I have a resolution which I wish to offer.

"*Resolved*—That this Convention values most highly the opportunity afforded its members of visiting Palo Alto and of enjoying its attractions on tomorrow, October 17th, and so far as possible its members will avail themselves of it; that the thanks of the Convention are hereby tendered to San Francisco Bankers for choosing such a practical mode of entertainment, and to Senator and Mrs. Stanford for their hearty co-operation and hospitality. And be it further

"*Resolved*—That the thanks of the Convention are due and are hereby heartily tendered to the President, Thomas Brown, and the affable and obliging Secretary, Geo. H. Stewart, for the able manner in which they have conducted the business of the Association and the proceedings of this Convention; and to the Bankers of San Francisco for the very cordial manner in which they have received and entertained their visiting brethren."

Duly seconded and carried.

W. W. Phillips, of Fresno: The proposition comes up to submit to the Convention at large, the question as to where we shall meet next year. I am willing to submit the proposition, as there are two other candidates for the location besides my town.

W. D. Woolwine, of San Diego: I move that, in taking the vote, each member respond for the place that he favors.

Lovell White: I second that motion.

A. C. Henry, of Oakland: If the gentlemen will please withdraw that motion for a few minutes, there is another matter that I would like to have this Convention have a rap at first. Will you withdraw your motion?

Mr. Woolwine withdraws motion, Mr. White consenting.

The Chairman: The next business in order is Miscellaneous and Unfinished Business, which will embrace that.

A. C. Henry: There is another serious question to come up. That is the question of the bonds that will be issued by the irrigation districts. That is a question that this Convention of bankers should take up, in my judgment, and argue, submit it, and determine what shall be done. I think that we should arrive at some decision, and either give these bonds a good send-off, or know what is to be done. I desire to bring the question up before this house, and move that the Chairman of this Convention appoint a committee of seven of the bankers of this State, locating them in different parts of the State: and, when a district in the State is formed and ready to issue its bonds, or after its bonds are issued, the President of the Association shall appoint a committee of three or five, out of that committee, to visit the locality, examine the land, examine the ditch, and examine all the proceedings under the Wright law that have been had, and see whether or not these proceedings conform thoroughly to the Wright law, and make a report to this committee. My object in that, gentlemen of the Convention, is this: we will know the benefit that has arisen in this State by the irrigation system. You gentlemen in the Central portion of this State, and in the Southern portion of the State, don't understand it any better than we do; because, years and years ago, before a great many of you young men ever came into the banking business, we knew the position that the Counties of Los Angeles, San Diego, Santa Barbara, San Bernardino and other counties there, occupied, twenty-five and thirty years ago. Since that time, by the energy of their people and the people that have gone into that country, they have adopted a large system of irrigation, and you all know the benefit of it. You men that live there know more about the benefits than we do, but we appreciate and know what it is. Take some portions of San Joaquin county; take Fresno county, where, we all know, twenty-five and thirty years ago land couldn't be sold for two dollars and a half an acre, and they are now selling it at one hundred and one hundred and fifty dollars an acre. The Chairman of this Convention knows the position that these counties occupied at that time, twenty years ago, as well as I do. Now, this whole portion of the country, the greatest portion of the San Joaquin valley, the greatest portion of the Santa Clara valley and the Salinas, of the Sacramento valley, is all waiting today and striving for the waters that are in the streams and in the mountains; and, under the law that has been passed by Mr. Wright, it is said, all over the State, almost any district, of from twenty to thirty or a hundred thousand acres, by an issue of twenty-year bonds, payable in ten years at six per cent. interest, can build these ditches and give the farmer and land holder, whoever he is, large or small, an opportunity to increase his land in value from fifty to five hundred per cent. That, we all know, is the fact; but the great question comes up, as has been well said by a gentleman who spoke yesterday, that here are bonds which have been placed upon the market and been worn in the pockets until they are all frayed out at the edges. When we ask that foreign capital or our own capital be invested in these bonds, what is the first question that is asked? It is, "Are the bonds that are issued by this corporation or by this district secure? Are they what we believe to be permanent security, so that when money is advanced and put into them, it can be got back?" The large bond holders of Europe and other foreign countries care nothing particular about getting rich, but they want something that is secure; they want to know that, at the end of that twenty years, or whatever the time the bonds are issued for, they will be sure to get their money back. Now, I think it is the duty of this Convention to adopt some plan, either by appointing a committee or by some other plan, so that when capital from a foreign country, or from our own country, or from our own cities, comes to California to be invested, we can assure the money lenders of the character and standing and security of this bond proposition; that we, as bankers, through our committee, or through the Bankers Association, after the examination of these districts and a report is made out, can say, "Our committee, of the Bankers Association of California, has examined that property; and their report is, that it is good security." Now, every man knows our first object is to get all the population we can; second, to get all the capital we can possibly get into the State of California; because the capital that we have at the present time, and the majority of the capital that has been in this State for the last thirty years, is the capital that we have produced ourselves, either from the mines or from the land; but a few hundred thousands of capital have come from the Eastern States or from Europe into the State of

California, for certain reasons that have been spoken of here before. Now, it is our duty to encourage this great enterprise, so that all the districts will have a fair opportunity to give their bonds a chance and get capital invested; because there is nothing, in my judgment, aside from the Nicaragua Canal today, that is of as much interest: and that is not of as much interest to us older people as it is to the younger ones. I believe that by that process, by the confirming of it or something of that kind, it will be of great benefit to our people at large and get the bonds disposed of. Therefore I make the motion: My motion is, that the Chair appoint a committee of seven of the bankers of this State, located in different portions of the State—and you may extend it—that the chairman of that committee appoint three or five to visit the locality of any district formed under the Wright law, examine the land, examine all the proceedings of the corporation or of the district, and see by their examination that the bonds upon the land and the way the corporation or district has been formed is all legal and correct, and make a report on it, either in favor of or against it.

J. K. Wilson, of San Francisco: I would suggest that the gentleman put it in writing.

J. A. Clayton, of San Jose: I understand that we have to wait for a decision of the courts in the matter. If that is the fact, it would be a matter of suspense at this time, until that decision is rendered, to go into this matter.

A. C. Henry: If we have got to wait until we get a decision on that bond question—the question of the Wright bill, the question of the irrigation bonds—if we have got to wait until we get a decision on that point in the United States Supreme Court, then there will be many of us, whose hair is silvered over with the frosts of many winters, in our graves: because the Supreme Court is now eight years behind in its work. After this committee has made its report, after they have looked into it, and say that the provisions of the Wright bill have been performed, and our Supreme Court has declared it is constitutional, that is all we can do. If there is a question comes up between us and the Supreme Court of the United States, that is another matter.

J. A. Clayton, of San Jose: Is it your idea that they should be entitled to call in legal aid?

A. C. Henry: Certainly, sir; to be paid by either the corporation or by the district.

A. C. Bingham, of Marysville: I do not intend or wish to antagonize that resolution; only, as a business man, I somewhat question whether the report of such a committee would meet with the practical result of accomplishing the end which the gentleman desires. I realize the importance of this irrigation question; not particularly in my section—still I understand it is of great value to the State. The institution with which I am connected sometimes invests in securities. Suppose this committee should be appointed and should report that they had examined the scheme and reported on it entirely as a satisfactory investment; we cannot invest in those bonds, and I doubt very much whether the banks generally in the State would invest in those bonds. It seems to me, if it could be arrived at, the most practicable proposition would be this: there are several very large savings institutions in the city of San Francisco which invest largely in securities in the shape of bonds; the Hibernia Bank has invested very heavily in securities, in United States bonds and in your State bonds. Now, suppose some irrigation district takes those bonds to some large institution here—as the Hibernia Bank, or the Savings and Loan Society, or the San Francisco Savings Union—and say: "Here, gentlemen, we have bonds; we believe they are absolutely good; if you will have your attorney, if you will have your expert go and examine our condition, see just what we have, and find that it is a highly satisfactory investment, we request that you will take one hundred thousand or one hundred and fifty thousand dollars of our securities; if not, of course we cannot expect to place them." If any bank wished to take them, after an examination of that kind, I think, it once being known, the other banks of the State, and parties having money to invest, would be very liable to be willing to invest. But the mere report of a committee—I should doubt whether it would get at the point we wish to arrive at.

A. C. Henry: I will thank the gentleman if he can suggest any better plan.

Frank V. McDonald: I made some remarks on that same subject this morning, that brought forth a reply similar to that one. I think I will have to follow it with a few words. Now, it seems to me we have had this irrigation question up for several years, off and on; we have been writing it up enough to fill volumes; and, if it is to reach a practical shape, it has got to be done by the practical support of all the bankers of the State. It is not fair to place all the burden on one man. I think this is a first-rate proposition, and we are perfectly satisfied in our mind that it is. Now, here is a proposition representing millions of dollars. They talk about ten millions; it may go into the hundreds of millions; nobody knows to what extent these irrigation bonds may go. Now, it is necessary that the bankers of this State go into this; that every bank in the State should either make an investment in these bonds, or help to place them on a solid footing with other investors, if they all consider this to be such an important thing for the State. Now, under those conditions, I will renew, in a little different manner, what I said this morning: that, if the Chairman will appoint a committee, as Mr. Henry has suggested, and that committee of bankers, who are practical business men, who know how to deal with securities and know what securities represent—if they will make a favorable report on any single proposition, or any number of propositions, under this Wright irrigation law, and the bankers of this State will agree to take a million dollars of those bonds, distributed around in this way; I repeat that we will take fifty thousand dollars. Now, after those gentlemen have agreed to do this, and that committee is satisfied, there is nothing to prevent us from making our investigations. This bankers' committee would be satisfactory, I think, but I should go and make an examination myself. The great thing is that a certain number of bonds should be placed in this community, so that we can simply say, "Here are a million dollars of bonds all bought." That is an unanswerable argument. It doesn't require whole volumes of explanation. Therefore, Mr. Chairman, I think that the motion that this gentleman makes is a very good one. And we should, furthermore, have the understanding with the bankers here that, if this committee is not sufficient, some other will be; and if we get a favorable report, that they will all lend their financial aid; that if they will take some of the bonds, then the placing of the others will be a mere bagatelle; with the whole State supporting it, why, the placing of the bonds, in this community or elsewhere, will be easy.

A. C. Henry: The object, gentlemen of the Convention, was to bring this matter up, have the committee appointed, for the prestige it will give to the bonds. Just as Mr. McDonald says: it don't prevent you from examining for yourselves; it don't confine any capitalist to this one way of determining the standing of the bonds; but if this committee has made an examination, and made a report, it gives the bonds a prestige for other people to work upon. Now, I understand the question brought up by Mr. Bonebrake was, whether the irrigation district law was Constitutional or not. The Supreme Court of our State decides that.

E. C. Sessions, of Oakland: I think it is entirely proper for this Convention to express its sentiment on this subject. It is one of great importance to this State, and one which I recognize the importance of as to its bearing upon the future of the State. At the same time, it occurs to me that the method proposed is hardly likely to accomplish the object. Is it proper for us to appoint a committee for such a purpose as this, which shall bind this Convention, as our representatives? Is it easy to find a committee in this Convention which will want to serve? Is it easy to find men who will want to assume the responsibility of examining the proceedings, and the regularity of the proceedings, and all the other questions which it will be necessary to determine, beside the question of the regularity of the issue of any bonds? It seems to me that there will be some difficulties in the way. A remark has been made here that, if some of the San Francisco savings banks would only buy these bonds, that their endorsement would be what is wanted. I have heard that remark made a number of times. The bank with which I am connected has bought large amounts of bonds. At the same time, this has occurred to me, and perhaps it has not occurred to those gentlemen: that savings banks are trust institutions, and they are called upon to see that the funds of their depositors are invested safely. We conclude—and it seems to me there is force in it—that it is not possible for banking institutions to give credit to any security. It is policy to buy only an accredited security; and gentlemen who feel interested in having this subject enlarged upon, and these bonds accredited, can, as individuals—and it is entirely proper and right that we should do so—advocate the credit of these bonds. And this point I want to call your attention to: as savings bank and trust company directors, we are not called upon to accredit any security, but to purchase only an accredited security; after they are accredited, then it is the duty of a savings institution or trust company to come in and buy those securities; prior to that, as individual bankers—as individuals—it is our duty to establish the credit of any security or any enterprise which we think is of interest and benefit to the community at large.

Geo. H. Stewart, of Los Angeles: I do not believe that this resolution should be passed, and for the following reason: that, while most of us, I believe, look with very favorable eyes upon Irrigation bonds, hoping that their status will be established so that we can safely recommend them, it is equally true that the conditions surrounding their payment have never yet been exploited; and until that is done, I do not think any commendation we can give them will materially aid their establishment on a better footing.

James Patterson, Jr., of Perris: As I understand, there has been a committee of bankers appointed on these bonds—I believe Mr. Brown, and Mr. McDonald, of San Francisco, and Mr. Wilson, the lawyer, are the committee—to report favorably on any bonds that are satisfactory.

The Chairman: There is no proposition of that kind.

Jas. Patterson, Jr.: Just as individuals.

The Chairman: The suggestion was this: that the bankers named appoint a competent engineer to make examination, an engineer in whom they had faith and confidence, and also attorneys to pass upon the validity of the securities offered. Those are the only two things that we are asked to pass upon.

A. C. Henry: Now, Mr. Chairman, that is exactly what I asked; but I don't see the objection of my friend Mr. Sessions, here. That has been done by a few districts.

The Chairman: That was done at the request of the irrigation districts, and these gentlemen acted.

A. C. Henry: Now, the proposition I make is not going to cost this Bankers Convention anything at all; and I don't see that it is going to do any harm, after they have made their report. No corporation or district is going to ask this committee to go up there to do it for nothing. Pay them, if they will take anything, for making this examination. Then that report can be taken for what it is worth. It will be some benefit to all of us, as Mr. McDonald says. He admits that that will assist him; then, if he is not satisfied, he can send all the experts he desires to; and if he wants Mr. Brown, or Mr. Hall, or any other engineer, to go, he can do it. If any question comes up, we should express our opinion, and not be afraid. Now, if this was going to do any harm, I wouldn't advocate it. I know it will be a good thing for the State. It will give encouragement to the irrigation portions of the State to go ahead; and as far as the benefits are concerned, it is not worth while for me to repeat them, because every man knows them.

A. D. Childress: Question, Mr. Chairman.

The Chairman: Gentlemen, the question is on the adoption of Mr. Henry's resolution. The resolution has been reduced to writing. The Secretary will read.

Secretary reads:

"*Resolved*—That a committee of seven be appointed by the Chair, to be called 'Committee on Irrigation Bonds,' whose duty it shall be to pass on Irrigation bonds when requested by any district; the expense, however, to be borne by the district."

Viva voce vote had, and division of the house called for.

The Chairman: Division is called for. The ayes will please to rise.

The Secretary: Twenty-nine, Mr. Chairman.

The Chairman: The noes will please arise.

The Secretary: Thirteen, Mr. Chairman.

The Chairman: The resolution is adopted. The next matter is the appointment of the Committee. How shall it be appointed?

A. C. Henry: The Chair can take his time to appoint the Committee. There is no necessity for appointing it now.

W. W. Phillips, of Fresno: I move that we call the roll upon the question of location for the next Convention.

The Chairman: Let me appoint that Committee first? I will appoint A. C. Henry, of Oakland; Bryant Howard, of San Diego; W. P. Harrington, of Colusa; Wm. M. Eddy, of Santa Barbara; Frank V. McDonald, of San Francisco; E. F. Spence, of Los Angeles, and Frank Miller, of Sacramento.

W. P. Harrington: I would like to be excused.

E. F. Spence: I ask to be excused. My business will not permit me to devote the necessary time to the work of the Committtee.

A. C. Henry: Mr. Chairman, I am surprised that these gentlemen from the Southern portion of the State should refuse to act on this Committee. If you all are going to resign, I don't see what we can do. The very irrigation question has made you—made you, completed and finished, from top to bottom. [Applause.] Now, when the question comes up, and you are asked to serve on a Committee to spend a few days, you haven't got time. My business confines me as much as any man's, but I think when a great question comes up for the benefit of my community, and I am called upon, I consider it is my duty to set my business to one side and attend to it; and I hope that no other man will get up and say, "I haven't got time." [Applause.]

E. F. Spence: It is the first time that I ever heard that a Los Angeles man was finished. He says that we are made from top to bottom—we are made complete. But I withdraw my resignation. I will do the very best I can.

A Delegate: With the permission of the gentleman who spoke about the place of next meeting, I wish to speak of a matter. We have been very highly pleased in listening to the able addresses delivered before this Convention, and I for one would not feel satisfied to go home without having a copy of those papers; and I would like to ask if any provision has been made for their publication, and, if not, would recommend that this be attended to.

The Chairman: The proceedings are to be published. The next business in order is location of the next Annual Convention of this Association.

Here the roll was called, members responding by naming place favored. The result as tallied was as follows: San Jose, 17; Fresno, 26; Sacramento, 18. The Secretary was proceeding to announce the vote, when he was interrupted:—

E. F. Spence: I wish to change the First National Bank of Los Angeles from San Jose to Fresno.

W. D. Woolwine, Cashier First National Bank, San Diego: I will change my vote from San Jose to Fresno.

Bryant Howard, of San Diego: Representing the Bank of Oceanside, and the Consolidated National Bank of San Diego, I will change my votes also from San Jose to Fresno.

A. D. Childress, of Los Angeles: I will change my vote from San Jose to Fresno. I move that the vote be declared unanimous in favor of Fresno.

A. C. Bingham, of Marysville : I second the motion to make the vote unanimous in favor of Fresno, and at the same time extend to you a standing invitation on behalf of Sacramento, at any and all times.

Motion to make vote in favor of Fresno unanimous, carried.

A. D. Childress: Mr. Chairman, I move that Mr. C. E. Palmer, Cashier of the Union National Bank, of Oakland, be sent as a delegate to the Convention of the American Bankers Association, at New Orleans, November 11th and 12th.

W. D. Woolwine, of San Diego: I second the motion.

The Chairman: Gentlemen, you have heard the motion of Mr. Childress.

Motion put and carried

W. W. Phillips, of Fresno: *Mr. Chairman and Gentlemen* On behalf of Fresno, I wish to extend our hearty thanks for the large vote in favor of Fresno, and the unanimous vote afterwares. We promise you a good time, and we will set them up handsomely.

The Chairman: Is there any other Unfinished Business?

Frank V. McDonald: I wish to ask the experience of the members here on that mortage tax. I want anybody who has had any experience with it, as some of the older bankers here may have had. There is a case that we have been working up for some time, and I thought perhaps they could devise a solution.

The Chairman: It is under the head of Unfinished Business, I suppose.

A motion was made that Mr. McDonald be heard on the subject mentioned by him, and motion was carried.

Frank V. McDonald: It is just this: As you know, the mortgagee is supposed to pay the mortgage tax. Now, in the case of placing a series of first mortgage bonds upon the property that is not included in a public corporation or quasi public corporation, it comes under the head of individual or private individual property. I would like to know what expedient has been used by other people in placing such mortgage bonds, to avoid the complication of the mortgage tax; because, if the mortgagee pays the tax, why then the purchaser of a mortgage bond might, under some circumstances, be actually defrauded out of the whole bond by the mortgagor paying the tax and charging it against him: so that the purchaser of those bonds wouldn't know exactly whether he was going to get his regular rate of interest on the bond, and, at the end of the time, his principal. Now, that is a very delicate matter. We would like to find the most convenient way of meeting this difficulty. I don't exactly see what expedient others have used in that connection, and I would be very glad of any suggestions.

The Chairman: I think your question is a legal conundrum. There are some attorneys here who might enlighten us on the subject.

Frank V. McDonald: I didn't know but some of them had already gone through the workings; and, if they had, I would be glad of their information.

A Delegate: While I don't profess to be an authority in the matter, I have given some little consideration to that subject. As I understand the law, a quasi public corporation is not to offset—that is, it is not allowed to offset—its debts. A quasi public corporation is a railroad, gas company, water company, or any other company of that nature which is semi-public in its character, acting under franchise, and receiving the right to use streets and so on; it is public to a certain extent. That corporation is obliged to pay taxes on its entire property, and consequently to tax its mortgage as well as its property would be double taxation; so I think the question is made plain there, that no assessor attempts to assess the mortgage given by a quasi corporation. But the bonds given by a private corporation—I cannot see in what way it stands any different from a mortgage given by an individual. By the law of the different states, a private corporation shall be treated the same as a private individual. For instance: a milling company, flouring mill, or something of that kind, if it belongs to Mr. A. B., and he execute a mortgage on it, that mortgage shall be deemed as an interest in that property and shall be assessed as a portion of it. Now, if he can, by simply incorporating himself into a private corporation, change the entire aspect of the thing, it would seem a little singular. I think there have been some bonds issued by private corporations which have not been assessed as an interest in the property—the mortgage has not—for the reason that the corporation that issued the bonds has voluntarily returned all of its assets to the assessor; and consequently the assessor, getting all the property, has not assessed the mortgage. There is a chance there, again, it seems to me, for a discussion; and that question never has been brought forward, I think, in any court, as yet.

Lovell White, of San Francisco: I think the thanks of this Convention are due to the Chamber of Commerce for its civility. I make that motion.

Motion seconded and carried.

W. D. Woolwine, of San Diego: I would also move that the thanks of this Convention be tendered to the reporters and the Press. I make the motion, that the thanks of the Convention be extended to the Press of this city and elsewhere for the courtesies extended to the Convention.

Motion seconded and carried.

Motion to adjourn made and carried.

The Chairman: I declare the Convention adjourned, *sine die*.

It was deemed appropriate to invite the State Board of Bank Commissioners, consisting of A. Gerberding, W. H. Knight and C. H. Dunsmoor, also the National Bank Examiner for this District, Col. W. H. Chamberlain, to be present and take part in the proceedings. All these gentlemen accepted the invitation, and, with the exception of Mr. Dunsmoor (who was unavoidably absent), were present at most of the sessions and assisted in many ways in making the meetings interesting.

Social Features.

EXCURSION TO PALO ALTO AND LELAND STANFORD, Jr., UNIVERSITY.

On Saturday, October 17th, by invitation, the delegates with their ladies took the 8:30 train from Third and Townsend Streets. The party filled three cars, and were met at Menlo Park by Senator and Mrs. Stanford, who escorted them through the grounds at Palo Alto. The visitors were entertained by an exhibition driving of the horses, after which they were escorted to the extensive grounds occupied by the Leland Stanford, Jr., University, and were shown through the buildings by President Jordan.

Shortly after noon the guests were welcomed by Senator and Mrs. Stanford at their home, and entertained at a bountiful lunch. Hon. E. F. Spence, of Los Angeles, in behalf of the visitors, expressed their appreciation of the entertainment, and Senator Stanford responded briefly, expressing his pleasure at the opportunity to entertain such a body of representative men.

The excursion returned to San Francisco about 4 o'clock

BANQUET AT PALACE HOTEL.

SATURDAY EVENING, OCT. 17th.

In pursuance of the invitation extended by the San Francisco Bankers, through the Chairman of their Entertainment Committee, Mr. James A. Thompson (see pages 19 and 62), the invited guests and delegates assembled shortly after 6 o'clock in the parlors of the Palace Hotel, and at 7 o'clock were seated in the large dining hall on the main floor.

The decorations were novel and picturesque: consisting of palms and ferns dispersed about the room, and strips of tan bark covered with Tokay and Black Prince grapes and golden-hued chrysanthemums.

A notable feature of the occasion was the use of California rieslings, sherries, sauternes and clarets, in preference to imported wines.

The music was conducted by Henry Heyman, with an orchestra of twenty-five selected musicians, pleasantly relieved by the "Bohemian Quartette," consisting of M. Fortescue, Clarence Howland, F. G. B. Mills and Chas. B. Stone.

I. W. Hellman, of the Nevada Bank, Vice-President of the Association, presided, in the absence of Mr. Thomas Brown.

In place of the customary menu card the following unique "Statement" was presented:

STATEMENT OF THE CALIFORNIA BANKERS ASSOCIATION,
OCTOBER 17TH, 1891.

RESOURCES.	LIABILITIES.
Huitres d'Est en Coquille	Grand Festival March...... ....*G. Sourlet*
Consomme a la Princesse	(Composed expressly for this occasion.)
Canapes Caviar a la Russe	Festival Overture... ....*Leutner*
Escallope de Foie Gras a la Diplomate	Amontillado Sherry
Filet de Sole a la Normande	Selections—"Faust,"...... ....*Gounod*
Pommes Croquettes	Inglenook Riesling
Filet de Bœuf a la Chatelaine	Waltz—"La Serenata,".......... .....*Granada*
Poulet a l'E arlotte, Venitienne	Sauterne Souvenir, Cresta Blanca
Crepinette Faisan a la Castillane	Intermezzo and Valse -"Naila,".........*Delibes*
Sorbet au Champagne	Napa Valley Private Stock Claret
Caile roti	Gavotte—"Ingenue,".....................*Arditi*
Salade a l'Italienne	Hedgeside Cabernet
Haricots Verts an beurre	Polka—"The Daisy,"................... *Arditi*
Pouding Comtesse	Pommery and Greno Sec
Gelee Mogador	Intermezzo—"Cavalleria Rusticana,"...*Mascagni*
Glaces Napolitaines	Dry Monopole
Petits Fours	Ballet—"Feramors,"..................*Rubenstein*
Gateaux Assortis	Ruinart Brut
Pieces Montees	Spanish Dance...... ....*Moszkowski*
Fruits	
Fromage	National Popourri.......................*Tobani*
Cafe Noir	

Music under the direction of Mr. Henry Heyman

We hereby certify that the above is a true Statement of the condition and affairs of the California Bankers Association.
     GEO. H. STEWART,
        Secretary.
                                THOS. BROWN,
                                      President.

Bank Commissioner Gerberding acted as master of the toasts, and proposed them in felicitous style. He began by swearing in all the guests to tell the truth, "so help me Alameda." Calling for the first toast, he said that the bankers had discussed every topic under the sun pertaining to finances until the subject seemed to have been squeezed dry; what they wanted now was a "new scheme". The best place to go for a new scheme, he thought, was outside of the banking fraternity. The bankers have exhausted their last "resource," and it would be fruitless to call on any one of them. It must be suggested by an outsider; one thoroughly familiar with finances, yet able to look at the subject through other glasses than those worn by bankers. He knew of no better man of that character than Irving M. Scott.

Mr. Scott's ready response was: "Gentlemen, the best new scheme I can possibly suggest is, 'loan your money to a man who needs it most'." He added that the undying cry of bankers had always been "collaterals." "For heaven's sake, let us have something *without* collaterals." If the bankers cared to profit by his suggestion, he knew of no way they could be of more usefulness to the public. Following a serious vein, Mr. Scott expressed a very warm sentiment in favor of a single monetary basis; namely, gold. It is the single gold standard that makes the Bank of England respected by all the world. He hoped to see the day when the California banks would stand on the same footing.

Mayor Sanderson responded very gracefully to the toast "Our City." for there are few who can sound the praises of San Francisco better than the Mayor.

E. F. Spence, of Los Angeles, responded in a merry vein, to "The Ladies," and was aided by George H. Bonebrake, of Los Angeles.

J. D. Redding, who was "neither stockholder nor depositor," told what he saw at the Bankers Convention in England as distinguished from a like Convention in France. He approved of the French banking system as against the English ; in fact he generally favored "Frenchy" things.

Ex-Governor Perkins responded pleasantly to the toast "Overdrafts," and George T. Bromley told what he knew about "After Banking Hours." Being uncertain what the toast master announced he asked again, and said he felt relieved that it was not "After Banq-ueting Hours"; he had known such hours when one lamp post in hand was worth two in the next block.

W. P. Harrington of Colusa. Lovell White of San Francisco, W. W. Phillips, Louis Einstein and C. Walters of Fresno, P. B. Fraser of Stockton, and others, were called upon, and responded in appropriate and humorous vein. It was nearly midnight when a motion to adjourn *sine die* was finally entertained.

B 13

THE ORGANIZATION OF THE CALIFORNIA BANKERS ASSOCIATION WAS THE RESULT OF A CONVENTION OF CALIFORNIA BANKERS AT LOS ANGELES, MARCH 11, 12 AND 13, 1891, CALLED BY THE LOS ANGELES CLEARING HOUSE. A MAJORITY OF THE PROMINENT BANKERS OF CALIFORNIA WERE PRESENT, NINETY-FOUR BANKS BEING REPRESENTED. FULL PROCEEDINGS OF THIS CONVENTION WERE PUBLISHED IN PAMPHLET FORM, WHICH CAN BE HAD ON APPLICATION TO THE SECRETARY, GEO. H. STEWART, CARE OF BANK OF AMERICA (formerly Los Angeles County Bank), LOS ANGELES.

THE NEXT MEETING (SECOND ANNUAL CONVENTION) WILL BE HELD AT FRESNO, PROBABLY IN OCTOBER, 1892 (see page 101). THE EXACT DATES TO BE FIXED BY THE EXECUTIVE COUNCIL.

CONSTITUTION AND BY-LAWS

OF THE

CALIFORNIA BANKERS ASSOCIATION

DECLARATION.

In order to promote the general welfare and usefulness of banks and banking institutions, and to secure uniformity of action, together with the practical benefits to be derived from personal acquaintance and from the discussion of subjects of importance to the banking and commercial interests of this State: especially in order to secure the proper consideration of questions regarding the financial usages, customs and laws which effect the banking interests of the entire State, and for protection against loss by crime: we have to submit the following Constitution and By-Laws for the CALIFORNIA BANKERS ASSOCIATION:

CONSTITUTION.

ARTICLE I.

This Association shall be called the CALIFORNIA BANKERS ASSOCIATION.

ARTICLE II.

SECTION 1. Any National or State Bank, Trust Company, Savings Bank, Banking Firm, or individual, doing a banking business within the State of California, may become a member of this Association, upon the payment of such annual dues as shall be provided by the By-Laws, subject to the approval of a majority of the Executive Council, and may send one delegate to the annual meeting of the Association; and any member may be expelled from the Association upon a vote of two-thirds of those present at any regular meeting.

SEC. 2. Delegates shall be: an officer, or director, or trustee, of the institution they represent; or a member of a banking firm, or an individual doing business as a bank.

SEC. 3. Delegates shall vote in person; no voting by proxy shall be allowed.

SEC. 4. All votes shall be viva voce, unless otherwise ordered; any delegate may demand a division of the house.

ARTICLE III.

Section 1. The administration of the affairs of the Association, not otherwise delegated, shall be vested in the President, First Vice-President, Secretary, Treasurer, one Vice-President for each County which may be represented in this Association, and an Executive Council : who shall be elected at the annual meeting, and who shall serve until their successors are chosen or appointed. The Executive Council shall be composed of nine members, divided into three classes, one-third of whom shall be elected annually.

Sec. 2. Immediately after the first adjournment that occurs in the session of the annual Convention, the delegation from each county shall meet and make nominations for Vice-Presidents of the Association.

Sec. 3. The Vice-Presidents shall have the supervision of the business of the Association in the counties where they reside. The banks in each county may organize under the Vice-President of the county, and form a Committee for local matters; but such Committee shall have no power to in any manner bind or effect the interests of the organization. Such local Committee may fill any vacancy occurring in the Vice-Presidency during the year.

Sec. 4. A majority of the Executive Council shall constitute a quorum for the transaction of business.

Sec. 5. Special meetings of the Executive Council may be called by request of three of its members, giving two weeks notice to the Secretary, desiring him to call such special meeting. The Executive Council shall have power to fill vacancies that may occur in its own body.

Sec. 6. The Executive Council shall provide:

First—For keeping the records of the proceedings of their own meetings, as well as that of the Association annual or special meetings.

Second—They shall submit to each annual meeting a report covering their own official acts, as well as a statement of any new or unfinished business requiring attention.

Third—They shall make full statements of the financial condition of the Association.

Fourth—Submit an estimate of the amount required to carry on the affairs of the Association according to their judgment of the business to be done, and recommend means for raising money to carry out such plans as may be resolved upon by the Association.

Sec. 7. The Secretary shall make and have charge of the records of the Association, as well as those of the Council, and of the correspondence of the Executive Council and Standing Protective Committee; and shall promptly send to each member of the Association a synopsis of reports received by him of attempted or accomplished crime against any member of the Association. Such records shall be the property of the Association, and be held subject at all times to the order of the Executive Council.

Sec. 8. The Treasurer shall receive and account for all moneys belonging to the Association, but shall pay out moneys only upon vouchers approved by the President of the Association and counter-signed by the Secretary.

ARTICLE IV.

Section 1. The Executive Council shall appoint a Standing Protective Committee of three persons, whose names shall not be made public. The said Committee shall control all action looking to the detection, prosecution and punishment of persons attempting to cause, or causing, loss by crime to any member of the Association.

Sec. 2. The said Committee, when called upon for aid by any member of the Association, through the Secretary, shall forthwith take such steps as it shall deem proper to arrest and prosecute the party charged with crime; provided, however, that no expense or liability shall be incurred beyond the amount of funds in the Treasury especially appropriated for that purpose.

Sec. 3. The said Committee is prohibited from compromising or compounding with parties charged with crime or with their agents or attorneys.

Sec. 4. All detectives and legal expenses and costs will be paid by the Association out of any money in the Treasury especially appropriated by the Executive Council for that purpose; subject, however, to the approval of a quorum of the Executive Council.

Sec. 5. All members of the Association, when called upon by the Secretary in behalf of the Protective Committee for information or aid, shall promptly respond by giving all assistance in their power; and all members shall, at all times, notify the Secretary, who shall promptly notify the Committee, of any attempted or accomplished crime reported to him as likely to effect other members of the Association.

ARTICLE V.

Section 1. Annual meetings of the Association shall be held at such times and places as shall be determined by the Executive Council. Special meetings may be called by the said Council if, in their opinions, circumstances require them; giving two weeks notice of time and place of meeting, together with the subject-matter of business to come before such special meeting. The Executive Council shall meet to arrange the order of business on the day preceding any general meeting of the Association.

ARTICLE VI.

Section 1. The expenses of the Executive Council, in carrying out the business of the Association to be done by them, shall be provided for by the annual dues of the members of the Association; provided, however, that the Executive Council shall have no authority to incur or contract, on behalf of this Association, any liability whatever beyond the annual dues hereby authorized, and only that for the purposes hereby designated.

ARTICLE VII.

Section 1. Resolutions and subjects for discussion (except those referring to points of order or matters of courtesy) must be submitted in writing to the Secretary, for reference to the Executive Council, at least ten days before any general meeting of the Association ; but any person desiring to submit any resolution of business in open Convention can do so, upon a two-thirds vote of the delegates present.

ARTICLE VIII.

Section 1. Any one failing to pay within three months the annual dues for carrying on the business of the Association, shall be considered as having withdrawn from membership ; but may be reinstated upon application to the Secretary, and paying all dues in arrears, with consent of the President.

ARTICLE IX.

Section 1. This Constitution may be altered or amended at any annual meeting by a vote of two-thirds of the members present : notice of the proposed amendment having been first submitted to the Secretary at least ten days before the annual meeting, to be placed by him before the Executive Council, that they may arrange for bringing it before the Convention under the regular order of business.

BY-LAWS.

SECTION 1.   The annual dues of the Association shall be considered due at the beginning of the year, which year shall commence with the regular annual meeting; it being understood that absent members from such annual meeting shall not forfeit their membership nor the right to become members, provided they comply with the Constitution and By-Laws and remit the amount of the dues to the Secretary within one month after such annual meeting.

SEC. 2.   The annual dues of all members shall be Ten (10) Dollars.

Index.

California

Bankers

Association

1892

PROCEEDINGS

OF THE

SECOND ANNUAL CONVENTION

OF THE

CALIFORNIA BANKERS ASSOCIATION

HELD AT

SAN FRANCISCO, SEPTEMBER 5TH AND 6TH,

1892

CONSTITUTION AND BY-LAWS,
LIST OF OFFICERS AND MEMBERS,
ETC.

"No opinions expressed, principles advocated, theories advanced or policies suggested by any party or person, however presented, shall be deemed to have had the indorsement of this Association, except the question of so indorsing shall have been referred to a standing or special committee; shall have been reported upon by such committee, and shall have been specifically voted upon, receiving a majority of the votes of those present at an open session of a Convention of the Association.

"This item of the Constitution shall be published in every report of the proceedings of any Convention, and where indorsements are given the fact shall be noted in the report of proceedings in that behalf."

Sec. 2, Art. VII.

FULL INDEX **AT BACK** OF PAMPHLET

✦   ✦   ✦

TIMES-MIRROR
PRINTING AND BINDING
HOUSE

THE organization of the California Bankers Association was the result
of a convention of California Bankers at Los Angeles, March 11th,
12th and 13th, 1891, called by the Los Angeles Clearing-house. A majority of the prominent bankers of California were present, 91 banks
being represented. Full proceedings of this Convention were published
in pamphlet form. copies of which can be had on application to the
Secretary.

.*.

The First Annual Convention was held in Chamber of Commerce
rooms, San Francisco, October 14th, 15th and 16th, 1891. Full proceedings of this Convention were published in pamphlet form.

.*.

The next meeting (Third Annual Convention) will be held at
Fresno, probably in October, 1893, the dates to be fixed by the Executive Council.

Officers Elected 1891

PRESIDENT,
Thomas Brown, Bank of California, San Francisco.

VICE-PRESIDENT,
Isaias W. Hellman, Nevada Bank, San Francisco.

SECRETARY,
Geo. H. Stewart, Los Angeles County Bank, Los Angeles.

TREASURER,
G. W. Kline, First National Bank, San Francisco.

EXECUTIVE COUNCIL.

TERM EXPIRES, 1892.

W. M. Eddy, Santa Barbara County National Bank, Santa Barbara.
T. S. Hawkins, Bank of Hollister, Hollister.
W. D. Woolwine, First National Bank, San Diego.

TERM EXPIRES 1893.

A. D. Childress, Chairman; City Bank, Los Angeles.
N. D. Rideout, California State Bank, Sacramento.
Lovell White, San Francisco Savings Union, San Francisco.

TERM EXPIRES, 1894.

C. E. Palmer, Union National Bank, Oakland.
W. W. Phillips, Farmers Bank of Fresno, Fresno.
A. L. Seligman, Anglo-Californian Bank, San Francisco.

1891-2.

MEMBERS

AT DATE OF SECOND ANNUAL CONVENTION

ALAMEDA COUNTY.

J. West Martin, - - Vice-President
President, Union Savings Bank, Oakland
Bank of Livermore - - Livermore
California Bank and Trust Co. - Oakland
First National - - - "
Oakland Bank of Savings - "
Union National - "
Union Savings - "
Bank of Haywards - Haywards
Bank of Alameda - Alameda

BUTTE COUNTY.

Charles Faulkner - - Vice-President
Cashier, Bank of Butte County, Chico
Sacramento Valley Bank - Biggs
Bank of Butte County - Chico
Bank of Chico - "
Rideout Bank - - Gridley
Bank of Rideout, Smith & Co. - Oroville

COLUSA COUNTY.

W. P. Harrington - - Vice-President
Cashier, Colusa County Bank
Colusa County Bank - - Colusa

CONTRA COSTA COUNTY.

L. C. Wittenmeyer, - Vice-President
President, Bank of Martinez, Martinez
Bank of Martinez - - Martinez
Bank of Antioch - Antioch

EL DORADO COUNTY.

Mierson & Jewell - Placerville

FRESNO COUNTY.

Louis Einstein, - Vice-President
President, Bank of Central California, Fresno
Bank of Central California - Fresno
Farmers' Bank of Fresno - "
First National - - "
Fresno National - "
Fresno Loan and Savings Bank - "
People's Savings Bank - "
Bank of Madera - Madera
Bank of Sanger - Sanger
Bank of Selma - Selma

GLENN COUNTY.

Bank of Orland - Orland
Bank of Willows - Willows

HUMBOLDT COUNTY.

J. W. Henderson, - Vice-President
President, Humboldt County Bank, Eureka
Bank of Arcata - - Arcata
Bank of Eureka - - Eureka
Humboldt County Bank - "
Randall Banking Co. - "

KERN COUNTY.

S. W. Wible, - - Vice-President
President, Bank of Bakersfield.
Bank of Bakersfield - Bakersfield
Kern Valley Bank - "
Producers' Savings Bank - "

LAKE COUNTY.

H. C. Boggs, - - Vice-President
President, Farmers' Savings Bank, Lakeport
Farmers' Savings Bank - Lakeport

LOS ANGELES COUNTY.

E. F. Spence, - - Vice-President
President, First National Bank, Los Angeles
Alhambra Bank - - Alhambra
Bank of America - Los Angeles
California Bank - "
City Bank - "
East Side Bank - "
Farmers and Merchants Bank - "
First National - "
German American Savings Bank - "
Los Angeles National Bank - "
Los Angeles Savings Bank - "
Main St. Savings Bank and Trust Co. - "
National Bank of California - "
Savings Bank of Southern California - "
Security Savings Bank and Trust Co. - "
Southern California National Bank - "
State Loan and Trust Co. - "
First National Bank - Pasadena
Pasadena National Bank - "
San Gabriel Valley Bank - "
First National Bank - Pomona
Peoples' Bank - "
First National - - Santa Monica

MERCED COUNTY.

C. Loudrum, - - Vice-President
Vice-President, Merced Bank, Merced
Commercial Savings Bank - - Merced
Merced Bank - - "
Merced Security Savings Bank - "

MONTEREY COUNTY.

J. D. Carr, - - - - Vice-President
President, Salinas City Bank
Monterey County Bank - - - Salinas City
Salinas City Bank - - - - "

NAPA COUNTY.

G. E. Goodman, Sr. - - - Vice-President
President, J. H. Goodman & Co. Bank, Napa
Bank of Napa - - - - - Napa
Jas. H. Goodman & Co. Bank - - "
Bank of St. Helena - - - St. Helena
Carver National Bank

NEVADA COUNTY.

Citizens' Bank - - - - Nevada City

ORANGE COUNTY.

W. H. Spurgeon, - - - Vice-President
President, First National Bank of Santa Ana
Bank of Anaheim - - - - Anaheim
Bank of Orange - - - - Orange
Commercial Bank - - - Santa Ana
First National - - - - "
Orange Co. Savings, Loan and Trust Co. "
Bank of Tustin - - - - Tustin

PLACER COUNTY.

T. J. Nichols, - - - - Vice-President
Cashier, Placer County Bank, Auburn
Placer County Bank - - - Auburn
W. & P. Nicholls - - Dutch Flat

SACRAMENTO COUNTY.

W. E. Chamberlain, - - Vice-President
Of the National Bank of D. O. Mills & Co.
California State Bank - - - Sacramento
Farmers' and Mechanics' Savings B'k "
National Bank of D. O. Mills & Co. "
Peoples' Savings Bank - - "
Sacramento Bank - - - "
J. H. Burnham - - - Folsom

SAN BENITO COUNTY.

T. W. Hawkins, - - - Vice-President
Cashier, Bank of Hollister
Bank of Hollister - - - Hollister
Farmers' and Merchants' Bank - "

SAN BERNARDINO COUNTY.

John W. Davis, - - - Vice-President
President, First National Bank, Colton
First National - - - - Colton
Ontario State Bank - - - Ontario
First National - - - - Redlands
Savings Bank of Redlands - "
Union Bank of Redlands - "
First National - - - Riverside
Orange Growers' Bank - "

Riverside Banking Company - - Riverside
Riverside National - - - - "
Bank of San Bernardino - - San Bernardino
Farmers' Exchange Bank - - "
First National - - - - "
San Bernardino National - - "

SAN DIEGO COUNTY.

Jerry Toles, - - - - Vice-President
Vice-President, First Nat. Bank, San Diego
Bank of National City - - National City
People's State Bank - - - " "
Bank of Oceanside - - - Oceanside
Perris Valley Bank - - - Perris
Consolidated National - - San Diego
First National - - - - "
San Diego Savings Bank - - "
State Bank - - - - San Jacinto

SAN FRANCISCO CITY AND COUNTY.

H. Wadsworth, - - - Vice-President
Cashier, Wells, Fargo & Co. Bank
American Bank and Trust Co.
Anglo-Californian Bank, Limited
Bank of California
Bank of Sisson, Crocker & Co.
California Safe Deposit and Trust Co.
Crocker-Woolworth National
First National
German Savings and Loan Society
Hibernia Savings and Loan Society
London, Paris and American Bank, Limited
London and San Francisco Bank
Mutual Savings Bank
Nevada Bank of San Francisco
Pacific Bank
People's Home Savings Bank
San Francisco Savings Union
Sather Banking Co.
Savings and Loan Society
Security Savings Bank
Tallant Banking Co.
Wells, Fargo & Co.'s Bank

SAN JOAQUIN COUNTY.

Name of Vice-President not yet received.
Bank of Lodi - - - - Lodi
Farmers' and Merchants' Bank - Stockton
First National - - - - "
Stockton Savings Bank - - "
Stockton Savings and Loan Society "
San Joaquin Valley Bank - - "

SAN LUIS OBISPO COUNTY.

McD. R. Venable, - - - Vice-President
President, Commercial Bank of San Luis Obispo
Citizens' Bank of Paso Robles - Paso Robles
Commercial Bank - - - San Luis Obispo
First National Bank - - " "

SANTA BARBARA COUNTY.

A. L. Lincoln, - - - - Vice-President
Cashier, First National Bank of Santa Barbara
Commercial Bank - - - Santa Barbara
First National - - - - "
Santa Barbara County National - "
Santa Barbara S. & L. Bank - - "
Bank of Santa Maria - - Santa Maria
Bank of Lompoc - - - Lompoc

SANTA CLARA COUNTY.

B. D. Murphy, - - - Vice-President
Pres., Commercial & Savings Bank, San Jose
Bank of Gilroy - - - - Gilroy
Bank of Los Gatos - - - Los Gatos
Commercial Bank of Los Gatos - "
Bank of San Jose - - - San Jose
Commercial and Savings Bank - "
First National - - - - "
Garden City National - - "
Security Savings - - - "
Union Savings - - - "

SANTA CRUZ COUNTY.

J. J. Morey, - - - Vice-President
Cashier, Pajaro Valley Bank, Santa Cruz
Bank of Santa Cruz County - Santa Cruz
City Bank - - - - "
Pajaro Valley Bank - - Watsonville

SHASTA COUNTY.

C. C. Bush, - - - Vice-President
Vice-President, Bank of Shasta Co., Redding
Bank of Shasta County - - Redding

SISKIYOU COUNTY.

Fred E. Wadsworth, - - Vice-President
Cashier, Siskiyou County Bank, Redding
Siskiyou County Bank - - Yreka
Bank of A. B. Carlock - - Fort Jones

SOLANO COUNTY.

Jos. R. English, - - Vice-President
Cashier, Vallejo Commercial Bank, Vallejo
Vallejo Commercial Bank - - Vallejo
Bank of Dixon - - - Dixon
Bank of Sui-un - - - Suisun

SONOMA COUNTY.

J. W. Wilson, - - - Vice-President
Cashier, Bank of Healdsburg
Bank of Healdsburg - - Healdsburg

STANISLAUS COUNTY.

O. McHenry, - - - Vice-President
President, First National Bank, Modesto
First National - - - Modesto
Bank of Oakdale - - Oakdale

SUTTER COUNTY.

Geo. Ohleyer, - - - Vice-President
Sec. Farmers' Co-operative Union, Yuba City
Farmers' Co-operative Union - Yuba City

TEHAMA COUNTY.

J. S. Cone, - - - Vice-President
Cashier, Bank of Tehama Co., Red Bluff
Bank of Tehama County - - Red Bluff

TULARE COUNTY.

A. J. Harrell, - - - Vice-President
Manager, Harrell & Son, Visalia
Bank of Lemoore - - - Lemoore
Farmers' and Merchants' Bank - Hanford
Bank of Tulare - - - Tulare
Harrell & Son - - - Visalia

VENTURA COUNTY.

E. B. Foster, - - - Vice-President
President, Bank of Ventura
Bank of Hueneme - - Hueneme
First National - - - Santa Paula
Bank of Ventura - - - Ventura
William Collins & Sons - - "

YOLO COUNTY.

C. W. Bush, - - - Vice-President
Cashier, Bank of Yolo, Woodland
Bank of Winters - - - Winters
Bank of Yolo - - - Woodland

YUBA COUNTY.

A. C. Bingham, - - - Vice-President
Cashier, Decker, Jewett & Co., Marysville
Decker, Jewett & Co. Bank - Marysville
Northern Cal. Bank of Savings - "
The Rideout Bank - - - "

HONORARY MEMBERS

A. Gerberding - - - - State Bank Commissioner.
C. H. Dunsmoor - - State Bank Commissioner.
W. H. Knight - - - State Bank Commissioner.
W. H. Chamberlain - National Bank Examiner for California.

OFFICERS ELECTED 1892

PRESIDENT,
ISAIAS W. HELLMAN, The Nevada Bank, San Francisco.

VICE-PRESIDENT,
E. F. SPENCE, First National Bank, Los Angeles.

SECRETARY,
GEO. H. STEWART, Bank of America, Los Angeles.

TREASURER,
G. W. KLINE, First National Bank, San Francisco.

EXECUTIVE COUNCIL,

TERM EXPIRES, 1893.

A. D. CHILDRESS, Chairman; City Bank, Los Angeles.

N. D. RIDEOUT, California State Bank, Sacramento.

LOVELL WHITE, San Francisco Savings Union, San Francisco.

TERM EXPIRES, 1894.

C. E. PALMER, Union National Bank, Oakland.

W. W. PHILLIPS, Farmers Bank of Fresno, Fresno.

A. L. SELIGMAN, Anglo-Californian Bank, San Francisco.

TERM EXPIRES, 1895.

W. P. HARRINGTON, Colusa County Bank, Colusa.

GEO. E. HERSEY, Bank of Gilroy, Gilroy.

J. H. BARBOUR, Consolidated National Bank, San Diego.

1892-3.

BANKS REGISTERED AT THE CONVENTION

NAME.		REPRESENTED BY
	ALAMEDA.	
Bank of Alameda.		J. E. Baker.
	ANTIOCH.	
Bank of Antioch.		R. Harkinson.
	AUBURN.	
Placer County Bank		T. J. Nichols.
	BIGGS.	
Sacramento Valley Bank		G. K. Smith.
	BAKERSFIELD.	
Kern Valley Bank		Sol Jewett.
	COLUSA.	
Colusa County Bank		W. P. Harrington.
	DIXON.	
Bank of Dixon		S. G. Little.
	DUTCH FLAT.	
W. & P. Nicholls		Wm. Nicholls, Jr.
	EUREKA.	
Humboldt County Bank		J. W. Henderson.
	FRESNO.	
Bank of Central California		Louis Einstein.
Farmers' Bank of Fresno		John Reichman.
First National Bank		O. J. Woodward.
Fresno National Bank		H. D. Colson.
Peoples' Savings Bank		Chester Rowell.
	GILROY.	
Bank of Gilroy		Geo. E. Hersey.
	GRIDLEY.	
The Rideout Bank		E. E. Biggs.
	HANFORD.	
Farmers' and Merchants' Bank		B. A. Fassett and H. Nathan.
	HEALDSBURG.	
Bank of Healdsburg		Jno. Wallace Wilson.
	HOLLISTER.	
Bank of Hollister		T. S. Hawkins.
Farmers' and Merchants' Bank		Wm. Palmtag.
	LIVERMORE.	
Bank of Livermore		H. H. Pitcher.
	LOS ANGELES.	
Bank of America		Geo. H. Stewart and Chas. Forman.
City Bank		A. D. Childress and R. G. Lunt.
Farmers' and Merchants' Bank		I. W. Hellman, Jr.
Los Angeles National Bank		F. C. Howes.
Savings Bank of Southern California		J. H. Braley.
Southern California National Bank		L. N. Breed.
State Loan & Trust Co.		John Bryson, Sr.
	LOS GATOS.	
Commercial Bank of Los Gatos		J. R. Ryland.
	MERCED.	
Merced Bank		J. Howell.
Merced Security Savings Bank		W. W. Westbay.
	MARTINEZ.	
Bank of Martinez		L. C. Wittenmeyer.

NAME.		REPRESENTED BY
	NATIONAL CITY.	
Bank of National City		C. B. Whittelsey.
	NAPA.	
James H. Goodman & Co. Bank		E. S. Churchill and Geo. E. Goodman.
	NATIONAL CITY.	
Peoples' State Bank		Henry Shaubut.
	NEVADA CITY.	
Citizens' Bank		E. M. Preston.
	OAKLAND.	
California Bank & Trust Co.		A. C. Henry.
First National Bank		A. D. Thompson and L. G. Burpee.
Oakland Bank of Savings		W. W. Garthwaite.
Union National Bank		C. E. Palmer.
Union Savings Bank		J. West Martin.
	OAKDALE.	
Bank of Oakdale		J. Haslacher.
	ORLAND.	
Bank of Orland		R. B. Murdock.
	PASADENA.	
First National Bank of Pasadena		A. H. Conger and H. I. Stuart.
Pasadena National		T. P. Lukens.
	PASO ROBLES	
Citizens' Bank of Paso Robles		A. F. Horstman.
	POMONA.	
Peoples' Bank		Jno. H. Dole.
	RED BLUFF.	
Bank of Tehama County		Charles Cadwallader.
	REDLANDS.	
Union Bank of Redlands		R. C. Wells.
	REDDING.	
Bank of Shasta County		C. C. Bush.
	RIVERSIDE.	
Riverside Banking Co.		J. A. Brenneman.
Riverside National Bank		S. C. Evans.
	SACRAMENTO.	
California State Bank		N. D. Rideout.
Farmers' and Mechanics' Saving Bank		Edwin K. Alsip and B. U. Steineman.
Nat. Bank of D. O. Mills & Co.		Frank Miller.
Peoples' Savings Bank		Wm. Beckman.
Sacramento Bank		Ed. R. Hamilton.
	SAN BERNARDINO.	
Farmers' Exchange Bank		S. F. Zombro and Richard Gird.
First National Bank		Joseph Brown.
	SALINAS CITY.	
Monterey County Bank		Luther Rodgers.
	SAN DIEGO.	
First National Bank		W. D. Woolwine.
San Diego Savings Bank		O. J. Stough.
	SAN FRANCISCO.	
American Bank & Trust Co.		J. W. Farren, Jr.
Anglo-Californian Bank, Lmtd.		A. L. Seligman.
Bank of California		Thomas Brown.
Bank of Sisson, Crocker & Co.		Geo. W. Scott.
California Safe Deposit & Trust Co.		S. P. Young.
First National Bank	S. G. Murphy, G. W. Kline, Jas. Moffitt and E. D. Morgan.	
German Saving & Loan Society	L. Gottig, A. H. R. Schmidt, Geo. Tourny, Wm. Herrmann	
Hibernia Savings and Loan Society		Robert J. Tobin.

NAME.	REPRESENTED BY
Mutual Savings Bank	James A. Thompson.
Nevada Bank	I. W. Hellman and J. F. Bigelow.
Pacific Bank	W. S. Morse and R. H. McDonald, Jr.
Peoples Home Savings Bank	J. E. Farnum.
San Francisco Saving Union	Lovell White and Etta Averill.
Sather Banking Co.	James K. Wilson.
Savings and Loan Society	S. C. Bigelow.
Security Savings Bank	S. L. Abbott, Jr.
Tallant Banking Co.	John McKee.

SAN LUIS OBISPO.

Commercial Bank	Hy. Brunner.
First National Bank	F. B. Jack.

SAN JOSE.

Bank of San Jose	T. Ellard Beans.
Commercial & Savings Bank	James W. Findlay.
Union Savings Bank	H. W. Wright.

SANTA ANA.

Commercial Bank	N. Palmer.

SANTA CRUZ.

City Bank	W. D. Haslan.
Bank of Santa Cruz County	F. G. Menefee.

SELMA.

Bank of Selma	J. A. Stroud.

SANTA BARBARA.

First National Bank	A. L. Lincoln.
Santa Barbara Co. Nat. Bank	E. S. Sheffield.

SANTA PAULA.

First National Bank	C. H. McKevett.

ST. HELENA.

Carver National Bank	A. L. Williams.

STOCKTON.

First National Bank	H. H. Hewlett.
Farmers' & Merchants' Bank	P. B. Fraser and D. S. Rosenbaum.
Stockton Savings Bank	Sidney Newell.

SUISUN.

Bank of Suisun	R. D. Robbins.

TUSTIN.

Bank of Tustin	W. S. Bartlett.

VENTURA.

William Collins & Sons	D. Edward Collins and J. S. Collins.
Bank of Ventura	E. P. Foster and J. A. Walker.

VISALIA.

Harrell & Son	A. J. Harrell.

VALLEJO.

Vallejo Commercial Bank	John R. English.

WATSONVILLE.

Pajaro Valley Bank	J. J. Morey.

WILLOWS.

Bank of Willows	B. H. Burton.

WINTERS.

Bank of Winters	E. E. Kahn.

WOODLAND.

Bank of Yolo	H. P. Merritt and C. W. Bush.

HONORARY MEMBERS

A. Gerberding	State Bank Commissioner.
C. H. Dunsmoor	State Bank Commissioner.
W. H. Knight	State Bank Commissioner.
W. H. Chamberlain	National Bank Examiner for California.

The Convention of 1892 was, by vote taken in 1891, and consent of Executive Council, located at Fresno, and so announced. The Annual Convention of the American Bankers Association for this year having been secured for San Francisco, partly at least through the efforts of this Association, the Second Annual Meeting was changed from Fresno by consent of its bankers so as to fully harmonize with the National Convention, and located in San Francisco, as follows:

PROCEEDINGS

OF THE

SECOND ANNUAL CONVENTION

OF THE

CALIFORNIA BANKERS ASSOCIATION

HELD IN THE

CHAMBER OF COMMERCE ROOMS, SAN FRANCISCO.

FIRST DAY.

MONDAY, SEPTEMBER 5, 1892.

The convention was called to order at 2 o'clock P. M. by Thomas Brown, president of the Association.

The Chairman: Gentlemen, I take pleasure in introducing to you the Honorable E. B. Pond, president of the Chamber of Commerce of San Francisco, who will make the opening address.

Mr. Pond spoke as follows:

Gentlemen of the California Bankers Association:

It affords me pleasure, on behalf of the Chamber of Commerce and your fellow-members residing here, to cordially welcome you, individually and collectively, to San Francisco.

Your business is so closely allied with the commerce of the country that it seems to me peculiarly fitting that your deliberations in reference to the matters pertaining to your own intricate business, as well as, incidentally, the great business interests of our State and its business industries, should be conducted here in this Metropolis, as well as in the rooms of this Chamber.

And, gentlemen, do not for a moment think that your presence here, or the presence of such a body of able, enterprising and trained business men, whose interests and relations are so closely allied with the prosperity of our State, can cause but a ripple upon the ordinary life of our city. The discussions by your body of the great and important questions of the day, whether matters exclusively connected with your own affairs, or the construction of the Nicaragua Canal and the advantages to accrue from it, the transportation question, the question of the issue and sale of irrigation bonds, or the more chimerical schemes of Senators Stanford, Jones and Stewart for flooding our

country with cheap money, will certainly, coming from you, have a greater
influence than those of any other body of men that could be brought together,
as you are from all parts of the State and your interests are directly and
closely connected with its prosperity.

I welcome you then, gentlemen, as men whose influence must be felt on all
these great and important questions; as men upon whose judgment much
depends as to the success or failure of business projects. You are the custodians of the money—the capital of the State; without your consent nothing
moves—with it follows prosperity and enterprise.

I welcome you then most cordially, believing that your deliberations and
conclusions in matters appertaining especially to your own interests as bankers
will tend to encourage and promote all those varied interests which will cause
this to be a great and powerful commonwealth. I greet you, gentlemen, one
and all, old friends as well as new, and hope and trust that your labors will be
both pleasant and profitable, socially as well as in a business way, and, on your
return to your homes, that you will carry with you many pleasant recollections
and renewed bonds of personal friendship. [Applause.]

The Chairman: Mr. Frank Miller of Sacramento, representing the
banks of Northern California, will respond.

Mr. Frank Miller, Cashier of the National Bank of D. O. Mills & Co.,
Sacramento, spoke as follows:

Mr. President and Gentlemen of the Convention:

In the harvest season, when the weather is hot and dusty, your country
cousins often think with envy of the city bankers who are enjoying the sea
breezes. In the wet and dull days of winter we men of the interior think of
our brother bankers in the Bay City who do a large business by day and have
the best of entertainments in the evening.

When we come here singly or collectively we always receive a warm welcome.

It is my pleasant task to thank you sincerely for these welcomes in behalf
of Northern Californians. We represent one-half of the area of this State
and one-third of its population and wealth, allowing equal thirds to Southern
California and San Francisco.

It is well known that our sympathies are with San Francisco, yet that we
trade largely at the East. The wheat does go through your clearing-house, but
the fruit products (some $20,000,000 worth) are of equal value, and you see
little of them.

It would be interesting to collate from all banks in the State, outside of
San Francisco, a statement of the New York exchange which they sell to San
Francisco during the year, and also a statement of what they buy. I think the
purchases and sales will nearly offset each other. If this be so, then we might
infer that the fruit products are exchanged by the interior with the East for
goods, and San Francisco gets no commission on this outgo or income.

This business cannot leave the straight line to Chicago and go through San
Francisco unless better terms are given. Some concessions must be made by
San Francisco.

Allow me to suggest that obstacles might be removed that now stand in the way of increasing loans from your city to the interior. Trade follows loans, and if you send your money into Northern and Southern California more freely and more safely than heretofore your merchants will get more business.

In this line of thought, it seems to me that the Legislature should be asked to adopt the Torrens Act* for registering titles, as used in Australia and other British colonies. The Government guarantees titles and issues a certificate to the owner of the land, so that title can be transferred on the books like a certificate of bank stock. Abstracts are not needed.

The attorneys in this State are charging $200,000 yearly for reading abstracts in the making of sales and loans. This expense is never-ending and it is always increasing. The Torrens Act can reduce this expense to $50,000, or less, per annum; it will assist in the subdivision of large loans and large tracts of land; for every transfer is now circumscribed by an abstract of formidable dimensions and a charge of almost one per cent on the value of the land every time the title is read.

After the first expense of governmental examination and guarantee there will be no abstract, and the cost of transfers will be less than one-fourth of one per cent.

The borrower can apply to lenders of all kinds and in all places, and the only question between them will be: What is the value of the property? At present an existing loan cannot change to another lender unless his rate is about one per cent lower, because of the expense of transfers.

If it is the policy of San Francisco to diminish the tolls for wharfage, it is just as politic to diminish the tolls for lawyerage.

By the end of this century this State may be worth $4,000,000,000, and owned by two millions of people. The bonds of friendship and commerce are worth strengthening between all the citizens of this great State. Let us love one another and buy and sell with each other.

_____

*NOTE.—The admirable system of land transfer originated in Australia by Sir Robert Torrens and is now adopted also by Tasmania, New Zealand, British Columbia and part of Canada.

Its purpose is to make the transfer of land as simple as the transfer of bank stock, and the title of the holder as free from danger or difficulty as ordinarily the title of the holder of bank stock is to the shares he holds.

The act provides for the establishment of a land registry, under the control of officers to be known as "Masters of Titles." All land transactions may be registered.

A title may be registered as absolute or possessory. If an absolute title is required the applicant will not be registered as the owner of the fee simple unless the title is approved by the Masters of Titles. The first registration of a person as owner of any land with an absolute title will vest in that person an estate in fee simple in the land, subject to any incumbrances entered on the register. If a possessory title is required, the applicant will be registered as owner of the fee simple, on giving such evidence of title as may be required. The registration of any person as first registered owner of land, with a possessory title only, will not affect the enforcement of any estate, right or interest adverse to or in derogation of the title, either subsisting or capable of rising at the time of registration. Should it appear to the Masters of Titles that an absolute title to land sought to be registered can only be established for a limited period, or subject to reservations, they may, on the application of the person applying to be registered as owner, except from the effect of registration any estate, right or interest arising before a specified date, or arising under a special instrument, or otherwise particularly described in the register. A title granted under such conditions is to be called a qualified title. The Masters of Titles must give to the first registered owner a "land certificate," and this certificate must say whether the title of the owner is "absolute," "qualified," or "possessory." An insurance fund is created to indemnify persons that suffer loss through misdescription, omission, or other error, in any certificate of title, or in any entry on the register. The fund is provided by levying a tax of a quarter of one per cent on the value of the land, on the first certificate of title being granted, in addition to registration fees. Any question as to the liability of the fund for compensation is to be determined by the Masters of Titles.

The chief benefit obtained is the _indefeasible nature of the title_ obtained, together

The Chairman: Mr. James K. Wilson, president of the Sather Banking Company, will respond for Central California.

Mr. Wilson addressed the convention as follows:

On behalf of the central portion of the State, in this assemblage of representative bankers of that part of the financial world which is located in California, I feel grateful to respond, as best I may, to the invitation with which you have honored me.

"The central division of California." What are we to understand by that expression? By natural topography it embraces that portion of California whose watersheds terminate at the Golden Gate: that portion whose golden fountains gave the State a world-wide fame and made it a central point of observation on this continent.

I am gratified to stand on this occasion as the representative of the thriving cities and towns of this portion of the State, and in their name return thanks for the kindly and generous words that have been expressed in the address of welcome.

This, very properly, may be regarded an auspicious occasion, for, as you all know, this State Convention of Bankers is the precursor of the National Convention of Bankers soon to be held in San Francisco. These conventions are called at the natural entrepot of this State of many possibilities, which nature appears to have planned for the emporium of the Pacific Coast, and where is provided every requisite for extensive commerce.

In the name of the bankers of the middle division of California, it is my pleasure to say to the bankers of the northern and southern divisions that we are happy to meet you here in San Francisco, and to unite with you in the consideration of important matters which may come before this convention.

The interchange of thought, and the closer personal acquaintance which are the outgrowth of occasions like this, tend to broaden our views and awaken new interests. While each of us must, in our individual capacity, act in an independent manner and adjust our business to local conditions and requirements, there may be times when good results will be obtained through combined action, when threatening situations in finance may be tided over and perhaps serious consequences averted.

Nothing is more timid than capital in times of danger. A knowledge, therefore, of each other, because we are custodians of capital, is an element of strength not to be overlooked and the importance of which should not be undervalued.

I am sure we have come together with an earnest desire to develop some

---

with the speed and certainty of transfer, and the abrogation of the necessity of abstracts of title.

Dwight Olmstead, Esq., of New York has published a report on the system.

Under the system above described a purchaser or mortgagee would have, when the title was warranted, simply to deal with the registered owner, and upon the removing any caveats or inhibitions there might be on the register affecting the land, to pay his money to and take his conveyance or mortgage from the registered owner; and thus he would be saved all the delay and expense of investigating the title. On the other hand, when the title was unwarranted, the title anterior only to first registration would have to be investigated in the usual way; but in that case, also, the delay and expense of proving the title, subject to first registration, would be saved. For these and other reasons it is considered the plan affords great facilities for the sale and transfer of land.

See Jones on Torrens System, Toronto, 1886.

See Fitch before Ohio Bar Association, Weekly Law Bulletin for August 22, 1892.

thing that may prove beneficial to us as factors in the finances of the State.
and directly and materially aid in the growth and permanent prosperity of this
great commonwealth.

With this thought in mind, will you indulge me if I take this opportunity for
suggesting some things to which, in my judgment, the representatives of the
financial institutions of the State may properly give attention?

In the broad sense of the term, what are the bankers of a country or of a
State? and what their relation to industrial development? What do we, who
are gathered in this convention, represent? What are banking-houses? Are
they not the Reservoirs into which empty the streams and rills which spring
from the various industries, and from which radiate accumulated capital to
nurture and foster all those industries?

Banking institutions properly have the reputation of being conservative.
From their very nature they must be conservative. They receive from the
people respect and confidence, and the people demand from them in return
strict service of ability and integrity.

The banker occupies a unique position in the world; into his possession and
to his keeping go the fruits of labor; the fortunes of widows and orphans; the
earnings of great corporations, and the revenues of States and nations, which
he must ever keep busy in safe investment and yet hold in readiness for sudden
demand. Possessing tremendous powers, privileges and responsibilities, the
banker must be conservative. He must be slow and cautious in his action that
he may do no wrong to those whose agent he is.

In view of these facts it appears to me that the bankers of every State hold
the possibilities of great good or of great evil; that they can do much to advance a State, and have equal power to impede its progress.

If this be true, may I not venture to ask "What are some of the duties of
the bankers assembled in this convention?" May we not properly make inquiry whether there be any means within our special reach whereby we can assist in the improvement of industrial conditions and in the general welfare
of the State?

I have observed that on the 1st of July, 1892, there was on deposit in the
several banking institutions of San Francisco the sum of 132½ millions of accrued capital, due depositors. Of this amount 3½ millions were in the national, nearly 27 millions in the commercial, and over 102 millions in the
savings banks, with 6¼ millions due to outside banks.

I also find that the aggregate capital of all these banking institutions is a
little over $35,000,000, 2½ millions being that of the national banks, 28¼
millions that of the commercial, 4½ millions that of the savings banks.

It appears to me that within these surprising facts there lie questions of
the deepest interest to all the people of the State of California, among them
the question whether there be anything which the banking and commercial
men of the city of San Francisco can do to change this financial condition.

Every business man in California realizes the fact that what this State
most needs is more people. They also know that there are vast estates of the
best and most desirable lands which are unavailable at the present time to settlers of more moderate means.

Is it possible to devise any way whereby those lands may be opened to settlement, and the vast accumulation of inactive capital may be set in motion to the benefit of the State?

During the period it has been my privilege to be associated with banking interests, I have had occasion to give attention to matters and conditions which seem to me to lie at the foundation of general business affairs and which relate to the progress of the State. Endeavoring to obtain a clear and comprehensive insight into them. I have repeatedly asked myself whether the banking institutions of California have done their full duty; whether they are doing all that they might do, and, may I not say. all they ought to do. to assist in the development of the possibilities which lie within our reach?

Regarding the vital forces of trade and commerce, am I not justified in saying that they live, move and have their being within well established and irresistible laws? Trade and commerce, speaking in a general sense. are neither controlled nor influenced by the passions, prejudices nor preferences of men. Each and both seek their own welfare and follow only those channels wherein lay their greatest advantages; they permit nothing to interfere with or impede their progress when once they are set in motion, and yet both of these gigantic creations are frail and timid and easily wounded unto death.

I think that I am also warranted in saying that nature has made and appointed the great seats for commerce in every country, and she has also, to some extent, formed their feeding channels, which she will not consent to have clogged. And I speak in the broad sense as a Californian when I say that I am convinced that nature made and appointed the bay of San Francisco for the seat of a gigantic commerce—a commerce which will cover the vast seas which have long been waiting for its appearance. Furthermore, that nature has bountifully provided within this State the conditions and means in variety of soils and climatic features for the creation and maintenance of that commerce.

But the commerce of a country depends on something more than raw materials and natural productions. It must have the assistance of mechanical and manufacturing industries. It appears to me that a great present need in California is manufacturing industries of various kinds. With her numerous natural resources and her possibilities in production, California should be dependant on no other State or country. Mills and factories should be in operation throughout our State. What would be the result of such a condition of affairs on all our people? I have thought, gentlemen, that the bankers of California might possibly and safely assist in the inauguration of such an era and reap benefit therefrom.

Let us premise that the wool which California produces, or might produce, is absorbed and manufactured into cloths within the State; that all the hides and skins were tanned and made into boots and shoes; that the valleys, which are eminently fitted for it, were planted with mulberry groves and the raw silk that could be produced therefrom were spun and woven into rich and delicate fabrics in our cities and towns; and that other industries were busy in pouring out their products to swell the commerce we wish to see and find way into the markets of the world. What would be the result of this in the harbor of San Francisco. and all the harbors along our coast?

In other States banks have frequently been among the foremost agents in encouraging the establishment of manufactories and other much desired industries; they have been prompt to lend a helping hand to those who desired to engage in enterprises calculated to develop the resources and agencies within their State and to assist them in times of severe trials.

Is there anything we can do to assist in bringing about that growth, prosperity and progress in our State, which we all desire to witness? I have sometimes thought that the bankers of California have before them great possibilities for doing good work in the business world of the State, and the results of this convention or the good accomplished will be as far reaching as you make it. The banking institutions of the southern section can do but little; those of the northern section can do but little, and even those of the middle section, to which all the streams of capital tend, can of themselves do but little in this work; but the united institutions of the whole can do much, and if I rightly understand the business men of this city and State, we shall find them prompt to respond to, and coöperate with, whatever may be here suggested. We hear the statement that all the industries and interests of California are shackled hand and foot because of the modes and means of transportation.

Gentlemen, California is a great State, and it takes a large body time to get in motion, but when it does move its power is irresistible.

There is another power which will have something to say regarding transportation, and that is the power of supply and demand, which is much greater than that of any humanly devised institution. Supply and demand will not long submit to any detrimental interference with their proper movements. Whatever may be necessary to their convenience they will have, and they are all-powerful to supply their needs.

They furled the sails over the old wooden hulls and set fiery heated monsters at work in those of steel; they stretched the cables for their use over the floors of the seas; they have fretted the face of every country with roadway, for the iron steed made his pathway over desert waste and through the mountains' heart; they have wedded the two tideless seas by the Suez Canal, and they will find the means to serve their ends throughout this broad land.

With healthful competition, supply and demand have formed a triple alliance which no other combination can break or shake; and they will open every needed line of passage from the Golden Gate to the rock-bound coast of New England; and many of us here will see the liquid band which will unite the Atlantic and Pacific at Darien.

The Chairman: Mr. A. D. Childress of Los Angeles will respond on behalf of the bankers of Southern California.

Mr. Childress, president of the City Bank of Los Angeles, spoke as follows:

When the traveler first enters Southern California through the narrow gateway of San Gorgonia Pass, the transition from the treeless, arid and desolate wilds of the Colorado Desert produces a sensation of surprise and delight never to be forgotten. The truth of the old saying, that "It is always darkest just before the dawn," is fully verified, for, tired and weary after a hot and dusty journey thousands of miles over desert wastes and burning sands, his eyes are suddenly gladdened by the sight of purling streams of dancing water, and orchards of the orange and lemon, the fig and the apricot.

It is a refreshing scene, never to be forgotten, when one gazes out the car window upon fields of snow high up on the hoary tops of San Jacinto and San Bernardino, while all around is the bloom and beauty of almost tropical luxuriance.

The sudden change from a cheerless desert to a semi-tropic clime is bewildering. His eyes rest at pleasure upon lofty mountain tops, the home of ice and snow kings, as well as upon sun-kissed and fertile valleys, rivaling the Arcadia of the ancients. Here to him is paradise; all around him is the Eden of his brightest youthful dreams. As he is whirled onward he is greeted with the perfume from a veritable world of flowers; his cheeks fanned by the balmy breezes of an eternal springtime. Here is Southern California, "Our Italy," the paradise of the world. Here is our sunny southern clime, where the morning-glory and century plant submit to the same conditions and flower with equal frequency; where the rose and lily are free from the environments of the hothouse, and the tree geranium evidences perpetual summer.

Here is El Dorado for the invalid and aged, where restored health is given to the one and extended life to the other; a land of perennial sunshine, where the buoyancy and ambition of youth is augmented and the day star of hope never sets; where the misfortunes and disappointments of life are ameliorated and the terrors of death and extinction forever shut out.

Ours is a unique corner of the earth; a singular region, unparalleled for happy conditions on the face of the globe.

A study of its physical conditions develops and establishes the fact of the permanency of its climate, its equability and freedom from blizzards and cyclones, and extremes of heat and cold, characteristics of other lands and climes.

Shut off from sympathy with other countries by high mountain ranges and desert wastes of vast extent, it possesses its own climate, unaffected by external changes. The osculation of Colorado's scorching heat with the Pacific's bracing cold manufactures that perfection of temperature which is a blessing to animal life and vegetation, and always exempt from "import duties" and "McKinley bills."

The area of the southern counties constituting Southern California, namely, Kern, Los Angeles, San Bernardino, Santa Barbara, San Diego, San Luis Obispo, Orange and Ventura, is 57,860 square miles, of which 22,385 is mountains, 29,380 is desert, leaving only 5805 square miles in valleys out of such a vast scope of territory.

This small area is adapted to all productions of a semi-tropic clime, in fact, vies with other lands and countries in tropical luxuriance. Within a few short years the prairies where the Indians hunted and the coyote dwelt have become orchards bending under the weight of golden apples of the Hesperides.

The fame of this wonder-land spread so far and wide within the last decade that it increased in population more than 200 per cent. The immigration has not been of the usual pioneer element, poor in mind and purse, on the westward march for the speedy accumulation of wealth or repairing broken fortunes; neither has it been confined to the physically weak and impotent, with frames wasted by the ravages of some dread disease, but, as a rule and not the exception, an unusually intelligent and cultivated people, with refined tastes and habits, whose actual presence compel thrift and enterprise and stimulate the mind to higher and nobler impulses and exertions.

The total population of Southern California in 1880 was only 79,551, whereas in 1889 by census report it had swelled to 227,232, an increase of say 150,000 souls in less than ten years.

The assessed valuation of the combined eight counties in 1880 was only $41,460,218, which was increased to $199,934,416 in 1889, a grand difference of 159 million dollars within a short decade. Since then there has been the same ratio of material development of the whole country, the bloom and beauty of which is so bewildering that it is beyond the power of anyone to adequately picture or describe.

The fame of Southern California has gone out over the whole land. Wherever the English tongue is spoken in every quarter of the habitable globe the names of our beautiful towns and cities are household words, and the products of our orange groves, vineyards and ranches are looked upon as coming from fairy or wonder-land. Who has not heard of San Diego, the city of bay and climate, the Naples of America, whose crescent ocean front, blue as the summer sky and flecked with snow-capped, dancing wavelets, together with its mesa, foot-hill and picturesque mountain ranges in the background, afford a panorama of loveliness alone worth traveling across continents to look upon. Who has not heard of San Bernardino and Riverside, two beautiful inland cities at the base of snow-capped mountain ranges, literally surrounded by orange groves whose luscious yellow spheres dot the rich, green foliage like golden stars, and yield their happy owners princely annual incomes not equaled anywhere. Riverside, a creation of the past fifteen years, even in 1890 shipped 1253 carloads, or 358,341 boxes of oranges and, gauged by the annual income from its orchards, enjoys the enviable reputation of being the richest agricultural community of its size in the whole world. Who has not heard of delightful Santa Barbara, where the commingling of sea and mountain air tones up the weary system and gives renewed vigor and health to the invalid; whose annual flower festival has become historical for its unique and gorgeous pageantry and earned for it the appropriate name of the "Flower Kingdom." Who has not heard of our Queen City, Los Angeles, the birthplace of the California Bankers Association, second only to the State's great metropolis in population and commercial importance, whose phenomenal growth within the past seven years has no recorded parallel. From a thriving town of 22,500 people in 1885 it has grown to be a city of beautiful residences, the dwelling place of over 60,000 happy and contented people. In July, 1885, there were only four commercial banks in Los Angeles, having a total capital of $500,000, with a surplus of $600,000. The combined deposits of the four banks amounted to $3,128,000, whereas in July of this year (1892) the number of commercial banks has increased to thirteen, with a combined capital of over $3,300,000, a combined surplus of over $1,395,000 and the large sum of over $7,500,000 deposits. Besides the thirteen commercial banks, there are at present five prosperous savings banks, with a total capital and surplus of $390,000, and combined deposits of $3,275,000, as against two institutions in July, 1885, with a total capital of only $42,000 and total deposits of only $142,000.

2

These figures show the gratifying increase of banking capital within the past seven years to be $4,943.000, with the corresponding increase of deposits of over $7,505.000.

Situated midway between the lofty Sierra Madre Mountains and the shores of the peaceful Pacific, surrounded by the fertile and unrivaled valleys of the San Fernando, San Gabriel and Santa Ana, Los Angeles has no rival in her varied charms and attractions, and stands the unchallenged metropolis of Southern California. Who has not heard of lovely Pasadena, the future home of James G. Blaine, with her fields of golden yellow poppies, the emblem of our Association; San Luis Obispo, Ventura, Pomona, Ontario, Santa Ana and a host of other beautiful towns, all jewels in the crown of our wonder-land's fame and glory.

No less wonderful than the great influx of people and wealth poured into the lap of Los Angeles during the last seven years has been the astonishing increase in number and wealth of all financial institutions in Southern California.

From statistical reports the bank deposits of Southern California exceed $22,000,000. a showing rarely if ever equaled by a country which a score of years ago was regarded as a sheep pasture and little better than a desert waste. This sum of $22,000,000 is over 11 per cent of the total deposits in all the banks of California, which exceed $198,000,000. When we consider that in 1885 there were only nineteen banks in Southern California. with a combined capital of $1,540,000 and total deposits of $4,999,000, and contrast them with the eighty-five banks which exist today with a combined capital of $11,-500,000 and deposits of over $22,000,000, it is difficult to realize the grand growth and increase which statistics prove beyond doubt.

Facts like these plainly illustrate the relative importance of Southern California compared with the remainder of our Golden State. Without raising any question of climatic superiority or relative greatness, it is not impertinent to remark that the press and people of Northern and Central California are scarcely sensible of the rapid advancement in both wealth and population of their sister section. Our growth and prosperity within the past ten years has been phenomenal, and I am glad to announce to you today that the wheels of progress are still well oiled and turning many revolutions to the minute. Without rivalry, without braggadocia, we throw out the challenge of competition to our sister sections and "bid defiance to our foes." The whole grand State of California is the Mecca toward which numerous eager, straining eyes are turned. They see the land of promise and long to dwell where milk and honey flows. The electric spark, the panting engine and the press, those three mighty civilizers, are doing noble duty in carrying the news of our boundless and inexhaustible resources to the hungry and waiting thousands. Within the confines of this empire of itself all the reasonable expectations of human life can be more than met and satisfied. Whether in the lofty altitudes, the lowlier valleys or down by the rolling sea, there are combined the conditions of soil, climate and surroundings which induce happiness in this life if it can anywhere be found. It is not an idle prediction to make that within twenty-five years California will be the richest, most prosperous country in our glorious Union and in all the world. To San Francisco, the city of the Golden Gate, whose hospitable portals are always open to California's sons and daughters, and to the stranger as well, Southern California gives the meed of praise. Your cordial greeting on this occasion, your words of welcome so freely and heartily spoken, cause us to feel that home is everywhere.

> That it is where the day star springs,
> And where the evening sun reposes;
> Where'er the eagle spreads his wings
> From Northern pines to Southern roses.

Mr. Thomas Brown, cashier of the Bank of California, San Francisco, and president of the California Bankers Association, then delivered the following address:

Gentlemen of the Convention:

There are many subjects that might appropriately be considered in an address which custom imposes upon the president in opening proceedings of a convention like the one which has called us together at this time.

There are live issues of various kinds which demand our attention, and these should receive careful consideration at our hands before adjournment.

While not neglecting the social amenities of an occasion like the present, we should remember that we have met to further other and more serious purposes.

Our business is necessarily of an advisory character, yet, if we can agree what is best to be done in the matter of any of the issues that may be presented, the influence of our united action will do something to mold public opinion, and we all know that public opinion is the fulcrum which moves the world.

The Executive Committee has arranged a programme of the topics to be presented, and it is hoped that there will be the utmost freedom in the discussions which may follow.

Notwithstanding the great progress of the nineteenth century, there are still many unsolved problems in finance and business.

There are many unsettled questions about immigration and transportation and currency inflation that ought to be cleared up before the end of the present century.

There are numerous local issues of vital importance relating to the development of the material interests of the State that ought to be considered and acted upon at the earliest practicable opportunity.

What can be done to improve the irrigation and transportation interests of the State may well claim attention and such action as we can decide upon.

Changes concerning our methods of doing business are pertinent to this hour and place, provided the suggestions are in the line of enlarged usefulness and greater protection to the various interests involved.

It is not my purpose to indicate in detail the work of this convention. Nevertheless the hope is expressed that something may be accomplished before we adjourn.

It has been charged that California bankers are too conservative for the age in which they live; that they are lacking in enterprise; that their methods are too inelastic for the business emergencies of the times; that they are wanting in sympathy and coöperation.

It is not denied that we are conservative. That element has saved us and others a great deal of trouble.

The banker who guides his business into safe channels of activity and so on to success is apt to be credited with conservatism, and he is entitled to it.

That, however, should not be the measure of his praise.

Conservative banking has much to do with creating and maintaining a high standard of mercantile honor, while so-called liberal banking is not infrequently loose banking, the inevitable results of which are demoralization, failure and dishonor.

Banking and commerce are so intimately allied that the standard of either is the standard of both, and it is the province and duty of the banker to pitch the standard and put it on a safe plane.

While California bankers share many ideas and pursue many methods in common with those in the same profession in other parts of the country, they have their peculiarities. Many of them have grown up with the State, and, therefore, thoroughly know its needs and purposes.

They early planted themselves on solid financial foundation. No banks of issue have ever been allowed. We have extracted our money circulation from the rocks and rivers of the State, and have had plenty to spare to less favored States. Thirty years ago we refused to give hospitality to the Government greenback as money, because opposed to depreciated currency.

Our action at that time subjected us to the charge of disloyalty, but subsequent events proved that ours was the most loyal State in the Union, because loyal to honest money.

Our course at that time could not stop the issue of greenbacks, but the pickets along the State line brought them to a halt, and allowed them to enter only for what they were worth.

We refused to adapt commercial values in this State to the vagaries of the greenback, and thus saved our people much trouble and hastened the day of specie resumption on the other side of the country. The shrinkage in values incident to that change, and the many and grievous embarrassments that followed, left no trace of sorrow here.

Our record for honest money is clean and straight. We not only shut out the overvalued greenback in the days of its depreciation, but when the country was being flooded with trade dollars manufactured at a discount on their face value, we drove them from circulation between two suns by declining to receive them except at their commercial value.

When other silver coin became so plentiful as to be cumbersome, our bankers sought relief through Congressional action, providing for the redemption of the overvalued redundant currency.

In these and other ways the bankers of the State have exhibited a conservatism in full touch with the times, thus demonstrating their ability to cope with the financial issues of the day.

We are not sure but what the silver question, the greatest financial problem of the world today, will have to be settled by California bankers. The trade dollar, as a scheme for getting rid of the surplus silver of the country, was a California idea, and if unscrupulous parties had not attempted to put the coins into domestic circulation, the proposition would have been a success.

It may not be generally known that the present silver law is the outcome of a suggestion by a California banker in 1881, and embodied in a pamphlet and sent to members of Congress in that year. After reviewing the rapidly disappearing national bank note and the necessity for an enlarged use of silver, the pamphlet suggested the following:

"Just at this point the proposition comes in to utilize silver ingots by making them the basis of Treasury notes to supersede the national bank notes, which must ere long be given up for want of security."

Nine years later that idea was incorporated in the silver law adopted by Congress in July, 1890. This law was meant to absorb the surplus silver product of the country, and had its operation been confined to American silver it would have been a much greater success. In the past two years it has taken out of the market 108,000,000 ounces of fine silver and put into circulation over $100,000,000 in Treasury notes.

A trial of two years has demonstrated that this law should now be repealed, or there should be a prohibitory tariff on foreign silver in whatever form it may seek entrance.

From the great mass of information on the silver question which has been printed in the past twenty years, and from this country's experiment in silver coinage and in the purchase of fine silver for Treasury notes, two or three things are evident beyond any dispute.

One of these is that there is not enough of gold or silver to transact the business of the world in either one of these metals separately.

The world produces and uses more silver than gold. Both metals have been almost universally used as money from the foundation of the world.

What God hath thus joined together, it is not the part of human wisdom, after an experience of six thousand years, to separate.

During the past two hundred years the ratio between these metals has varied from 14.14 to 24.80. It is only during the past twenty years there has been a wide divergence between the two. From 1687 to 1813 there was a difference on only a little over two points. At one time during that interval 14.14 ounces of silver was equal to an ounce of gold; while at another time it required 16.25 ounces of silver to equal an ounce of gold. These extremes were marked by an interval of forty-three years.

In the past twenty years these extremes have been 15.63 to 24.80. Such a marked depreciation in one of the monetary metals of the world has caused great distress in silver-using countries and great apprehension of evil throughout the world.

In this connection the calling of an international monetary congress for the readjustment of gold and silver, which has now been agreed upon by the leading nations, is a wise step in the right direction.

Without attempting to outline the action of that body, we may say it ought not to consider its work complete until it has made such an equable adjustment of the metals as will insure their largest possible use interchangeably.

If a single country can maintain a parity between these two metals on the basis of 15½ or 16 to 1, as in France, and also in the United States, it will not be difficult for the world at large to maintain such parity on any new adjustment that may be agreed upon.

The great difference which has come between these metals in the past twenty years suggests the absolute necessity of new relations. It is probable that twenty ounces of silver to one of gold would be a fair adjustment.

The silver question will not be settled until it is settled on the basis as broad as the world.

Either the various governments must regulate the amount of silver that shall be used for money purposes, or open the mints alike to the free coinage of both metals on a fixed ratio, making the same international and interchangeable.

Action along either of these lines, if ratified by the proper legislative bodies of the various countries represented in the forthcoming monetary congress, would settle this irritating question for a long time, if not forever.

To prevent one nation from unloading its silver upon another in the event of giving that metal an international character, it would be well for the Monetary Congress to fix the proportions of the metals that might be used in liquidating obligations between one country and another, to the end that there should be no violent disturbance of the equilibrium in the holdings of these metals.

Whatever the result of the congress or whatever the action of our own Government, California has little cause for uneasiness, since its specific contract law protects all alike.

In conclusion, allow me to congratulate the banks of California on having done so much to shape the financial policy of the country along right and therefore safe lines. We may move slow, but we are always sure of our footing.

It took us a quarter of a century to establish a clearing-house, but when it was found that one was really needed, it came into existence.

It took us forty years to find out whether we needed a State Bankers Association, but although we did not organize until March, 1891, this is the third time we have come together in this capacity in eighteen months.

There can be no question but what some good will grow out of these gatherings. The coming together of bankers from all parts of the State, representing such diversified interests, must be of advantage in many ways.

The better we understand each other and the wants of our State, the more intelligently can we act, and the more powerful will be our influence in furtherance of the objects we may seek to accomplish.

The Chairman: I will declare the convention open for business. The secretary will proceed with the roll-call.

The secretary called the roll, and, after footing up the register, announced that it showed 112 representatives present, representing 82 banks.

Complete list of delegates [133] and banks represented [108] will be found in front of Proceedings.

The Chairman: The next business in order is the report of the Executive Council.

Mr. A. D. Childress, chairman, read the annual report of the Executive Council as follows:

Mr. President and Members of the California Bankers Association :

GENTLEMEN: The machinery of the California Bankers Association has run with alarming smoothness during the past year, as the business of the Executive Council has been conducted by correspondence, and no matter of enough importance has sprung up to call the members from different parts of the State to sit in council. We beg, therefore, to submit the following report as summing up our official acts, to-wit:

After the election of San Francisco by the American Bankers Association as the place for this year's annual meeting, and September 7 and 8 as the dates for the convention to be held, your council conceived that it would be wise to change our place of meeting so that the State bankers would be enabled to attend both conventions in one trip. With the hearty approval and consent of the bankers of Fresno, which had been selected as the place for this year's meeting, this was accordingly done, and San Francisco enjoys the distinguished honor of having two bankers' conventions in the brief space of one week. The Fresno bankers, however, reserve the right to have the convention next year in consideration of their self-denial, and your Executive Council cheerfully granted the concession.

From the secretary's and treasurer's reports, which we have examined and approved, you will see that the financial condition of the Association is satisfactory. Our income, which is derived solely from annual dues collected from the members, is sufficient to pay all expenses.

A balance of $741.45 remained in the treasury from last year, and the sum of $1600 has been received as income this year, while the total expenses have been only $1260.23, leaving a balance of $1081.22 on hand.

There is no necessity to increase our revenues by any other method of taxation.

The membership of the Association has increased from 161 to 170 during the past year. There have been three lapses and two failures. The Association this year, for the first time in its history, bears the shock of financial failure of one of its members, viz., the California National Bank of San Diego, and records with regret and sorrow the death by suicide of the president of the California National Bank.

The appointment of a standing Protective Committee was duly made in the early part of the year, in compliance with the constitution.

On account of difficulties contended with heretofore we recommend the adoption of the following amendment to the constitution, to be known as Section 2 of Article VII, which is as follows, to-wit:

"No opinions expressed, principles advocated, theories advanced or policies suggested by any party or person, however presented, shall be deemed to have had the indorsement of this Association, except the question of so indorsing shall have been referred to a standing or special committee; shall have been reported upon by such Committee, and shall have been specifically voted upon, receiving a majority of the votes of those present at an open session of a convention of the Association.

"This item of the constitution shall be published in every report of the proceedings of any convention, and where indorsements are given, the fact shall be noted in the report of proceedings in that behalf."

We have authorized the purchase of 175 lappel buttons as a distinctive badge to be worn by members of the Association at our conventions, recognizing in the design the California poppy as an appropriate emblem.

We compliment our worthy secretary upon the zeal he has displayed in forwarding the interests of the Association, and attribute our prosperity and large membership to his persistent energy and "letter writing."

We recommend the adoption by the Association of the following resolution, to-wit:

"WHEREAS, the California Bankers Association has already put itself on record as heartily favoring the construction of the Nicaragua Canal; and,

"WHEREAS, an American company has been chartered by the Government of the United States for the construction of the Nicaragua Maritime Canal, and is now engaged in the work of construction; therefore, be it

"Resolved, That the California Bankers Association, having in view the great and permanent benefit of this work to the finances, commerce and industries of the Pacific Coast, and to the entire Republic, respectfully requests the American Bankers Association meeting at San Francisco on September 7 and 8, 1892, to pass resolutions in favor of an 'American canal under the control of the American Government,' and recommending the enterprise to the good will and financial support of the American people."

On account of the interest that the State Bank Commissioners and the National Bank Examiner have always taken in giving this Association a standing with the bankers throughout the State, and their zeal and energy displayed in its success and prosperity, we recommend that they be made honorary members. Respectfully submitted.

A. D. CHILDRESS, Chairman Executive Council.

Mr. C. C. Bush, vice-president of the Bank of Shasta County, Redding: I would ask if a motion for the adoption of the report of the Executive Council is in order?

The Chairman: It is.

Mr. Bush: I move the adoption of the report as read.

I. W. Hellman, president Nevada Bank, San Francisco: I second the motion.

Lovell White, cashier San Francisco Savings Union: I would like to ask if that motion includes the adoption of everything contained in the report or whether a separate vote is necessary on the different recommendations? There are three resolutions or recommendations. Now, does this report carry it all, or have we to vote specifically on each recommendation?

The Chairman ruled that adoption of report would carry all.

After some parliamentary skirmishing the Executive Council retired and amended their report (as printed above) as to the resolution referring to the Nicaragua Canal, whereupon, on motion of John Reichman of Fresno, the report as amended was adopted.

During the discussion on the adoption of the report, Capt. William L. Merry of San Francisco, by request, addressed the convention upon the subject of the Nicaragua Canal, and spoke as follows:

Mr. Chairman and Gentlemen of the Convention:

I thank you for the privilege of explaining to you the condition of this project as to its control.

It is a matter of history that the Arthur administration made a treaty with Nicaragua for the construction of a canal by the United States Government, with a joint sovereignty of two and one-half miles on each side of the canal, with the right to fortify.

That treaty was by the Senate of Nicaragua adopted, and in our Senate, before it had received action, it was withdrawn by President Cleveland at the suggestion of Secretary Bayard, for the reason alleged that it was feared it might create foreign complications.

It is not my privilege to know exactly what the President meant by this, but I apprehend that he referred to a treaty whereby the United States is bound to share with Great Britain the control of that canal in case it is constructed, which our Government claims is invalid and which Great Britain claims is still in force. At all events, the correspondence was terminated without a satisfactory conclusion.

After the failure of that treaty Nicaragua made a contract with a company of American citizens for control by private capital. That company, after paying $100,000 in evidence of good faith for the concession, organized for construction, and is now before the American people and at work.

Now, that company is not endeavoring, as the Senate Committee upon Foreign Relations, and, as the President also, has repeated, to obtain Congressional action in respect to this matter. It has been the thought of the best men in the United States; men like Mr. Evarts, Mr. Edmons, and Senator Morgan of Alabama, irrespective of party—it has been their sentiment that the United States should control that work, and, in accordance with that view, they have introduced a bill for that purpose, using this company as an intermediary for construction. That bill is drawn for the express purpose of removing the objections which President Cleveland and Mr. Bayard made to the Frelinghuysen treaty; they propose to obtain Government control through the intermediary of this company in a manner that Great Britain or any other country cannot object to, and so that the United States will construct the canal without violation of our treaty obligations.

Now, that matter of control is illustrated by that bill. I will explain the bill to you directly. It states, in the first place, that the company shall hypothecate with the United States Government, in the hands of the Secretary of the Treasury, seventy per cent of its capital stock, carrying with it voting power; six per cent of the capital stock belongs to Nicaragua, one and one-half per cent to Costa Rica, making seventy-seven and one-half per cent absolutely taken away from the control of the company, and the voting power belongs in that stock. The company is also obligated to elect only eight directors, Nicaragua elects one, the United States six. With the voting power in the hands of the Secretary of the Treasury, as you will see, the Government of the United States controls the election of every director of the company except the one director named by the Government of Nicaragua.

In addition to that, there are further clauses of this character to control the situation. As the work proceeds the President of the United States appoints five engineers of the Topographical Corps, who are obligated to examine the work every sixty days and report upon what work has been done, and, on that

3

work done as reported by these engineers, the guaranty three per cent bonds of the company are paid over by the Government.

I may say that these three per cent guaranty bonds are printed by the company, turned over to the Secretary of the Treasury, and remain in his possession during the entire construction of the canal and are so paid out.

The Government also has the right of purchase of this seven-tenths of the capital stock at any time prior to the maturity of the bonds, at par, holding them as security until those bonds mature.

There are one or two other clauses also controlling the matter of tolls.

But the fact remains that Nicaragua retains her sovereignty in this bill, instead of the joint sovereignty with the United States. Now, it is obviously the duty of Nicaragua, as any government would exercise it, to maintain her sovereignty, and it has put into the concession to this company that it shall not be sold to any government or any foreign power. They don't want it sold to Great Britain, or France, having a remembrance of what France did in Mexico, and for that reason they have put this clause into this charter, which she has granted to this company. How, then, can this company absolve itself from its duty to Nicaragua, and turn over to the United States or any other power the right which it has acquired from this government?

You will see that the purpose of this bill is controlled by the American Government. There is not any question in this world as to the feeling in that particular. The company does not contest that fact at all. The company desires the work constructed, and it is willing to let the control of that work rest in the United States with the voting power of the stock. In fact, the company concedes everything that the United States has asked it to concede.

I may say that the Senate Committee on Foreign Relations, with the consent and advice of the President, last spring sent for Mr. Miller, the president of the construction company, and they said to him, "Senator Miller, we understand that you are negotiating in Europe for the sale of your securities." He said, "Yes, gentlemen, I am." They said, "But, Miller, you must not let this thing go to Europe." He said, "Gentlemen, that is good advice. I am patriotic, as you are, but what am I to do? We have spent between $5,000,000 and $6,000,000. The work must go on. I can get the money in England, and if you do not want me to go there, what do you suggest?" "Why, Miller, Congress must legislate." "But," he said, "gentlemen, Congress moves very slowly and with great uncertainty. Now, what am I to do?" In answer to this they suggested to him the floating of a $5,000,000 loan, if necessary, to keep this work going until Congress could be made to legislate; that they would demand legislation for American control. Under that proposition this loan is before the public here; under that proposition it is to be floated. The only question is the matter of construction: Shall it be constructed by the Government itself, as our dry-docks are, as our postoffice is to be? Those are questions of propriety, time and money. We cannot point with any degree of pride to the slow and expensive construction of our dry-docks, our Government works; but, here is a proposition to construct this work under the immediate control of the President of the United States, and under the control of the Secretary of the Treasury, voting the majority of the stock, electing every director of the company, in fact, complete control, except that the Government does not build it and does not exercise sovereignty over the canal.

Now, my friend speaks about the Government owning the canal. Why? Nicaragua is a foreign power. Although, in a military point of view, she is weak, she has as many rights as any nation, and if we try to interfere with her sovereignty we will find other nations stepping in our path in that respect. How can we, then, ask a foreign government to absolve itself from its duty and give away its territory and let us come in there and build a canal because we want to? In fact, the right was given us. What did we do with the right when it was given us? We threw it aside. Now, the second time, would she permit herself to be placed in the position to be denied what she suggested we should take before? Particularly when she has given an agreement with a company to construct the canal independent of that. As a friendly government she is willing that the United States should control. She says: "Come here and build it and control it by any legislation you like; you construct the canal and control its management. We gave you the right of joint sovereignty and you discarded it; we are willing now, but the sovereignty remains with us unless you make good the Frelinghuysen treaty. We know that it was a European nation or some other influence that prevented your doing so before."

Government control through the intermediary of a Government committee, by joint sovereignty, we have discarded when we had the opportunity to secure it, and now it cannot be had.

I will say this, further, if it could be had, the company would willingly waive their position and let this Frelinghuysen treaty be renewed, but Nicaragua would not ask for it. You cannot get a sovereign power to ask a second time that a treaty be renewed which has been discarded and thrown out of the Senate without action.

You recollect when we bought St. Thomas that the Government made a treaty which enabled Congress to purchase that island, but when it had purchased it the house refused to appropriate the money and it fell through. Did Denmark ever ask us to buy it after that?

This is a practical question. You know that this coast is suffering intensely in the matter of transportation, cheap transportation. Without it this city is suffering and the State is suffering, and when we approach this question we should approach it as practical men and seek a practical solution.

This charter says that it may be amended or rescinded at any time Congress may desire. It gives the company no power whatever, for the Government exercises its control, its practical government control. The words of the resolution are "American canal, under American control." I can imagine how that language was used. Gen. Grant, in the North American Review, in 1881, said: "I recommend to my countrymen an American canal, under American control." [Applause.]

Now, what he meant by "American control" I do not know, but I presume he meant the control by the American Nation for American commerce.

If the gentlemen had any objection to that resolution it is better for them to suggest an amendment and make it more rigid, make it more binding. Mr. Sherman and his associates in the Senate have made it as binding as they knew how; let these gentlemen make it still more binding. But while we are quarreling about these matters time passes. We have to go around Cape

Horn. 15.000 miles, for relief. Had that Frelinghuysen treaty been adopted and passed, that canal would have been constructed years ago.

Now the country wants it. It can get it only under the conditions of an intermediary company, by constructing that canal under the control of the United States Government. and if you do not do that, gentlemen, what is the position? Just as sure as the sun shines. if that is not done, it will be done by English capital. and then who will own it? Didn't Great Britain buy and own the Suez Canal stock, which is now declaring twenty per cent dividends? If this stock is offered in Europe it will be bought there, and when that comes to pass what will occur? What occurred in the Suez when they bombarded Alexandria and said: "Gentlemen, this canal is closed, you cannot come through here at present, we are not ready for you," and when they desired they withdrew their ironclads and resumed traffic.

That is the position. You have had offered government control; you threw it away. But now, control by the Government can be had under conditions so that the company has no power to hurt commerce; no power. if it desired, to inflict upon commerce a high toll.

Another point. A canal is not a transportation company. A canal company holds a toll. it holds a gate, and a low price for the use of that gate. They started at Suez at $2.50 a ton and they decreased the tariff to $1.75 per ton. They were not obligated to do this. They did it of their own volition and for their own benefit. That is precisely what will occur here. It is not a transportation company that can charge all the traffic will bear.

Gentlemen, I thank you for your attention. I only desired to explain to you the conditions of this enterprise. You cannot have the construction of this canal through joint sovereignty; you threw away that opportunity when you had it; you cannot get it again except through this company. If this company desired to give up its rights it is doubtful whether Nicaragua would permit it. You can have the work controlled by the Government. which shall be as rigid as legislation can make it. If you reject that. the result will be that you will have English control. There is not the slightest doubt about that in my mind.

Gentlemen, I thank you.

The Chairman: The next business will be the report of the secretary.

Here George H. Stewart, cashier of the Bank of America. Los Angeles. secretary of the Association. read his annual report, which was as follows:

To the Officers and Members of the California Bankers Association:

GENTLEMEN—Delightful memories still cling to us of the excursion to Palo Alto and elegant banquet at the Palace Hotel tendered to our delegates last October by the San Francisco bankers. This may account in some measure for the genial feeling now pervading the Association, further evidenced by the large representation and the glowing words to which you have just listened.

Two days more, and the American Bankers Association will convene in this city, and for the first time on the Pacific Coast. It is partially due to our efforts that the convention was located here. In consequence. after the return of the secretary from New York, in March, our Fresno bankers, waiving all claim to the convention, asked our Executive Council to set our meeting here, and at a date to best contribute to the success of the national event.

Upon adjournment we expect to take some part in the other convention, and enjoy the satisfaction of assisting to make enjoyable to our visitors from other States a day or two of relaxation. We cannot do more than wish them as good a time as we had last year.

Now, all this sounds very well, but, a few figures, by way of variety, should be thrown in.

We closed the last convention with 161 members, five of these have severed their connection since, viz: The California National, of San Diego, by reason of its unfortunate suspension; the University and Citizens Banks of Los Angeles, and the Bank of Paso Robles and Bank of Commerce, San Diego, by limitation. In place of these, fourteen banks have acquired membership, viz:

Bank of Lemoore, Lemoore.
Orange Growers Bank, Riverside.
Producers Savings Bank, Bakersfield.
San Joaquin Valley Bank, Stockton.
Savings Bank of Redlands, Redlands.
Commercial and Savings Bank, Merced.
City Bank, Santa Cruz.
Citizens Bank, Nevada City.
First National Bank, San Luis Obispo.
Bank of Sisson, Crocker & Co., San Francisco.
The Bank of San José, San José.
Bank of Oakdale, Oakdale.
Mierson & Jewell, Placerville.
Farmers and Merchants Bank, Hollister. making the present membership 170.

The year has been specially notable in developing twenty-nine new banks, which have been licensed and commenced business in California since October 1, 1891, and there are "more in the bushes." State bankers' associations have largely increased in number. At the date of my last report fifteen were in operation, while now eight more are listed, viz: The Ohio, Illinois, Kentucky, West Texas, Arkansas, Wisconsin, Illinois Private and Colorado Bankers Association.

To refer particularly to matters which should be in a secretary's report, he has drawn thirty-nine warrants on the treasurer, aggregating $1260.23, and has collected in dues the sum of $1600, which has been duly turned over to the treasurer.

The Executive Council authorized me to receipt to all new members joining after July 1 as if membership was acquired at the date of this convention; therefore, the thirteen new members, remitting since July 1, have been given receipt until the annual meeting in 1893, the annual dues of all other members being now payable, to cover until that date.

The printed proceedings of our first annual convention were somewhat delayed in publication. many members forgot to register. some omitted to hand into the secretary resolutions and other data, and complications occurred in other ways. After considerable effort the data was obtained, and, if the members derived half the pleasure in receiving the pamphlet that the secretary did in getting it off his hands. I congratulate the members.

It is proper here to acknowledge the renewed obligations under which the secretary, in particular, rests to the Board of Bank Commissioners, for courtesies and attentions during the entire year. The local press and banking publications have shown a very friendly attitude, the inaccuracies which have crept into unofficial reports being traceable to other causes.

Allow me, in view of the eloquent remarks of the gentlemen who have opened our convention in such auspicious manner, to congratulate the Association at large that it has so little to regret and so much to hope for. May the existence of our organization and the lives or our delegates be sufficiently long to wear out, on similar occasions, the association badge with which you are provided. The golden poppy (California's adopted floral emblem), upon which the initial letters of our name are fused, suggests to me that this Association should ever be identified with California's substantial interests, and while endeavoring to imitate its modest individuality, as a collective body, can we not stand forth, as do the poppies, worthy the attention and admiration of all?

Respectfully submitted,

GEORGE H. STEWART.

On motion of John McKee of San Francisco, seconded by C. C. Bush of Redding, the secretary's report was received and placed on file.

G. W. Kline, assistant cashier of the First National Bank, San Francisco, treasurer of the Association, then read his annual report, as follows:

To the California Bankers Association, City:

GENTLEMEN—I beg leave to submit herewith a statement of my account for the year ending September 3, 1892:

Balance brought forward from account rendered October 13, 1891 ... ... $741.45
Membership fees received from 160 banks and bankers............. ...... 1600.00

Total Receipts..$2341 45
Paid secretary's warrants Nos. 28 to 66 inclusive (which are returned
herewith) amounting to.. ... 1260.23

Leaving a balance of cash on hand...............................$1081.22
Respectfully submitted.   G. W. KLINE, Treasurer.

On motion, the treasurer's report was received and placed on file.

The secretary then read the report of the Committee on Irrigation Bonds:

George H. Stewart, Secretary California Bankers Association:

DEAR SIR—Since the appointment by the Association of the Committee on Irrigation Bonds but one case has been submitted to it for its action. This was the case of the Anaheim Irrigation District. On the 28th of January last at the request of the Board of Directors of said district, I appointed as a sub-committee to examine the same the following named members of the Committee on Irrigation Bonds, viz: Messrs. Bryant Howard of San Diego, W. M. Eddy of Santa Barbara, and E. F. Spence of Los Angeles. The said sub-committee personally inspected the said district and made strict inquiry into all matters affecting the value of the bonds proposed to be issued, formulating a series of questions relative to the subject to which specific answers were required, and which answers were attested by the resident engineer as well as prominent citizens of the district. As a result of such investigation said committee were able to report as follows:

"We believe the Anaheim Irrigation District is legally constituted and all the requirements of the law have been complied with, and all the transactions affecting the validity of the bonds issued are bona fide, but as your committee has no legal official standing, we deem it best to state that as citizens of California, taxpayers and bankers, we can unhesitatingly say that the security to the bondholders is ample, at the same time qualifying this remark that the purchaser of the bonds should make thorough investigation of all things necessary to be considered for his protection.

"In conclusion I desire to say that in the questions hereinbefore mentioned, every point affecting the question at issue appears to be covered, and in my opinion they may well serve as a guide, if not as a model, for formulating the reports of future similar committees. Respectfully submitted,

"A. C. HENRY, Chairman of Committee on Irrigation Bonds."

On motion of C. C. Bush of Redding the report was received and placed on file.

The Chairman: The appointment of committees will be left to the Executive Council, who will meet tomorrow morning at 9:30 o'clock.

William Beckman, president People's Savings Bank, Sacramento: Mr. Chairman, as there is a little lapse in the proceedings just at this time, I will say, in listening to the roll-call today, I was sorry to see that San Francisco so poorly responded. In the name of Fresno bankers—I don't live in Fresno—I wish to give a cordial invitation to San Francisco bankers to be present in Fresno, a year from now, and I will guarantee that every Fresno banker will second my invitation. I am really sorry to see that you folks right here should not respond to this convention more freely than you have done.

The Chairman: I am sorry that there should not have been a better attendance of the San Francisco bankers.

A. D. Childress, of Los Angeles: Mr. Chairman, our convention is honored today by the presence of Mr. William H. Rhawn, president of the National Bank of the Republic, of Philadelphia, and also of the American Bankers Association, and I know that the convention will be pleased to have him make a few remarks to us on the subject of banks in general.

Mr. Rhawn spoke as follows:

Mr. President and Gentlemen of the California Bankers Association:

The worthy chairman of your Executive Committee has done me too much honor. I am merely a warhorse, chairman of the Executive Council of the American Bankers Association, and not the president. I wish that you might have had before you General Nelson, our president, as I am sure he would have had something to say to entertain you. I have been thirty-five years an active worker in the ranks, but have never been accused of being a public speaker. I traveled some 4000 miles to get here, and I now realize what has been for years the dream of my life, to see the Pacific Coast and to make the acquaintance of your worthy president, with whom I have been a correspondent, in Philadelphia, for a quarter of a century, without ever having had the pleasure of taking him by the hand, until today. And upon seeing him I was quite surprised at the very striking resemblance that he bears to the President of the United States. [Applause.] I am very sure that neither of the gentlemen have any reason to complain at my having said so. [Renewed applause.]

I desire to say that I am extremely pleased to thus meet with the gentlemen composing the California Bankers Association, and am more than gratified with the compliment which I perceive in the fact of your meeting at this time, during the same week with the American Bankers Association, and, as the chairman of the Executive Council, I am bold to express the thanks of that Association for the great honor that you have done us in holding your convention at this time, having changed the place of meeting from the city that you had previously decided upon for this purpose. I am sure that every member of the American Bankers Association from elsewhere—and I hope you are all members of the Association, as well—will appreciate this compliment as I do. I therefore tender you their thanks.

This is the first time in the sixteen or seventeen years of the existence of the American Bankers Association that it has ventured so far away from the place of its birth, Philadelphia, where it sprung into existence during the Centennial year: this is the first time that it has ventured upon the shores of the Pacific. We have never yet had a meeting farther west than Kansas City. I have done what I could, as an humble instrument, to bring this about, and it is therefore with very great gratification that I realize that we are about to have this convention in the greatest city of the Pacific Coast; the city which to me, in the few days that I have been able to look at it, appears as one of the marvels of the age, a city of such magnitude and beauty and doing such large business, in banking—as the figures in your little pamphlet which is placed in my hands show—with ships in the harbor that I saw as I approached it, and many lines of communication traversing and gridironing your city, all demonstrate.

I am glad to be among you, and I hope that you are all-members of the American Bankers Association, as well as of the California Bankers Association, and that you will all be present at our convention, and, if there are any that are not members of the American Bankers Association, I take pleasure in inviting you to become such. At any rate, I invite you to attend our convention.

There is a subject, Mr. President, that I would like to touch upon, in connection with the business of the American Bankers Association, if I may be privileged to do so.

Two or three years ago the American Bankers Association took up the subject of the higher education of bankers. To illustrate, I will take my own case. When my boy became old enough to go to the university I wanted him to have a higher education. He said, "Father, what is the use of me going to the university? I have a good common-school education. I don't want to be a lawyer, nor a doctor, nor a clergyman. I want to go into the bank."

"Well," I said, "my son, if you go through a course in the University of

Pennsylvania you will make a better banker." But I couldn't persuade him, and the consequence was he came into the bank without having taken a course in the university, and to my mind he will be so much the poorer banker.

When my cashier's son, who was younger, was old enough his father spoke to him in the same way, but the answer was the same: "I don't want to be a lawyer, nor a doctor, nor a clergyman; I want to be a banker."

"Well," his father said, "my son, I want you to go to the University of Pennsylvania and go through the Wharton School."

In the meantime, since the time I had spoken to my son on this subject, a school had been opened in connection with the University of Pennsylvania for the education of business men; that is to say, that a man might take a course in the university and finish in the Wharton School, getting an education that would fit him to be a banker, railroad man, insurance man, or a journalist. There was no such school when I wanted my boy to go to the university, and, therefore, I couldn't appeal to that school. My cashier's son saw the force of the argument, and he went through that school. When he came out he had learned something, and he decided he would not be a banker and chose journalism as his profession. [Laughter.]

I may say in regard to the Wharton School, that it was founded by Mr. Joseph Wharton, one of our most liberal citizens of Philadelphia, who gave $100,000 for the purpose, to which he subsequently added $25,000 more for a library. He was a gentleman who had not received a collegiate education, but he felt the necessity of it, and desired that every young man who possibly could should have such an education, even though he might not want to be a lawyer, a doctor or a clergyman.

After our Kansas City convention the American Bankers Association had a little money on hand, which they still have, I am happy to say. Some one suggested the establishment of an institute for bankers. Seeing that that would simply result in a rivalry between New York and Chicago, to say nothing about Philadelphia and Boston, or San Francisco, it was suggested that a better thing might be done in endeavoring to promote the organization of schools like the Wharton School in connection with every college and university of the land, as far as it might be possible to do so, encouraging men like Mr. Wharton to give of their wealth to the founding of such schools. It was felt that the American Bankers Association would be doing a good work in fostering such a spirit and endeavoring to secure the establishment of schools of this kind in connection with every university in the land. Therefore, at Saratoga at our annual convention, Prof. James, of the Wharton School at Philadelphia, was invited to deliver an address, and he did so, in which he very clearly showed the necessity of the founding of such schools.

The bankers of the next generation will probably have to cope with men in every branch of life who have received the benefit of higher education, and they should be able to keep up with the procession. Men who have been educated in such schools should be the leaders among the banks. The presidents and cashiers and under-officers of the banks in the next generation will probably be—I may say there is scarcely a doubt that they will have to be. They should take a position in the banks of the present generation. There should be progress in this as well as in everything else.

4

The American Bankers Association has endeavored to disseminate this idea, and this last summer Prof. James was sent to Europe to investigate the schools there, and he is to deliver an address, if he gets here on time, at our convention. I lost him somewhere on the road. He returned from Europe two days after I left Philadelphia. He has not reached here yet, but I hope he will be here in time to give us the benefit of his investigations in Europe on the subject of education of business men. It is a subject that is very dear to me, and I hope that all of you will be interested in it and make it a business to come and listen to Prof. James's address.

I desire to thank you, gentlemen, for your attention. I have taken up rather more time than I intended to. [Applause.]

On motion of I. W. Hellman of San Francisco the convention adjourned until tomorrow, at 10 o'clock a.m.

SECOND DAY.

Tuesday, September 6—Morning Session.

The convention was called to order at 10 o'clock a.m., by Chairman Thomas Brown.

The Chairman: The Executive Council will now announce the committees appointed.

Lovell White of San Francisco: Mr. Childress, president of the Executive Council is absent today, and it devolves upon me to read this report.

The Executive Council recommend that C. B. Whittelsey of National City, James W. Findlay of San José and F. G. Menefee of Santa Cruz constitute the Auditing Committee for the ensuing year; and for the Nominating Committee, to present names to this convention for officers and members of the Executive Council: L. N. Breed of Los Angeles, H. H. Hewlett of Stockton, S. P. Young of San Francisco, Charles Cadwallader of Red Bluff and Ed R. Hamilton of Sacramento. For the Committee on Resolutions, who are to examine papers that are read here, with a view to their indorsement by this convention: John Richman of Fresno, Frank Miller of Sacramento and James D. Phelan of San Francisco.

On motion of O. J. Stough of San Diego the report of the Executive Council was received.

C. E. Palmer of Oakland: I would suggest that the Nominating Committee be allowed until 2 o'clock to make their report. They want to hear these papers read, and it might take a little too much time to wait for their report.

On motion of Mr. Palmer that the Nominating Committee be allowed until 2 o'clock to report, seconded by W. D. Woolwine of San Diego, it was so ordered.

The Secretary: The following telegram has been received from Monrovia:

"GEORGE H. STEWART,
        "Bankers Association, San Francisco:
                "Doctor will not allow me to take the trip to attend convention.   I most sincerely regret this.
                                                "E. F. SPENCE."*

The Chairman: The next business in order is the resolutions.

Lovell White: Mr. President, I suppose that any paper that has been read here, approval of which by this convention is requested, is of the nature of a resolution and will go to the Committee on Resolutions, and, as I propose to ask the indorsement of this convention to what I have to say on taxation, I presume it may come in at this time.

The Chairman: I think it very proper for it to be referred to the committee.   Mr. Lovell White will now address the convention.

Lovell White of San Francisco spoke as follows:

SOME MISTAKES OF THE TAX GATHERER.

It is not the purpose of this paper to show the uselessness of taxing mortgages as a means of distributing the burden of taxation; that such taxation has no effect is well understood by many, but until the fact is recognized by at least a majority of the voters of the State, it may be well to let those incapable of good, sound thought in this behalf indulge in the (to them) pleasing hallucination that the taxation of credits affords relief to the debtor class.

The assessment and collection of mortgage taxes costs the counties, cities and towns of the State in their corporate capacities, some $200,000 actual money disbursed for requisite stationery, and for hire of additional clerks.

Tl is item, important even to the wealthy State of California, was probably not fully considered by the framers of our revenue system, and it would, perhaps, be eliminated at an early day except for the fact that political bosses must have places at their disposal in the offices of assessors and tax collectors as a reward for the services of their adherents.

It being understood that the taxation of mortgages is a luxury for which payment must be made—with their taxation for State and county purposes there is relatively little fault to be found—rates of taxation do not vary much year by year, and interest rates can be fixed by estimate to meet them without doing much injury to either party.

To be sure there is the trouble and annoyance of making two returns to the assessor instead of one, and of two payments to the tax collector when one should serve, and there is also increased expense for the hire of additional clerks in the offices of the assessors and tax collectors, to be paid by the different counties—no inconsiderable amount—but, perhaps, all this personal inconvenience and public expense is compensated by the abiding satisfaction felt by those unskilled in political economy when they reflect that mortgages are taxed.

---

*Mr. Spence died at Los Angeles on the morning of September 19, 1892.   Resolutions of the Los Angeles Clearing-house are printed on another page.

While the taxation of mortgages is non-effective for the purposes that were in view when the new constitution was adopted, it cannot be said that it is positively injurious to either party to a loan, but such is not the case with municipal taxation of the same instruments, or of their taxation for special purposes, such as building school-houses, opening roads, etc.

Municipal taxes are relatively uncertain quantities. In some cities and towns they are limited by the charters or by law, but in a majority of cases they are at the discretion of the authorities, with the result that a tax one year may be one-half of one per cent and the next it may mount up to two, three, and even four per cent, as has been the case in some instances when public improvements of note have been undertaken at the cost of the municipality.

The uncertainty as to rate, coupled with the annoyance of making returns to two assessors and paying taxes to two collectors, has for its effect that money-lenders will not loan their funds on town property, except in the long established cities of very considerable population.

It is a well-known fact that the real estate owners in many new and thriving cities of California cannot secure loans from the institutions of the State engaged in the business of money lending.

Like usury laws in their operation, the attempt at legislation supposed to be in favor of the debtor has deprived the property-owner most in need of a loan of all chance of borrowing money.

As a rule the building of school-houses, the opening of new roads and like operations enhance the value of the real estate taxed to cover the expense.

When property is encumbered, the gain results to the mortgage debtor; in it the mortgagee has no part or lot, and to tax him for a share of the cost is precisely equivalent to compelling him to assist his debtor in the erection of his dwelling.

Why a mortgage creditor should be taxed for building a school-house and exempt from contributing to the expense of street improvements in a city is one of the many anomalies of our revenue laws.

The absurdity for taxing mortgages for special purposes needs but one illustration to be appreciated.

An owner of land in the San Joaquin Valley sold a large body to an association of colonists, taking a small cash payment and notes secured by mortgage for one year for deferred payments.

Within a year those thrifty colonists organized a school district, levied a tax and built a school-house costing $5000, the mortgage creditor, as his share of the tax, paying very nearly the whole cost, consuming practically the whole sum of interest by him received.

This was in effect a swindle, but one countenanced by the law and which may be repeated at the expense not only of the vender of lands, but of a creditor who lends money solely for the sake of the interest.

Fortunately for the business interest of the State mortgagees appreciate the injustice of requiring their creditors to pay special taxes, and neither expect nor demand of them so to do.

The moral sense of the debtor is superior or his business insight clearer than those of the good and wise men who frame our constitution and make our laws.

There is another form of credits which the State seeks to tax to the direct and serious detriment of the taxpayer. to-wit: the bonds issued for State, county and municipal indebtedness.

That it is absurd for a State to tax its own borrowing power must be conceded by every sensible person who will give the subject serious attention.

If governmental obligations are liable to taxation there must be added to what would otherwise be the rate of interest the tax rate. else the obligations will not find purchasers.

In other words. the Government must first pay its creditors in form of increased interest, the full rate it may claim to have returned in form of taxes.

Now, if such return was made. the public would be injured to the extent of cost of paying out with one hand while receiving with the other. but such is not the case, for as a matter of fact nine-tenths of the bonds escape taxation; some few are caught. say those loaned by money-lending corporations compelled to report their securities. and in the hands of administrators. executors, guardians. etc.

The total indebtedness of the counties of this State was, on June 30, 1890, $6,727,484. as per report of State Controller.

To this amount may safely be added for debts of cities. towns and school districts fifty per cent, say $3,363,742. making a total of $10,091,226.

Upon this large sum the taxpayers pay interest one and one-half per cent per annum. say $150,000 higher than the rate that would be demanded by bond buyers except for the fact that county. city and municipal bonds are taxable under the law. and as already mentioned. not one-tenth of the amount is returned to the public in form of taxes paid on bonds.

The escape from taxation is due to the fact that bonds are held by non-residents and by local parties with elastic consciences who contrive to shirk their share of the burden of supporting government.

Non-taxable bonds are a favorite investment; witness the prices at which United States and other exempt bonds are sold—place a tax on them and they cease to be desirable, for there is no competition for their purchase—they cease to be the next thing to cash—cash items as they are sometimes called. Not being readily salable in the market. they do not find a full place on the list of securities that savings and provident institutions may purchase or upon which they may loan money.

Competition for securities of any one class is the prominent factor in reducing the rate of interest thereon—the taxation of bonds diminishes the competition at least one-half. the result being a positive loss to the community for the benefit of bondholders non-resident or those within the State skilled in the matter of evading taxes.

Bonds of irrigation districts to the face value of $5,000,000, more or less. are seeking a market in this State, but they cannot be placed. the chief objection being that they will be taxable in the hands of purchasers.

For the same reason. bonds of various school districts linger in the hands of agents and brokers.

The wealth of the State would be increased by the watering of its arid lands, and sound public policy requires that facilities for education be afforded all the children in the commonwealth. but. important as these matters are, they must give way to the paramount necessity that no credits must be allowed to escape taxation.

It is often said of laws enacted or in contemplation that their tendency or effect is or will be to make the rich richer and the poor poorer.

This is eminently true of the taxation of bonds of irrigation and of school districts remote from centers of population. The tax is paid in the form of increased interest by real estate owners who stagger under their burdens, and is realized, if at all, by affluent counties and municipalities where reside the wealthy who invest in the purchase of bonds.

This paper is intended as a statement of points for consideration by this convention and by the public—no attempt has been made to support the positions taken by argument for the reason that lengthy papers are not supposed to be in favor with this Association.

For reasons herein given and others that may be urged, the revenue laws of the State should be amended in at least two particulars.

Mortgages should be exempted from taxation, except for State and county purposes.

Government bonds, by which is meant those on which interest is paid by a tax collected from the inhabitants of the State or from those of any fractional part thereof, should be absolutely free from taxation.

Such amendments would benefit the money-lenders and investors only by extending the field for the satisfactory employment of money.

The chief benefit would result to parties having occasion to borrow money on city or town property, and to inhabitants of municipalities and school districts where the public necessity compels the issuance of bonds.

If it is in order, I move that this paper be referred to the Committee on Resolutions, just appointed, with a view to its indorsement by this Convention.

Mr. White's motion being seconded and carried, it was ordered that the paper read by him be referred to the Committee on Resolutions.

The Chairman: We will now hear from Mr. E. S. Sheffield, of Santa Barbara.

E. S. Sheffield, cashier Santa Barbara County National Bank, of Santa Barbara:

Mr. President and Gentlemen of the Convention:

I have the honor to read to you this morning a paper on

THE DEVELOPMENT OF BANKING.

The chief reason for the existence of a business enterprise, from the point of view of its promoter, is that it produces profit; and the ways in which its profits come, determine the direction of its development.

Banking profit is made by lending, not money, but the banker's own credit, which, when loaned, takes the form of deposits, or of circulating notes; and he enables it to be used as money, by buying or exchanging it for real money, whenever its holders desire. Although a portion of it only is thus redeemed, the offer of redemption fixes the value of the whole, in the same way that the buying price of wheat fixes the value of all wheat capable of being marketed. So, but it yields a profit in proportion to the size of the fund kept to redeem it. If the redeeming fund or reserve must be large, the profit is less: if small, the profit is greater. It is, therefore, toward the lessening of the reserve — the more complete utilization of credit — that the business of banking has a tendency to develop.

The proportion needed of reserve to liability is determined by the degree of credit established and the skill of management exercised. The one acts by lessening the need; the other, by making more effective whatever is kept. The strength of the first, largely induced through an appeal to the imagination, is increased by the second, which more directly affects the pocket.

With perfect credit, save to settle balances, no reserve would be needed; with no credit, the reserve must equal the liability; consequently the proportion required is almost wholly a matter of feeling. Any proportion, however great, which fails to allay the apprehensions of the community, is insufficient. And, since the ability of banks to redeem all obligation as needed, depends on the willingness of the holders to wait redemption until needed, the confidence of one holder must be sustained by knowledge of like confidence in others. This is why a note issue is less desirable to banks than an equivalent in deposits. Circulating notes get into the almost exclusive possession of people who are not familiar with the mechanism of banks, in whom credit has not yet reached the stage of development attained by the depositing class.

Being poor judges of credit, such people are apt to run from an extreme of confidence to a panic of distrust. Owing to these characteristics, should panic occur, the notes are suddenly precipitated in a mass for redemption. To be prepared for this, a larger reserve must be maintained than is needed to guarantee deposits.

While it is perfectly true that through the use of credit bankers' profits come, it is no less true that its use must not be attempted until surely gained. It is not the banker's opinion, but the public sensitiveness that must be consulted. He who, presuming on credit, lends from his reserve too freely, is "killing the goose that lays the golden egg." Credit is more intangible than air; it must be coaxed and followed, never pushed or led: it cannot be manufactured; it grows, and grows slowly. Each year of faithful performance of promise adds an increment of strength to it: every failure to redeem obligation is a shock, partially paralyzing it. Still skillful management may do much to hasten its growth.

On the continent of Europe a real, or fancied, state guarantee is utilized to impress the imagination; in Great Britain giant banks, with a multitude of branches, similarly affect it; in the United States, where the banks are numerous and independent, but small, government regulation and inspection is supposed to assist. But the most powerful agency to strengthen credit experience has proven to be union.

This is seen in the massing of the reserves of the English banks at the Bank of England, where the imposing effect of an enormous quantity of money, available to liquidate bank obligations, steadies the nerves of the holders of those obligations, and prevents apprehension giving way to panic. It is also seen in the pooling of the reserves of the clearing-house banks of New York, through the issue of clearing-house certificates, of which there have been several instances; and again, in the Suffolk bank redemption system of New England—the parent of that devised for the national banks—which established confidence through the daily testing of credit.

The growth of credit in this country and also in England has proceeded so far that, already, whenever solvent banks unite to sustain credit, even in times of unreasoning panic, they succeed.

Witness the admirable treatment of the panics of 1860, of 1873, of 1884, and again of 1890, by the associated banks of New York. Witness the magical effect first produced on credit in London in 1825, when the Bank of England, holding the combined reserves of the English banks, decided in the midst of a panic, to lend them freely, an expedient repeated in each recurring crisis. Who doubts the value to credit of the mutual examination and the weekly statement of the New York clearing-house banks; and, although less effective, are not the examinations of national banks by Government agents worth, in favorably affecting credit, infinitely more than their cost?

What has been partly done by legislative authority, can be more perfectly accomplished through association. Given a union of banks, widely extended over the country, formed somewhat on the plan of the New York Clearinghouse Association, mutually agreeing to do business on certain safe lines, to submit to frequent examination by experts and periodical publication of condition; to combine reserves whenever the apprehensions of the public need allaying; and to take uniform and simultaneous means to prevent the exhaustion of floating capital in seasons of lessened production; would not the individual banks composing such an association enjoy a degree of credit, capable of utilization under an assurance of security, that would soon appear in their profit and loss accounts?

Such an association for self-protection would require in all its members a condition of solvency and the practice of safe methods.

This would discourage bad banking, weeding out of the association and ultimately out of the business unsafe institutions. Expulsion from such an association would be fatal to the credit of the expelled member, and lead to loss of business. Such an association once formed would grow, or would give rise to similar associations. Accretions of banks would strengthen it, until finally, no bank could command credit enough to do a profitable business outside; competition with institutions whose credit was superior would be hopeless.

A greater degree of safety could be expected from the operation of such an association than from any device imposed by statute. Examinations would mean far more than by State agency. Experts themselves, its members would be more capable of judging the character of the business conducted by the individual banks; could more effectually cure defective methods; and, being competitors, vitally interested in the solvency of each, their supervision over each other would in essentials be more strict.

Whether the union of banks suggested should take the form of one association, or of a number of rival ones, is not material; there are advantages in both. In the former there could be greater strength, but it might inspire the wish to reap the advantages of monopoly; if the latter, competition would remore danger of monopoly, and afford opportunity for the trial, side by side, of differing methods.

Perhaps a union of banks at money centers with their country correspondents, and a subsidiary union of the former through their respective clearing-houses, would be the natural course of development. Indeed, whatever of approach to association we already have, has begun on these lines.

But if we wish to set banking credit on an adamantine rock—to completely utilize it—some way must be devised to mutually insure deposits.

If all depositors felt absolutely sure that no loss could come to them by entrusting their means to banks; if bankers themselves felt the same degree of security as to their own deposits with other banks, reserves would become, not obsolete, but inactive, and could be diminished with safety.

Their use would be little except as a measure of value. No waste would then be incurred shifting coin from place to place as now. A depositor's money is equally effective to make payments while in the vaults of a bank as in his pocket: so, a balance due in one city or country could as effectually make payment in another as if transferred by shipment. Reserves, held in Calcutta, Hong Kong, London or New York, could remain in their respective places of deposit and their ownership only move. In this way the reserves of the entire banking world could be massed at the money centers, to guarantee or liquidate the liabilities of banks. Cost of exchange having been eliminated, the funds of the world would stand at a par. Rates of interest would tend to equalization through the greater mobility of capital, and the evil effects of bankruptcy, both by lessening in amount, and by being spread over a greater area, would be minimized.

Utopian as this may seem, it is the tendency of the business; changes as marvelous as this, to the eyes of the last century, have already taken place. Each year sees a smaller percentage of coin moved to payment made; and the time may come when it will not move at all.

It is not to be expected that so intimate a union as this implies could be brought about suddenly; nor would it be desirable that it should. Bankers have much to learn in the field of associated action before the proper conditions are understood; the true way is to attain it through a cautious and gradual approach.

The banker's reserve consists of two parts. One, maintained as a guarantee fund, drawn upon only when credit is failing or when the fixing of capital goes on more rapidly than a declining production warrants. The other, utilized to settle balances.

Skill of management is shown in effective measures applied to check the drain upon the former, and in the adoption of good devices to economize in the use of the latter. Before discussing the measures needed to check the drain on the guarantee fund, let us get a clear idea of the causes producing it.

We have heard that the small boy "cannot eat his cake and have it, too." Now, the skillful banker apparently can. He lends his money, and still has it to lend again. With him, it is observed, that as loans increase deposits increase correspondingly. The explanation is, that although seeming to do so, he does not in fact lend money; he lends credit; that is, he lends orders which will procure the things wanted by his borrowers or their assigns. And by basing his loans on things his borrowers have, or soon will have, to sell, he is enabled to cancel both loan and credit as the exchanges of things proceed, by offsetting one against another.

If a banker lends to borrowers to use in making permanent improvements, to fix capital, in other words, and the amount so invested exceeds his borrower's surplus production, or savings, he is lending out of the reserve—the heart-blood of the bank; and because the proceeds of such loans, directly or indirectly, are expended for things from elsewhere, and the salable product for cancellation is wanting, they will not, like loans of credit, reappear in the deposits. The banker, then, is truly lending money, but he lends as a capitalist, not as a banker, and receives capitalist's not banker's profits.

Such loans it is the banker's duty in his own interest to discourage; and so long as the State prohibits the application of the proper remedy he should select his borrowers, as an insurance company selects its risks, that the fixing of capital may not to his detriment take place.

The fixed capital of the country—that part invested in permanent improvements—increases year by year by conversions into it of surplus products or savings. If savings rapidly increase, a stagnation in business termed over-production can only be avoided by converting them more rapidly. Yet, as it is impossible to reconvert fixed into consumable capital should there occur a deficiency, in place of a surplus at a time when there is not a sufficient margin of floating capital to prevent stringency in the money market, and the banks fail to intervene, property will depreciate and financial interests suffer. At such time a drain sets in upon bank reserves; commodities being what banks have lent in the absence of other commodities for offset, real money is taken.

If the fixing of capital now continues loans expand while reserves fall—this is the tell-tale.

When a deficiency occurs, a check to the conversion into fixed capital is needed; and this check bankers, who are the chief dealers in capital, should be permitted to give by advancing the rate of interest sufficiently to make the fixing of capital an unprofitable operation.

Interest, even though it be usury, like price, has a beneficial function to perform. As price regulates the relative use of things, interest can regulate their general use. Let us examine how price acts beneficially, and the likeness to it of the action of interest.

A Robinson Crusoe, alone on a desert island, sees with his own eyes the condition of his granary, and limits consumption to the size of his harvest. Not so with the people of a large community; other eyes than physical are needed; each individual, subsisting by exchanging his own product for that of others, sees the condition of his own alone. If scanty, he raises the price; others, because of the higher price, consume less of it. So, by adjusting price to scarcity and consumption to price, the smaller product lasts until reinforced by a new production, which the higher price has stimulated; and the distress incident to scarcity is first palliated and then relieved. Just as produce dealers alleviate distress in times of scarcity, when, foreseeing light crops, they bid against each other, buy them up, and for their own profit advance prices, thereby inducing the necessary economy in consumption before dearth brings suffering, so bankers, by advancing the rate of interest in seasons of scant production of capital, may lessen the financial distress that always attends scarcity. Under the incentive of a higher rate capital is used with greater economy. Loans are reduced, or paid, and speculation is checked; released where it can be spared, it is available where it cannot be dispensed with, and enterprises that fix it will absorb it slowly or stop. Not only this, but individuals having means available to convert into fixed capital will refrain from such conversion, tempted by the better rate obtainable for loans.

Interest on money is a rent paid for the use of the things procured by its agency, and which by use can be made to produce a return that must exceed the interest to be paid, or the transaction would not take place; to advance the rate to a point where it exceeds the profit on fixed capital is the natural palliative for troubles arising from a scant production of capital, and is far less damaging than would be an undiscriminating reduction of loans. To advance it, also, when distrust exists, makes credit money less plentiful, and as it grows less in proportion to the reserve, adds to the appearance as well as the fact of safety. The refusal to loan on good security implies weakness, invites distrust, and if general leads to panic. Loans should always be obtainable at some rate, yet even were usury laws repealed banks could not act alone: one bank cannot continue discounting while all others cease; as already suggested, some bond between banks needs be forged, through which uniform action can be had.

While it obviously is the interest of bankers to absorb into their reserves all the real money of the community, that the credit money which they create may rest on a broader foundation, it is equally their interest to substitute their own methods of payment for all others; because, as these methods tend to a more economical use of that part of the reserve held to settle balances, it is equivalent to increasing its size. Bankers can only do this by making payments more cheaply, as well as more conveniently, than can others.

So late as 1875 it was the custom of the banks of the large commercial city of Liverpool to charge their depositors a commission of one-eighth to one-quarter per cent for the mere labor of paying their checks. The result was, that the bulk of the payments necessitated by the immense trade of the city were made with actual cash. A large volume of money which might otherwise have remained in the banks, swelling their deposits, adding to their profit and increasing their safety, was passing from hand to hand at great risk and expense. This commission, which is simply a charge for local exchange, can be defended on the ground only that the service is worth paying for; and on this ground only can some other charges for exchange be defended. Now, a charge for exchange is a species of friction in the machinery of banking, which, to the extent that it exists, defeats the great object for which bankers strive.

In anticipation of the time when it may be possible to abolish a rate for exchange between different countries, let us see if we cannot make progress in that direction as respects domestic exchange.

The problem of the collection of country checks has long worried the banking mind. Solution after solution has been proposed, but since the worry continues it evidently does not stay solved. Experience has taught that a wonderfully cheap way to make payments is to offset, or cancel, credit by credit, calling on the reserve to eliminate balances only.

Whatever we do in the logical line of banking method is cheaply done. It is the exceptional that is costly. Let us then cease treating country checks as exceptional things. Let us pass them through the clearing-houses at money centers, even though a separate daily clearing be demanded. Let customers' checks have printed on them the names of all clearing correspondents of the banks whose form it is. Let the correspondents of the country banks at such centers take all checks drawn upon their client-banks which appear in the exchanges of such city and debit and remit daily to each its respective checks for proper credit.

For country banks it would be much simpler to settle such remittances by entry and acknowledgment than to remit separately to many different places, as now.

For city banks it would be vastly more convenient to send all such checks daily to the clearing-house than to undertake separate collection. Their goodness could not, of course, be known so soon as local checks, but the difference would be merely that of time, which, on the average, would be less than by the present method. An objection might be raised that the city correspondent would be reluctant to advance the sums needed to make these clearings; one answer is that little money would be required. For, just as do city clearings, country clearings would on the average balance themselves.

But the effective answer is, that city banks already hold the very funds out of which these checks are now paid, placed with them partly for that purpose; so that it is solely a question of doing the thing, directly or indirectly. Again, let the habit of clearing country checks once be established, these balances would increase; for the aim of all bankers is to place their funds at the point where the demand upon them is to be made. It is an economy of time and expense to keep the larger stocks of money at the money centers, so every device which tends in that direction leads to the final form the banking interest is to take.

It is not needful to explain to city bankers the relative economy of settlement by clearing to settlement with each bank separately. The same economy would be found in clearing country checks. As no charge for collection of local checks is made, none should be made for country checks. The cost of providing funds to meet them should be borne by the country banker; most of them now supply their depositors with exchange free; all, with few exceptions, in their own interest should do so. By multiplying the reasons favoring deposits, deposits increase; furnishing exchange free is enlarging the convenience of the bank to the depositor. He finds, that in addition to safe storage for his money, he gains the use of it at distant points without expense, which he could not do outside of banks. He is thus encouraged to become a steady and permanent depositor, and his balance supplies the means to make these distant payments.

It is often thought that much depends on legislation to increase the safety of banks. The fact that the interests of the public are vitally connected with money matters, leads to the opinion that government should regulate. Unquestionably, if goverment were both wise and omnipotent, it might advantageously do so, but, being neither, it is hopeless to expect good from it.

The American Bankers Association long indulged the hope of favorably in-

fluencing legislation. Whether that hope survives, after years of disappointment, I do not know. Certain it is, that whatever the bankers of the United
States agree in wanting, that particular thing they cannot get from Congress.
Legislators are apt to regard the advice of bankers as interested; such advice
frequently is interested, and the average legislator is not qualified to discern
when it is not. Consequently legislation is generally harmful; it could not be
otherwise. Law-makers, inexperienced in banking, are imagined to be more
skillful than those who have made it a life study, and their interference puts
the business in leading-strings, which prevent a healthy development.

What have law-makers in their ignorance done? Taking advantage of the
usual indefinite term, describing the commodity bankers deal in, they have, by
legal tender and coinage acts, commanded it to be something different from that
intended.

Regulations intended to augment the circulation of banks, have, in the end,
operated to restrict it.

Regulations expressly designed to give confidence in the issues of banks,
actually did give rise to a belief in the power of law to bestow value, and,
through such belief, threatened the evils of fiat money, and a fluctuating
standard.

Before the war State laws regulating the establishment of banks operated
to bring into the business designing and inexperienced men, and by giving them
an apparent State certificate established for them a credit they were unworthy
of, and then, when they failed to fulfill their promises, other laws suspended
their obligation to do so, and thus kept them in a business they did not understand. By failing to compel fulfillment of their contracts, they thwarted the
natural action of the instinct of self-interest, which would have sifted the bad
from the good. And above all, like the fabled viper that "bit the hand that
warmed it", they have blindly struck at usury, their best defense against the ills
of bankruptcy arising from an undue fixing and waste of capital.

In fact, the history of American bank legislation is a shameful tale of unwise stimulation, of unwarranted privilege, of unhealthy restriction and of law-
produced distress. It has caused the spread of false theories, because, under it,
true principles had little chance to develop and become understood through
the experience of a natural growth.

The superiority of a natural development to Government regulation is seen
in the fact that all we now have of value to the business came in that way.
Attention has been called to the New York Clearing-house Association's
method of combining to resist panic to its habit of examination and its frequent
publication of condition, and to the Suffolk bank redemption device.

These are the more modern contributions, but the whole minutiæ of the
business devised to economize reserves, to convenience depositors, and to inspire confidence, is of voluntary growth.

Why cannot we trust that agency in the future, which in the past has done
so much for us? Why should banking more than shoemaking, than merchandising, or than farming, need Government regulation?

Is it not true that no one, not even a banker, can foresee the precise direction or degree of development that must take place to meet the ever-multiply-
ing, ever-varying wants of the public? And if so, is not both stimulation and
restriction harmful?

Let alone, banking will follow the natural course; unable to get profit without rendering a corresponding service, it will develop to serve the public more faithfully.

It has been said that the best legislation of the British Parliament of late years has been the repeal of former legislation. As much might be said of American legislation should all laws pertaining to money and banks be repealed.

Believing that the evils attributed to free banking are due to the interference of the State, resenting the opinion that our business unregulated is dangerous to the community, and desiring to be freed from the obloquy always thrown on a class supposed to be privileged, let the bankers of the United States ask nothing from the law, but to be placed on the same plane where stand our fellow-citizens in other lines of business—nothing for ourselves but what we can equally ask for all; for, as is well said by the poet:

> "That which is asked for self alone
> Is asked for the meanest creature known."

The Chairman: We will now hear from Mr. C. E. Palmer of Oakland.

Mr. Palmer addressed the Convention:

IMPRESSIONS OF A DELEGATE.

A year ago I was appointed delegate from California to the American Bankers Convention to be held at New Orleans November 11 and 12, 1891.

In speaking of my observations and experiences as a delegate to that convention, I think you will pardon me if I deviate from "strictly business" axioms and pass unnoticed such subjects of special interest to business men as irrigation bonds, mining industries, mortgage taxes, free coinage of silver, the Nicaragua Canal, the Pacific cable and other subjects of like interest, and leave the preparation of papers on these topics to maturer minds.

My aim is rather to tell of what I saw and thought; and, by way of deduction therefrom, to impress upon my fellow business men the importance of occasional recreation to health and happiness.

It was through the kindness of Mr. Childress, our worthy and esteemed president of the Executive Council, that I was chosen by this Association to attend the annual convention at New Orleans.

When Mr. Childress asked me if I would go, I was so profoundly amazed that I did not consider the responsibility attending the honor about to be conferred upon me.

The compliment was so unexpected and flattering, it touched my vanity so strongly, that I could not say emphatically No.

So in the rush of closing the convention, and through the generosity or politeness of the members in omitting to nominate someone in opposition, I was unanimously elected.

The next day, as I met my old friends and acquaintances, I began to realize the gravity of the situation.

I wondered what they thought of me going on so important a mission.

The first time after my appointment, when I met Mr. Sessions, president of the Oakland Bank of Savings, he congratulated me very cordially. I next met Mr. Garthwait, the cashier of the same bank; after he had asked me a few unimportant questions about how I was chosen, he spoke very pleasantly and kindly of the affair and wished me a pleasant time.

I next met another cashier of our city: he said: "What is this I see in the papers about your going to New Orleans?" I briefly stated the case to him. He then asked, "Do we bankers have to pay your expenses?" Fearing what might come next, I hastily replied that they did not. He had nothing further to say.

Mr. Martin, president of the Union Savings Bank, was the next to meet me with a twinkling eye. He stroked his flowing beard very gracefully and cordially congratulated me in his usual polite manner.

The expression assumed by some of my boyhood acquaintances, however, was a little peculiar. They were evidently nonplussed; but I bore my blushing honors with dignified demeanor, and it soon became an established fact that I should attend the convention in that quaint old city, famed for its Creoles and its carnivals.

One of our tellers had not taken his vacation, and my going at this time imperiled his chances of getting his usual summer outing. You can imagine his looks and feelings. My appointment touched him in a tender spot, and had it not been for the hearty encouragement and very willing assistance of Mr. Prather, the president of our bank, I am sure I would have declined the honor and remained at my post; and so have lost the most pleasant, and I believe the most profitable, three weeks of my life.

Up to the moment of my departure I wanted to back out; I thought I ought not to leave my work for others. I thought of several things, private and public, that might require my attention. At last with the greatest reluctance I started, five days before the date of the convention.

I will not occupy your valuable time by relating the incidents of the trip, but I must be permitted to say that much of the pleasure attending it sprang from the agreeable company met on the way, particularly that of Hon. E. F. Spence (president of the First National Bank of Los Angeles) and his estimable wife, who joined our party at Los Angeles. They, too, were on their way to New Orleans.

Mr. Spence knows how to travel and enjoy all the changes and charms and extract all the sweetness possible. His puns, jokes and anecdotes almost transformed the Colorado desert, and made it bloom as the rose; and with the flashes of his fruitful fancy the Texas norther became like a San Francisco zephyr.

From San Antonio to New Orleans we traveled through immense fields of rice, cotton and sugar cane, growing on a soil as rich and fertile as the sun ever shone upon.

Reaching our destination on the fifth day from Oakland, we stopped at the old historic St. Charles Hotel, the headquarters of the Bankers Association.

One of our party remarked, upon our arrival, that at 11 o'clock "the great Louisiana lottery drawing would take place." So we all went down to the opera-house and witnessed it.

Afterward we visited the cemeteries, which attract all sightseers. From

the nature of the soil all the tombs are above ground.   Some are very costly
and beautiful structures of marble, iron and brick.

We then visited Lake Ponchartrain, a great pleasure resort, about five
miles north of the city.

The most important sight, however, of New Orleans, and perhaps the most
picturesque to be seen in America, is the French Market, which comprises
several buildings on the levee near Jackson Square.

The city is not rich in architecture, but there are a few noteworthy buildings.   Chief among these is the custom-house, built of Quincy granite.

Wednesday, November 11, the convention assembled.   There were present
about 150 delegates.   Among them were prominent bankers from nearly all
the States.

There were some very able papers read; but as you have probably all seen
an account of the proceedings, I need not comment on them further than to
say that the entire two days' programme was particularly interesting to me.

The social features of the convention seemed to be in experienced and
energetic hands.   The principal clubs of New Orleans were thrown open to all
the delegates and everything that could conduce to their comfort was most
lavishly bestowed.

There was a special performance of *Rigoletto* given at the French Opera-
house in honor of the Association, and tickets were presented to all the delegates and to the ladies accompanying them.

Only those who have visited New Orleans and attended the grand French
opera, can appreciate what a treat we had, for no other city in America sup-
ports such opera.

As it was my first visit to the South, the excursions to the immense sugar
plantations, the great works of machinery for making sugar, and the beautiful
homes of the wealthy planters, gratified my curiosity and afforded me unusual
pleasure.

For hospitality and courteousness I am now convinced the Southern people
are unequaled.

I was not at all anxious to leave the sunny South and its varied attractions.
I was impressed with its productiveness, I was charmed with its natural
beauties.

Another thing that impressed me deeply, during this excursion, was the
grandeur and resources of our country.

One cannot pass through the great State of Texas without giving it a
thought, for the resources and varied products of Texas are beyond the comprehension of the average man.   I think, in respect to products and outward
features, the difference between our States—as for instance between California
and Vermont, or between Florida and Montana—is as great, I imagine, as between England and Egypt, or between Europe and Africa.   We have, in a
sense, the world within our borders.

I became so impressed and enthused over the beauties and possibilities of
this great continent, that when we reached San Antonio, Tex., on our return
trip, we ran down to Laredo, a little town on the Mexican border, and there
bought tickets for the City of Mexico.

On our way down we stopped over Sunday at the beautiful historical old city of Monterey, with its flowering gardens, running springs and streams of limpid water, its plazas and parks enlivened with bands of music playing in every direction, and soldiers everywhere—it seemed to me as if half the population were soldiers.

Our next stop was at the great City of Mexico, the oldest city perhaps on the continent, with a population of about 450,000. After sight-seeing a couple of days we ran down to Vera Cruz, passing through Puebla (the home of the Mexican onyx), also through Cordova, where we wandered through the immense coffee plantations, fields of bananas, pineapples and cocoanut palms. On this little run we had an imposing view of the snow-capped crests of several extinct volcanoes, two of them looking down on the City of Mexico from an altitude of over 17,000 feet.

After stopping over Sunday in the City of Mexico, we turned our faces homeward. I found the vegetable products of the country varied in the extreme, owing to the diversified climate.

The productiveness of Mexico is, perhaps, unsurpassed by any other country on the globe.

The soil produces all the cereals and all the fruits of the United States and Europe.

Among the cereals the most abundant is Indian corn, which grows almost everywhere — in some places two crops a year. This is eminently a Mexican staple, serving as nutriment for man and beast and forming the "staff of life" when made in the form of cakes called tortillas.

The Mexicans claim $5,000,000 per year for their coffee; $10,000,000 to $12,000,000 for their cotton, etc., etc.

Nature has certainly showered her gifts upon the republic with a lavish hand.

Her mines are practically inexhaustible, and her forests rich in every variety of precious woods.

Her most populous cities are at an altitude of from 6000 to 8000 feet.

I would enjoy telling you more of the interesting features of Mexico, but I know these benches are hard, and many think more of the social features than they do from nature's resources and of figures and statistics. So I will relieve you of further patient endurance in listening to this subject, and take up another by way of conclusion.

Upon my return home I resumed my regular duties, feeling that bankers' conventions were a grand success.

I felt better myself, and I felt better toward every one around me.

Right here is where the true value of these conventions comes in; for as sure as you live, to succeed in life a man must have a healthy body and a cheerful mind; and too close confinement will not produce these. But recreation, change of scenery and the enjoyment of travel promote pleasant thoughts and develop a taste for the beauties of nature, such as abound in our own Golden State.

We should all visit Yosemite, Lake Tahoe, Yellowstone, the hundreds of other places where we might hold undisturbed communion with nature in all her primitive beauty, simplicity and grandeur.

6

The necessity of the president and cashier always being at their desks is greatly imaginary.

The deposits will not decrease nor the loans increase.

The chief officers should throw some of the responsibilities on others, and teach them the details of the business.

We are all liable to sickness or accident, and where would your bank be without any one who is familiar with your duties.

Try it once or twice a year.

Lay aside your burden for a time and I am sure you will find a great change in your disposition; you will find renewed enjoyment in your home with your family and with your friends.

You will greet your clients more cordially; they will all think more of you; they will readily discern that your mind is more cheerful. Expand your ideas and your business will grow in proportion.

If you are not amiable to others you cannot expect them to be agreeable to you.

I claim that this advice, if followed, will prove a good business investment, as well as a lasting pleasure.

Try it, gentlemen, and if it improves you as it has improved me, you will be more than doubly paid.

You will find the pleasures of recreation grow, trip by trip, until you are ready to exclaim, with that wise mathematician of old. "Eureka."

It is difficult for me to speak of these fascinations, as they have been impressed upon me, and yet avoid the use of terms that are liable to the suspicion of exaggeration.

But while we are taking such good care of ourselves, we must not forget the teller and book-keeper.

If you will allow me one moment more, I will give you the benefit of my thoughts in this particular also; I believe these attaches of the bank should have their regular annual vacation of say two weeks, to be spent among the mountains or in communion with Nature in her most cheering phases.

When you get a good man, who has arduous duties to perform, do not fear to give credit where credit is due. Let him have a taste of the real joys of life. We are always ready to criticise, but never to praise, to exact, but seldom to yield. We love to point out a mistake, but how loathe we are to applaud a thing well done. How short-sighted is such a policy. What is there more stimulating in the hard business world of today than honest approval openly given.

I believe there are men in office or bank to whom an honest "you have done that well" would mean more than any addition to salary. Everybody's goal is not the almighty dollar. A good man is never spoiled by an honest word of praise. Let us be free to give encouragement when occasion requires.

I take this opportunity of thanking you, gentlemen, for my very enjoyable trip. My modesty forbids me claiming any credit, but it is rather a strange coincidence that the next American Bankers Convention following my appearance in that body in New Orleans should be held in California. But I most generously and cordially waive all the honors naturally accompanying that achievement, and ask this honorable body that they be transferred to our worthy friend, Mr. Spence, who did so much to make my trip a source of pleasure and of profit to myself.

A. Gerberding of San Francisco: I am requested by Mr. Thompson, the chairman of the Committee on Entertainment of the American Bankers Association, to state to you that this evening between the hours of 8 and 10 o'clock there will be an informal reception in the parlors of the Palace Hotel.

This meeting tonight is merely for the purpose of making our Eastern friends acquainted with our California bankers who may be present in the city at the time. The committee has felt that while their work has been to prepare entertainment for our Eastern friends, that all the California bankers belonging to this Association should stand in with them and help them through. Therefore, it is requested that you be present this evening and help us in the pleasant duty of introducing our friends and getting acquainted with them.

I wish to state further that on Friday next an excursion about the bay has been arranged for, and on that excursion you are expected to be part of this committee and stand in with us.

Tickets for that excursion are to be had from the registry clerk at the door, and it is suggested that the excursion will be more delightful if you bring your wives and sisters and aunts and cousins, and possibly other people's wives.

And, as Mr. Palmer has just said that he succeeded in bringing the American Bankers Association to San Francisco, I will state that the committee has succeeded in making Friday a legal holiday; therefore there is no excuse for your remaining away, you can all go on the excursion and have a pleasant time. [Applause.]

E. M. Preston of Nevada City: Mr. President, in the addresses that have been delivered this morning there have been a number of practical suggestions as well as much that is instructive and entertaining.

One of the practical suggestions, it seems to me, is worthy of very serious consideration and of adoption by this convention, and that is the one that is contained in the address by the gentleman from Santa Barbara in regard to the clearing of customer's checks. It seems to me that that ought to be referred to the proper committee, with a view to bringing it before this convention for adoption. I move that the portion of the address delivered by the gentleman from Santa Barbara referring to a clearing-house for customers' checks to be referred to the committee, with that purpose in view of having it adopted by the convention.

Mr. Preston's motion was seconded, and, on vote being had, was carried.

C. C. Bush of Redding: I would ask if there is anything before the convention until the hour of adjournment, 12 o'clock?

The Chairman: I know of nothing, sir.

C. C. Bush: Well, sir, I move that there be a little reunion, a general introduction held right here, so that we may be able to get acquainted with one another, and that Mr. Stewart or some one else who is well acquainted introduce the various members to anyone they wish to meet. I find it very embarrassing after seeing gentlemen here to meet them on the street and be unable to call them by name or locate them. We might have a little reunion here and be introduced to one another. I think it would be not only pleasant, but beneficial in the end.

John Reichman of Fresno: I second the motion.

The Chairman: I think that is a very good suggestion. I understand that Mr. Gerberding, the Bank Commissioner, will undertake to make everybody acquainted.

Mr. Bush's motion being put to vote was carried.

On motion, the convention took a recess until 2 o'clock P. M.

AFTERNOON SESSION.— SEPTEMBER 6, 2 O'CLOCK.

The convention was called to order at 2 o'clock P.M.

The Chairman: Gentlemen of the convention, we will have an address by Mr. James D. Phelan of San Francisco on the subject of "The World's Fair." [Applause.]

James D. Phelan of San Francisco:

Mr. President and Gentlemen of the Convention:

I am associated with the local management of the World's Fair and that is my apology for speaking upon this subject, having been requested by the secretary.

On account of the peculiar character of this organization, composed altogether of bankers, financiers, I thought it would be most interesting and advantageous to you to know something of the business of the management of the World's Fair, rather than rhetorical passages, sentimental illusions, perhaps, to the event which we are about to celebrate at Chicago, and, as little has been known of the management of the fair, by reason of the fact that the people in Chicago work very quietly and very effectively, and, as the facts I will state were brought out recently by the investigating committee appointed by Congress, when the Columbian Exposition asked for more money, the information which I give you might be said to be new.

It is hardly proper, though, in referring to the World's Fair, not to make some reference to the event, and I see, in referring to the event, that I may point a moral which will be of interest to this convention.

Perhaps the discovery of America is the most important event in secular history. Columbus was the man and the occasion was at hand, and, still, wherever he went, he received very little aid, very little encouragement, and, as you are aware, he first proposed to his own townspeople the distinguished honor of the discovery of America, the discovery of the new world, the existence of which he had no doubt; but they rejected his plans and described them as chimerical, futile. He then went to Spain, and, through the aid of Isabella, he was enabled to reach the sovereign, Ferdinand, and, after considerable ne-

gotiation, in which very few men took much interest, he was allowed some
1,140,000 pieces of silver, called marvides, and a draft was made on the
people and the shipping of the port of Palos, in Spain, to provide him with a
crew and to provide him with three ships, within a very short time. That is
the way they had in those times. Of course, the people of Palos, who did not
know Columbus or have any confidence in his plan, refused to do anything of
the kind, but proceeded in a negative or desultory sort of way, not wishing to
put themselves in opposition to the king. It was a critical moment for Columbus and his plan, and, at that time, a very wealthy man, a financier, for aught
I know, a banker, certainly a large ship-owner and ship-builder, by the name
of Pinzon came to the aid of Columbus, and, respecting the ships, they were set
aside for his use; he provided three new vessels out of his own means, he pro-
visioned them for a year out of his own means, and, to the amount received
from the crown, he added 500,000 more pieces of silver. Such was his confidence in Columbus, such was the character of his mind, as to seize the idea of
its possibilities, long before the discovery, and give it the means, fruition and
accomplishment.

We may regard the discovery of America as a great speculative undertaking,
because Columbus had a contract with the Spanish crown by which he was to
receive but a small portion of the wealth that awaited him in the West. But
this banker, this man of money, actually had no written or even verbal agreement with Columbus, so far as history shows, for a share of the profits or for
financial reimbursement. He must have known, considering the stupendous-
ness of the undertaking, that his name would, and I think his name should, go
down in history, side by side with that of the discoverer; but we never hear
his name mentioned, because the man who originates the idea, and perhaps
correctly—history has always done so—receives all the credit; but he needed
credit from his banker, to carry out that idea, and that credit, happily, Columbus
got. And that is why we are here, that is why America was discovered.

That event is fittingly celebrated by a world's fair, because a world's fair
is an acquainting of one people with another, the introduction of new ideas,
the commingling of nationalities, a making patent to all of what theretofore
remained hidden in commerce and trade; and it is singularly proper that a
world's fair should be the form of this celebration which is to signalize the
quadro-centennial of the discovery of America, and perhaps Chicago is a very
fitting place for it to be held. I don't know of any city in America that better
represents American energy and enterprise than Chicago. Everything there is
on a gigantic scale, and that city will be a grand exhibit in itself. The fact that
Chicago is an interior city will also add very much to the success of the exposition, from the point of view of the observer, because it will compel foreign
peoples to travel from the seaboard, and that trip over a thousand miles, for a
day and night, in sumptuous palace cars, passing through a diversified country,
affording a view on the way of Niagara Falls, will be another exhibit of American progress and American enterprise.

There is only one circumstance which is at all likely to cause a failure of
this vast undertaking, greater than any other fair ever laid out or planned,
and that is the introduction of cholera into this country, either this year or in
the spring. It is a very serious matter, and, although Chicago is an interior
city, this in no way lessens the danger of contagion spreading in that part of

Illinois, for the reason that the sanitary condition of Chicago is not good. Last fall the Chicago river backed up to an extent unprecedented. The water supply of the city of Chicago is derived from the lake at points two miles and four miles from the shore, and such an overflow interferes with the water supply. At a time when the population of the city is greatly augmented the danger would be increased, and, if the cholera should threaten the world at the opening of the fair, I am afraid that the World's Fair would have to be postponed, and, as you can't postpone enthusiasm, I think this would seriously affect the finances of the fair, if not cause a financial disturbance which would be very serious to those people who have made large investments. These are the dangers that are threatened, unless the cholera is turned aside by improved sanitation or by the grace of God.

We must regard this as a business venture, and I will take that view of it in discussing it with you here this afternoon.

The Paris Exposition buildings covered a comparatively small space. The buildings which are planned for the World's Fair cover 159 acres of land, and the largest buildings, the Manufacturers and Liberal Arts buildings, cover 30 acres alone. Then there are immense spans, 380 feet from point to point, rising some 250 feet and extending over a building 1700 feet long, which is the largest building ever constructed in the world, giving an unobstructed view of 1700 feet by 380 feet, which is due to the magnificence of these arches and their extent, extending from one point to another 380 feet. Engineers have gone from all over the world to see that building. Everything connected with the exposition is in proportion. The cost is no small item, and it is the figures which will probably most interest you. I have from Chicago this week authenticated reports which I will be glad to submit to you.

It will cost for construction and to open this vast exposition, $15,911,-459; for the departments, to March 1, 1892, $608,385; temporary organization, $90,675, making a total cost of $16,610,519, to open the exposition.

That is their great struggle now, to get the money to open the exposition.

A list of the operating expenses until the closing of the exposition, by departments, shows these figures:

For construction $2,263,905
The executive 80,425
The secretary's office 55,148
The legal department 25,520
The auditor 51,675
The World's Congress auxiliary 41,350
The treasurer 74,125
Medical and surgical department 41,248
Ways and means 184,000
Press and printing 7,000
Committee on Ceremonies 422,900
Traffic manager 39,415
Grounds and buildings 13,850
Agriculture 85,923
Horticulture 112,103
Live stock 220,985
Fish and fisheries 25,185
Mines and mining 67,295
Machinery 92,987
Transportation 68,517

```
Manufactures.................................................. $    86,788
Electricity...................................................      84,449
Fine arts....................................................      244,787
Liberal arts.........................................$100,000
Music.................................................. 491,966   591,966
Ethnology, archæology, etc................................      157,094
Forestry.............. ..................................       31,808
Publicity and promotion ...................................      228,900
Foreign affairs......................................  ........   50,000
Insurance, buildings...............................$230,000
                Accident ...................... 6,235           236,235
Rent and other office expenses after October 30, 1892...........   25,000
Expenses, except rent, and not otherwise estimated.............   160,000

                                                              $22,481,102
Add 1 per cent for expenses of various kinds not anticipated.....  224,811

    Grand total of expenditures...............................$22,705,913
```

You will appreciate these figures when you remember that at the great Paris Exposition of 1889 the total receipts were only about $9,000,000.

Now, as against that, the income is a very interesting study.

I don't know that it is generally understood that, by act of Congress, approved by the President in April, 1890, the World's Columbian Commission was organized, and, at that time that body, which consisted of two members from each State in the Union and eight at large, divided equally between the great political parties, was authorized to receive the buildings from the World's Columbian Exposition, which is an organization under the laws of the State of Illinois. The duty of the commission created by Congress was to deal directly with the exhibitors, and with foreign exhibitors more particularly, and it was their duty to receive the buildings, which were to be provided and paid for by the World's Columbian Exposition, as distinguished from the commission created under the laws of the State of Illinois.

Now, that commission started out to raise the money for carrying on this fair, and they got public subscriptions to 550,000 shares at $10 a share, which made $5,500,000. Then they induced the city of Chicago to bond itself for $5,000,000. Then they endeavored to get money from the United States Government, the history of which movement is familiar to you on account of it being but recently mentioned in the newspapers. They started out with the intention of getting $10,000,000, and finally they said they would be satisfied with $5,000,000, and, when the opposition increased, they said that they did not want a pure donation, but that they would mortgage the gate receipts for the amount, and, in the confusion of the last days of Congress, a compromise was effected which shows, certainly, the skill of the Chicagoan in financiering, because they actually got their $5,000,000 as a pure donation, without any conditions and without mortgaging their gate receipts; so their receipts from all sources are not incumbered or in any way out of the reach of the subscribers to the original fund, who will probably derive large amounts in dividends. It was done by a compromise by which 5,000,000 half-dollar souvenir pieces were freely given to the World's Columbian Exposition for the purpose of carrying out their plans, and they at once, by judicious advertising and by news-paper notices or proposals, brought about an offer to buy the $2,500,000 for

$4,000,000. They worked up a sentiment and gave sentimental value, which bankers never understand or know, to these souvenir coins, of $2,500,-000, in about ten days, and the sales have actually been made. Mr. Shepard of the Mail and Express of New York, bought $10,000 worth, receiving for $10,000, 10,000 50-cent pieces, but they were souvenir pieces and he was satisfied with the sentimental value which had been added, knowing that there would be probably 30,000,000 people attend the fair and there would be a demand for them.

It is hardly to be understood that such a real enhancement of value occurred, but they put in their official statement, "United States Government appropriation, 500,000 souvenir coins, $2,500,000 premium on coins $2,-500,000," making $5,000,000, which we add to the subscription of $5,000,-000, the bonds of the city of Chicago $5,000,000. Then comes salvage, which is estimated low, $1,750,000; income from various sources, interest, refunds, etc., $500,000; gate receipts, $200,000 per day, 150 days, 30,000,-000 people at 50 cents each, $15,000,000; concessions, $2,642,000.

The Paris Exposition, which was a stupendous undertaking and which was the greatest up to the present time, received only $434,000 from its concessions.

The World's Fair concessions of $2,642,000 are made to private concerns, to carry on various kinds of business and manufacture articles of interest to the people, which will find a ready sale to the market, and these concessions have been granted, as a rule, on the basis of 25 per cent of the gross receipts, to be returned to the local directory, as we call it, of the World's Columbian Exposition Company of Chicago.

There is one item of the concessions, popcorn, which seemed to surprise every one. I happened to be in Chicago at the time invitations for proposals for the sale of popcorn were made. Bidders were required to put in certified checks of $10,000 each, and on that occasion twenty-five men competed for the privilege of the sale of popcorn, putting up, pending the decision of this momentous question, $250,000. Finally the concession was granted to a man on the basis of the return of 62½ per cent of the gross receipts to the commission, he offering that in lieu of a cash payment of $75,000, and they accepted the 62½ per cent. There seems to be a demand for popcorn in that part of the world.

I have a list of the concessions which have been given: Barre Railway, American Glassware, Street in Cairo, Street in Constantinople, "Puck"—that is the New York illustrated paper, "Puck." One of the conditions of the concession to "Puck" is that no religious or political allusion be made to anyone, which takes the pucker out of "Puck." Ten per cent of the gross receipts is to be paid for the privilege of giving "Puck" a place on the grounds. Next on the list are Esquimau Village, Intramural Railway, Lake Transportation, Lagoon Transportation. By lake and lagoon transportation one can pass from one building to another. They charge a fee for passage from one place to another by this means. You may also move around the grounds by the Intramural railway. Then come the Observation Tower, Mineral Spring Waters, Panoramas, of which there are two, Captive Balloon, Chocolate and Cocoa Houses, Venetian Glass Factory, Austrian Street, Japanese Bazar, Chinese Theater,

Hungarian Café, Moroccoan Village, Algerian and Tunisian Village, Dahomey Village. Ice Railway, South-Sea-Island Settlement, East Indian Village. Amer, ican Indian Village, Bohemian Glass Palace. Then come the restaurants-cafés, etc., which will pay $3,250,000; entertainments. $300,000; miscellaneous, $1,000,000; making a grand total of $40,042,000.

In regard to the income, you will notice that the popular subscription to date is $5,600,000. This is given as a net amount, the exposition anticipating a loss of about 6 per cent on the total amount subscribed from deaths, failures, etc. This amount of loss, therefore, is not included.

The bonds issued by the city of Chicago are upon the same basis as the stock subscriptions. They are to be repaid pro rata with the stockholders The dividends to be returned to the city are not to exceed the $5,000,000 furnished. This practically makes the stock subscriptions $10,600,000.

The balance in favor of the exposition at its close will be approximately $18,000,000. This is to be returned as follows: Five million dollars to the city of Chicago, and the remainder, $13,000,000, to the stockholders, who have subscribed $5,600,000, which, you will see, leaves approximately $8,000,000 to be returned as dividends, in excess of the amount subscribed.

The Chicagoans had in view the immense receipts to be derived from this undertaking. The figures are glowing, but, with a very high rate of loss (not anticipated), the stockholders in Chicago are justified in being reasonably sure of a return of full value for subscriptions made. When they enter an undertaking of this kind, it is reasonable to suppose that they have some way of getting out. which I never appreciated until I studied these figures, but there will probably be a balance of $8,000,000 in favor of the subscribers, who are principally citizens of Chicago.

Of course they take all the risks in the matter, and they are also ready in an undertaking of this kind to borrow money from any source in order to carry out their plans.

I saw, the other day, a reference to the characteristics of the people of the different States of this country which I thought pertinent. The astronomical situation of Mars developed that there were probably inhabitants thereon. A paragrapher of Boston said, "Well, if there are people on Mars, we will learn something from them." New York said, "If Mars is populated we will sell something to them," and Chicago said, "If there are people on Mars we will borrow from them."

You will notice that the total amount necessary to open the exposition is $18,000,000. The available funds on hand are approximately $15,000,000. This leaves a deficiency of $2,400,000 to be raised for immediate use. It is the purpose of the exposition to issue bonds, bearing 6 per cent interest. for this amount, these bonds to be paid on or before May 1. 1894, at the option of the exposition.

The directors have never felt that the undertaking would not be a financial success, but the financial problem has been to secure the necessary funds for a proper opening of the gates. Of course, if the receipts anticipated are realized, there will be no difficulty, if the full amount necessary to open the exposition be secured.

7

If you will compare these figures with those of the Paris Exposition you will find that the outlay to open here is approximately $10,000,000 in excess of the actual outlay which was required to open the gates there.

At the Paris fair, in 1889, there were 55,000 exhibitors; it was open 183 days; there were 28,149,000 admissions at the gate, and the whole receipts were $8,300,000.

The estimates upon the various concessions are based upon information gleaned from all possible sources.

It might be interesting to you to know the manner in which the attendance is figured. If you draw a circle around the city of Chicago, having a radius of 500 miles, you will find that, within that circle, there lives a population of 20,000,000 people; also that each person within that circle can go to Chicago and return for not to exceed $10 each for railroad fare.

The exposition, therefore, assumes that the total number of admissions will be equal to one and one-half the population within the described circle. This number of admissions, distributed over the civilized world, will, you see, make a very small percentage of the total population. It will, in fact, reduce it to a very reasonable percentage of the people who are in a financial position to travel in luxury and see that which pleases them most.

You will also notice that the estimate of income from restaurants is $3,250,000. The history of former expositions teaches us that the total receipts by restaurants within any exposition is equal, approximately, to the total receipts of said exposition. This is a very peculiar coincidence, which has been established by facts and figures in all recent European expositions.

Assuming these figures to be correct, and we having established the basis that all restaurants and cafés must pay a tax of not less than 25 per cent of the gross receipts, the estimate is approximately correct.

There are numerous other channels through which a very material income will be derived, but, in order to allow for shrinkage which may occur in the estimate given, those items are not quoted.

We have seen, then, the immense fund which will be raised for the purpose of this exposition.

In addition to that, the States and Territories of the Union have actually raised and are now expending some $3,182,500.

I have an authentic list of the States and Territories that have made appropriations, and the amounts, but will simply say that Illinois has made the largest appropriation, it being $800,000; that of New York, Pennsylvania and California follow, with $300,000 each, and the least State appropriation is that of Delaware, $10,000. These appropriations, thirty in number, aggregate $3,182,500.

California passed a law appropriating $300,000, and, at the same time, giving the counties of the State the privilege of raising money, in such amount as they saw fit, in proportion to their class. Now, these counties have either appropriated or shown a desire and an intention, through their boards of supervisors, of appropriating some $150,000, the items of which I will submit to your secretary.

In closing I will say that this seems to be a great opportunity for California. We are very remote from the Eastern seaboard, from the centers of population and wealth, and we have a State which is worthy of exhibition. I think, in every department, hardly without an exception, California may make an exhibit which will vie with the best, and in two or three win prizes against the world, and, when that becomes known, it will be, so far as we are concerned, a great advertising medium, and California will be benefited.

Since the last census we know that the Sacramento Valley, probably one of the richest sections of the world, has not increased appreciably in population for years. What we desire out here is population to develop our resources, and a market in the East and Europe for the sale of the products of the soil. While the World's Fair will attract settlers, by reason of the show California will make, at the same time it will make a market for our products if our enterprising people will take advantage of all the opportunities which will be given them.

The easy and natural growth of California, its periods of transition from one stage of development to another, is a subject which will admit of striking illustration. Note the period of growth, covering but the short space of our State's life, or less than fifty years. Wonderful to narrate, the upbuilding of the commonwealth and its development have all been accomplished within the memory of the living: the admission of the State, then the stages of development of the country, the marvelous production of gold, followed by agriculture, giving a stupendous output of gold, wheat and other cereals, and all of them being produced at one time. The most remarkable fact of all is that, while we pass from one stage to another, it is not by the abandonment of any; side by side, live stock, mining, agriculture, horticulture, find abundant room, generous rivalry and greatest development.

Why should California be modest, unless we regard modesty as the chastity of merit? [Applause.]

C. C. Bush of Redding: I was very much interested in the gentleman's address. I would like to know, however, if I understood correctly, that in the handling of $66,000,000 he stated the charges for legal services were only $25,000. I would like to have that verified by the gentleman's direct assertion if it is true that the law is as cheap as that in Chicago.

Mr. Phelan: They have an attorney under salary, at $6000 a year, Benjamin Butler, and his tenure of office being but one year, the difference between $6000 and $25,000 is the sum for contingent expenses.

The Chairman: Gentlemen, we have present here today Mr. Nelson, president of the American Bankers Association. I know the convention would like to have a few remarks from him.

Richard M. Nelson of Selma, Ala.:

Mr. President and Gentlemen:

I returned on the Sunday night preceding the 25th of August from 11,000 miles of travel; I found a considerable quantity of correspondence lying on my table, and, among the letters I opened I found one from this Association kindly inviting me to be present here with you and to make an address. Within seventy-two hours, therefore, I started for California. I wrote no special acceptance because I thought if I did you might expect a formal address, and you will readily appreciate that a man who has traveled 11,000 miles is not in very good condition to prepare an address. Then, another thing, I am not eloquent, and I don't write a good hand, of which I had an evidence today from the secretary of the Executive Council, who was trying to read an indorsement that I put on a paper and utterly failed.

Therefore, it is that I am here not to make you an address, but to say how very pleased I am to meet you, how very much as the president of the American Bankers Association—and voicing, I know, the feeling of every member of that Association. I appreciate the courtesy you have shown us by having your convention at the same time, or very nearly the same time, as our convention, that we may shake hands with you all, look into your faces, believing that by our acquaintance we may learn something of you, and you learn something of us.

I had intended, Mr. President, to have been here yesterday, but the first thing that happened to us after we crossed Mason and Dixon's line was to be stolen. I thought that business had stopped, about twenty-six or twenty-seven years ago, when about a million of you Northern gentlemen came down with shotguns in your hands, and persuaded us that slavery was wrong; but we were very neatly stolen in Chicago; we thought we were coming here by the Union Pacific, and didn't discover to the contrary until about thirty-six hours afterward.

However, as we came by the Denver and Rio Grande, you can conceive that we were not very much displeased with having been taken away from our original route. Then, again, I was very anxious to come on, but some of the party concluded that they would like to stop at Reno. Well, you know and I know that Reno is not like 'Frisco, although they treated us very courteously, but we stayed much longer than we expected from the fact that a bull, with that habit peculiar to bulls, having more valor than discretion, concluded that he would try and butt the train off the track. The bull fell by the wayside, and so did the train. The bull hasn't yet recovered, but the train has, and we are here. [Applause and laughter.]

Mr. President, I take it that these meetings of ours have their chief good in bringing men together, the social feature. We cannot meet without learning something, one from another. We come together and we part. If we stayed always in our homes we are apt to think, as did a young gentleman who lived in the county adjoining the one in which I was raised, in North Carolina, whose sweetheart had done as sweethearts sometimes do, sent him to the right about. He concluded that he would drown his sorrow by traveling around the world—by indulging in that of which I have had so much in the last sixty days. The first day he got off twenty-five miles, and the next fifty miles, but, within the week he was seen again in his former haunts. Somebody said, "Well, John, I thought you were going to travel around the world." "Well," he said, "I didn't know the world was so —— big."

Now, the way for us to find out how big the world is, and how small we are, is to travel, is to meet people. The more people we meet the more enlarged our views become, and the broader we become, the more able are we to deal with whatever may be presented to us.

I trust, sir, that the meeting of this Association, the meetings of the all State Associations, now twenty in number, and the meeting of the National

Association, all of them, will bring about that very broadness which I think is necessary to this American people. We are very apt, in the South, to think that cotton is king. You in California are very apt to think that gold is king, and you are pretty near right, but over in Colorado they think that silver is king. They told me over there that they were going to send President Harrison to the White House again—President Harrison, who, I am told, bears a remarkable resemblance to the president of the California Bankers Association. [Applause.] And I put it that way, gentlemen, as did Mr. John Ingersoll, on one occasion, when being asked if he was a brother of Robert Ingersoll, said, "No, sir. Robert Ingersoll is a brother of mine." In the West they think that wheat is king, and in the East—well, they think that all manner of things that you and I and the West haven't got, are king

Mr. President and gentlemen, there are a great many things that I think we and our Associations should discuss, which, as a rule, we do not discuss; practical questions, questions with regard to our every-day business, particularly those banes of all bankers, collections and par points. If we can get at some plan by which we can reduce the great and growing number of banks that do business for glory and add to the diminishing number of those that do business for profit, if we can do that by our meetings, we shall have accomplished a great deal, and I say to you that, from my own experience in our own Association in Alabama, I think our meetings are beginning to have that effect.

There are a great many of those things that we might discuss with profit to ourselves. Take the option bill, for instance. I will not say anything about the silver bill, because it seems to have died an untimely death, and possibly we had better write over it "requiescat in pace," until some of our friends in Congress, who are in earnest in all they do about the silver bill, will undertake to pursue a different course.

I am very much afraid, Mr. President—I am a silver man—that the silver men are like the agitators across the water, in Ireland; their meat and bread is agitation; whenever this silver matter is settled, their meat and bread is gone—so is their reputation before the public.

I would like, Mr. President, if I could say something to the gentlemen before me that would interest them. I would like that I were eloquent, because eloquence is so rare a virtue that it sometimes becomes effusion, and then it ceases to be eloquence.

When I was elected president of the American Bankers Association, at Kansas City, you know we had established the rule of rotation in office by not allowing anybody to be eligible for reëlection, and I remarked, as I was presented to the Association, that it seemed that they admired rotundity as well as rotation in office. I admire rotation in speakers, Mr. President and gentlemen, and I thank you for your attention, and will take my seat. [Applause.]

The Chairman: Gentlemen of the convention, we have with us to-day Prof. James of the University of Pennsylvania, who is in charge there of the department in relation to the higher education of business men. We should like to have a few remarks from him.

Professor Edward J. James of Philadelphia:

Mr. President and Members of the California Bankers Association:

I respond very gladly to the invitation of your presiding officer to say a few words on the question which interests me very greatly, and which I trust is not without interest to you.

As you will infer from the remark of the speaker, I am not a practical banker, indeed. I am not even a theoretical banker, and, as a college professor, you doubtless are well enough aware of the conditions of our American college life to know that I have very little personal use for the banker. If a college professor can get enough together to take care of himself and family from day to day he is quite satisfied, and very rarely has occasion to call upon the banker to act even as a saver of his deposits.

However, I am very much interested in the subject of a broader and higher general financial education, and I have given some years of my life to the attempt to attract public interest to that in our college and university work.

No country in the world has more need of a sound financial education in general than the United States. Not because our people do not know enough about finances; not because, as a country, we are not successful, not because we have not great financial enterprises that have been carried through with rare skill to success, but because, in no place in the world is the general financial interest of the country so nearly dependent upon the intelligence of the average man. You, as bankers, know well enough that the loans, in which you do very much of your business, depend, to a very large extent, upon the ideas of the average man as to the functions of a bank in the community, and you also know that there is a very general misunderstanding of the functions of banks and monetary institutions in general throughout the country. Certainly we need this general education, and we need it in various ways and in various directions, and, as a college man, I have tried to secure from our institutions in this country a recognition of the importance of the study of industrial questions as an integral and necessary part of a college course. The question has been discussed sometimes, as it should be, by the honorable president of the American Bankers Association, as to the functions of bankers' associations of this sort. You have, doubtless, discussed it here, and it has been discussed in other banking associations. You formulate plans for looking after legislation of interests to the bankers alone and the general industrial interests of the country.

Now, as the gentleman has said, from the meeting of banker with banker good results must come. Certainly no Eastern banker can come into this Western country and study carefully the conditions from which your banking practices have been evolved, the reason for the development in different lines, without going back a wiser man, and carrying with him some ideas which he can use practically in his business at home. And certainly no banker from here can go into the East and study the conditions of banking there, without coming back in some way benefited. In a country like this the public, as a whole, is dependent very largely upon what bankers, as a class, are willing to do in the way of educating the public. It is no uncommon thing to find some of the greatest newspapers in this country taking up with the most heretical doctrines upon subjects of banks and banking. It is no uncommon thing to find political parties doing the same thing. Now, the people to whom many look for the correcting of these things are the bankers, and, if you do not at least assist in the development of sounder doctrines, it is not surprising if we find it difficult to educate the general public.

There is still back of this a further educational function, an opportunity to reach the people, further back, at their heads, namely, in the schools and colleges. And it is in that work that I have been specially interested, and it is that to which I should like to call your attention.

You have here, within an hour's ride in either direction from San Francisco, two of the most magnificent educational institutions that the world knows today. The University of California and the Leland Stanford, Jr., University, I think I may say, stand side by side with the very highest institutions of their class, and they are kept there today by your interest in higher education.

Now, inside of a great university we have very much of the same sort of conflicting materials, the same sort of ebb and flow of passion and wisdom that we find outside of the university. A college board of trustees, a college president, find themselves beset from morning till night by college professors who represent, in the proper way, as they should, a special subject each, who think it is absolutely essential that the institution should establish professorships in this or that department: one thinks we need, above everything, the development of Greek archæology, or, if we are going to keep our institutions abreast of the times we must have a museum; another urges the claims of this department or that to a professorship and a museum. And so it goes.

Now, the men, of course, who are conducting these institutions are putting forth their best efforts for the good of such institutions and to secure for those institutions in the university and collegiate world everything which properly belongs to them. But, today, if you were to go into some of our American colleges and take no notice of the buildings and surroundings, the electric lights which may be used to light the lecture-room, and the various modern devices, but simply pay attention to the subjects discussed, you would imagine you were in the class-room of a German professor of the fifteenth century. Now, we are asking simply today that these modern subjects, that the great field of commerce and finance and banking, of everything that pertains to this great side of modern life, with all the difficult questions which are associated with it, shall become constituent parts of a college and university education.

Thanking you for the kind attention which you have given me, I beseech from you an interest in this subject, and that you shall hold up the hands of your institutions on this Coast, especially these two I have mentioned, in their efforts to secure at least a fair representation of the great modern side of human life. [Applause.]

The Chairman: The next business in order is the report of the nominating committee. Mr. Breed will make the report for that committee.

L. N. Breed of Los Angeles:

To the Chairman and Members of the California Bankers Association:

GENTLEMEN—Your committee appointed to select and present for your consideration the names of members for offices of this Association for the ensuing year beg leave to report as follows:

We recommend for president, I. W. Hellman of San Francisco.

For vice-president, E. F. Spence of Los Angeles.

For secretary, Geo. H. Stewart of Los Angeles.

For treasurer, G. W. Kline of San Francisco.

For members of the Executive Council for three years: W. P. Harrington of Colusa, George E. Hersey of Gilroy. and J. H. Barbour of San Diego.

For delegate to the American Bankers Association Convention, 1892, Lovell White of San Francisco.

Delegate for 1893, W. P. Harrington of Colusa.

On motion of C. E. Palmer of Oakland, the report was adopted, and the persons named therein for the respective offices mentioned were declared elected.

The Chairman: The committee on resolutions is now prepared to report.

Mr. John Reichman of Fresno:

Mr. President and Gentlemen of the Convention:

The other members of the committee did not show themselves. Mr. Miller has left the city for the time being; Mr. Phelan was here but a few minutes, and had to read a paper, therefore could not act with me.

I have written up a report, so that the convention could act upon this matter at once, because I know the time is short.

Your committee on resolutions. to whom was referred the paper of Mr. Lovell White on "Some Mistakes of the Tax Gatherer", and that portion of the paper of Mr. E. S. Sheffield on the "Development of Banking", relating to the clearing of country checks in San Francisco by the correspondents of the banks upon whom the checks are drawn, would most respectfully report as follows:

The paper of Mr. White is very full and complete. and the recommendation therein contained, to wit, "Mortgages should be exempted from taxation, except for State and county purposes", and the recommendation, to wit, "Government bonds, by which is meant those on which interest is paid by a tax collected from the inhabitants of the State. or from those of any fractional part thereof, should be absolutely free from taxation", should meet the hearty approval of this convention. and we recommend the adoption of this paper as the sense of this convention on the subjects.

On the matter of collecting country checks. contained in the very excellent paper of Mr. Sheffield, which we commend as a fine literary article, abounding with truisms which it would be well for the members of the convention to study. we would report that the short time allotted to this committee. and we may say, this convention. is not sufficient for the proper investigation and solution of the problem. We would, therefore, recommend that the matter be referred to the Executive Council for its consideration, and report to the next convention. Respectfully submitted,

John Reichman, Chairman.

On motion of C. E. Palmer of Oakland, the report of the committee on resolutions was adopted as read.

C. C. Bush of Redding: Mr. Chairman, I would ask if a resolution is in order before this convention?

The Chairman: Yes, sir.

C. C. Bush: I will offer the following:

WHEREAS, the subject of the higher education of business men is now receiving increasing attention from the colleges and universities in this country, and,

WHEREAS, it appears that the advice and assistance of practical men is desired in this movement, therefore, be it

Resolved, that the president of this Association appoint a committee of three to confer on this subject, and report to this body at its next meeting as to what it may be able to do in the promotion of higher business education.

In offering this resolution, Mr. President, I beg of you not to confine yourself to parliamentary law. I do not wish to be appointed on this committee, because I am not able to follow up what is to be done. The object is to appoint a committee to see what can be done. I move that the resolution be adopted.

Motion of Mr. Bush being seconded, it was carried.

The Chairman: I will name for that committee Mr. C. C. Bush, Mr. C. E. Palmer, and Mr. E. S. Sheffield.

C. C. Bush: Mr. Chairman, if you will persist in overruling my objection, please put Mr. Palmer first.

The Chairman: I don't know of any handsomer gentleman in the house, or a better one than yourself for chairman of that committee.

Gentlemen, we are about to close the proceedings of this convention. Is there any gentleman present who desires to make any motion before we close? If not, I will now declare the convention adjourned, sine die.

FRACTIONAL CURRENCY.

A hearty reception was accorded all the addresses, which will repay perusal.

+ + +

Fresno is a grand place for fruit and hospitality. The weather is cool there by October.

+ + +

The personal courtesies shown by San Francisco bankers to delegates were highly appreciated.

It is not much of a trick to prepare the index for this book, but it will be found a great convenience.

Monday being a legal holiday, the San Francisco bankers were in attendance almost to a man.

The social features of our Convention were combined with those of the National Convention to the great advantage of both.

It is already time to prepare for our third meeting at Fresno in 1893. If an idea strikes you, write it down and develop it for the occasion.

+ + +

The Chamber of Commerce rooms were placed at the disposal of the Association this year, as last, without charge other than mere incidentals.

+ + +

Our delegates, whether members or not of the American Bankers Association, were made welcome on the excursion around the Bay, Sept. 9th.

+ + +

Frank Miller, of National Bank of D. O. Mills & Co., Sacramento, was elected Vice-President for California of the A. B. A. for the ensuing year.

+ + +

A number of our delegates omitted to register, and in consequence their names do not appear in the list of representatives on pages vii, viii and ix.

The Executive Council held their regular meeting on Saturday, the third inst., at the Bank Commissioner's office. A very full attendance was present.

+ + +

The tasteful program, with lithograph cover in unique design, was the work of the Union Lithograph Company, and furnished with their compliments.

+ + +

The San Francisco press devoted considerable space to data concerning the Convention, and their reports of the proceedings were careful and accurate.

+ + +

Next year at Fresno, the Metropolitan bankers being away from the immediate demands of business, will doubtless take a more active part in the proceedings.

+ +

The lapel button (the initials C. B. A. and the "California Poppy" enameled on solid silver) adopted and worn at the Convention, was much admired for its beauty and good taste.

+ + +

Our delegates attended in force the informal reception to Eastern bankers and delegates to the Convention of the American Bankers Association at Palace Hotel, Tuesday evening.

+ + +

Wm. H. Rhawn, President of the American Bankers Association, after addressing the Convention on Monday, remarked that the California bankers were a body of fine looking men.

+ + +

The office of the Board of Bank Commissioners was a sort of rendezvous for the California bankers, and the courtesy shown by the Commissioners and their Secretary will not soon be forgotten.

+ + +

The services of Mr. P. H. Maxwell, the stenographer, who has "taken" our proceedings this year and last, were secured by the "American Banker" of New York to report for them the Convention of the American Bankers Association.

+ + +

A one and one-third rate on all Southern Pacific lines was secured for our delegates. For the correction of many irregularities and liberal interpretation of the conditions in the certificates, the delegates are under obligation to the General Passenger Agent's Office.

Thomas Brown. the retiring President, expedited the business of the Convention. permitting an early adjournment on Tuesday afternoon. At the National Convention he was elected a member of the Executive Council of the American Bankers Association for the ensuing year.

+ + +

The "Midsummer Jinks" of the Bohemian Club in their "Sequoia grove" was a rare treat to those of our delegates who had the good fortune to be present. The ceremonies and music in the midst of the grand redwoods were rendered most impressive by the great image of "Buddha" (over fifty feet high), the costumes of the participants. and the eloquent addresses.

+ + +

Mr. B. Singer, the wide awake representative of the "American Banker" was present among the gentlemen of the Press. The notes taken by him were so full that, when printed in the "special edition" with report on the Convention of the American Bankers' Association, the reader will have about all the information practicable in advance of our official pamphlet.

+ + +

The excursion on the Bay, in which nearly fifty of our delegates participated as members of the American Bankers Association, and many others by invitation of the Committee. was a most enjoyable affair. The steamer Encinal left the wharf at 10 o'clock and carried away, besides the wealthy bankers and their families, a most lovely selection of California's fairest daughters and bright young men, who hope to be bankers some day.

All the chairs in the cabin of the steamer had been taken out and put on the upper deck, both fore and aft, and seats were at a premium. On the lower deck forward was seated Von der Mehden's orchestra, which discoursed sweet music while the crowd swarmed aboard. Finally every one was on board (except the last man) and the lines were cast off. Handsome Captain Rogers blew his whistle and the Encinal glided gracefully out of the slip to the inspiring strains of "A Life on the Ocean Wave." The steamer headed down the bay toward Hunter's point, while the sun made desperate efforts to get out and show himself. He was not to blame for trying to get out, for the array of loveliness on the upper deck was dazzling enough to make the shrewd financiers forget the $20 pieces they left at home. The fair ones did not mind the sun's absence in the least and the cabin was deserted.

At 11 o'clock lunch was announced, and it was found that even bankers eat. Down the forward stairs the party trooped, the band playing a march the while. On the lower deck numberless tables were prettily arranged for parties of four, six and a dozen or more. Fore and aft of the engine room were large tables on which were scattered in profusion fruits and

cereal products of California, and the banquet hall was draped with stream-
ers of green and orange and hung with ferns. California wines sparkled
on the tables, and the scene was an animated one.

While the menu was being discussed the band played selections from
"Cavallera Rusticana", "Lucia de Lammermoor", "Il Trovatore",
Orpheus", "Tannhauser", and other operas. There were fifty waiters to
supply the wants of those present and everything went off merrily and
well. The following menu was served:

EXCURSION

OF THE

AMERICAN BANKERS ASSOCIATION

STEAMER ENCINAL.

MENU

Shrimp Salad   Chicken Salad
            Roast Chicken
Fillet of Beef   Sirloin of Beef
        Ham   Tongue
        Pickles   Olives
            Sandwiches.

DESSERT.

Vanilla and Strawberry Ice Cream
        Nut Cake   Almond Cake
Cocoanut Cake   Lady Fingers   Macaroons
        Fruit Cake

While the party was making merry over the good things of life the
steamer was getting on up the bay. She went as far as Mare island, and
then came down on the other or western side of the bay, passing through
Raccoon straits, past Tiburon and Sausalito out near Lime point and back
to the wharf, landing a crowd highly pleased with the day's diversion.

LETTER WITH RESOLUTIONS ON THE DEATH

— OF —

HON. E. F. SPENCE,

VICE-PRESIDENT OF THE ASSOCIATION.

To the Members of the California Bankers Association.

GENTLEMEN: The Los Angeles Clearing-house, at a special meeting held this day, adopted the following resolutions of respect:

WHEREAS, It has pleased Divine Providence, at an early hour this morning, to remove from us by the hand of death the President of this Association, a man of national reputation, our fellow banker and friend, Hon. E. F. Spence, be it therefore

Resolved, That this Association has lost an able officer, whose efforts have always been directed toward the success of the business interests of the Clearing-house, and the promotion of friendly and social spirit among its members; and be it further

Resolved, That we appreciate the sterling qualities of our friend as a successful banker; as a man of thoughtful mind and broad views; and as a friend whose loss we keenly feel; and be it further

Resolved, That a copy of these resolutions be transmitted to the wife and family of the deceased; to the California Bankers Association, of which he was Vice-President; to the American Bankers Association, of which he was an executive officer; to the First National Bank of this city, of which he was for many years President; to other banking institutions of which he was an officer; to the Press of this city, and be spread upon the records of this Clearing-house.

A. D. CHILDRESS,
GEO. H. STEWART,
GEO. L. ARNOLD,
Committee.

Mr. Spence having been elected our Vice-President at the recent Convention in San Francisco, it is fitting not only to transmit to you the above resolutions, but also to recognize the loss our Association has sustained in the death of its second officer, who presided over the deliberations at the time our Association was formed, and has ever since taken the heartiest interest in its success.

Yours very truly,

GEO. H. STEWART, Secretary.

Los Angeles, Cal., September 19, 1892.

CONSTITUTION AND BY-LAWS

OF THE CALIFORNIA BANKERS ASSOCIATION.

DECLARATION.

In order to promote the general welfare and usefulness of banks and banking institutions, and to secure uniformity of action, together with the practical benefits to be derived from personal acquaintance and from the discussion of subjects of importance to the banking and commercial interests of this State : especially in order to secure the proper consideration of questions regarding the financial usages, customs and laws which effect the banking interests of the entire State, and for protection against loss by crime : we have to submit the following Constitution and By-Laws for the CALIFORNIA BANKERS ASSOCIATION :

CONSTITUTION.

ARTICLE I.

This Association shall be called the CALIFORNIA BANKERS ASSOCIATION.

ARTICLE II.

SECTION 1. Any National or State Bank, Trust Company, Savings Bank, Banking Firm, or individual, doing a banking business within the State of California, may become a member of this Association, upon the payment of such annual dues as shall be provided by the By-Laws, subject to the approval of a majority of the Executive Council, and may send one delegate to the annual meeting of the Association ; and any member may be expelled from the Association upon a vote of two-thirds of those present at any regular meeting.

SEC. 2. Delegates shall be : an officer, or director, or trustee, of the institution they represent ; or a member of a banking firm, or an individual doing business as a bank.

SEC. 3. Delegates shall vote in person ; no voting by proxy shall be allowed.

SEC. 4. All votes shall be viva voce, unless otherwise ordered ; any delegate may demand a division of the house.

ARTICLE III.

SECTION 1. The administration of the affairs of the Association, not otherwise delegated, shall be vested in the President, First Vice-President, Secretary, Treasurer, one Vice-President for each County which may be represented in this Association, and an Executive Council : who shall be elected at the annual meeting, and who shall serve until their successors are chosen or appointed. The Executive Council shall be composed of nine members, divided into three classes, one-third of whom shall be elected annually.

9

SEC. 2. Immediately after the first adjournment that occurs in the session of the annual Convention, the delegation from each county shall meet and make nominations for Vice-Presidents of the Association.

SEC. 3. The Vice-Presidents shall have the supervision of the business of the Association in the counties where they reside. The banks in each county may organize under the Vice-President of the county, and form a Committee for local matters; but such Committee shall have no power to in any manner bind or effect the interests of the organization. Such local Committee may fill any vacancy occurring in the Vice-Presidency during the year.

SEC. 4. A majority of the Executive Council shall constitute a quorum for the transaction of business.

SEC. 5. Special meetings of the Executive Council may be called by request of three of its members, giving two weeks notice to the Secretary, desiring him to call such special meeting. The Executive Council shall have power to fill vacancies that may occur in its own body.

SEC. 6. The Executive Council shall provide:

First—For keeping the records of the proceedings of their own meetings, as well as that of the Association annual or special meetings.

Second—They shall submit to each annual meeting a report covering their own official acts, as well as a statement of any new or unfinished business requiring attention.

Third—They shall make full statements of the financial condition of the Association.

Fourth—Submit an estimate of the amount required to carry on the affairs of the Association according to their judgment of the business to be done, and recommend means for raising money to carry out such plans as may be resolved upon by the Association.

SEC. 7. The Secretary shall make and have charge of the records of the Association, as well as those of the Council, and of the correspondence of the Executive Council and Standing Protective Committee; and shall promptly send to each member of the Association a synopsis of reports received by him of attempted or accomplished crime against any member of the Association. Such records shall be the property of the Association, and be held subject at all times to the order of the Executive Council.

SEC. 8. The Treasurer shall receive and account for all moneys belonging to the Association, but shall pay out moneys only upon vouchers approved by the President of the Association and counter-signed by the Secretary.

ARTICLE IV.

SECTION 1. The Executive Council shall appoint a Standing Protective Committee of three persons, whose names shall not be made public. The said Committee shall control all action looking to the detection, prosecution and punishment of persons attempting to cause, or causing, loss by crime to any member of the Association.

SEC. 2. The said Committee, when called upon for aid by any member of the Association, through the Secretary, shall forthwith take such steps as it shall deem proper to arrest and prosecute the party charged with crime; provided, however, that no expense or liability shall be incurred beyond the amount of funds in the Treasury especially appropriated for that purpose.

SEC. 3. The said Committee is prohibited from compromising or compounding with parties charged with crime or with their agents or attorneys.

SEC. 4. All detectives and legal expenses and costs will be paid by the Association out of any money in the Treasury especially appropriated by the Executive Council, for that purpose; subject, however, to the approval of a quorum of the Executive Council.

SEC. 5. All members of the Association, when called upon by the Secretary in behalf of the Protective Committee for information or aid, shall promptly respond by giving all assistance in their power; and all members shall, at all times, notify the Secretary, who shall promptly notify the Committee, of any attempted or accomplished crime reported to him as likely to effect other members of the Association.

ARTICLE V.

SECTION 1. Annual meetings of the Association shall be held at such times and places as shall be determined by the Executive Council. Special meetings may be called by the said Council if, in their opinions, circumstances require them; giving two weeks notice of time and place of meeting, together with the subject-matter of business to come before such special meeting. The Executive Council shall meet to arrange the order of business on the day preceding any general meeting of the Association.

ARTICLE VI.

SECTION 1. The expenses of the Executive Council, in carrying out the business of the Association to be done by them, shall be provided for by the annual dues of the members of the Association; provided, however, that the Executive Council shall have no authority to incur or contract, on behalf of this Association, any liability whatever beyond the annual dues hereby authorized, and only that for the purposes hereby designated.

ARTICLE VII.

SECTION 1. Resolutions and subjects for discussion (except those referring to points of order or matters of courtesy) must be submitted in writing to the Secretary, for reference to the Executive Council, at least ten days before any general meeting of the Association; but any person desiring to submit any resolution of business in open Convention can do so, upon a two-thirds vote of the delegates present.

SEC. 2. No opinions expressed, principles advocated, theories advanced or policies suggested by any party or person, however presented, shall be deemed to have had the endorsement of this Association except the question of so indorsing shall have been referred to a standing or special committee; shall have been reported upon by such committee and shall have been specifically voted upon, receiving a majority of the votes of those present at an open session of a Convention of the Association.

This item of the constitution shall be published in every report of the proceedings of any convention and where indorsements are given the fact shall be noted in the report of the proceedings in that behalf. (Sec. 2 adopted Sept. 5th, 1892.)

ARTICLE VIII.

SECTION 1. Any one failing to pay within three months the annual dues for carrying on the business of the Association, shall be considered as having withdrawn from membership; but may be reinstated upon application to the Secretary, and paying all dues in arrears, with consent of the President.

ARTICLE IX.

Section 1. This Constitution may be altered or amended at any annual meeting by a vote of two-thirds of the members present : notice of the proposed amendment having been first submitted to the Secretary at least ten days before the annual meeting, to be placed by him before the Executive Council, that they may arrange for bringing it before the Convention under the regular order of business.

BY-LAWS.

Section 1. The annual dues of the Association shall be considered due at the beginning of the year, which year shall commence with the regular annual meeting ; it being understood that absent members from such annual meeting shall not forfeit their membership nor the right to become members, provided they comply with the Constitution and By-Laws and remit the amount of the dues to the Secretary within one month after such annual meeting.

Sec. 2. The annual dues of all members shall be Ten (10) Dollars.

INDEX.

Three copies of this pamphlet are sent to every bank a member of the Association. Additional copies may be had on application to the Secretary.

PROCEEDINGS

OF THE

THIRD ANNUAL CONVENTION

OF THE

CALIFORNIA BANKERS ASSOCIATION

HELD AT

SAN FRANCISCO, FEBRUARY 22d, 23d, and 24th,

1894

CONSTITUTION AND BY-LAWS,

LIST OF OFFICERS AND MEMBERS,

ETC.

FULL INDEX AT BACK OF PAMPHLET

BRUNT, PRINT,
533 CLAY STREET,
SAN FRANCISCO.

OFFICERS ELECTED 1894.

PRESIDENT.
LOVELL WHITE, San Francisco Savings Union, San Francisco.

VICE-PRESIDENT.
I. G. WICKERSHAM, First National Bank, Petaluma.

TREASURER.
G. W. KLINE, Crocker-Woolworth National Bank, San Francisco.

SECRETARY.
R. M. WELCH, San Francisco Savings Union, San Francisco.

CHAIRMAN OF EXECUTIVE COUNCIL.
George H. Stewart, Bank of America, Los Angeles.

EXECUTIVE COUNCIL.
President and Vice-President, members *ex-officio*.

TERM EXPIRES, 1895.
C. E. PALMER, Union National Bank, Oakland.
A. L. SELIGMAN, Anglo-Californian Bank, San Francisco.
S. PRENTISS SMITH, Bank of California, San Francisco.

TERM EXPIRES, 1896.
W. P. HARRINGTON, Colusa County Bank, Colusa.
GEO. E. HERSEY, Bank of Gilroy, Gilroy.
JAMES A. THOMPSON, Donohoe-Kelly Banking Co., San Francisco.

TERM EXPIRES, 1897.
GEORGE H. STEWART, Bank of America, Los Angeles.
H. H. HEWLETT, First National Bank, Stockton.
N. D. RIDEOUT, Rideout Bank, Marysville.

MEMBERS
AT DATE OF THIRD ANNUAL CONVENTION

ALAMEDA COUNTY

J. E. Baker ....*Vice-President*
Cashier, Bank of Alameda

Bank of Livermore.................	Livermore
California Bank........	..........Oakland
First National Bank......	Oakland
Oakland Bank of Savings	....Oakland
Union National Bank...............	Oakland
Union Savings Bank....	.........Oakland
Bank of Haywards..	Haywards
Bank of Alameda...............	Alameda

BUTTE COUNTY

Charles Faulkner ....*Vice-President*
Cashier, Bank of Butte County, Chico

Sacramento Valley Bank................	Biggs
Bank of Butte County......	Chico
Bank of Chico......	......Chico
Rideout Bank	Gridley
Bank of Rideout, Smith & Co...	Oroville

COLUSA COUNTY

W. P. Harrington .... *Vice-President*
Cashier, Colusa County Bank

Colusa County Bank	Colusa

CONTRA COSTA COUNTY

L. C. Wittenmeyer ....*Vice-President*
President, Bank of Martinez, Martinez

Bank of Martinez...................	Martinez
Bank of Antioch	Antioch

EL DORADO COUNTY

Mierson & Jewell................ .... Placerville

FRESNO COUNTY

H. D. Coburn .... *Vice-President*
President, Fresno National Bank, Fresno

Bank of Central California.....	Fresno
Farmers' Bank of Fresno	... Fresno
First National	Fresno
Fresno National Bank	......Fresno
Fresno Loan and Savings Bank	......Fresno
People's Savings Bank	Fresno
Bank of Sanger	... Sanger
Bank of Selma ..	Selma

GLENN COUNTY

B. H. Burton .. .. *Vice-President*
Cashier, Bank of Willows

Bank of Orland .. ..Orland
Bank of Willows...	Willows

HUMBOLDT COUNTY

Wm. Carson ....*Vice-President*
President, Bank of Eureka

Bank of Arcata..........	...........Arcata
Bank of Eureka...... ..	.........Eureka
Humboldt County Bank	Eureka
Randall Banking Co...	..........Eureka

KERN COUNTY

Sol. Jewett .... *Vice-President*
President, Kern Valley Bank

Bank of Bakersfield....	....Bakersfield
Kern Valley Bank...........	..Bakersfield
Producers' Savings Bank	....Bakersfield

KINGS COUNTY

Farmers' and Merchants' Bank........Hanford

LAKE COUNTY

H. C. Boggs.................... *Vice-President*
President, Farmers' Savings Bank, Lakeport

Farmers' Savings Bank........	Lakeport

LOS ANGELES COUNTY

L. N. Breed ....,*Vice-President*
President, Southern California National Bank,
Los Angeles

Alhambra Bank..	........Alhambra
Bank of America	..........Los Angeles
California Bank	....Los Angeles
East Side Bank...................	Los Angeles
Farmers' and Merchants' Bank	...Los Angeles
First National Bank..	Los Angeles
German American Savings Bank..Los Angeles
Los Angeles National Bank........Los Angeles
Los Angeles Savings Bank ......Los Angeles
Main St. Savings B'k and Trust Co., Los Angeles
National Bank of California..... ..Los Angeles
Savings B'k of Southern California. Los Angeles
Security Savings B'k and Trust Co.. Los Angeles
Southern California National Bank, Los Angeles
State Loan and Trust Co.......... Los Angeles
First National Bank . ...Pasadena
Pasadena National Bank........... Pasadena
San Gabriel Valley Bank	Pasadena
First National Bank....	Pomona
Peoples' Bank	.... Pomona
First National Bank.	Santa Monica

MERCED COUNTY

C. Landram ....Vice-President
Vice-President, Merced Bank, Merced

Commercial Savings Bank ....Merced
Merced Bank ....Merced
Merced Security Savings Bank ......Merced

MONTEREY COUNTY

J. J. Field ....Vice-President
Vice-President, Bank of Monterey

Monterey County Bank...........Salinas City
Salinas City Bank ....Salinas City
Bank of Monterey ....Monterey

NAPA COUNTY

George E. Goodman, Sr............Vice-President
President, Jas. H. Goodman & Co., Bank

Bank of Napa .... Napa
Jas. H. Goodman & Co. Bank.........Napa
Bank of St. Helena........ ......St. Helena
Carver National Bank ....St. Helena

NEVADA COUNTY

E. M. Preston...... ....Vice-President
President, Citizens' Bank

Citizens' Bank.....................Nevada City

ORANGE COUNTY

W. H. Spurgeon............ .....Vice-President
President, First National Bank of Santa Ana

Commercial Bank ....Santa Ana
First National Bank.... ......Santa Ana
Orange Co. Savings, Loan & Trust Co. Santa Ana
Bank of Tustin ....Tustin

PLACER COUNTY

D. W. Lubeck.................. .....Vice-President
Vice-President, Placer County Bank, Auburn

Placer County Bank.... ....Auburn
W. & P. Nicholls........ ....Dutch Flat

RIVERSIDE COUNTY

M. J. Daniels........ ....Vice-President
President, Orange Growers' Bank

Perris Valley Bank.... ....Perris
First National Bank.... ....Riverside
Orange Growers' Bank.............Riverside
Riverside Banking Co..........Riverside
Riverside National Bank ... .Riverside

SACRAMENTO COUNTY

W. E. Chamberlain.... .... Vice-President
Of the National Bank of D. O. Mills & Co

California State Bank ....Sacramento
Farmers' & Mechanics' Savings B'k, Sacramento
National Bank of D. O. Mills & Co., Sacramento
Peoples' Savings Bank.......... Sacramento
Sacramento Bank ... .Sacramento
J. H. Burnham....................... ....Folsom

SAN BENITO COUNTY

T. W. Hawkins.... .... Vice-President
Cashier, Bank of Hollister

Bank of Hollister ... .Hollister
Farmers' and Merchants' Bank. Hollister

SAN BERNARDINO COUNTY

H. B. Smith. . ...Vice-President
Cashier, First National Bank of Colton

First National Bank........ .. ..Colton
Ontario State Bank............ .. Ontario
First National Bank ....Redlands
Savings Bank of Redlands........ .Redlands
Union Bank of Redlands....... Redlands
Bank of San Bernardino .. San Bernardino
Farmers' Exchange Bank......San Bernardino
First National Bank. ....San Bernardino
San Bernardino National Bank, San Bernardino

SAN DIEGO COUNTY

E. M. Powers .... Vice-President
President, Bank of Commerce, San Diego

Bank of National City...........National City
Peoples' State Bank ....National City
Bank of Commerce.................San Diego
First National Bank..............San Diego

SAN FRANCISCO CITY AND COUNTY

Thos. Brown....... ....Vice-President
Cashier, Bank of California

American Bank and Trust Co.
Anglo-Californian Bank, Limited
Bank of California
Bank of Sisson, Crocker & Co.
California Safe Deposit and Trust Co.
Crocker-Woolworth National Bank
Donohoe-Kelly Banking Co.
First National Bank
German Savings and Loan Society
Grangers' Bank
Hibernia Savings and Loan Society
Humboldt Savings and Loan Society
London, Paris and American Bank, Limited
London and San Francisco Bank
Mutual Savings Bank
Nevada Bank of San Francisco
Peoples' Home Savings Bank
San Francisco Savings Union
Sather Banking Co.
Savings and Loan Society
Security Savings Bank
Tallant Banking Co.
Wells, Fargo & Co's Bank

SAN JOAQUIN COUNTY

H. H. Hewlett.... ....Vice-President
President, First National Bank of Stockton

Bank of Lodi.... ....Lodi
Farmers' and Merchants' Bank ......Stockton

First National Bank ....Stockton
Stockton Savings Bank ....Stockton
Stockton Savings and Loan Society ..Stockton
San Joaquin Valley Bank.............Stockton

SAN LUIS OBISPO COUNTY

R. E. Jack.......................Vice-President
    County Bank of San Luis Obispo
Citizens' Bank of Paso Robles.....Paso Robles
California Mortgage & Savings Bank
    ....San Luis Obispo
Commercial Bank ... . San Luis Obispo
First National Bank...........San Luis Obispo

SANTA BARBARA COUNTY

A. L. Lincoln.....................Vice-President
    Cashier First National Bank of Santa Barbara
Commercial Bank......   Santa Barbara
First National Bank ....Santa Barbara
Santa Barbara County National. Santa Barbara
Santa Barbara S. & L. Bank. ....Santa Barbara
Bank of Santa Maria ....Santa Maria
Bank of Lompoc .... Lompoc

SANTA CLARA COUNTY

J. W. Findlay .... Vice-President
    Vice-President, Commercial and Savings
    Bank, San Jose
Bank of Gilroy..................... ...Gilroy
Bank of Los Gatos ... .Los Gatos
Commercial Bank of Los Gatos ...Los Gatos
Bank of Palo Alto ....Palo Alto
Bank of San Jose.................San Jose
Commercial and Savings Bank ... San Jose
First National Bank ....San Jose
Garden City Bank and Trust Co. ...San Jose
Security Savings Bank ....San Jose
Union Savings Bank ... .San Jose

SANTA CRUZ COUNTY

W. T. Jeter....................Vice-President
    President, Bank of Santa Cruz Co., Santa Cruz
Bank of Santa Cruz County ...... Santa Cruz
City Bank....... ....Santa Cruz
Pajaro Valley Bank .... .Watsonville

SHASTA COUNTY

C. C. Bush ....Vice-President
    Vice-President, Bank of Shasta Co., Redding
Bank of Shasta County ....Redding

SISKIYOU COUNTY

Fred E. Wadsworth.......... .....Vice-President
    Cashier, Siskiyou County Bank, Yreka
Siskiyou County Bank...... ....Yreka
Bank of A. B. Carlock............ Fort Jones

SOLANO COUNTY

R. D. Robbins....................Vice-President
    President, Bank of Suisun
Bank of Dixon ....Dixon
Bank of Suisun . ...Suisun

SONOMA COUNTY

L. W. Burris................ ....Vice-President
    Cashier, Santa Rosa Bank
Farmers' and Mechanics' Bank. Healdsburg
Bank of Healdsburg ....Healdsburg
First National Bank...... ....Petaluma
Santa Rosa Bank ....Santa Rosa
Sonoma Valley Bank .. ..Sonoma

STANISLAUS COUNTY

O. McHenry ....Vice-President
    President, First National Bank, Modesto
First National Bank.... ....Modesto
Bank of Oakdale .... Oakdale

SUTTER COUNTY

G. W. Carpenter .... Vice-President
    President Farmers' Co-operative Union, Yuba City
Farmers' Co-operative Union ... Yuba City

TEHAMA COUNTY

J. S. Cone.................... ....Vice-President
    Cashier, Bank of Tehama Co., Red Bluff
Bank of Tehama County ....Red Bluff

TULARE COUNTY

S. Mitchell ... ... Vice-President
    Cashier, Producers' Bank, Visalia
Bank of Tulare......... ....Tulare
Producers' Bank .. .. Visalia

VENTURA COUNTY

J. S. Collins ....Vice-President
    Cashier, Wm. Collins & Sons, Ventura
Bank of Hueneme... ... Hueneme
First National Bank ....Santa Paula
Bank of Ventura .... Ventura
William Collins Sons ... ... Ventura

YOLO COUNTY

C. W. Bush ....Vice-President
    Cashier, Bank of Yolo, Woodland
Bank of Winters .... Winters
Bank of Yolo........ .....Woodland

YUBA COUNTY

J. H. Jewett................ ...Vice-President
    President, Decker, Jewett & Co., Marysville
Decker, Jewett & Co. Bank .. Marysville
Northern Cal. Bank of Savings ....Marysville
The Rideout Bank . ...Marysville

Banks Registered at the Convention.

NAME		REPRESENTED BY
	ALAMEDA.	
Bank of Alameda	·	J. E. Baker.
	ALHAMBRA.	
Alhambra Bank	·	J. M. Elliott.
	BAKERSFIELD.	
Bank of Bakersfield	· ·	J. J. Mack.
	CHICO.	
Bank of Butte County	·	Chas. Faulkner.
	COLUSA.	
Colusa County Bank	·	W. P. Harrington.
	DIXON.	
Bank of Dixon	· ·	S. G. Little.
	FRESNO.	
Farmers' Bank of Fresno		John Reichman and A. Kutner.
	GILROY.	
Bank of Gilroy	·	George E. Hersey.
	HAYWARDS.	
Bank of Haywards	· · ·	J. E. Crooks.
	HEALDSBURG.	
Bank of Healdsburg	·	Jno. Wallace Wilson.
Farmers' and Mechanics' Bank	·	Geo. H. Warfield.
	HOLLISTER.	
Bank of Hollister · · ·	·	T. S. Hawkins.
Farmers' and Merchants' Bank	· ·	A. Tonn
	LIVERMORE.	
Bank of Livermore	·	H. H. Pitcher and John Taylor.
	LOS ANGELES.	
Bank of America ·	· ·	George H. Stewart.
Farmers and Merchants Bank		I. W. Hellman, Jr.
First National Bank · ·		J. M. Elliott.
Main st. Savings Bank and Trust Co.		J. B. Lankershim.
Southern California National Bank	·	L. N. Breed.
	LOS GATOS.	
Commercial Bank of Los Gatos	· ·	J. R. Ryland.
	MARTINEZ.	
Bank of Martinez	·	L. C. Wittenmyer
	MARYSVILLE.	
The Rideout Bank · ·	· ·	C. S. Brooks
Decker, Jewett & Co. Bank	· ·	J. H. Jewett.
	MERCED.	
Merced Bank	· ·	John W. Howell.
	MODESTO.	
First National Bank	· ·	O. McHenry.
	MONTEREY.	
Bank of Monterey	· ·	T. J. Field.

NAPA.

Jas. H. Goodman & Co. Bank	Geo. E. Goodman.

NEVADA CITY.

Citizens' Bank	D. E. Morgan.

OAKLAND.

California Bank	S. M. Babbitt and J. Greenhood.
First National Bank	P. E. Bowles and L. G. Burpee.
Union National Bank	C. E. Palmer, W. H. High, Jr.
Union Savings Bank	J. West Martin.

ORLAND.

Bank of Orland	R. B. Murdoch.

OROVILLE.

Bank of Rideout, Smith & Co.	N. D. Rideout.

PALO ALTO.

The Bank of Palo Alto	B. Parkinson.

PASADENA.

First National Bank	A. H. Conger
Pasadena National Bank	T. P. Lukens.
San Gabriel Valley Bank	Frank C. Bolt.

PASO ROBLES.

Citizens' Bank	A. F. Horstman.

PETALUMA.

First National Bank	I. G. Wickersham.

SACRAMENTO.

California State Bank	W. E. Gerber.
Farmers' and Mechanics' Savings Bank	B. U. Steinman.
National Bank of D. O. Mills & Co.	Frank Miller.
Peoples Savings Bank	Wm. Beckman.
Sacramento Bank	Ed R. Hamilton.

SAN DIEGO.

Bank of Commerce	G. W. Jorres.
Merchants' National Bank	Levi Chase.

SAN FRANCISCO.

American Bank and Trust Co.	Jas. J. Fagan.
Anglo-Californian Bank, Ltd.	I. Steinhart.
Bank of California	S. Prentiss Smith.
Bank of Sisson, Crocker & Co.	Geo. W. Scott.
Crocker-Woolworth National Bank	G. W. Kline.
Donohoe-Kelly Banking Co.	James A. Thompson.
First National Bank	S. G. Murphy.
German Savings & Loan Society	Edw. Kruse, A. H. R. Schmidt and Geo. Tourny.
Humboldt Savings and Loan Society	Henry F. Fortman.
London, Paris & American Bank, Ltd.	C. Altschul and Sig. Greenebaum.
Mutual Savings Bank	Geo. A. Story.
Nevada Bank of San Francisco	I. W. Hellman and John F. Bigelow.
San Francisco Savings Union	Lovell White.

SAN JOSE.

Commercial and Savings Bank	J. W. Findlay.
Union Savings Bank	H. W. Wright and Ant. Friant.

SAN LUIS OBISPO.

County Bank	J. Goldtree.

SANTA CRUZ.

Bank of Santa Cruz County	W. T. Jeter.
City Bank	W. D. Haslam.

SANTA BARBARA.

First National Bank	James W. Calkins.

SANTA MONICA.
Bank of Santa Monica — Robert F. Jones.

SANTA PAULA.
First National Bank — C. H. McKevett.

SANTA ROSA.
Santa Rosa Bank — L. W. Burris.

SELMA.
Bank of Selma — D. S. Snodgrass.

ST. HELENA
The Carver National Bank — A. L. Williams.

SONOMA.
Sonoma Valley Bank — Fred'k T. Dahring.

STOCKTON
Farmers and Merchants Bank — P. B. Fraser and D. S. Rosenbaum.
First National Bank — H. H. Hewlett
Stockton Savings and Loan Society — H. H. Hewlett
Stockton Savings Bank — Sidney Newell.

SUISUN.
Bank of Suisun — R. D. Robbins.

VENTURA.
Wm. Collins & Sons — D. Edward Collins and J. S. Collins.

VISALIA.
The Producers Bank — S. Mitchell.

WILLOWS.
Bank of Willows — W. P. Harrington.

WINTERS.
Bank of Winters — J. B. McArthur and E. E. Kahn.

WOODLAND.
Bank of Yolo — C. W. Bush.

WATSONVILLE
Pajaro Valley Bank — J. J. Morey.

YUBA CITY.
Farmers' Co-operative Union — G. W. Carpenter.

HONORARY MEMBERS.

W. H. Knight — State Bank Commissioner.
C. H. Dunsmoor — State Bank Commissioner.
J. B. Fuller — State Bank Commissioner.

CONSTITUTION and BY-LAWS

CALIFORNIA BANKERS ASSOCIATION

DECLARATION.

In order to promote the general welfare and usefulness of banks and banking institutions, and to secure uniformity of action, together with the practical benefits to be derived from personal acquaintance and from the discussion of subjects of importance to the banking and commercial interests of this State: especially in order to secure the proper consideration of questions regarding the financial usages, customs and laws which affect the banking interests of the entire State, and for protection against loss by crime: we have to submit the following Constitution and By-Laws for the CALIFORNIA BANKERS ASSOCIATION:

CONSTITUTION.

ARTICLE I.

This Association shall be called the CALIFORNIA BANKERS ASSOCIATION.

ARTICLE II.

SECTION 1. Any National or State Bank, Trust Company, Savings Bank, Banking Firm, or individual, doing a banking business within the State of California, may become a member of this Association upon the payment of such annual dues as shall be provided by the By-Laws, subject to the approval of a majority of the Executive Council, and may send one delegate to the annual meeting of the Association: and any member may be expelled from the Association upon a vote of two-thirds of those present at any regular meeting.

SEC. 2. Delegates shall be: an officer or director, or trustee of the institution they represent: or a member of a banking firm, or an individual doing business as a bank.

SEC. 3. Delegates shall vote in person: no voting by proxy shall be allowed.

Sec. 4. All votes shall be *viva voce*, unless otherwise ordered; any delegate may demand a division of the house.

ARTICLE III.

Section 1. The administration of the affairs of the Association, not otherwise delegated, shall be vested in the President, First Vice-President, Secretary, Treasurer, one Vice-President for each county which may be represented in this Association, and an Executive Council; who shall be elected at the annual meeting, and who shall serve until their successors are chosen or appointed. The Executive Council shall be composed of nine members, divided into three classes, one-third of whom shall be elected annually. The President and First Vice-President shall be *ex-officio* members of the Executive Council.

Sec. 2. Immediately after the first adjournment that occurs in the session of the annual Convention, the delegation from each county shall meet and each for itself elect a County Vice-President.

Sec. 3. The Vice-Presidents shall have the supervision of the business of the Association in the counties where they reside. The banks in each county may organize under the Vice-President of the county, and form a Committee for local matters; but such Committee shall have no power to in any manner bind or affect the interests of the organization. Such local Committee may fill any vacancy occurring in the Vice-Presidency during the year.

Sec. 4. A majority of the Executive Council shall constitute a quorum for the transaction of business.

Sec. 5. Special meetings of the Executive Council may be called by request of three of its members, giving two weeks' notice to the Secretary, desiring him to call such special meeting. The Executive Council shall have power to fill vacancies that may occur in its own body.

Sec. 6. The Executive Council shall provide:

First—For keeping the records of the proceedings of their own meetings, as well as of the Associations annual or special meetings.

Second—They shall submit to each annual meeting a report covering their own official acts, as well as a statement of any new or unfinished business requiring attention.

Third—They shall make full statements of the financial condition of the Association.

Fourth—Submit an estimate of the amount required to carry on the affairs of the Association according to their judgment of the business to be done, and recommend means for raising money to carry out such plans as may be resolved upon by the Association.

SEC. 7. The Secretary shall make and have charge of the records of the Association, as well as those of the Council, and of the correspondence of the Executive Council and Standing Protective Committee; and shall promptly send to each member of the Association a synopsis of reports received by him of attempted or accomplished crime against any member of the Association. Such records shall be the property of the Association, and be held subject at all times to the order of the Executive Council.

SEC. 8. The Treasurer shall receive and account for all moneys belonging to the Association, but shall pay out moneys only upon vouchers approved by the President of the Association and countersigned by the Secretary.

ARTICLE IV.

SECTION 1. The Executive Council shall appoint a Standing Protective Committee of three persons, whose names shall not be made public. The said Committee shall control all action looking to the detection, prosecution and punishment of persons attempting to cause, or causing, loss by crime to any member of the Association.

SEC. 2. The said Committee, when called upon for aid by any member of the Association, through the Secretary, shall forthwith take such steps as it shall deem proper to arrest and prosecute the party charged with crime; provided, however, that no expense or liability shall be incurred beyond the amount of funds in the Treasury especially appropriated for that purpose.

SEC. 3. The said Committee is prohibited from compromising or compounding with parties charged with crime or with their agents or attorneys.

SEC. 4. All detectives and legal expenses and costs will be paid by the Association out of any money in the Treasury especially appropriated by the Executive Council for that purpose; subject, however, to the approval of a quorum of the Executive Council.

SEC. 5. All members of the Association, when called upon by the Secretary in behalf of the Protective Committee for information or aid, shall promptly respond by giving all assistance in their power; and all members shall, at all times, notify the Secretary, who shall promptly notify the Committee, of any attempted or accomplished crime reported to him as likely to affect other members of the Association.

ARTICLE V.

SECTION 1. Annual meetings of the Association shall be held at such times and places as shall be determined by the Executive Council. Special meetings may be called by the said Council, if, in their opinion, circumstances require them; giving two weeks' notice of time and place of meeting, together with the subject-matter of business to come before such special meeting. The Executive Council shall meet to arrange the order of business on the day preceding any general meeting of the Association.

ARTICLE VI.

SECTION 1. The Expenses of the Executive Council in carrying out the business of the Association to be done by them, shall be provided for by the annual dues of the members of the Association; provided, however, that the Executive Council shall have no authority to incur or contract, on behalf of this Association, any liability whatever beyond the annual dues hereby authorized, and only that for the purposes hereby designated.

ARTICLE VII.

SECTION 1. Resolutions and subjects for discussion (except those referring to points of order or matters of courtesy) must be submitted in writing to the Secretary, for reference to the Executive Council, at least ten days before any general meeting of the Association; but any person desiring to submit any resolution of business in open Convention can do so upon a two-thirds vote of the delegates present.

SEC. 2. No opinions expressed, principles advocated, theories advanced or policies suggested by any party or person, however presented, shall be deemed to have had the endorsement of this Association except the question of so indorsing shall have been referred to a standing or special committee; shall have been reported upon by such committee and shall have been specifically voted upon, receiving a majority of the votes of those present at an open session of a Convention of the Association.

This item of the Constitution shall be published in every report of the proceedings of any convention and where indorsements are given the fact shall be noted in the report of the proceedings in that behalf.

ARTICLE VIII.

SECTION 1. Any bank failing to pay within three months the annual dues for carrying on the business of the Association shall be considered as having withdrawn from membership; but may be reinstated upon application to the Secretary, and paying all dues in arrears, with consent of the President.

ARTICLE IX.

SECTION 1.   This Constitution may be altered or amended at any annual meeting by a vote of two-thirds of the members present ; notice of the proposed amendment having been first submitted to the Secretary at least ten days before the annual meeting, to be placed by him before the Executive Council, that they may arrange for bringing it before the Convention under the regular order of business.

BY-LAWS.

SECTION 1.   The annual dues shall be due and payable at the commencement of each calendar year.

SEC. 2.   The annual dues of all members shall be Ten ($10) Dollars.

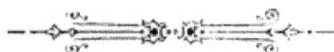

PROCEEDINGS

OF THE

THIRD ANNUAL CONVENTION

OF THE

CALIFORNIA BANKERS ASSOCIATION

HELD IN THE

CHAMBER OF COMMERCE ROOMS, SAN FRANCISCO.

FIRST DAY.

THURSDAY, FEBRUARY 22, 1894.

The convention was called to order at 10 o'clock A. M. by Isaias W. Hellman, President of the Association.

The Chairman called upon Lovell White, Cashier of the San Francisco Savings Union, to deliver the address of welcome.

Mr. White spoke as follows:

Mr. Chairman, and Gentlemen of the California Bankers Association:

It is my unpleasant task to apologize for the absence of Hon. L. R. Ellert, Mayor of San Francisco. It is a very disagreeable duty to lament the absence of a star. Mr. Ellert, as Chief Magistrate of the City of San Francisco, was to have given strength and honor to this convention, but he has declined.

He is said to be a modest man, so he takes himself out of the way. I suppose he realizes the trite saying that "speech is silver, but silence is golden." He is like a great many other men, he can perform good executive work, but he is bashful and timid, like heroes who have won honors in battle, when it comes to appearing before the public.

If Mayor Ellert had been here probably he would have suggested

that this weather is exceptional; he would have talked about the mild-
ness of our climate and the beauty of San Francisco. You come here
now and you find the weather cold and inhospitable.

But the bankers of the city welcome you. They are happy to see
you, and I believe they will try to make your visit with us as pleasant
for you as the circumstances permit.

I regret the necessity of saying this little without any preparation
whatever, but it is simply an apology for the absence of Mayor Ellert.
[Applause.]

The President: *Gentlemen of the Convention:* I am sorry that
I have not the privilege to respond to an address from Mayor Ellert.
He has disappointed us, but I hope that other speakers, delegates from
the country, will be able to compensate us for it.

It affords me great pleasure to be able to welcome you here to-
day, and I hope that this meeting will be of as much benefit to us as
those which have preceded it, and that it will help to cement closer
feelings of good-fellowship between the bankers of the State.

During the past year marvelous changes have taken place in the
financial condition of the country, and a lifetime's experience has been
crowded into that brief period. Banks, one after another, closed their
doors. Factories have stopped working and trade generally has
become paralyzed. I do not propose to enter into the causes that have
brought about this crisis. Sufficient is it to say that confidence was
shaken in the whole of the United States, and all classes and all trades
were injured by it. The crisis affected us here in California in a peculiar way, because we are so far off from financial centers. Ordinarily
bankers' balances in New York or Chicago could easily be transferred
here, but by reason of the great scarcity of the circulating medium in
the Eastern centers, we were even refused by our corresponding banks
in New York to have our own funds transmitted to us.

Another great hardship for California was that the Treasury Department, which had previously made transfers of money from New
York to San Francisco by telegraph, had, during the height of the
panic, even refused to do that. Notwithstanding all this, we certainly
can be proud of how well our banks have weathered the storm. California has, by reason of the unbounded resources of its soil, climate
and mines, stood the brunt of the financial storm better than many
States in the Union. Most of the banks which, during the panic, had
to suspend, have reopened their doors. To-day the only ones remaining closed are four, two of which should really have been closed long
before, and would probably have suspended under any circumstances.
The shrinkage in values of cereals, fruits, silver, in fact of all products, points to a contraction of trade.

Commercial as well as savings banks are again feeling the favorable effect of a change, and deposits are on the increase, especially in
the moneyed centers. I do not ascribe it entirely to the increase of
trade, but partly to the emptying of stockings and the depleting of
safe-deposit boxes from the coin lodged therein during the panic.

Since money has again become much easier to obtain, it would not be amiss to call to the attention of our capitalists the fact that this is the time to aid in establishing manufacturing enterprises, thereby giving employment to many idle men.

A lasting benefit which is the direct result of the panic is the new regulation of the Associated Banks of San Francisco, which does away with the old system of overdrafts, probably the most dangerous feature of our Western banking system—a custom which had nothing to recommend it and one contrary to all sound banking principles.

The late crisis has also demonstrated that large deposits by wealthy people in savings banks are a danger to a bank. When money becomes stringent and rates of interest advance it is the capitalist who at once takes advantage of the situation and withdraws his funds. In doing so he depletes the reserve of the bank and upsets all previous calculations or arrangements. In the Eastern States, where savings banks have been established a number of years, the law regulates the maximum amount which a depostor can have to his credit. I understand that in the State of New York the maximum is $3000. Similar laws should be passed by our next Legislature, and under no circumstances should a savings institution be permitted to accept in the aggregate more than $10,000 from any one depositor.

I will not take up more of your time with my suggestions. Many other subjects appertaining to business will claim your attention, and I hope you will all return to your counting-rooms with broader views, looking back with pleasure and profit to this, our third meeting in council.

The next in order is the report of the treasurer.

The Secretary: Mr. Chairman, Mr. Kline, our treasurer, has not arrived, but he has sent me his report, with the request that I read it.

The California Bankers Association, City:

GENTLEMEN—I have the honor to submit herewith a statement of receipts and disbursements :

Balance of cash on hand at last report		$1,081 22
Received from memberships	$1,719	
Received from sales lapel buttons	13 50	
Received from warrant drawn in error	25	1,778 50
Total receipts		$2,859 72
Paid secretary's warrants Nos. 67 to 121 inclusive, returned herewith		1,939 49
Balance of cash on hand February 22d, 1894		920 23

Respectfully submitted,

G. W. KLINE, Treasurer.

The Chairman :   The next in order is the secretary's report.

To the Officers and Members of the California Bankers Association:

GENTLEMEN—Since the adjournment of our last Convention in September, 1892, three different secretaries have served the Association.   Mr. George H. Stewart resigned in July last, and was succeeded by Mr. A. D. Childress, who in turn resigned in October following, and was succeeded by the present incumbent.   The books, records and effects of the secretary's office surrendered by Mr. Childress were found in perfect order.

At the date of our last Convention 177 banks were enrolled as members of the Association.   Since then the following nine have joined :

Grangers Bank of San Francisco.

Humboldt Savings and Loan Society.

Donohoe-Kelly Banking Company of San Francisco.

Bank of Monterey.

Bank of Palo Alto.   .

California Mortgage and Savings Bank of San Luis Obispo.

First National Bank of Petaluma.

Bank of Commerce of San Diego.

Farmers and Mechanics Bank of Healdsburg.

Four banks, the San Diego Savings Bank, the State Bank of San Jacinto, the Vallejo Commercial Bank and the Bank of Lemoore failed to pay the annual dues required to maintain their membership; one, the Bank of Orange, resigned, and six, the City Bank of Los Angeles, the Bank of Anaheim, the Pacific Bank, the Consolidated National Bank of San Diego, the Bank of Oceanside and the Bank of Madera are in liquidation.   The present membership of the Association is therefore 175.

From the secretary of the State Bank Commissioners it is learned that at the present date there are in the State of California recognized and doing business :

National Banks........ 35
Incorporated State Commercial Banks...... 179
Incorporated State Savings Banks.. 61
Private Banking firms.. 15

A total of..290

Of these, 30 National Banks, 110 State Commercial Banks, 29 Savings Banks and 6 private banking firms are members of this association.

Of the 115 remaining, 3 National Banks, 40 State Commercial Banks, 27 Savings Banks and 6 private banking firms, 76 altogether, have each a capital stock of less than $100,000.

The dues collected after the close of the Convention of 1892 have been considered as payment in full to the end of 1893.   It is the intention in future to collect the dues annually with the commencement of each calendar year.   No call for the dues of 1894 has yet been made, it being deferred by order of the Executive Council until after the adjournment of this Convention.

The receipts, $1,753.50, shown by the Treasurer's report, represent $1,610 collected since his report of September 5, 1892, for dues to the end of 1893, and $130, dues for 1894, collected from 8 new members joining since January 1st of this year and 5 members renewed, together with $13.50 from sales of the Association lapel button.

The expenditures, $1,914.49, shown by the Treasurer's Report represent disbursements for 17 months, from September 1st, 1892, to January 31st, 1893, segregated as follows:

Cost of 211 Association lapel buttons $316 50
Expenses of Convention of 1892...................................... 164 37
Printing and distributing proceedings of same................ 255 50
Expenses of members of Executive Council attending meetings.. 134 80
Expenses of Secretary's Office, including salaries, stationery,
   printing, postage and incidentals............................... 1,043 32

All of which is respectfully submitted,

R. M. WELCH, Secretary.

On motion of Lovell White of San Francisco, seconded by Wm. Beckman of Sacramento, the reports of the Treasurer and Secretary were referred to the Auditing Committee.

The Chairman: We will now listen to the report of the Executive Council.

Lovell White read the report of the Executive Council as follows:

Mr. President and members of the California Bankers Association:

In May last, Mr. Childress, then Chairman of the Executive Council, appointed the following gentlemen to represent California in the World's Congress of Bankers and Financiers held at Chicago during the week commencing with the 19th of June following.

DELEGATES.

S. G. Murphy,	First National Bank,	San Francisco.
Norman Rideout,	The Rideout Bank,	Marysville.
W. W. Phillips,	Farmers Bank,	Fresno.
W. M. Eddy,	Santa Barbara Co. Nat'l Bank,	Santa Barbara.
O. H. Churchill,	Nat'l Bank of California,	Los Angeles.

ALTERNATES.

A. D. Thomson,	First National Bank,	Oakland.
C. W. Bush,	Bank of Yolo,	Woodland.
O. J. Woodward,	Fresno National Bank,	Fresno.
F. P. Morrison,	First National Bank,	Redlands.
W. D. Woolwine,	First National Bank,	San Diego.

Otherwise the efficient action (gratefully remembered) of the secretary left little demanding the attention of the Council until July 6th. On that date Mr. Stewart, much to the regret of the members, addressed a circular letter to the Council tendering his resignation and giving reasons therefor so conclusive as to compel its acceptance. At the same time it was determined by correspondence between the members that Mr. A. D. Childress, then chairman of the Council, should succeed to the office of secretary, and on July 20th Mr. Stewart reported that he had turned over to Mr. Childress all matters pertaining to the office.

At a special meeting held in San Francisco, on the 29th of July, Mr. Childress resigned as chairman and a member of the Council, and the vacancies thereby created were filled by the election of the undersigned as Chairman and Mr. George H. Stewart as a member.

At the same time it was decided that, in view of the unsettled conditions existing in financial circles, it was inexpedient to fix a date for the holding of the third annual Convention of the Association.

Early in October Mr. Childress finding it impossible to give any attention to the duties of Secretary resigned and the Council communicating by letter appointed Mr. R. M. Welch of the San Francisco Savings Union in his stead.

At the request of certain members a meeting of the Council was called for November 18th in San Francisco to again consider the holding of the third annual Convention.

When, after the Convention of 1892 had been assigned to Fresno, the bankers of that city waived their claims thereto in order that the Convention might be held in San Francisco in connection with the Convention of the American Bankers' Association, it was understood that Fresno should be considered to have a prior claim to the next Convention.

At the suggestion of the Council, however, the claims of Fresno were again generously waived and it was decided to hold the Convention in San Francisco at this time to afford the delegates the additional attraction of the Midwinter Fair.

At the same meeting Mr. W. W. Phillips of Fresno resigned as a member of the Council on account of his retirement from banking circles, and Mr. S. Prentiss Smith of the Bank of California was elected in his stead.

A special Committee was then appointed consisting of Messrs. S. Prentiss Smith, N. D. Rideout and C. E. Palmer, to have in charge the arrangements for this Convention.

The duties of that Committee have been well performed and to the members the thanks of the Convention are due.

It was also decided, on the suggestion of our President, Mr. I. W. Hellman, who was present, to recommend that our By-Laws be so amended as to provide that the annual dues be payable at the commencement of each calendar year.

Our present By-Laws relating to dues read as follows:

" SECTION 1.   The annual dues of the Association shall be considered due at
" the beginning of the year, which year shall commence with the regular annual
" meeting; it being understood that absent members from such annual meet-
" ing shall not forfeit their membership nor the right to become members, pro-
" vided they comply with the Constitution and By-Laws and remit the amount of
" the dues to the secretary within one month after such annual meeting."

It is proposed to strike out the entire section and substitute therefor the following:

" The annual dues of the Association shall be due and payable at the com-
" mencement of each calendar year."

It is also recommended that the Constitution be so amended as to provide that the president and first vice-president shall be *ex-officio* members of the Executive Council.

Reference is made to the reports of the treasurer and secretary for a showing of the financial condition of the Association.

The balance in the hands of the treasurer together with the annual dues to be collected for 1894 will, it is believed, be ample for all possible contingencies of the Association during the present year.

The State Bank Commissioners and the National Bank Examiner for California having been elected at our last Convention honorary members of this Association, it is in order for us to recognize as members J. B. Fuller and W. B. Wightman, the successors respectively of State Bank Commissioner Gerberding and National Bank Examiner Chamberlain retired.

At our last Convention certain recommendations relating to the clearing of country checks at money centers, being part of a paper presented by Mr. E. S. Sheffield, were referred to the Council for consideration. A supplementary report in this behalf prepared by Mr. George H. Stewart, others concurring, will be presented later on.

All of which is respectfully submitted.

LOVELL WHITE,

Chairman.

On motion of George E. Hersey of Gilroy, seconded by Wm. Beckman of Sacramento, the report of the Executive Council was ordered received and placed on file.

The Chairman: The following gentlemen are appointed on the various committees:

Auditing Committee: W. E. Gerber of Sacramento, J. M. Elliott of Los Angeles, and O. McHenry of Modesto.

Committee on Resolutions: Frank Miller of Sacramento, H. W. Wright of San Jose, H. H. Hewlett of Stockton, C. S. Brooks of Marysville, and A. H. R. Schmidt of San Francisco.

Committee on Nominations: E. R. Hamilton of Sacramento, C. W. Bush of Woodland, P. E. Bowles of Oakland, L. W. Burris of Santa Rosa, John Reichman of Fresno.

Lovell White: There is fortunately, or unfortunately, quite a number of papers to be read. The reading and discussion of these may occupy more time than will be at our command in the two days. There is one paper, by Mr. Sheffield of Santa Barbara, which is quite long, and it is speculative, we may say, rather than practical. That paper has been printed and a pile of copies of it lies on the secretary's table. It has been suggested that it would be well to distribute copies of that paper, for the reason that we may not have time to hear it read. If each of the delegates will take a copy of the paper, the subject treated by it can be discussed at our leisure, when the subject of the paper comes up in due course. That may save us perhaps half an hour.

I believe the authors of the other papers will be here and read them. Mr. Sheffield, unfortunately, is absent.

George H. Stewart of Los Angeles: Mr. Chairman, Mr. Sheffield's paper having been presented to the Executive Council and having passed through their hands and been printed, and Mr. Sheffield being absent, I move that it be accepted and opened to later discussion, just as if read.

Mr. Stewart's motion was seconded and duly carried, and it was so ordered.

W. E. Gerber of Sacramento: Mr. Chairman, in looking over the programme as prepared by the Committee of Arrangements, I find that, in order to bring a matter before the convention which I wish to present, I will have to do so at the risk of being declared out of order. The subject is one which I do not believe can be properly brought up and discussed at a meeting of this kind.

It has been suggested by the interior bankers that we request of the members of the Clearing House Association that they grant us an audience at some time agreeable to them. The discussion will no doubt be a short one. I am requested to ask the chairman to make arrangements with the Clearing House to meet the interior bankers in session at any time during this convention. I do not believe that the subject is one which can be properly brought before a body of this character, and I would ask the chairman to endeavor to make such arrangements, and announce the time at which the Clearing House will give us an audience, any time during the next two days. If the matter is discussed at a meeting of this kind, in open convention, there will be many arguments and propositions submitted, and probably nothing more, and we will go home without accomplishing anything. On the other hand, if the members of the Clearing House will meet the interior bankers in the manner suggested, it is believed that we can reach some definite conclusions.

The Chairman: For what purpose shall I ask a meeting of the Clearing House? I must give a reason.

Mr. Gerber: As I stated in the beginning, I don't know but what I am entirely out of order in making any remarks upon the subject, but, inasmuch as you have asked for it, Mr. Chairman, I will state that I hurriedly wrote a little circular and sent it to the different bankers in the State, pertaining to the subject which I thought was of sufficient importance to warrant us in asking the members of the Clearing House to grant us a hearing. This circular is now in the hands of Mr. Stewart. I don't know that it is pertinent to read it here. I think, if the chairman will look at it, he will agree with me that it is a subject that should properly come before the members of the Clearing House Association and the interior banks, at a meeting by themselves. If you will allow me, Mr. Chairman, I will present this to you. [Hands paper to the chairman.]

The Chairman : This is contrary to the late action taken by the Clearing House, so much so that if this is the only reason why you want me to ask them for a hearing, I would consider it useless, unless the Convention here takes it up. If the Bankers Convention now in session takes up the subject, and desires me to do as suggested, I will do so. The bankers in San Francisco, the Clearing House banks, have all agreed to do away with overdrafts, in every way, shape and form, and you will notice by my report that I am personally opposed to overdrafts. Now, if the Convention desires me to take this action, I desire to be instructed by the Convention to ask the Clearing House to come together. I cannot call them together, but if the Convention desires it, I can ask them to give a hearing.

Wm. Beekman of Sacramento · Then, Mr. Chairman, I will make that motion—that you be requested to ask the Clearing House to give the interior bankers a hearing, and we will take a vote on it, to bring this matter before the Clearing House Committee, or whatever you may call it, and ask them to appoint a time, if they wish to do so, for a hearing upon this question. My motion is that the Clearing House be asked to give a hearing to the interior banks at such time as is agreeable.

Mr. Gerber : Mr. Chairman, I desire to correct the statement made, that this conflicts with the recent resolutions passed by the members of the Clearing House, in so far that it is an attempt to do away with overdrafts. I do not believe that the circular has been correctly read by the chairman, and I want the matter, when voted upon by this Convention, to be properly understood. I say in the circular that I believe the custom of allowing overdrafts is a pernicious one. I say that overdrafts are wrong. I say that the resolution passed is in the direction of safe and conservative banking. But I do not want the members to vote upon the question without understanding it perfectly. There are other matters there that I think are of sufficient importance to warrant the interior banks in asking for a hearing before the Clearing House Association.

The motion being seconded, was voted upon and duly carried.

The Chairman: It is so ordered. I will endeavor to secure a hearing for you. Are there any other impromptu matters?

J. B. Lankershim of Los Angeles:

Mr. Chairman and Gentlemen of the Convention: I have a communication from Los Angeles bankers, and I think it would be appropriate at this time to introduce the same to the notice of the Convention. It will take but a very few minutes to do so.

The Chairman: Proceed.

Mr. Lankershim: I will state, preliminarily, that this address is from seven savings banks of Los Angeles. They are banded together under the name of the Los Angeles Savings Banks Association. We formed this association in June last. There was a panic among all the banks then, and the savings banks came together and decided to form a union, so that they should all do business on the same basis, so that a depositor in one bank should have no advantage over a depositor in other banks. We formed our union on the 20th of June, and the day following we insisted upon notice for payment of deposits, made a rule that no money should be paid without regular notice of six months upon time deposits, and sixty days on ordinary deposits. The action subsequently to that resulted very harmoniously. All the savings banks passed through the panic without the least trouble. In the month of December last we came to the conclusion that we were ready to pay depositors without further notice, and after January we resumed the loaning of our money. We have meetings monthly. Last Monday the association of savings banks met and adopted some resolutions and I was asked to bring them before the Convention of the California Bankers Association here, showing what we have done.

I will state that this association is composed of the following banks, including all the savings banks in Los Angeles: The Security Savings Bank & Trust Company, German-American Savings Bank, Los Angeles Savings Bank, Savings Bank of Southern California, The Union Bank of Savings, The Columbia Savings Bank, and the Main Street Savings Bank and Trust Company. The membership consists of one member from each bank, but each bank has the right to bring in other officers to take part in discussions.

Mr. Lankershim read as follows:

In recent years the managers of the various savings banks of the city of Los Angeles have been much annoyed by vexatious experiences, common in all cities wherein a uniform method of conducting the banking business is not in vogue.

Recognizing that the savings banks are trustees of the money of the mass of the people, and that they are custodians of large deposits, and that there are a few necessary rules to which every savings bank must adhere in order to conduct business safely, these experiences gave rise to the feeling that an organization of the savings banks which should sustain the same relation to the individual members as the Clearing House does to the commercial banks, would be productive of great good, not only to the bank members of the organization, but also to the community at large. This sentiment finally culminated in the issuance of a call for a meeting of representatives from each of the savings banks, with a view to effecting such an organization. This meeting was unanimous in opinion, and preliminary arrangements were there made, and later on the organization known as "The Los Angeles Association of Savings Banks" was effected July 1, 1893.

The object of this Association is to promote the efficiency and security of savings banks by a harmonious and united action in regard to the requiring of notice for the withdrawal of money; in regulating the time that deposits must remain to be entitled to interest; to fix the rate of interest to be paid semi-annually to depositors, and to advise and counsel in regard to conducting the business in a legitimate manner, so that the interest of depositors, borrowers and stockholders may receive the proper attention. Such other regulations are found in the constitution and by-laws as provide for the proper management and conduct of the Association.

The Association includes all Savings Banks in the city—all having found it to their interest to join. The German-American Savings Bank and Trust Co., Security Savings Bank and Trust Co., Los Angeles Savings Bank, Savings Bank of Southern California, Union Bank of Savings, Columbia Savings Bank, and Main Street Savings Bank and Trust Co. constituting the list.

The membership consists of one officer from each Bank composing the Association, but each of such officers has the right to bring any other officer or Director with him to the meetings, and take part in any discussion, but each Bank represented has only one vote. The term Savings Bank is defined in the constitution so as to restrict the membership to banks doing a legitimate Savings Bank business. An Executive Committee is provided to look after the general affairs of the Association, to receive applications for membership, and to look after the interests of the Association in general when not in session. The meetings are held regularly once a month, usually in the evening, as that seems to be the most convenient for all the Bankers, and has the advantage of giving the members plenty of time without being recalled to look after business matters.

Although this Association is but a few months old, having been organized in July last, the work already done has been productive of much good and has been very satisfactory. "In union there is strength," and in this union the benefits have been especially manifest during the trying times of the past few months, when the wisdom that comes from counsel and united efforts has been of great help to all members of the Association. All phases of the business, advertising, methods of book-keeping, methods of figuring interest and other minor matters have been more or less discussed, and benefits invariably derived therefrom. The work of the Association has been harmonious throughout, and the membership is encouraged therefore in looking forward to enlarged and continued usefulness.

J. B. LANKERSHIM.
President Los Angeles Association Savings Banks.

I think, owing to the fact that there are only one or two gentlemen here that are connected with the savings banks of Los Angeles, we would like to tender to this Convention this memorandum as a communication from the savings banks of Los Angeles to this Convention, and as such I offer them.

The Chairman: Very well. The secretary will take the memorandum.

Here the Convention adjourned until Friday, February 23rd, at 10 o'clock A. M.

SECOND DAY.

FRIDAY, FEBRUARY 23—MORNING SESSION.

The Convention was called to order at 10 o'clock A. M., by President Isaias W. Hellman.

Lovell White: Mr. Chairman, will you allow me to make one remark? In speaking yesterday and apologizing for the absence of Mayor Ellert, I used language which perhaps admits of the construction that I meant he was evading the responsibility of speaking here. Such was not the fact. He could not have come. The circumstances did not permit of his being here. Could he have been here, I know he would have spoken ably and well, and done justice to the occasion and himself.

The Chairman: The first business in order this morning is the supplementary report of the Executive Council.

Lovell White: The Executive Council submit the report of its sub-committee on a suggestion presented at our last Convention by Mr. E. S. Sheffield of Santa Barbara and then referred to the Council.

Mr. George H. Stewart of Los Angeles has handled the matter, and here is what he has prepared. It has received the concurrence of several members of the Executive Council. The savings bank members of the Council are not concerned in this matter. It was left to the commercial people. Mr. Stewart will read his paper, with your permission.

The Chairman: Proceed, Mr. Stewart.

George H. Stewart of Los Angeles then read as follows:

The matter of "Collecting Country Checks" contained in the paper entitled "Development of Banking," read at our last Convention by Mr. E. S. Sheffield of the Santa Barbara County National Bank, was referred by the Committee on Resolutions to the Executive Council for consideration and report at this meeting. It has become my duty to prepare its report.

Mr. Sheffield said in part (see proceedings 1892, pages 45 and 46):

"The problem of the collection of country checks has long worried the banking mind. Solution after solution has been proposed, but since the worry continues, it evidently does not stay solved. * * * Let us pass them through the clearing houses at money centers, even though a separate daily clearing be demanded. Let customers' checks have printed on them the names of all clearing correspondents of the banks whose form it is. Let the correspondents of the country banks at such centers take all checks drawn upon their client-banks which appear in the exchanges of such city and debit and remit daily to each its respective checks for proper credit." * * *

"An objection might be raised that the city correspondent would be reluctant to advance the sums needed to make these clearings; one answer is that little money would be required. For, just as do city clearings, country clearings would on the average balance themselves."

"But the effective answer is, that city banks already hold the very funds out of which these checks are now paid, placed with them partly for that purpose; so that it is solely a question of doing the thing directly or indirectly. Again, let the habit of clearing country checks once be established, these balances would increase, for the aim of all bankers is to place their funds at the point where the demand upon them is to be made." * * *

"It is not needful to explain to city bankers the relative economy of settlement by clearing to settlement with each bank separately. * * * As no charge for collection of local checks is made, none should be made for country checks. The cost of providing funds to meet them should be borne by the country banker; most of them now supply their depositors with exchange free: all, with few exceptions, in their own interest should do so. By multiplying the reasons favoring deposits, deposits increase; furnishing exchange free is enlarging the convenience of the bank to the depositor. He finds, that in addition to safe storage for his money, he gains the use of it at distant points without expense, which he could not do outside of banks. He is thus encouraged to become a steady and permanent depositor, and his balance supplies the means to make these distant payments."

There is no doubt depositors will agree with Mr. Sheffield's position, and can be depended upon for assistance in "multiplying the reasons favoring deposits." The customer would like to do his entire local and distant financeering without expense; would be pleased to have his bank combine the security of a safe deposit box, the guarantees of an insurance company, the conveniences of a stationery store, the facilities of an express company, the counsel of a lawyer, and the services of an agent—all without expense or trouble to him. The senseless competition among banks existing in this State previous to the panic of 1893 appears to be intensified rather than modified, and favors doing anything and everything for the customer *without charge*, except, perhaps, loaning him money, if his deposit can be secured.

I hope it is unnecessary to remark that while such a course may seem proper to many bankers, who have, until recently, been successful in other lines of business, and may in some cases result in an apparently prosperous business, the plan must strike every thoughtful and conservative man as calculated to lower the standard which should be demanded in bankers, and inevitably tends to unsafe— even dangerous methods. A condition of things better than the present must exist if the resulting damage can be limited to those responsible therefor. Practical illustrations have not been wanting since our last Convention, and if the bankers of California will have the good sense to permit the experience and failure of others to teach the needed lesson, both themselves and the public will be the gainers.

Believing that each branch of banking should contribute its profit in proportion to the cost and risk of operating, and realizing that the opportunities for kiting checks are already too numerous, the writer must voice the sentiment of this Council that *as a policy*, the clearing or handling of country checks at par and without limit should be discouraged—a matter extremely difficult of accomplishment, as the man to be favored by the bank and the drawer of the check are merged in the one depositor. He therefore sends his check to the city creditor, who raises little, if any objection, because as a depositor he is in position to throw the burden on his own bank, which in turn insists on passing along the item at par to its correspondents and their connections until it reaches the drawee bank. The latter deprived of the profitable sale for its exchange on the one hand, and forced to provide funds at distant points without notice on the other, takes its reward in the satisfaction of having customers able and willing to calculate the exact time a deposit will be necessary to provide for the returning check without the services of a notary.

In view of the foregoing, this report would suggest that, without reference further to our belief that the indiscriminate floating of country checks should be discouraged, our efforts be confined to making as safe, expeditious and economical as possible the handling of business in this direction, which the members of our Association are now compelled to transact. Each bank in receiving country checks must protect itself,—

First—Against the bank from whom received—for items returned " not good."

Second —Against the bank to whom sent—for items proving " good."

The Executive Council would therefore report that in its judgment:

1. The clearing of country checks through the Clearing Houses of California is practicable by arrangement and under suitable restrictions.

2. That in such case the Clearing House By-Laws be so amended as to provide indemnity, in behalf of the clearing hourse bank accepting the country checks through the clearing, against the default of both sender and drawee bank.

3. That the listing in full of items by each bank in the course of their travel seems to us a useless burden, and that all detailed registration shall be done by sending bank, on proper form of ticket to accompany each check, permitting ready listing by numbers only at later stages.

4. That some uniform rule be adopted which will cause checks to travel through regular channels where safeguards can be provided, and the standing of the endorsers and drawee bank known.

5. That any provisions adopted shall in no case be compulsory, but shall merely provide a uniform method available to those banks who may desire.

It was my first intention to suggest in detail my conclusions as to the suitable form of ticket to accompany check, and other blanks required to conform to the above, but I have concluded to await favorable action of this Convention on this report before submitting them.

GEO. H. STEWART,
Of Executive Council.

On motion, the report of the Council on Mr. Sheffield's suggestion was adopted.

The Chairman: I expected to hear some discussion of that subject.

We will now listen to the report of the Committee on Higher Education of Business Men, C. C. Bush of Redding, Chairman.

The Secretary: Mr. Chairman, Mr. Bush is not here. I have a letter from him requesting that I present the report in his behalf.

It reads as follows:

To the California Bankers' Association:

GENTLEMEN :—At your last annual meeting the following Whereases and Resolution were adopted—viz.

WHEREAS, the subject of the Higher Education of Business Men is now receiving increasing attention from the colleges and universities in this country, and

WHEREAS, it appears that the advice and assistance of practical men is desired in this movement, therefore, be it

RESOLVED, that the President of this Association appoint a Committee of Three to confer on this subject, and report to this body at its next meeting, as to what it may be able to do in the promotion of Higher Business Education.

C. C. Bush, of the Bank of Shasta County, C. E. Palmer, of the Union National Bank of Oakland, and E. S. Sheffield, of the Santa Barbara County National Bank of Santa Barbara, were appointed such committee, and they herewith submit their report :

As soon as circumstances admitted, your Committee obtained a limited number of copies of the address of Prof. James, of the Wharton School of Finance and Economy, in the City of Philadelphia, delivered before the American Bankers' Association, at Saratoga, N. Y., and submitted it to the consideration of prominent bankers, educators and business men of the Pacific Coast, requesting their views on the subject of the " Higher Education of Business Men."

At first we met ready and encouraging responses ; unfortunately, before many who no doubt would have replied had done so, the financial stringency invaded our Coast, and a school was forced upon us, wherein but few had even learned their A, B, C's, and while the education received therefrom may not have been of the desired higher kind, it no doubt was impressive, and will be lasting to the members of this association and many others.

How very few anticipated or were prepared for the events of the past year? Can we find or establish a school wherein proper preparation may be had to ward against like financial disasters in the future? If so, it is our plain duty to ourselves and the world at large, to put forth every reasonable exertion to found such an institution.

As before intimated, the opinions of the many we are unable to submit to you, but we can assure you that those we do are invaluable for the soundness of the views expressed and the encouragement they give us, that we are in line for the benefit of would-be business men, and consequently mankind in general.

SAN FRANCISCO, March 28th, 1893.

Mr. C. C. Bush, Chairman, care of Bank of Shasta, Redding, Cal.

DEAR SIR :—I beg to thank you for the copy of Prof. James' address before the American Bankers' Association at Saratoga, but as I will leave in a few days for Japan, there is little time left for the perusal of the same, and it is hardly possible that I can give the matter my attention, and therefore cannot comply with your request until my return.   Yours truly,

L. GOTTIG.

This association, no doubt will agree with your committee ; when they say that it was most unfortunate that Mr. Gottig's health after his return was of such a nature to the day of his death that he was unable to carry out his intention and comply with the request of your committee.

PALO ALTO, April 10th, 1893.

Mr. C. C. Bush, Redding, Cal.

DEAR SIR :—In reply to your kind circular letter of March 27th, permit me to say that I am fully in sympathy with the views of Dr. James in regard to the Higher Education of Business Men. I am well acquainted with Dr. James and have been familiar with his views and the plan of the Wharton School of Finance for some time. It is in the plan of this institution to carry out so far as may be the ideas of Dr. James, and to develop in connection with the University and its Department of Finance the same work which is carried on so well in the Wharton School. To this end we have appointed Dr. Edward A. Ross of Cornell, Professor of Administration and Finance. His work, together with that of Dr. Amos G. Warner in Applied Economics will probably meet the demand in this direction on this Coast for some time to come. There seems to me no good reason why a college should not give the Higher Training of business men and merchants just as well as of lawyers and engineers.   Very truly yours,

DAVID S. JORDAN.

WOODLAND, April 14th, 1893.

Judge C. C. Bush.

DEAR SIR :—I beg to acknowledge your letter of yesterday enclosing Prof. James' Address. I was much impressed with his ideas at the time of its delivery in San Francisco. There is no question about the advantages to be derived from Schools of Finance nor in my judgment about the success which would follow their inception. The only question to be considered is, is there anything in the educational line more essential for us on this Coast to devote our energies toward? We are lamentably backward as compared with the older states in the direction of technical training. A vast field is open before us. I believe that every effort in any direction of technical training should receive the encouragement and assistance of the scholar and capitalist.   Yours very respectfully,

C. W. BUSH.

SACRAMENTO, CAL., April 15th, 1893.

Hon. C. C. Bush, Chairman Comm. Cal. Bankers' Association :—

DEAR SIR :—I am honored by your letter of 13th, and a copy of Prof. James' Address.

I am reading one or two elementary law books and answering questions propounded by the managers of a "school" in Detroit.

In the course of a few years, if I persevere, I shall not be a lawyer, but perhaps I shall be a better banker. So I have come to the conclusion that a "Correspondence School" for bank clerks would be a good thing, and while it should include some law it should also include some arithmetic.

Arbitration of exchange is out of the line of the great number of us, but we are often asked as to comparative value of bonds : thus, if the country sells its 6 per cent. bonds at 110, and its 5½ per cent. bonds at 105, is the one result equal to the other?

A "Correspondence School" would cover many things in which we are rusty.

It would be like a bank examination, and regarded as an ordinary piece of necessary routine. The man who could not progress through such a course of questioning should not expect promotion : having graduated in this preliminary school and thereby laid claim to permanent employment, he would next look at a higher course ; and finally, he might even understand the Silver Question in the abstract (for we are all convinced it is a nuisance in practice.)

To repeat, I believe in a system of instruction and reading which shall be proven by a series of questions through the mail, checked off by a competent instructor. The system to begin at the root of the tree of knowledge and rise as high as you please. Respectfully,

FRANK MILLER.

CHICO, CAL., April 28th, 1893.
George H. Stewart, Esq., Secy. California Bankers' Assoc'n, Los Angeles, Cal.

DEAR SIR :—The subject of a Higher Education for Business Men is certainly one deserving the most thoughtful consideration. We are in the midst of an era of special schools. For the past quarter of a century the tendency has been in the direction of special and practical instruction for those seeking to qualify for the business activities of life, outside of the so-called learned professions. In my judgment these special lines of instruction should be encouraged and expanded. If the mind of a young man is carefully prepared and instructed in the general principles of his chosen occupation, as well as in the enlightened experience of others, he will the more clearly discern and more readily and intelligently adapt himself to the every-day practical duties that press upon him.

It seems to me, therefore, that the Resolutions adopted by the California Bankers' Association (a copy of which you enclose) are full of pertinent suggestion, and if followed will result in establishing a higher standard of business intelligence.

Very truly yours,

JOHN BIDWELL.

BERKELEY, May 8th, 1893.
Hon. C. C. Bush:

DEAR SIR :—Your letter of last month presented so novel a question that I could not reply at once; and a pressure of duties has delayed me so long as to

make me seem discourteous. I have been seeking light from my University associates. The conclusion I reach is something like this:

1. A School of Finance *would* be a desirable thing.

2. To make it effective, on higher lines than those of the " Business Colleges "
and " Commercial Schools " that have sprung up, there should be thorough studies
in political economy, portions of a law course, finance, etc.; such studies as belong
to one of our existing college courses.

3. There could be grafted on our college courses a new college, embracing those
studies, and also a considerable part of what we call our "culture studies." Modern
languages are needed for the higher business interests. History, English litera-
ture, the plainer applications of the natural sciences, and other studies, would go
to form a broad-minded, intelligent man, fit to be an ornament to any business
position. By a proper adjustment of studies, one could take with profit a two
years' course in such studies, a three years' or a four years' course. The full four
years would qualify him for an honorable college diploma.

Of course I am speaking of something much higher than what is commonly
called a " business education." I am thinking of a business turn given to a fully
educated man.

4. *We* have no funds to establish such an additional course; are the bankers
and business men ready to help us to do it? Probably three-fourths of the studies
are given here now. The other fourth would have to be added—in such special
studies as are mentioned by Prof. James. I remain,

Yours very truly,

MARTIN KELLOGG.

SANTA BARBARA, CAL., Dec. 11th, 1893.

My Dear Mr. Bush:—

I have yours of 6th inst. While not dissenting from your view that practical
work in the bank is indispensable, I yet think it desirable that the two Universities
of California so arrange their courses of study that students intending to pursue
business careers may not be disadvantaged as to those fitting themselves for professional work. I would suggest submitting the letters received from the two
Presidents with a resolution recommended for the adoption that it is the sense of
the Convention that the Universities should adapt their studies to this end.

Deriving their support most largely from the business community it certainly
is not too much to ask.   Sincerely yours,

E. S. SHEFFIELD.

SAN FRANCISCO, December 12th, 1893.

C. C. Bush, Esq., Bank of Shasta Co., Redding, Cal.

DEAR SIR: There has recently been published in book form, a series
of lectures by Dr. Sherwood, of the Wharton School, given as a University Extension
Course, under the patronage of the Bankers of Philadelphia. Mr. Wm. H. Rhawn,
in his introduction to the book says, "If it shall aid and encourage educators, bankers and others throughout the country to undertake a like work, its publication will
not have been in vain."

Here in San Francisco there is a very decided and growing interest in University Extension work. The University of California this winter is conducting three courses in this city, one of which is in Economics, under the direction of Prof. Plehn, a clear and forcible lecturer. * * *

It has occurred to me that it would be possible to arrange with the University of California for a similar course, devoted exclusively to Finance and the history and theory of money, during the winter of 1894-5, under the auspices and patronage of the California Bankers' Association, the lectures to be afterwards published in pamphlet form for distribution among the members of the Association.

No inquiries have been made by myself as to the possibility of carrying out this plan.

I merely take the liberty of offering the crude suggestion for the consideration of your Committee. Very truly,

LOVELL WHITE,

Chairman Executive Council, Cal. Bankers' Association.

BERKELEY, January 27th, 1894.

Mr. C. C. Bush, Chairman, Redding, California.

DEAR SIR :—The letter of your committee, concerning a course of lectures "devoted exclusively to finance and the history and the theory of money," dated, December 16th, and addressed to President Kellogg, has been handed to me for consideration and reply. I have discussed the proposition with other members of the Department of History and Political Science, and find that it may be possible to arrange such a course as you describe. This, however, we cannot definitely determine till the question of the appointment of a needed additional instructor in this department shall have been settled.

I shall be pleased to receive further details of your proposition.

Very truly yours,

BERNARD MOSES,

Professor of History and Political Economy.

Besides these letters, we read you an extract from an editorial in the Bankers' Magazine, January 1892.

" The opinion has been prevalent among business men that there was not " much need for careful training in order to succeed in any business pursuit. Too " often, when a young man has asked his superior for advice on the subject, he " has been told : " Do as I have done and you will succeed," and yet this advice, " if followed, in most cases would have brought forth very unsatisfactory results. " The difficulty with the adviser in such cases is, that he does not comprehend the " natural difference between himself, mentally and otherwise, and the person who " seeks his advice. Methodical Training is needed, not so much for exceptional " characters as for average ordinary men, who constitute by far, the larger num- " ber engaged in business. What shall be done to equip them more perfectly for " their intended pursuit? Now the experience of the most successful men usually " furnishes no correct ground work for our reasonings with respect to others ; and " the reasons why it does not may be briefly given.

" Until the present time the natural resources of our country abounded on
" either side, and, therefore, with a little aptitude and energy and self-denial, it
" has been easy for a large number of persons to acquire in a short period great for-
" tunes; but that time is passing away. Our natural resources while great, are
" not so easily transmuted into wealth as they were a few years ago. Fortunes
" can no longer be made in a day in railroads, banks, mines or lands. New con-
" ditions confront those engaged in business. Competition is infinitely keener
" than at any former time. The one great advantage, perhaps, which men of the
" present day possess is the greater abundance of capital which is always ready
" for investment in every enterprise that promises a fair return. Except this con-
" dition, all the others are less favorable for the acquisition of large wealth, and
" therefore, to succeed, a higher degree of ability, better training and more self-
" denial are needed than the successful merchants, bankers and other business
" men formerly practiced.

"If this be true, surely the need of a more systematic education in every kind
" of business is imperative, and bankers have not opened their eyes too soon to
" the need of it by those who are following or intend to follow the banking pur-
" suit. The conditions of success in the business are far more intricate than they
" ever were before, and a more careful study of them is necessary in order to insure
" a successful prosecution of it. The untrained man, therefore, is more likely to
" fail than the man who is able to study and understand these things."

You will also find over forty communications to the American Bankers' Association, printed in the proceedings of the New Orleans Convention of 1891, from
Bankers, Educators and Business Men, all of them encouraging and urging the
establishment of schools for Higher Business Education. Allow us to add an extract from Prof. James' admirable address delivered before the American Bankers'
Association in San Francisco in 1892.

"It is a commonly observed and much lamented fact that in many portions of
" the United States the proportion of boys in our Public Schools is decreasing, or
" at least is not increasing, as one interested in Public Education would like to see
" it, and that in all places the number of boys at school diminishes very rapidly
" as one goes up in the different grades.

" What is the reason of this phenomenon? One very important reason is, of
" course, that the economic condition of the mass of our people is such that they
" cannot afford to keep their boys in school after their thirteenth or fourteenth
" year. They must at that age begin to earn something. Of course it would
" make little difference to those who are absolutely obliged to quit, what the sub-
" sequent course of the school may be. But there are many boys whose parents
" could keep them at school some years longer if they felt that the advantage to be
" derived from such further schooling would overbalance the sacrifices they must
" make to render it possible. At present, the only higher school open to them is
" the ordinary literary high school, and while they would be glad if their children
" could get this additional training, they are not convinced that it is so valuable
" that they can afford the necessary sacrifice. Now, if there were a school of the
" same grade as the high school, with a curriculum so elaborated and adjusted as
" to prepare a boy immediately for practical commercial work, hundreds of
' parents would say that it is worth having. Our boys must take it. The result

" would be that a new class of boys would be reached by our educational system—
" a new line of interest enlisted in its behalf.

" This fact was strikingly illustrated by the establishment of the so-called
" manual training high schools in our various cities, such as Philadelphia, St.
" Louis and Chicago. An entirely new class of boys was reached; the public in-
" terest in high school system in general immensely increased, and the whole
" school system, public and private, strengthened.

" There is no doubt that if Commercial High Schools were established with
" three and four year courses, looking directly towards practical business life a
" similar result would show itself. New classes of the community would be inter-
" ested in our school system, and every part of the system would feel the beneficial
" effects of this new interest.

" It is exactly in this field that the movement for commercial education in
" Western Europe shows the most marked and satisfactory success. In Germany,
" France, Italy and Austria, a most excellent system of Commercial High Schools
" has been developed, which forms one of the most striking and valuable features
" of their educational systems. The full description of typical schools of this sort
" I shall give in the report to be submitted to you.

" I will only mention here the three-year course in the Commercial Academy
" in Vienna, which is one of the largest and most successful of these schools in
" Europe. This course embraces the study of accounting in all its different grades;
" of at least two modern languages, usually French and English, besides the
" mother tongue; of commercial geography, of history of commerce, of mercantile
" law and practice; of the history, distribution and modes of manufacture of
" commercial products; of money, banking and insurance; of political economy,
" of tariff legislation, of international exchange, etc., etc. In a word, the curriculum
" consists of such branches of study as have a pretty direct bearing upon the habits
" and customs of trade.

" Nor is the instruction a mere process of cramming in facts relating to in-
" dustry and commerce. It is given in such a way as to secure the largest educa-
" tional advantages from such material of instruction. Its aim is training in the
" habits and knowledge necessary or desirable for the business man; and I must
" say that the general knowledge of industry and commerce displayed by those
" boys from 15 to 18 would put to shame many a practical business man of years
" standing. It is not a free school. On the contrary, the tuition is high for Aus-
" trian conditions. In spite of this fact, it has in attendance on the three-year
" course over 600 boys; and that although there are other commercial schools in
" Vienna. This school is, moreover, not a government, but a private school. It
" is founded and conducted by a joint stock company of public-spirited citizens
" who chose the form of a corporation with shares as the most convenient system
" of organization.

" The instruction in this scoool in Commercial Geography and similar
" branches is excellent. Many of these subjects of instruction are absolutely
" unknown in our schools, either lower or higher; and while this school is only
" one (perhaps it is true), the best one, of many similar schools in Austria, we have
" not in the United States a single such school. Indeed, so far are we in this

" respect behind Austria, a country on which Americans are accustomed to look
" as in some respects centuries behind the times, that if one of you gentlemen were
" to offer the money to-morrow to open such a school, it would not be possible to
" find suitably prepared teachers for it in the United States of America.

"Of the students in the academy at Vienna it is safe to say that only a small
" part would be at school at all if this particular institution answering to their
" special wants were not in existence. It is also interesting to note that the bank-
" ers and other business men of Vienna appreciate the advantages of this school,
" as their applications for clerks, book-keepers, etc., etc., far outrun the ability of
" the school to satisfy them. What is true of the Vienna Commercial Academy is
" true of the other schools of like kind in Austria, of the schools of commerce in
" France, Italy, Germany, Switzerland, Belgium and Holland."

The consensus of opinion of all who have expressed themselves on the subject
is for such schools as we advocate. Your Committee are of opinion that the education to be had in such schools is not only advantageous from a business point of
view, but also makes a better citizen, a better son, a better husband, a better
father.

Therefore we urge upon your consideration the importance of Higher Business
Education for the better acquirement of this world's goods, more content and
greater happiness to the individual, better citizenship and more earnest patriots,
and to that end offer the following resolution:

Resolved, That the Executive Council confer with the President of the
Leland Stanford Junior University and the President of the University of California, and ascertain if in either institution there is a department such as this Association is striving for. If not, to ascertain if one can be added to said institutions
and on what terms. If this is found impracticable and beyond the reach of this
Association, then endeavor to arrange for a course of lectures in the city of San
Francisco, devoted exclusively to Finance and the history and theory of money
during the winter of 1894-5, under the auspices of this Association. The lectures
to be afterwards published in pamphlet form for distribution among the members
of the Association. Respectfully,

C. C. BUSH,
C. E. PALMER,
E. S. SHEFFIELD,
Committee.

The Chairman: Gentlemen, you have heard the report read.
What is your pleasure?

F. T. Duhring of Sonoma: Mr. Chairman, I move that the report be accepted and placed on file.

The Chairman: I should like to hear some discussion on the subject of that paper. It is certainly worth while.

J. B. Lankershim of Los Angeles: Mr. Chairman, I move, as an
amendment to the motion just made, that the report be received and
adopted. I think that would be more proper.

F. T. Duhring: I accept the amendment.

Lovell White: I suppose it is Mr. Lankershim's intention to have the resolution adopted as read.

J. B. Lankershim: To adopt it as read: yes, sir.

Lovell White: Especially the resolution?

J. B. Lankershim: My motion calls for the adoption of the resolution, in addition, to the report.

Motion, as amended, to receive and adopt the resolution and report, duly carried.

The Chairman: Is Mr. Benjamin C. Wright present? If so, we will be pleased to hear from him at this time.

Benjamin C. Wright of San Francisco addressed the Convention as follows:

Mr. Chairman and Gentlemen of the California Bankers Association:

I greatly appreciate the action of your Executive Council in extending to me an invitation to prepare a paper for this meeting, especially as I am not a banker, nor the son of a banker, nor connected with a bank in any way. I also am mindful of the honor conferred upon me in being placed first upon the programme to present a paper. I thank you in advance for your kind attention, which I know you will give.

BANK LESSONS OF 1893.

BY BENJ. C. WRIGHT.

Whoever undertakes to write up the business experiences of the people of this country for the calendar year of 1893 will have a most difficult task on his hands. To arrive at even approximately accurate conclusions, many factors outside of the year's operations and outside of the country must be considered, compared, analyzed and thoroughly digested. The business troubles of 1893 were not the outcome of trivial causes. The seeds were sown in other years. Last year was simply the reaping time for many people and many corporations. It is not by any means certain that all of the harvest has yet been gathered, though it is eminently proper to take a hopeful view of the situation. This characteristic of the American people has already tempered the business troubles of the past few months very materially. Hope is a prime element of confidence, and the latter is an essential factor in business capital. The best illustration of this happy combination brings about the most gratifying results.

Not one person in a thousand of the 65,000,000 people of the United States realized at the threshold of 1893 what was in store for the country, in a business way, during the year. To the great mass the prospects for a good average year were just as bright as they were twelve months before. Here and there a thoughtful person might be found, one accustomed to weighing cause and effect, who shook his head rather ominously as he looked out into the future. Even these persons, while admitting that they did not like the trend of business affairs, never for a moment realized the extent of the portending evils. The opening months of the year passed with very little apparent shrinkage in business. In fact, January, 1893, showed a larger business, as gauged by the bank clearings of the country, than any previous corresponding month for several years. February was nearly as good as in 1892, and better than any February in the three years previous to 1892. March was better than February, and better than any March in the previous four years. April was the lightest of the first four months, but not much under that month in 1892.

The first third of the year passed with really a better record, from a bank standpoint, than had been known for any corresponding period in several years. Thus far the January 1st prognosticators of evil had observed little to justify their predictions. The month of May was ushered in as smiling as usual, only a little more so, for the great Columbian Exposition, opened with much eclat at Chicago on the first day of that month, bid fair to dissipate the smallest and most distant cloud that might be seen in the business sky. That cloud was there, however, though at that time not larger than a man's hand. It came up from the Atlantic where the two rivers empty into the sea down by the Battery. Notice of its appearance was flashed over the wires of the country on the 3d of May, or within forty-eight hours of the opening of the World's Fair. As usual, the first wail emanated from Wall Street. The telegram sent broadcast contained these words: "The tension in the commercial community is great, but the general comment is one of surprise that there are so few failures. Everybody is looking for troubles to come."

When everybody is full of expectation, results are likely to follow. It was so in this case. Failures were announced before the going down of the sun on that 3d day of May. The next day brought a worse state of affairs in the great metropolis by the sea; and the third day, which was Friday, was denominated one of much peril. The fifth of May went into Wall Street's calendar as another Black Friday. There was a calmer feeling on the following day. On Monday the brokers' sheets passed all right, and some people thought that a good sign, and tried to make themselves believe that after all the trouble concerned only a few brokers, and that the worst was over. Such things are somewhat common to Wall Street, and so long as they are confined to that locality no great amount of sympathy is wasted over the occasion. But those who took that superficial view of the matter were utterly incapable of grasping the situation. The outburst was not from any local cause, but naturally focalized at the great money center.

On the very next day after the Wall Street operators had been consoling themselves with these reflections, the scene of trouble was transferred to another and distant city, hundreds of miles to the west. Chicago had been heard from. While all was going on merrily at the World's Fair in Jackson Park, there was trouble in the city. It was in the Chemical National Bank, just the place, perhaps, to look for an explosion, though no one had ever thought of that before. The bank had received the endorsement of the World's Fair Directory, and it was advertised as the only bank to have a branch on the World's Fair grounds. The Chemical National was converted from the Chemical Savings in December, 1891. It was capitalized at $1,000,000. As soon as the suspension was reported, a Washington telegram was sent out to the effect that the failure was not unexpected in that city in view of the recent report of the Examiner. It is the old story. Everybody knows a failure is anticipated after it has been publicly announced, though it is a queer acknowledgment for a Bank Examiner to make subsequent to the event.

The failure of the Chemical National Bank of Chicago was the beginning of last year's troubles among the banks of this country. Such a closing of banks as followed that event has never been known in this country. The trouble developed into a regular epidemic, and for weeks and months it was almost impossible to take up a daily paper and not be confronted with an announcement of another bank failure. The dispatches really became so monotonous as to be wearisome. The trouble in the banks covered a period of nearly six months. Most of the suspensions took place in May, June, July and August. For the first nine months of the year there were 585 bank suspensions, reported with assets of $183,185,389 and liabilities of $169,043,771. Such an incongruous statement of assets and liabilities was never made before for any corresponding number of corporations. It is something of an anomaly for an institution to suspend with assets in excess of liabilities. This, however, was quite a common feature in the bank failures in this country last year. It only proves that such suspensions were superinduced by a very unusual condition of affairs. Some really good banks found themselves as helpless to keep their doors open as those that had been poorly managed.

All classes of banks participated in the downfall, good, bad and indifferent, commercial, savings and trust, National, State incorporated and private. The contagion of bank failures was in the very atmosphere, and it swept from the seaboard to the remotest inland towns. Only four States were exempt from the devastation. These were Connecticut, Maine, Massachusetts and Maryland. The affected States were not treated in all parts alike. Some cities and large towns, supporting several banks, escaped entirely. It is a pleasure to know that several California cities and towns were in this complimentary list. Even our own city of San Francisco, with its thirty banks, representing over 60 per cent of the banking capital of the State, contributed only two suspensions to the record, and one of these banks has since resumed. Even that one would not have temporarily suspended if it had not been so closely allied to the one now in liquidation, which, although the oldest chartered bank in the State, was suspected of being in a weak condition, through unwise management, for some time. But for that fact, the other city banks would have stood in and sustained it as they did each other.

Various causes operated to embarrass the suspended banks. In many cases the trouble was the outcome of mismanagement, the result of ignorance of the proper principles governing the business, or criminal intent on the part of the executive officers. In the last analysis, however, all the banks, whether well or badly managed, suspended for the same cause, namely, the want of sufficient ready money to meet demand obligations. This factor is at the bottom of every business failure. There are times in the existence of every bank when nothing but money can keep its doors open. In ordinary times and under ordinary circumstances, all well managed banks keep sufficient money on hand to meet the average requirements of depositors and check-holders. Long experience has

taught bankers of all classes the safe limits along these lines, and prudent bankers
are ever careful to keep their margins at a safe average. Such an unexpected and
universal, and in many cases entirely uncalled-for demand on the banks for money
last year, was entirely without the experience or reckoning of every banker, even
with twenty-five years of experience behind him.

The real cause for this extraordinary demand for money was not its actual
need on the part of many making the demand, but the general fear of some portending evil which had enfeebled the life of business confidence. On the surface
the most potent factors in weakening confidence were the radical change in the
administration of governmental affairs and the agitation affecting the volume of currency. The very large majority by which the present administration was elevated
to power and the avowed purpose of the triumphant party concerning the sources
and volume of the government revenues accentuated the feeling of distrust along
that line. The opinions of the party were well known, and the fact of its having
full sway of all the branches of the Federal Government led many people to fear
the worst results from the promised radical change in the revenue system. The
agitation in Congress of the currency question, resulting as it finally did last November in suspending the operations of the compulsory Silver law, by which the
volume of money had up to that time been arbitrarily increased by an average
addition of $4,000,000 per month in paper money for over three years, did much
to tighten the purse-strings and to promote the hoarding of money by individuals.

But these were surface causes, all-powerful it is true, but not the only or perhaps the prime reasons for the condition of affairs which prevailed so prominently
in this country from May to November last year, and from the effects of which the
people have not yet recovered, nor is complete recovery expected for some time,
though no people emerge from their difficulties so courageously and so rapidly as
the American people. No doubt the causes leading up to the late business
troubles were the result of the unprecedented prosperity attending the agricultural and manufacturing industries of the people through a succession of bountiful crops and an unusually large and remunerative demand for our surplus
products from year to year, and to the impetus given to silver mining through a
compulsory purchase by the government of $2,000,000 to $4,000,000 per month
from March 1, 1878, to July 1, 1890, and afterwards through an enlargement of the
law requiring the purchase of 4,500,000 ounces silver per month, from August 13,
1890, to November 1, 1893, by which some $600,000,000 of new money was thrust
upon the country.

These two causes have been enriching the people of the country for the best
part of fifteen years as they were never enriched before during any corresponding
period since the Mayflower landed its little company of immigrants at Plymouth
Rock. The inevitable result of this immense addition to the wealth of the country
has been extravagance on the grandest scale ever known. This has not been confined to dress and personal living, but has permeated all branches of industrial
life. It has led to much overdoing in the matter of improvements of all kinds—
in the erection of tenements, residences, buildings for stores, offices and public
uses, in the construction of railways and many other forms of improvements. In
all these departments there has been a mortgaging of the future beyond reason,
because based on the false assumption that the times would always be just as good

as they were, and would even grow better from year to year. There is no analogy in this mundane sphere for such reasoning.

A check to these fancies has been coming on for some time, and every month up to the present has added new burdens and new complications. The result has not been so much a falling-off in productive resources as a decrease in the demand and remuneration for our supplies. Troubles abroad for the past two or three years and better crops abroad have decreased both the buying ability of our foreign customers as well as their demand on our surplus products. The result has been a diminished volume of export trade, diminished prices for American export products and diminished ability to pay for the heavy imports from abroad ordered in the midst of our prosperity and which had to be paid for afterwards. The cutting-off of millions of income from farmers and other producers through these causes in the past year or two has curtailed their expenditures by so much, and every manufacturer as well as every merchant, every professional man and every non-producer in all the walks of life has felt the pinch from the enforced economy on the part of those who had previously disbursed liberally.

The banks of the country last year were confronted with conditions rather than theories. The experiences developed in the trials through which they passed will be of value to the managers for many years. Lessons were learned that had not been mastered during the previous ten or fifteen years of clear sailing. Looked at in this light, the profit gained has probably been greater than the loss sustained. Certain inherently weak banks, because improperly managed, have been weeded out: never to be resurrected, it is to be hoped, under the old managements. Certain questionable practices in banks that were not blotted out, have been eliminated. The strong banks have naturally been made stronger on the same principle that an oak is strengthened by the fierce blasts that bends, but does not uproot. Bankers have found out their weak and strong points. They have learned who are their friends and who are their foes. It is reasonable to suppose that they will make the best use of these experiences. The people who patronize banks have also learned lessons along the same lines, which will long be retained in their memories.

One of the bank lessons of 1893 is to the effect that the country does not want any more of the chain bank system of banks, as operated by Dwiggins, Starbuck and others. The Columbia National of Chicago, the second bank to suspend in that city last May, was the reputed head of this system. The collapse of that bank involved upwards of thirty small banks which had been organized in Illinois, Indiana and Michigan, by Dwiggins and others, through the Columbia National, and the United States Loan and Trust Company. The plan was to lend these small banks $10,000 or $20,000 as capital with which to attract deposits from farmers and others in the neighborhood, the deposits to be forwarded to the central organization for use. The system was supposed to be an improvement on the English and French branch bank systems, and in the matter of lessened liability on the part of the central organization, it probably was. The chain bank system is not adapted to this country. Another illustration of the same system, with slight variation, was that introduced by E. Ashley Mears, in North Dakota, which also collapsed last May, and which has not been revived. That, however, was more of a family affair. The banks were mainly run by Mears and his relatives.

It is barely possible that some lessons have been learned about the adjunct bank system and mixed banking that will be profitable to all concerned. It has become common in this State for commercial banks to have a savings bank annex, as an offset to the mixed banking allowed under the law to all savings banks having a capital of $300,000. Some National Banks in this State have sought such alliances, but have been obliged to incorporate them under State laws, because National Banks are not allowed to loan on real estate. An unfortunate ending of such an alliance happened at San Diego two years ago, when the suspension of a National Bank brought to ruin its Savings Bank adjunct, which, but for such an alliance, would not have failed. Just what opinions the bankers of this Association have concerning these alliances and mixed banking is not known. It is the judgment of some not interested in banking in any way that there would be more cordial feeling all round and fewer embarrassments if Commercial Banks and Savings Banks attended strictly to the fields peculiar to each as primarily understood. In a country so well supplied with banking facilities, there is no need for either system to encroach upon the other, while such encroachments are often attended with danger.

One good result growing out of the strained condition of monetary affairs last year has been the abolishment, on the part of some of the banks, of the overdraft system. That has long been considered a weak and unsatisfactory feature in banking. It had been allowed to become proportionately large in this State where there has been such a disinclination to make notes. The San Francisco banks have been acting as a unit against allowing overdrafts since last September, and with good results to all concerned. The worthy President of this Association has decided opinions on this subject, and some banks in the southern part of the State have for some time discouraged overdrafts. If this Association have not already adopted a recommendation on this subject it should do so before adjournment, and every bank belonging to the Association should be impressed with the importance of not only at once abolishing the overdraft system, but of strictly enforcing the custom of note-giving on the part of all borrowers. Such a custom in the end is really as much in the interest of the borrower as the lender, and at any rate it is in keeping with ideas of sound banking.

The crisis of 1893 has taught the banks the necessity for a stronger bond of co-operation. In times of great trial, a really strong and well managed bank may find itself weak when attempting to stand alone. The New York, Boston and Philadelphia banks, as a rule, stood shoulder to shoulder in the trials of last summer. They did this by issuing Clearance House Certificates for settlement purposes, on the basis of 70 per cent. of hypothecated assets. The largest amount of these certificates outstanding at any one time was $60,690,000, of which the New York banks had $38,280,000, the remainder being about equally divided between Boston and Philadelphia. There is no doubt that this course averted much trouble. There was not a single bank failure in Massachusetts in the first nine months of 1893, and only 9 in Pennsylvania and 18 in New York, most of these being in the interior and nearly one-half private banks. The lesson along this line is for the banks to stand together. This does not imply that the shield shall cover dishonest or even inefficient bankers.

There should be a better understanding between the banker and the depositors. Want of confidence and co-operation between these two classes is what caused most of the trouble last year. After all, it is the depositor and not the stockholder that furnishes the bulk of the capital employed in the business. There are probably 10,000 banks and bankers in the United States. The Comptroller of Currency has reports from 9,466, but some did not report last year. The paid-up capital of these banks is $1,084,607,600, while the amount of deposits is $2,736,-836,100, and the aggregate resources $7,079,511,800. These figures show the important position which depositors sustain to the banking business of the country. Of course many of these depositors are also stockholders. This dual character puts an additional responsibility upon them to act considerately in times of financial strain. Any other line of conduct on the part of either a stockholder or depositor under such circumstances, may well be charged against them by the bankers at the proper time and in a practical way. It should be the aim of all concerned to hold the business up to a high level of honorable dealings all round. Bankers have it in their power to conserve all that is good and worthy of being upheld, and they owe it as a duty to the community to tone up honesty and integrity along all lines.

H. H. Hewlett of Stockton: Mr. Chairman, I move that the thanks of this Convention be extended to Mr. Wright, of the *Evening Bulletin* of San Francisco, for his very able address.

Mr. Hewlett's motion, being seconded, was carried by a unanimous vote.

The Chairman: If Mr. C. W. Bush of Woodland is present we will be pleased to listen to the reading of his paper on "The Relations That Should Exist Between City and Country Banks."

C. W. Bush of the Bank of Yolo, Woodland, spoke as follows:

Mr. Chairman and Gentlemen of the Convention :

I am suffering from a very severe cold, but I trust that you will bear with me.

The Relations that Should Exist Between City and Country Banks and the Advantages that Would Result from their Combined Action During Periods of Financial Stringency.

By C. W. BUSH, Cashier of the Bank of Yolo.

Many acute financiers contend, and with good reason, that the troublesome times for bankers are not yet passed. Whether or not their opinions prove to be true, while there remains a reason for them, it is needful that every safeguard should be employed to avert further disaster. After a battle weak positions are discovered. During the lull a good officer, profiting by experience, will strengthen them. A weak feature of banking in California, made very apparent during the monetary panic of last year, is the lack of co-operation and of uniform systems. Mr. E. S. Sheffield contributed to our last Convention a paper directly in line with my subject. Had his suggestions taken practical shape, there is no estimating the

benefits which would have accrued to our State. It is hoped now, that by
a re-presentation of the subject, we may be brought to a realization of the necessity for action. Could the experiences of the last few months have been anticipated,
a close relationship would have been formed between the San Francisco Bankers,
and an invitation to co-operate would have been extended to the country. With
the events of this period yet fresh in our minds, when we were compelled to bear
the burdens of the entire people, we can realize the benefits which would have
followed organization.

It is well that we should at first consider the relations as existing between
San Francisco Bankers, before formulating plans to embrace the country. Unless
their relationship is close, and their practices uniform, no successful general system can be maintained with the country. Each interior banker will be governed
by the requirements of his city correspondent to whom he looks for credit. It
was painfully apparent to us of the country, that these bankers were not leagued
for mutual protection during the panic. Had they been, the healthy reserves
which they are believed to have held, would have been combined, and the per-
emptory demands made on the interior would have been withheld. The complete and immediate suppression of business throughout the entire State would
not have followed. We are almost forced to the opinion, that the demands were
made under the inspiration of a timidity resulting from the weakness of an
isolated business method, without a careful consideration of necessities. It was
well known that the country bankers, in anticipation of the harvest immediately
at hand, had strained their credit to the last limit, and that by many the demands
made on them could not be met. A peculiar result followed—a general shifting of
city accounts; San Francisco was beseiged by interior bankers seeking money.
The lack of co-operation in the city was again apparent. At the expense of a
neighbor banker, new accounts were obtained, and advances made at increased
rates of interest by him who was in the enjoyment of a satisfactory reserve.
There was occasion for great alarm and for the employment of extreme caution.
The desire is to show simply, that by a concerted policy of indulgence by the San
Francisco bankers, opportunity might have been given the creditor to obtain returns from a reasonably abundant harvest, without requiring from him a complete
suspension of business. Later in the season, it is gratifying to know, a decided
and important co-operative action was taken, the effect of which will be of benefit
to every bank in the State. I refer to the discontinuance of the practice of allowing overdrafts. The interior will be compelled eventually to take the same action.

The Clearing House Association in itself furnishes a sufficient organization
by which the city bankers may be brought to a similarity of method. Assuming
that they will co-operate, they should maintain uniform relations with their country correspondents, based on conservative banking principles. The limit of credit
extended should be fixed by the ability of the borrower to secure. Tangible security in all cases should be exacted, which could be made available in time of distress. This rule, in connection with that abolishing overdrafts, would tend to a
wholesome and much needed restriction of the rapidly growing credit system.
There are certain other principles which should govern the conduct of our business,
irrespective of location. But for the restrictions placed on National Banks under
their admirable system, the results of the year would have been far more disastrous.

Before systems can be favorably presented, certain practical propositions, I may say, difficulties, must be successfully met. How may co-operative relations be established between the city and country? By what power can they be maintained, and under what guarantee of good faith? Can an organization be made desirable enough to make its membership general? And lastly, what should constitute the features of the organization? Before closer relations can be admitted to be practicable, it must be known that direct individual benefits will result. The interests of bankers, owing to location, and the nature of their business, are quite dissimilar. The question then arises: How will mutual benefit result from organization?

We will consider, at first, the benefits to accrue to the city banker. We will suppose, as a feature of a general system, that it will be decided that a certain percentage of capital or of deposits, or of both, shall be required to be held as a reserve, and that the city correspondent will be named as the depository for the country bank. Or, that the San Francisco Clearing House will decide to clear checks drawn on interior banks, and that a deposit will be required of the interior banker to meet contingencies. Or, that collections will be made without charge, except for actual expense incurred. These features alone would commend the organization to the city banker, especially so, as they would only apply to subscribing members. But there remains, in a general way, a much more important reason why the city banker should favor such a relationship. At certain periods of the year, we of the country, are borrowers. The lender has no better class of custom. We give our demand paper, which, under proper restrictions, will always be available as assets. It is greatly to the interest of the lender, that there should be proper regulations of method, based on the judgments of acknowledged financiers. The country banker would be benefitted by an improved credit, and strengthened by the adoption of improved methods, a condition difficult of attainment, except through a general system of co-operation, as there is to a certain extent a spirit of competition existing, which is fatal to conservative methods.

Assuming, then, that benefits will accrue to all, the practicability of an association is robbed of many of its difficulties. Articles of Confederation may be drawn, in which will be recited all details by which the subscriber agrees to be governed.

The question next arises, How will the agreement be enforced? A condition of success is, that the procedure shall be as simple as possible. There must be a head to the Association; probably, also, an Executive Committee, before whom complaint would lie, and which would have power of investigation and of passing sentence;—the penalty of violation to be suspension:— each case of suspension to be reported to all members, and the expense of investigation to be borne by the delinquent. These may be considered weak features of such an association, but the enjoyment of the certain practical benefits which will accrue to and remain with the subscriber will conduce to the faithful observance of conditions.

The last question for consideration is the all-important one. So important is it that its consideration should receive the utmost care and deliberation. What should be the nature of an organization? Should a project of Confederation be favorably considered at this Convention, time would not permit of a wise settlement of details, but by the appointment of a committee, with instructions to report at a subsequent assembly, and with full powers, the practicability of an organization may be determined on, and also the details for government.

There remains yet another branch of my subject to be considered—that of combined action during times of stringency. So closely are the two headings related that the discussion of one leads indirectly to the consideration of the other. The last branch, however, deserves especial attention. Just at this time, when the panic is fresh in mind, it is apparent to all that the lessons derived from it would lead to the idea of combination. A few months back we were all seeking assistance, but found that they who were able to furnish it were overburdened with applications. Our individual resources were inadequate to meet demands, and distrust arose; but by a combination of resources distrust would not have arisen, and demands would have diminished. A combination would have been a mighty power, sufficient to cope with any emergency, under proper and restricted methods of business. We have realized as never before the weight of responsibility resting upon us. The vital interests of the business world are in our keeping. Every bank suspension bears indirectly on all. By it all branches of trade are affected, so sensitive are the laws of trade to any untoward event. A system may be devised by which calamities may be averted. Certificates pledging the credit of the united Association may be issued, upon the deposit of adequate securities, which would be available to tide over temporary difficulty; for the redemption of which, in case of necessity, the securities pledged could be sold.

As with the plans of organization, the details of this system must be worked out. There are too many points involved to admit of their discussion within the limits of this paper.

Should this prove to be impracticable, what plan of co-operation may we suggest for times of stringency? I can think of none. There will remain but the ordinary procedure for him who has money to lend, to advance it upon terms and conditions to suit the exigency of the demand. If money cannot be had, the distressed banker must suspend or effect a possible compromise with creditors. The conditions become immediately serious for all. When banks discontinue lending, the depositor discharges that function. His demand the banker cannot ignore; a default here is fatal.

If we cannot co-operate, then it is all the more a necessity that correct methods should prevail, that reserves and adequate security for money loaned should be insisted on.

Owing to the present paralysis of business, and of weaknesses in the values of commodities, it is anticipated that there will be great shrinkages in property values. The indebtedness of our people has swollen into enormous proportions. The accretions of interest and shrinkage of values will result in the surrender of many pledges, unless from unexpected and improbable causes a reaction should set in. For each dollar of security surrendered, a dollar of banking capital becomes inoperative. There is hardly a bank in the country but will surrender a portion of its capital for unconvertible security. Considering the enormous landed indebtedness, the outlook is not encouraging. Just now we are having a breathing spell. Through extraordinary effort our resources have been strengthened, and there is no immediate necessity pressing us, but it is the duty of a financier to provide against possible calamity. No other defense appears to me so feas-

ible as a close alliance for mutual protection. Such a relation established, the
future will reveal a prosperous country and contented people, living on the natural
increase from labor, and legitimate investment, secure in the possession of the
same. The spirit of reckless gambling will have been exorcised by the banker,
who will have learned to discourage the indiscriminate use of money, and to
require deposits of security sufficient in amount to cover the debt and all possible
contingencies.

The Chairman: Mr. Frank Miller will now favor us with the
reading of his paper on "Unsecured Loans."

Frank Miller of Sacramento: Mr. Chairman and Gentlemen of
the Convention, about ten days ago Sacramento had a great literary
event. There are two commercial banks there, and one man out of
each bank was engaged, without the knowledge of the other, in doing
something—each one was preparing an essay for the bankers. They discovered that fact and they swapped papers. I speak of this so as to show
you that if you think there is any difference of opinion it is not a pre-
arranged one, and the paper that I have to present to you is entirely
pertinent to a man behind a bank counter and his immediate surroundings. I am not speaking of his bank counter, as connected with some
other bank counter. If I had undertaken to do so, that would have
taken more time. What I have to offer to-day is pertinent, I think,
to a man's own ground and his immediate custom. I speak of that so
that you will not think that Mr. Gerber and I had made a pre-arrange-
ment. This is one of those coincidences that in literary circles sometimes happens.

UNSECURED LOANS: TIME VERSUS DEMAND.

BY FRANK MILLER, PRESIDENT OF THE NATIONAL BANK OF D. O. MILLS & CO. OF
SACRAMENTO, CAL.

From the Report of the Comptroller of the Currency for 1893 (pages 120 and
152), we get some valuable facts.

Defining unsecured loans as those to which no collateral is affixed, and as
those which rest only on one or more signatures, we learn that 3,800 national
banks carry $12 of time (unsecured) loans to each $1 of demand (unsecured) loans.

In California, and especially in San Francisco, we learn that the ratio is very
different; our bankers carry only about half of their unsecured loans on time and
the other half is on demand.

Here is a wide difference, and we can profitably compare the two situations.

The Eastern ratio of 12 to 1 may have become established under the effect of
their usury laws, of which the penalties were once severe. Now they are trivial
and so seldom enforced that it can be inferred justly that the custom of writing
loans mostly on time is maintained by reason of merits in the custom itself, which

make time loans more satisfactory to both borrower and lender than one-day loans

The California ratio of 1 to 1 grew out of our recently condemned system of overdrafts. The panic of 1893 taught us to abandon these, but we have bettered ourselves only a little by accepting one-day loans in lieu of overdrafts. Neither should be cultivated in sound banking, and neither can exist except when and where high rates of interest may prevail.

We commence business in the morning facing the possibility that all our clients may call during the day, and expect to get loans, with the expectation also of re-paying at their own option. We have always had large reserves lying idle in vault, and a moderate volume of business. Much of our coin is kept to meet possible borrowers, and it results in educating our friends to make no provision for the future. We are expected to promise a line of accommodation of generous dimensions and privileges, retaining for ourselves the sole right to get the money back as best we can in case we need it.

Last year taught us all that a banker's promise to lend, and a borrower's promise to pay were of no value whatever in the presence of a general stringency. Lack of foresight in the creation of debts and the collection thereof is not good for any community. Promptness will be a winning card in the approaching days of large transactions and small profits. Sluggish bankers will have slow assets and will be left behind by those who conform to the larger experience of the majority.

Time loans are the best of assets; they are the heart of a banker's business. If carefully written and renewed they are safe and acceptable, not only to the borrower, but also to the banker. The banker can curtail their volume without damage, if he begins in season; where sudden stringencies arise he may be able to re-discount them with other banks, and he can even pay out such notes over the counter to panic striken depositors.

If the makers become insolvent, these notes are at no disadvantage. It is true that upon an account or demand-note an attachment can be issued, but our best clients will not need such remedies, and our poor clients will go into insolvency anyway, which dissolves attachments.

It is probable that California is entering upon a long future of lower rates of interest, and this, if it comes, will cause a complete cessation of overdrafts and one-day loans, unless they are secured by the best of collateral. As in the East our gross earnings will gradually shrink down to the line of expenses, and we shall no longer retain idle money for the possible wants of borrowers, nor will we give to small current balances, without compensation, the many facilities of our offices, as we have done heretofore.

From the Comptroller's report we find that the deposits in the National Banks amount to about two thousand millions. For one year their expenses were about sixty millions, and their losses about twenty millions. For the purpose solely of holding these deposits, about one-fourth, five hundred millions, was carried in unproductive cash.

The owners of these 3,800 National Banks accumulated a capital of one thousand millions, pledged it as security to their depositors, arranged offices, employed clerks, incurred an expense of sixty millions, and a loss of twenty millions during the year, in order to lend one thousand five hundred millions of other people's money. The report shows that they got six percent—some ninety millions—as interest. From this income should be deducted the outgo of eighty millions, and we find that ten millions are left as the inadequate compensation for the guaranty and labors and risks undertaken, by the capital of one thousand millions. This is a commission of one-half of one per cent. on the deposits.

These figures are proven by the report which shows that the net earnings on the capital have been seven per cent. This per cent is composed of six per cent. (which the capital could have earned in private hands), and the small commission made upon handling the immense mass of deposits for one year.

Expenses and losses cannot be reduced very greatly; clerks must be retained at such pay as will insure competent and honest service; losses will occur in spite of all precautions; all this without reference to whether the times are good or bad.

Wealth is accumulating, and individual money lenders materially cut down the bank rates for all kinds of loans.

Each banker may prove these ideas from his own books. His outgo will approach the sum of four per cent of his average deposits.

From his gross income he should deduct this outgo. The residue is his compensation as a banker. He should then compute his income upon his capital, on the supposition that he has gone out of the banking business, uses the sidewalk for his office, and is known as a private money lender who takes no risks. The comparisons would be interesting if they could be published.

The Eastern banks have given much attention to this problem, and know that they give services to depositors which can not be offered by individuals, or by any other class of institutions. They make their depositors pay indirectly for some of the costs of keeping their accounts and funds.

Each account is expected to show such a steady balance as will afford compensation above the cost of keeping it.

If the customer is a borrower he is expected to borrow enough to maintain a credit balance equal to one-tenth, or one-fifth of his loan. They lend only to people who can and will assist in increasing the line of deposit. This discipline can be enforced only by writing loans on time. Their notes bear no interest, usually, and are discounted.

The borrower gives several notes which mature at different dates, and is expected to accumulate a deposit which will cancel any note at its maturity, in case the bank cannot re-write it. The periods for which notes are written vary from fifteen days to four months. Bearing no interest they are promptly paid at maturity, or promptly re-written, or promptly put into a lawyer's hands.

It will be seen that by this system the assets of these banks are thoroughly revised at least three times each year.

In England the method is not exactly the same as in the United States. Some banks charge a commission of one-eighth or one-quarter of one per cent on all checks paid, and sometimes allow a small interest on a large credit balance.

Another view of the subject has been presented, which is based upon a division of the total expense for a year by the total number of checks paid. This may show that the cost of paying a check is 15 or 20 cents.

Therefore, for each check paid a credit balance of $5 should be held for one year; thus the man who issues 100 checks during the year should keep a minimum balance of $500 through the twelve months.

It is not possible for bankers to charge a rate of interest much higher than is got by individuals; we can make no combination of any kind; we can only state the situation clearly and encourage each other to follow the only possible courses left to us. These are the discontinuing of unprofitable forms of loans and the requiring of each account that it shall be self-supporting.

Mr. Miller: I arrived in town only a few minutes ago, and I don't know the rules of the Association very clearly, but, with your permission, I will read this resolution and ask your instructions afterwards.

The Chairman: Read it, please.

Mr. Miller: I sent this circular out, and with it this resolution, which I said I would offer:

Resolved, That this Convention approves the custom of writing all loans on time with the exception of those which are made to borrowers who reside outside the limits of this State; and we further approve the custom of writing time-loans without interest and deducting discount.

I believe that if this should be adopted it would greatly assist us, after a few years, towards the adoption of the Eastern custom. With your permission, Mr. Chairman, I will leave this resolution in your hands, to be brought before the Convention.

H. H. Hewlett of Stockton: Mr. Chairman, I move its adoption.

C. W. Bush of Woodland: I move that it be referred to the Committee on Resolutions for future action.

The Chairman: Does Mr. Miller accept the amendment?

Mr. Miller: I don't know whether the Convention is ready for this question or not, but it seems to me that it has no bearing upon any other question before the house. This is the practice in the East, and I prefer that the resolution should stand and let the matter be settled upon its merits.

The Chairman: Then I understand that Mr. Miller does not accept the amendment.

Mr. Miller: What is the amendment offered?

The Chairman: That the resolution be referred to the Committee on Resolutions for subsequent action on the part of this Convention.

John Reichman of Fresno: Mr. Chairman, I thought it was the custom that all resolutions offered before this body should be referred to the Committee on Resolutions for their report. Therefore, the resolution should take the usual course, which is to be referred to the Committee on Resolutions, getting their report this afternoon or tomorrow morning.

The Chairman: While that is the rule, I cannot accept it now, because there is a motion seconded, consequently I have to put the amendment to a vote.

Mr. Miller: Mr. Chairman, I would like to call your attention to the fact that Mr. Hewlett has seconded this resolution, and myself, with Mr. Hewlett and Mr. Wright, who has spoken on the subject, are on that Committee of Resolutions. Now, that is three out of five. If the resolution is to go to the committee simply to be reported back favorably, it seems to me that, in the interest of fair play, the Convention should take it as it stands and let it go without its going to the committee.

The Chairman: I think I will have to put the amendment to a vote first. Gentlemen, you have heard the amendment made by Mr. Bush of Woodland; what is your pleasure?

On vote being had the amendment of Mr. Bush was carried.

The Chairman: The amendment is carried, consequently there is no use of putting the original motion.

Mr. Lankershim's paper is in order to be read now.

J. B. Lankershim of Los Angeles:

Mr. Chairman, and gentlemen of the Convention:

The discussions thus far have been principally in regard to Commercial Banks. I suppose I ought to make an apology for reading a paper on the subject of Savings Banks when you have just had brought before you these important commercial questions, but the Savings Banks are certainly an important factor in finances, and I think it would be in order to make a few remarks in regard to them.

SAVINGS BANKS AND THEIR DIVIDENDS TO DEPOSITORS.

BY J. B. LANKERSHIM, PRESIDENT OF THE MAIN STREET SAVINGS BANK
AND TRUST CO., OF LOS ANGELES.

The savings banks of California are important factors in its financial world. About 70 per cent. of the total deposits in San Francisco are with them, leaving about 30 per cent. with the commercial banks. Just why this condition of affairs exists shall be the theme of this article.

The principal reason that savings banks have such large amounts deposited with them, is because of the high rate of interest paid to depositors as dividends. It attracts the money of capitalists in large sums, for they say we can make more, have fewer losses and pay less taxes if we deposit our money in Savings Banks. While this is no doubt true, would it not be better if these capitalists who are well versed in business matters were investing money in the industries of the State? Again, are not these deposits, in large amounts, a source of weakness rather than of strength? Such deposits could be prevented, or greatly reduced, by giving a more moderate rate of interest.

We know that a high rate of interest to depositors is not good for banks, for they must make their money by loaning it out, and must therefore charge a high rate to the borrower. He is the one that should have the advantage, for he borrows for the uses of commerce, merchandising, or the improvement of property. The lower the rate of interest the farther will his money go in these useful employments. Again, when rates of interest are low many capitalists are tempted to embark in new enterprises. As for the disastrous results of a high rate of interest, we have had a most striking object lesson in the last six months.

Now, let us see the effect of a moderate rate of interest to depositors. Most of the deposits in savings banks are, or should be, the surplus earnings of working men. As a rule, there are not a great many who depend entirely upon their dividends for a living, so that smaller dividends would not materially affect the depositor. It would also induce many capitalists who now have large sums in savings banks to invest their funds in some legitimate enterprise. While it might reduce the deposits of savings banks somewhat, the reduction would add to their stability, for a mere increase in deposits in a savings bank does not necessarily mean a strong bank, as this increase may come from large deposits or from unusual inducements, and be a source of weakness rather than of strength.

In order to show that a savings bank managed according to these ideas would be a model bank, I will refer to a well known bank in San Francisco, and to the Illinois Loan and Trust Company of Chicago. The latter does a very large business, and last year paid 4 per cent. to depositors. On January 1st, they announced that they would only pay 3 per cent. for 1894—and it does not seem to have affected their business. The rules and by-laws of all well conducted savings banks would allow, and are made with a view, of conducting business on the methods outlined in this paper. And it is a question for each bank to consider, whether it would not be better for them to step out of the race for large deposits and large dividends, and consider as its first principles, lower rates of interest to borrowers, moderate dividends to depositors and the stability of the savings banks.

The Chairman: The next paper to be presented is "Savings Banks—Their Mission and Duties," by Mr. Lovell White.

Lovell White, cashier of the San Francisco Savings Union, San Francisco, addressed the Convention as follows:

SAVINGS BANKS—THEIR MISSION AND DUTIES.

In their origin Savings Banks were eleemosynary in character, organized primarily for the safekeeping, while affording some returns in form of interest, of the funds of the poor, too scant in volume to permit of direct investment; and secondarily that these funds, of considerable amount in the aggregate, should be so massed as to become available to the borrowing class in community. Except as to the Secretary or other officer on whose time large demands were made, the officials rendered services without compensation, with the usual results that duties were neglected or were performed in a perfunctory manner, and that the best possible results in the way of interest were not attained by the depositor, while a large class of borrowers were shut out by restrictive laws, rules and regulations. Good men were usually in nominal control, but having no pecuniary interest to stimulate them in the discharge of their duties, the State was compelled for safety to step in and prescribe the nature and proportion of their investments, reducing the institutions to machines, and substituting for intelligent action automatic methods, with the consequence that usefulness has been impaired, the returns of the depositor have been small, and the deposits have been scaled down from time to time, and yet bankruptcy, in many cases has not been avoided.

In the Down East States, the savings institutions adhere to their original character, but as the Atlantic is left the people grow wiser; in the Western States the majority of the Savings Banks are capitalized, and when the Pacific Coast is reached their eleemosynary character is wholly lost, for here there is not an institution but has a capital stock, or its equivalent in the form of a reserve fund, in which the mass of depositors are not interested otherwise than as affording security for the safety of their deposits. There is not supposed to be a Savings Bank on the Coast where the rank and file of the depositors participate in the election of Directors or officers, or have any voice in determining the policy of the institution. That the banks are best served where those in control have a pecuniary interest in their prosperity is a fact that must be obvious to every one. There is no sense of duty that, as a stimulus to the best exercise of the faculties of the mind or the activity of the body, can compare with the sensitiveness of the pocket. Here the banks are organized primarily in the interest of the stockholders, with resulting and incidental benefit to the public—the eleemosynary has given place to the fiduciary; they are the agents, the factors, the commission merchants of the depositors, and as such, and not otherwise, do they owe allegiance to any one or to the community in general.

Sustaining the relation of fiduciary agents to a multitude of depositors who have no organization among themselves, and who consequently can have no representatives to protect their interests, it is eminently right and proper that the State, through Bank Commissioners, or otherwise, should so far supervise the operations of the banks as to see that they perform their part of the contract with the depositors as set forth in their respective by-laws, rules and regulations—and here the duties of the State cease. Beyond this there is no more occasion or justification for regulating a Savings Bank than for regulating a Commercial Bank, a manufactory, or a mercantile establishment. There are always those in community who have a sublime faith in the power of the law or in an expressed public opinion to adjust matters which, if left alone, will better adjust themselves—such parties would prescribe posture in prayer and limit the length of sermons in the pulpit. The Savings Banks of this city and State are under control, as a rule, of persons skilled in business affairs, men of good reputation, who have embarked portions of their capital in the guarantee funds of the institutions, and who are moved by every consideration that addresses itself to the well-balanced mind to conduct affairs with prudence; and yet these parties are continually counselled by relatively inexperienced persons as to the conduct of business, while the Directors and officers of Commercial Banks are left to grope in the dark, no advice being tendered them. That the first object of a Savings Bank should be the safety of the funds in its keeping, is a truth supposed to be recognized by all. When advice is offered that Savings Banks should carry larger amounts of cash, and should lend with greater caution, and insist upon more ample margins, the advice should be well received, although as an incident, a diminution in the rate of dividends must follow. But counsel has not been given from this standpoint. The constant suggestion has been that rates of dividends should be reduced to discourage deposits and thereby to encourage trade, manufactures and land speculations.

In this connection it is to be remembered that safety at best is relative only; there is no absolute safety for the twenty dollar piece a man has in his pocket, whether he is on the street, at his office or by his own fireside with his wife and other members of his family about him. The Scriptures say that "riches take to themselves wings," and they further remind us that "Thieves break through and steal." No Savings Bank can keep money on hand, or deposit it, or loan it with absolute safety. All is comparative. It is a peculiarity of money that each dollar requires watching; general supervision is insufficient: hence it is that the safety of moneyed institutions depends upon the capacity and honesty of those in control and not upon adherence to arbitrary rules. No set of rules can be adopted that will bind dishonest men, nor that will compensate for want of experience and ability of honest ones. Business is never automatic— live forces are required to keep the wheels in motion. Alexander T. Stewart conducted business successfully in New York for sixty years; within two years after his decease his successors found it necessary or advisable to retire—rules were not wanting, but brain power.

The ability that will preserve money in a savings bank, or elsewhere, from diminution is not all that is wanted. There must be faculty for increasing the store—there must be dividends. A low rate of dividend does not of itself signify safety of deposits. It may signify many other things—wastage, a large expense account, lack of enterprise, adherence to antiquated methods, etc. That the methods and policy of the savings banks of the State are not particularly open to attack should perhaps be inferred from the fact that they have survived the financial crisis of 1893, and it may perhaps be reasonably claimed in their behalf that what has served them in the greatest of American panics known to history will be found sufficient on a possible future occasion.

There are no natural antagonisms between commercial and savings banks, their spheres of action being quite distinct. It is the province of the former to furnish the means whereby the farmer is enabled to market his crops, the merchant to anticipate collections when goods are sold on credit, the manufacturer to realize on his wares so soon as they are ready for sale without awaiting the advent of a purchaser or the expiration of a term of credit. It is the mission of the savings banks to make farm productions in increasing quantity possible by enabling those of limited means to acquire land, and to stimulate the growth of manufactures and the march of improvements by purchase of the bonds and loans upon the stocks, of industrial and quasi public corporations. Briefly, it may be said, savings banks through their natural operations create wealth, the Commercial Banks handle it; each supplements and is the complement of the other. Savings Banks are creative, Commercial Banks administrative; when nothing is created there will be nothing upon which to administer.

Recently much has been said, mainly by parties interested, as will later appear, of the necessity or advisability of limiting the rate of dividends that may be paid on deposits, and of fixing the maximum of amounts that may be deposited in one name, with a view of inducing or compelling the owner of money to employ their funds in trade and in commerce, in manufacturing, or in the purchase and improvement of real estate.

As to rates of interest, the tendency of mankind is to hoard; and money is kept out of the ground, out of old stockings and out of safe deposit boxes only by the promise of accretions. Money seeks the best market and lowering rates here would only cause exportation or employment elsewhere. Rates of interest for ten years have not been high enough to attract any considerable amount of foreign capital—lower the rate, and what little foreign capital is here would leave. Concerted action of all the savings banks on the Coast, were anything of the kind possible, would not govern the rate of interest. If too high a rate was fixed, the funds of the banks would remain unemployed; if too low a rate, they would have no money to loan, for individuals would reclaim their money and handle it direct. Of all wild financial delusions that have ever obtained, the wildest one is that rates of interest ever have or ever will be determined by the State or by any association of its people; they are determined by the law of demand and supply, and as between lenders and borrowers that law is voiced by the borrowers; the latter may compel a reduction of interest at any time by collectively abstaining from borrowing. This is the secret of the reduction in rate from five per cent per month current in the early fifties. Money, or perhaps it should be said its use, is a commodity, and like other commodities, has no immutable and unchangeable value. At any given time it is worth just what it is worth in the market, and it is impossible to see how any movement can consistently be made to fix the price of money that does not at the same time fix the price of wheat, sugar, beeves, town lots, and rental of houses. Not only are the directors and officers of savings banks under obligation to secure for the benefit of their depositors current rates of interest on their loans, but their own self-respect demands that their acts shall show that they are not entire strangers to the principles of finance as expounded by Adam Smith, Ricardo, John Stuart Mill and other authorities on the subject of political economy. The question of interest on money has had the attention of the world from the days of the patriarchs to the present time. Moses, it appears by the record, allowed the Jews to take interest from a stranger, but not from their own people; but rates were not discussed. The laws of Rome allowed interest at rates two or three times as large as those now current in California. The three eminent writers above named and scores of others have written exhaustively on this subject of interest and have demonstrated that all attempts to control rates by legal enactment or by artificial means are as futile as was the attempt to control the price of bread during the French Revolution one hundred years since. And yet once a month, at least, some head bobs up serenely in this community, and, in ignorance of the lessons of history, the teachings of philosophy and the science of political economy, with childish simplicity, asks the savings banks to reduce the rate of interest.

As to amount, any one person may deposit with any one institution, the theory is that the unhappy possessor of money to a large amount, not being able to lodge it with the bank of his choice, will rush furiously forth and invest it in a commercial enterprise, in a manufacturing plant, in developing a mine, in subscription for the stock of a railroad or a navigation company, or in the purchase of real estate of his neighbor—the latter having the preference with the majority of the theorists. This theory will not hold water for many reasons, a few only of which need be mentioned. The funds lodged in large sums with savings banks are chiefly those of estates, widows, wards, non-residents, and of men advanced in life who have retired from active business. There is on deposit with the savings banks of this city several millions of dollars in the aggregate under control of the Judges of the Superior Court (the probate department taking the lead), and in many instances the sums are large, say in excess of one hundred thousand dollars—in such cases the money being distributed between several banks. If the honorable Judges cannot lodge this money with the savings banks, what shall they do with it? Is it any safer in a commercial bank, or is it in the interest of the business community that it be locked up in safe deposit boxes?

Take the case of absentees: Many persons proposing to be absent from the State for a few months, or perhaps years, leave money in large sums with the savings banks to be drawn against for expenses and to be available for business purposes upon their return. Is it proposed to detain such people at home, or as an alternative to compel them to appoint an individual as an agent?

So long as the funds of estates and others remain on deposit, they are a part of the loanable capital of the state, swelling the amount thereof and tending thereby to reduction in rates of interest; they are available in the way of loans for the developing and conducting of every variety of business enterprise, playing substantially the same part as they would if invested direct by the owners. Remove this class of deposits from the savings banks, and one-half of the amount thereof would disappear so far as their being of use in this State is concerned. The disappearing half would find its way to secret hoards, to safe-deposit boxes and to investment in securities foreign to California. The effect of this disappearance would be a scarcity of money that would forbid the making of new loans for months and probably for years.

The difference between an abundance and a scarcity of any commodity is not well understood. A diminution of five per cent in the customary quantity of any article in general use will render that article scarce, and advance abnormally the price of what there is in the market, while an increase of supply by the same percentage will make the commodity a drug and depress the price of all that is for sale. So it is with capital or with ready money; decrease the amount of loanable capital until only nine-tenths of the would-be borrowers can be supplied, and there is not partial but general distress; and rates of interest will advance, not simply one-ninth or one-tenth, but fifty per cent more or less. So it is with coined money; decrease the volume one-tenth, and there is general distress; not only is the one-tenth gone, but nobody seems to have any money. The year 1893 will, for a time at least, stand out in the history of the United States as the period of its greatest financial panic; and yet not ten per cent of the capital of the country had been withheld from use, and not ten per cent of its ready money had been withdrawn from circulation when the trouble commenced—the lock-up came later as the result of the scare.

The idea is harped upon that if the facilities afforded by the savings banks for the safe handling of money were withdrawn from capitalists, the latter would at once embark in trade or manufactures, in the building of railroads and steamships, or in the improvement of real estate, or, above all, in the purchase of lands and lots with or without improvements; but it is nowhere suggested that they would engage in agriculture in any of its branches; and yet the great need of the State is agricultural development; not of the kind that raises wheat or any other specialty and sells it below cost of production, but of the sort that makes homes. Farming in California to-day is a failure if upon it is based the hope that a fortune will be realized in five or ten years that will enable the operator to remove to a city and live at his ease; but it is not a failure when the object is to live on the farm, confining wants in the main to what the farm can supply and gradually accumulating the comforts and, to some extent, the luxuries of life. Abundance of rural population and diversified farming are the crying wants of the State. Raising of wheat as an exclusive crop impoverishes, and its cultivation as such has been abandoned by all the older States of the Union. California will follow suit by and by; as its people grow wiser, we will have a rural population of prosperous and contented farmers.

The farmer, and particularly the small one, is dependent on the savings banks for means wherewith to make a home. City capitalists do not lend in small sums, and the local ones demand excessive rates of interest. The enormous development of the agricultural and horticultural interests of this State in the past ten years is largely due to the savings banks of San Francisco—and who shall say that in fostering these interests they have not made the best possible use of the money with which they have been intrusted? Supposing a maximum limit is fixed for deposits in savings banks and that as a consequence a sum, large in the aggregate, is withdrawn; does anybody for a moment suppose that it will be invested in the various enterprises already suggested?

The construction of railroads and the building of steamships are specialties in which the general public, in the light of experience, will not engage. Will old men, widows and estates embark in trade, commerce or manufactures, and, if so, is it desirable that they should? In these employments capital must be supplemented by skill, by judgment, by training and youthful energy; when these are wanting, disaster inevitably results.

Is it desirable at the present time that capital be embarked in buildings in San Francisco? For twenty years, at least, buildings, whether for business or residence purposes, have been in excess of the needs of the inhabitants. Is any good purpose served by the erection of buildings to stand idle or take their tenants from those constructed some years since and which must thereafter remain unoccupied?

The suggestion urged with greater zeal is that the lessening of deposits in savings banks would help the real estate market. Is it desirable that such market be so helped? Is it in the interest of the community as a whole that real estate should be active, at advancing prices of course, as otherwise there would be no activity? Advance in price of land and lots is perhaps an evidence of general prosperity where they are bought for immediate use, but not so when purchased on speculation. Speculative purchases are evidences of boom times, and productive of boom prices, and booms, it has been demonstrated time and again in California and elsewhere, are worse in their effect than earthquakes or epidemics.

It is in the interest of the State and of the city of San Francisco that the prices of real estate should become or should remain low and that rents should be moderate. A party contemplating embarking in trade or in manufacturing enterprise considers the question of rent or cost of plant and of taxes, but not that of interest, for no man of well-balanced mind expects under such circumstances to borrow his capital to any great extent.

The community at large is not interested in the question whether there shall be frequent changes of ownership of real estate; the outcry in this behalf is from those who have lands or lots for sale, or who expect to make commissions through sales. A, B and C are real estate owners; D, E and F are capitalists; the first three wish to reverse the positions; they not only advise the second three to buy; assuring them that the investment is the best possible one to be made, but they call upon the moneyed institutions to reduce rates of interest or refuse deposits to the end that the second three may be in a sense compelled to buy. Is the public interested in the question of which three shall be capitalists and which real estate holders? Newspapers have long lent their aid; frequently corporations who deal in money are asked to assist holders of real estate to unload. If any good purpose was served by the unloading process, co-operation might be secured; but, until it shall be made to appear that the new capitalist will make a better use of his money than the old, title to real property, so far as the public is concerned, may as well remain unchanged.

Adam Smith, in the *Wealth of Nations*, lays down the principle that the best possible is done for the nation when each individual does the best possible for himself, and he bases this on the ground that a man will serve himself more faithfully than he will serve another and that consequently the community is best served where every man is his own master. Attempts to regulate business by legislation always fail of the desired effect, and resolutions adopted at public meetings to same end are a nullity when their bearing is upon third parties. Meddling is a habit with governments and with communities—that is, meddling with the course of events, meddling with the course of trade; it is ever without beneficial effect, and it would be fortunate if it could be said, without injury, but such is not the case. The legislators and the reformers always bungle—their efforts are akin to an attempt at repairing a watch for the moment out of order with a hammer and cold chisel.

Here and elsewhere, in regard to savings banks and otherwise, it may safely be admitted that business is not perfectly well balanced. This has been so from the beginning and will be so to the end of time; but inherent in the abuses, great or small, is the tendency to their own correction. In another day and with another generation there will still be a want of balance, but the preponderance and the deficiency will not be located at the same points.

The need of this and every other developing State is a capital in great quantity and circulating medium in large volume, and these can only be had in greatest abundance when the owners are least hampered in their employment.

It matters little who handles capital or who counts money if it is here and in use. Money controlled by commercial or savings banks, by insurance companies or by individuals, finds its way with unerring certainty to that point and that business where the need is greatest, provided its safety can be assured; and without such assurance there should and there can be no expectation of loans or investments.

The assertion that large capitalists are availing themselves to any considerable extent of the facilities afforded by savings banks for handling money is not supported by facts. The average of the deposits in the savings institutions of the city is considerably less than one thousand dollars, while if those of the whole of the State are included the average is still less. Now, if any considerable share of the aggregate of deposits is the property of wealthy people and is lodged in large sums, it must necessarily follow that each small depositor has but a trifle to his credit. Such is not the fact; deposits are graduated ranging from a single dollar upward, and there is no breach of regularity in gradation. There are no classes of depositors—the poor shade into the rich and there is no line of demarcation. There are few really large deposits in any of the banks and when there is one, almost without exception, there are behind it facts and circumstances that were they known would justify its lodgment and its receipt.

In this community savings banks have done their work well : they have been faithful and diligent, conservative and prudent, and yet not wanting in enterprise; they have crystalized into solid substance vaporous and straggling dollars that without their aid would have remained scattered or been dissipated and would never have been visible in the form of capital. Impair their usefulness or narrow their sphere by needless or mischievous restrictions, and a diminution of the total of available capital will follow; with diminution of capital will come financial distress, not partial but general, affecting and to an extent paralyzing every branch of business; and no class in community will feel the effect more seriously than operators in real estate.

Here the Convention took a recess until 2 o'clock P. M.

AFTERNOON SESSION—FEBRUARY 23.

The Chairman called the Convention to order at 2 o'clock P. M.

The Chairman: We have, next, a paper to be read by Mr. J. M. Elliott of Los Angeles.

J. M. Elliott, President of the First National Bank of Los Angeles, read the following:

SUGGESTIONS CONCERNING CERTAIN CHANGES IN THE STATE BANKING LAWS.

The following suggestions as to the enlarging of the powers of the Bank Commissioners are made in the hope that some law may be adopted which will put that body into a better position than it is at present for controlling certain banking elements within the State.

The writer feels satisfied that if the State Bank Commissioners had powers that should have been granted to them by law, several failures of State banks could have been prevented.

The time to stop poor banking is in its incipiency; but, unfortunately, as the law now stands, Bank Commissioners are powerless after having reported the matter to the Attorney-General, who may or may not, as he sees fit, carry out the suggestions made to him by the Commissioners.

The first change suggested is that the law requiring the banks to make reports be amended so as to abolish that part requiring them to report separately the amount of their capital stock.

Second, that published reports be called for five times during the year at a date which is already past, just as the Comptroller of the Currency calls for reports from the National Banks. If the dates as called for by the Comptroller could be adopted it would be an improvement.

Even State Bank Officers are human, and if they know that they have to make a report at some specified date there is a temptation to some of them to arrange for a more flattering statement than the average condition of the bank would warrant. In the other way there is no chance to know beforehand at what date a report will be called for, and the five reports would give the fair average condition of the bank during the year.

Another provision similar to that of the National Banking Law I think would be very serviceable: Many of the interior banks of really good reputation and management were until lately, at least, in the habit of keeping in their own vaults a very small proportion of cash, depending entirely upon a correspondent in the nearest large city for supplies when needed. A provision of the law requiring, say fifteen per cent. of cash to be kept on hand in the case of the Commercial Banks and a much smaller proportion in the Savings Banks would, I think, to some extent, remedy this evil.

Further, the law should be amended so as to enable the Bank Commissioners themselves to commence an action against any banking institution which is violating the law, or whose methods of banking are such as to render it plain to them that disaster would be the result of its continuance : also, that in cases of emergency the Commissioners by a unanimous vote, could close any banking institution.

Lastly, that the term of office of all the Commissioners be increased to, say eight years, and that at least two political organizations be represented in the personnel of the Board, and that the dates of the commissions of no two members should expire within twelve months of each other.

Frank Miller of Sacramento: Mr. Chairman, I desire to ask for a little change in the course of matters for a few minutes. The custom of banking which I referred to in my essay of this morning, as carried on in the East, I am not familiar with, except by hearsay. I have an opportunity to offer a witness, and, with your permission, I would like to ask for a few minutes' of the time of the Convention that we may be favored with an address by the witness I refer to, Mr. W. O. Hipwell, the Assistant Cashier of the Union National Bank of Chicago.

With your permission and the permission of the Convention, I would ask that he take the floor, to tell us how these matters are conducted in the East. I think his views would be of great benefit to us.

Wm. Beckman of Sacramento: I second Mr. Miller's motion.

By unanimous vote of the Convention, Mr. Hipwell was requested to address the meeting, and he spoke as follows:

Mr. Chairman, and Members of the Convention: [Applause.] Being a stranger in your city, I was rambling around this morning, when I was taken in by one of your bank men, an old friend of mine, Mr. Miller. I did not expect to have the privilege of being present here. Coming away from home for a rest, I thought I would throw shop to the wall altogether and not talk any shop. Mr. Miller got me to talking about something or other, about overdrafts and loans and so forth, and asked me to come in and look at the Convention, and I did not expect that you would ask me to address your body.

I do not know, in fact, what you expect me to talk about, or what I should speak about. Mr. Miller suggested the custom of Eastern banking. I have been connected with a national bank in Chicago for some thirty years now, the same bank all of that time. As regards country accounts, the Union National, of Chicago, with the exception of one other bank, the First National, I find, has had the largest number of country accounts there. We have been doing business in Iowa, Indiana and Wisconsin, and, as the years rolled on, we got into Colorado and away out into California. To-day I met four of our correspondents right here.

There is one thing about the custom of Eastern Bankers that I will mention, and that is, with country correspondents, as well as with their city banks, they will not allow overdrafts on any account. That is a matter that has been talked of with me several times to-day. I suppose you want to know something from me about that. If a banker in the country has some sudden demand upon him he must make a note with us in order to get the advances. But, if the funds are not used we allow him interest, in fact, allow interest all the time on balances, so that it makes very little difference with him as to whehter he makes a loan or makes an overdraft. [Applause.] In fact, making the loan, we look upon as the cheaper way for the country bank; he gets the loan at a lower rate than the rate at which an overdraft would be charged, if the city bank was in the habit of giving overdrafts. In the meantime you have your two per cent. on the money on deposit.

I understand the California banks do not allow overdrafts with their country banks. Perhaps I may be antagonizing some one, but I was asked merely to state facts, and those are facts. We are often asked, and especially by banks in the West—not very often, not at all I should say, in California—if they can overdraw their accounts by sending to us collaterals. Always our reply is, "No, sir." You can send your collaterals, perhaps, in some cases. We do not want your collaterals. You can make a note at ten days or thirty days, or payable on demand, if that will suit you better, and have the money to your credit, and if the money is unused, you have your two per cent. on it.

In the matter of exchange, I mean local or inland exchange, New York exchange. Of course, during the late stringency, we were obliged to make all kinds of rates on exchange. Usually our maximum and minimum rate on exchange in Chicago can never exceed eighty cents a thousand, for this reason, that is the express charge from New York. During June, July and August last, we frequently sold currency to New York, and we have received as high as thirty dollars a thousand; but that was owing to the peculiar circumstances existing in the country at the time. Chicago had plenty of funds all the time. Perhaps some persons say it was on account of the World's Fair, which threw the money from all over the world to us, and for that reason we were able to get on better than we otherwise would have done. Chicago is the "Windy City," and I suppose all the people from that city are inclined to be a little "windy," and talk a little more about their city than other people do; but I cannot say that it is a windy city after being three weeks in California. In every town I have visited they told me that was the Paradise. At this place, I can't think of the name of it—oh, down here below Los Angeles—San Diego, that is it—they told me that was the only place in California for a man to live in or do business in. I didn't like it there very well. I stopped there a little while and then ran away down into Mexico, to see if it was any better there, and didn't like it there very well. Then I went up to Los Angeles, and there, for the first time, I found a real live city in California. I intended to stop over at Fresno, but was thrown off by the wet weather, and now I have come to San Francisco, the metropolis, the beau ideal of all the West. We can go no further. Greeley said "Westward the Star of Empire takes its way," but, here, we can get no farther, unless we take in China, and the countries beyond the Pacific.

Gentlemen, I am very glad to have seen you and visited your beautiful city, and to have been so well met by the fraternity of which I have the honor to be a member. [Applause.]

The Chairman: Gentlemen, I am requested by the Manager of the Clearing House to inform you that the Clearing House Committee will meet the interior bankers to-morrow afternoon, at 1:30, in these rooms here, to discuss the subject brought up by Mr. Gerber.

Is Mr. Sheffield of Santa Barbara, here?

The Secretary: No, sir; he is not present.

The Chairman: Is Mr. Brunner of San Luis Obispo, here?

The Secretary: No, sir. I have a letter from Mr. Brunner, expressing his regret at his inability to be here, and asking that his paper be read. I can say now that neither Mr. Brunner nor Mr. Marble will be here. They have both written to us, saying they cannot attend.

The Chairman: What is your pleasure, gentlemen? Do you wish any of these papers read?

George H. Stewart of Los Angeles: Mr. Chairman, since these papers have been passed to print, I move that, in the instances where the author is absent, the paper be accepted as if read and opened to the same discussion to which they would be entitled, if read, unless the time of the Convention will permit their reading later on. Mr. Hewlett suggests that they merely be read by title. I am willing to accept that amendment to my motion.

Upon vote being taken, Mr. Stewart's motion, as amended, was duly carried.

The Chairman: It is so ordered. The Secretary will please read the papers by title.

The Secretary: We have first—

A PLEA FOR A RATIONAL CURRENCY SYSTEM.

BY E. S. SHEFFIELD, CASHIER OF THE SANTA BARBARA COUNTY NATIONAL BANK.

An oak, exposed to a storm, is strained from root to branch; decaying limbs break and in their fall carry to a common ruin smaller and weaker, though still sound stems. When the fury of the tempest ceases the tree remains, shorn of its defects and its strength revealed; what is left is sound and it will continue to live, adding new leaves and limbs of tougher texture as it gains in stature, strength and age. So with the banking system of the United States. The whirlwind of distrust that swept over the land last summer gave it a thorough test; pruned of its unhealthy and weaker members, it has emerged sound in root, body and limb; and having, unlike the Argentine, the Australian and the Italian systems, withstood the ordeal, now enjoys a perceptible gain in credit. So sound indeed, has it proven and so safely may it be left to grow to supply present and future needs, according to the tendencies already exhibited, that to discard it for another species or a newer planting, would be wanton waste.

There is little need to recount to bankers the history of last summer; it suffices to notice only the salient features of its events pertinent to the subject of this paper. The financial difficulties experienced seem due to the habit of legislative meddling with private contract—the effort to make that compulsory which in its very essence is voluntary. The original sin was the legal tender act of the war period, but the immediate cause, the persistent attempt to fix, by law, the price of a precious metal in defiance of the state of the market—as vain an undertaking as to regulate the force of the wind by act of Congress. When the storm came, the very restrictions imposed, as the acme of legislative wisdom, to prevent such difficulties, obstructed necessary measures for their relief and thus operated to aggravate them. The distress was mitigated through the wisdom and fidelity of the associated banks of New York and other money centers. These put into use a method of mutual insurance, the outcome of their own experience and sagacity, and through it established their credit on a higher plane. Although prohibited to loan when below the legal limit of reserve, they set the law at naught and loaned freely that they might save. Though forbidden, by an enactment that violates moral right, to coin their own credit, they assumed the burden of responsibility and coined it for their own use, thus releasing, for the service of their customers, their store of current money. And when, in the intensity of the prevailing distrust, this was hoarded, they, disdaining at such a time to consult the profit and loss account, bid a premium in the market for it to pay out again at par. Who can estimate the fortunes held intact, the homes saved, by their skillful and courageous acts? And who can estimate the greater beneficial results that might have been attained had they been free to act in the crisis as their judgment dictated?

When the National Banking System was established, it embodied what was then recognized as the best results of experience, acquired through years of mingled mistake, disaster and success, but, as if cast in an iron mould, it did not allow for the acquirement of further experience. The policy of the restriction on circulation has its warmest advocates among bankers, yet we see *one* instance of harm arising from it. The prohibition to loan when the reserve falls below the legal limit has seemed essential to sound banking, yet, if heeded during the recent panic, would have wrecked many whom its disregard saved. The terror of men in times of panic, lest funds may not be forthcoming for obligations soon to mature, the failure to meet which means ruin, leads them to hoard what current money comes within reach, thus tending to bring on the evil dreaded. The remedy for this fear, we have now learned, is to pour out money and credit like water—to loan on everything that is good security more freely than at other times, but to advance interest to such a rate as will induce an early repayment; yet, under the law, this remedy is unavailable.

The defects of the currency system provided by law are clearly seen, and much thought has recently been expended in the hope of perfecting it. The need of some system is generally conceded, though a few, dissenting from the general view, believe coin alone sufficient. That coin can be made to answer is not denied, but the cost will be greater. To use coin alone requires the investment of sufficient capital in the precious metals for that single use ; on the other hand, a paper currency, representing a claim on other forms of wealth, puts those forms to double use and in that measure economizes. By it, under security of commodities, commodities may be exchanged. Prudent bankers, however, hesitate to assume, singly, the responsibility of a note issue. The relation of note-holders and depositors to a bank, while theoretically the same, is in practice much different. Note-holders, as a rule, do not know the bank, its officers or the degree of credit it is worthy, and are not under obligations to it ; in seasons of distrust they very generally insist on redemption. The depositor, on the contrary, deposits through choice, under the idea of advantage to himself ; he generally is, has been, or expects to be a debtor to the bank for loans, or other favors ; he is acquainted with the standing of the bank and the reputation of its officers, consequently in a panic is less likely to make demands than the note-holder ; the depositor, too, is rarely a note-holder, for he converts his receipts of notes into deposits. For these reasons it is undesirable for isolated banks to issue circulation.

In the Clearing-House Certificate, a device of American bankers, there seems to exist the germ of a rational system. Originating in 1860 to meet an emergency suddenly arising, its most happy success gave promise of a solution of the currency problem then so perplexing ; but, soon stifled by the prohibitory tax on circulation other than National, it has remained dormant, reviving only, in successive crises, to palliate evils that the law-made system could not successfully deal with ; had it been left free to develop, it is not unlikely that it might have prevented many of the financial evils inflicted on us since that date, in particular those flowing from the superstition that government can make money having value, out of most anything. Exactly into what it might have developed it is impossible to say, but, it is believed, that a currency system similar to the one hereinafter suggested would lie in the natural course of development.

To create a good system there needs be added to present Clearing House Certificate methods, redemption features and a device to automatically vary the rate of interest to accord with the fluctuations in the supply of loanable capital. Under guarantee of a wider association of banks than those of a single city, it would seem impregnable in a panic, and thus would relieve banks of the anxieties connected with the care of an individual issue, as much as does now the national system.

It is desirable that whatever system is adopted, be an outgrowth of present banking methods, adapted to the National and State Banks already existing ; that the circulation provided be elastic ; that it be capable of expansion to keep pace with the growth of the country in resources ; that it be not made dependent on the existence of a symptom of poverty—the government debt—for its continuance; and that, above all, it be not directly the product of legislation, subject to frequent change through the misconceptions of legislators little skilled in finance ; at least, that legislation, if any is had, be permissive, not constructive. Such a system is here roughly outlined :

An association of banks not limited as to number.

Circulating notes to be issued by it under the joint guarantee of all its members.

The notes to be redeemable on demand, in gold, at the principal money centers.

A Redemption Fund, to consist of gold deposits into the treasury of the association by its members, induced by payment of interest made at pleasure and repayable on demand.

A ratio of reserve to liability at which it is desirable to maintain the Redemption Fund to be determined, then, to maintain it at that ratio, vary from time to time, the rate of interest to be paid for deposits; should the fund fall below the ratio, advance the rate ; should it rise above, lower the rate.

The notes to be put into circulation only by repayment of the Redemption Fund's deposits, (if preferred to gold) and loans of the association to its members on pledge of securities approved by its Managing Committee, as are now Clearing House Certificates. The rate of interest charged for loans to be the same as that paid for deposits and vary with it.

After payment of expenses and losses, the remaining profit to be divided among the banks in proportion to their respective capitals ; this would be something appreciable, for, should the ratio of reserve average fifty per cent. of the issues, the amount of interest received would double that paid. It is expected that the rate of interest would average as low, if not lower than that now paid by metropolitan banks on daily balances, and this would cover the whole cost—expenses included—to the borrowing bank, to be yet further reduced by the dividend accruing on its contribution to the guaranteeing capital. Loans should be terminable at the will of the borrowing bank, but should not be called in, except on failure to maintain margins, or where there is a separation from the association. The Managing Committee, however, should have power to call in a percentage of all loans outstanding, if needed to maintain the reserve ; and, as a last resort, to assess the guaranteeing banks, in proportion to capital, for the same purpose. The notes issued should not be the obligations of individual banks, but of the association, which should assume the whole charge of their preparation, issue and redemption. Under the plan proposed, the issue of circulation would appear as a loan of the united credit of all the banks to any individual bank, on the security of collateral, and at the market rate of interest, and would seem therefore, so far as experience indicates to possess the essential conditions of sound banking.

The association would logically begin with the Clearing Banks of New York ; these could invite such of their correspondents to join who would undertake to conduct business in the way approved as legitimate and safe. As membership aside from the assurance of safety in a crisis, would be advantageous, directly, on account of the share of profit inuring from the aggregate circulation, and indirectly through the greater local credit gained, it would not be difficult to induce banks to surrender methods regarded unwise, and confine themselves to the sound lines a wider experience has suggested ; a result, the attainment of which would greatly enhance the credit of the united banks.

Unrestricted by government regulation and left free to develop in accord with the wants of business, the association might, in time, assume an international character; banks connected therewith might gradually spread with the spread of American Commerce into Canada, Mexico, the commercial cities of South America and other countries.

As the proposed association is designed to further the interests of banks, it should have no direct dealings with the public, lest it should in some way enter into competition with them; both in its redemptions and in its borrowings for the reserve it should deal through its members; nevertheless, as the credit of the association would be higher than that of any single bank, enabling it to borrow at lower rates, and in panic times to retain deposits that individual banks could not control, it would be advisable to issue to its members certificates of deposit of the association for sale to the public, bearing a rate of interest slightly less than that paid on general deposits, the difference between the two rates to constitute a commission to the bank negotiating them, payable to it so long as they remain uncancelled; in this way the banks could make use of the higher credit of the association to lower the rate of interest. The certificates, too, would afford a low rate, convertible investment for trust funds and the reserve balances of savings banks, insurance and trust companies which will be much needed when the national debt is paid. To cover the expenses of redemption in the redemption cities, a commission could be allowed the banks making them.

Although, to the writer, an interest regulating device seems the most essential feature of any currency system designed to adjust itself automatically to the varying exigencies of commerce and to the alternate optimistic and pessimistic feelings of those engaged in it, it does not seem to be so regarded by those who have recently put forth views on the subject; it is therefore necessary to set out in detail the reasons which appear to require it. When the desired ratio of reserve to circulation and deposits is determined it can be maintained by varying the rate of interest paid for deposits and charged on loans; if the reserve falls, the fall may be checked and its rise induced by advancing the rate in successive steps until the rate which will effect the purpose is found; should the advanced rate cause the reserve to increase beyond the ratio desired, a lowering of the rate will aid to bring about the proper adjustment. That such would be the effect is known by the experience of the Bank of England, whose reserve is kept at the proper ratio by similar means; it is believed, however, that the method suggested would be more effective, because it is proposed that the variation in rate shall take effect on all loans, outstanding and new, by and to the association, and not simply on new loans as with the Bank of England, and doing this its fluctuations need not be so wide to produce the desired effect as in its experience.

A circulation, for the redemption of which there is no adequate incentive, and that costs little to issue, is liable at times to exceed the needs of commerce, and can only adjust itself to them by causing a general rise in prices. To guard against this, the motive for redemption and the inducement to issue must vary in strength from time to time, as the amounts presented for redemption indicate a redundancy or otherwise. A rise in the rate of interest would induce the presentation of notes for redemption, and the deposit of the resulting gold for profit; the same rise would make it less profitable to take out circulation and would lead to its retirement. The reverse effect would be produced by a fall in the rate; it would now become more profitable to take out circulation, and less profitable to retire or present it for redemption. The rise would increase the ratio of reserve, and the fall prevent its unnecessary increase. A rise, too, would induce the deposit of sufficient additional gold, upon which safely to increase issues in order to move the crops, or provide additional circulating medium during panic periods when other forms of credit are not available ; it would also insure its prompt retirement when the exigency passes.

The reserve would be a "finance meter ; " its fluctuations marking the state of trade. If decreasing, it would show either a spirit of speculation leading to over-trading, which a higher rate would check by lowering profits, or a diminution in production, likely to derange business unless economy in consumption is induced. If increasing, it would indicate a lack of enterprise needing stimulation by prospect of profit, or an over-production of consumable things that should be converted into fixed capital to prevent waste.

A surplus of consumable products may be converted into instruments of production (fixed capital) by withdrawing capital and labor from the production of consumable things, and applying them to the construction of other instruments of production, thereby increasing wealth ; if not done, too many consumable things are produced, prices fall, and the capital and labor engaged in their production are not sufficiently remunerated, businesses dependent on them suffer, these again affect others, until the depression becomes general. A deficiency in products for consumption, or conversion into fixed capital requires that they be consumed or converted with economy. As the lowering of the rate of interest would stimulate conversion by making it profitable, so a rise in the rate would discourage conversion. Should it at such a time continue through the construction of railroads, factories, &c., the way is paved for a financial revulsion, which, occurring, would still best be relieved by a rapid rise in the rate of interest. By such rise the united banks could safely place at the service of the business community their entire resources of credit secured by the wealth of the country pledged to them. The surety of obtaining loans when needed and their extra cost would induce their postponement until needed. The high rate would draw to the service of those needing from every quarter and aid to palliate the usual ill effects of a panic.

Financial panics are almost always caused by a continuance of the scale of business necessitated by a period of great production into one of small. The crisis is reached when banks can no longer bear the strain of supplying means for this unproductive trading and occurs because the symptoms of overtrading have not been detected soon enough and methods of checking it are absent. One marked symptom is a drain of gold, or whatever composes the reserves of banks. The export of gold is not of itself disadvantageous, for value therefor is received ; but when, as now, a structure of credit is based upon it, it has a value, to sustain credit, far exceeding its exchangeable value. For this reason only, it is desirable to retain enough gold to safely support bank deposits and circulation at the maximum figure required to effect the usual exchange of commodities. When in a locality the crops yield less than the average, the community dependent thereon must either consume less or must part with some of its previously saved money to buy things from elsewhere. Now if the price of money can be artificially raised, there will be a stronger inducement to consume less and what must be bought will cost less in money. In addition, whatever that community has to sell will find, on account of its greater relative cheapness, a readier market elsewhere and to the extent marketed diminish the export of money.

What is true of a village is true of a nation. If the export of gold may be checked by bidding higher for it, then the variable interest feature proposed will enable its export to be checked, just when and to the extent desired. And if capital may be so used as to prevent the occurrence of financial crises, then this feature too, as the endeavor has been made to show, will direct its application to the correction of tendencies that usually produce them.

A further means of protecting the reserve is available in the character of the securities taken from the individual banks as pledges to secure the circulation issued to them. A banker could logically divide all wealth into two classes, viz: *instruments of production* and *things produced*.

In the first would be placed land, buildings, railways, factories, ships, etc., etc. In the second all commodities to be consumed in the support and enjoyment of life.

Land, as a security for circulation, once thought desirable, is now, through unfavorable experience, discarded; yet, why it is unsuitable has seldom been told. The reason appears to be that it is generally owned by as many persons as can command the capital to do so; (the fact that it is always largely mortgaged is an indication that more hold it than have capital for the purpose) there being no further capital to invest in it but that arising from surplus production, there can be no market for it except through the capitalization of savings—a sale of land to purchase other land cutting no figure, as the two operations cancel each other; so when there is no surplus production and consequently no savings to capitalize, the market for land is destroyed; and it is just at such a time, if ever, that it needs be realized upon to sustain values. A few years of little or no surplus production, followed by one of deficiency, would wreck any currency scheme based on land. Government, state, municipal and railroad bonds, securities representing instruments of production, are now more generally suggested, but that there is inherent in these too, the same objection that lies against land, though less noticeable, because existing in less quantity, seems not to be suspected; yet, neither also is there capital to invest in these, but that arising from savings subject to capitalization; when there is need to realize on them, realization on any scale is impossible. It is otherwise with pledges of things produced for consumption. While the pledge of instruments of production is really only a pledge of the income derivable from them, that of consumable products is a pledge of their whole value. Land has value because of the things it will produce, consequently the thing produced is the value sought. Because of things produced transportation facilities exist and it is from them government revenue is derived. For them the people expend almost all their energies and for the reason that they must be consumed within a short time, if life continues, the market for them is never closed. As circulation would be issued to facilitate the exchange of things produced for consumption and in proportion to the extent that they are being exchanged, and as it will be redeemed and retired as the exchanges are completed, it would seem, if the reasons set forth weigh, that the ordinary discounts of commercial banks, based on consumable things in process of exchange, would supply the best, as it is the most logical form of security for its redemption.

It seems obvious that to open the way for the proposed system the repeal, or modification of the tax on circulation other than National, must be effected.

A fear prevails that repeal would entail the evils of "wild cat" banking; yet may not the proposed association itself be the most effectual bar to it? Its members, existing in every quarter of the land, would seek, in the ordinary routine of business, to convert at once into coin, every obligation received not yielding a revenue; notes of competing banks would be promptly presented for redemption, and in case of failure to redeem, the issuing institution would be closed by due process of law. But a greater safeguard would be that, as deposits are the most profitable part of the business, the desire to better credit in order to attract them, would lead to membership in a similar association. Indeed, such an association would be able to control the issues of the government itself! Holding the mass of the money of the country it could present for redemption from time to time sufficient of its obligations to compel the maintenance by the Treasury of the ratio of reserve believed by the banks to be prudent.

Every one has the moral right to give and receive any obligation freely agreed upon. To found a policy on the violation of right is surely a mistake; the evils sought to be avoided, may in a measure, be avoided, but other and greater evils are entailed. In the natural course the evils themselves suggest a cure which in time follows while the law-produced evils are avoided. At all events, it does not become a banker to suggest a privilege for his class, denied to others. Equity alone considered, the tax should be repealed; still, owing to the existence of the fear mentioned, a modification, opening the way to the proposed system, may be more likely of accomplishment. An amendment to the present act taxing State bank circulation, providing, that "issues of notes intended for circulation redeemable, at the option of the holder, in New York, Chicago, San Francisco and New Orleans, under the joint guarantee of State, National, or State and National banks, having paid-up capital aggregating one hundred million dollars or more, shall not be taxed," would remove legal obstacles to the proposed system, and would enable it to be put into operation without constructive legislation.

In one of Æsops fables is represented a carter stuck fast in the mud, who after vainly applying the whip fell on his knees and besought help of Hercules; the God, appearing, gruffly bade him "clap his shoulder to the wheel." Is there not in this a moral for us? So long as we fail to utilize all the means at our command, does it become us to beg assistance of Congress? Are we not apt, as experience teaches, asking for bread to receive a stone? We are not forbidden to co-operate; we are not forbidden to borrow and lend; and are even permitted, under a penalty, to issue circulating notes. The road is open to achieve all the benefits of the association recommended, save alone in the issue of circulation. Had it been in existence last summer, is it not likely that the united credit of all the banks, coupled with a sufficiently high interest rate, would have diverted into our own coffers that stream of gold, whose flow abroad startled the nation into a frenzy of alarm? Since the reserve feature, in its essence, is but a device to borrow on the credit of all and lend to those in need or who can with advantage use, would it not have been a natural and most effective means to combine and equalize the several reserves?—and have operated to prevent the runs which only isolated banks suffered? By calming the public fears, would not have been avoided that dearth of currency, experienced in money centers?—currency drawn therefrom to render more secure cautious country bankers compelled, singly, to face the storm. Would it not, too, have enabled the banks to expand their loans when the need was so sore, or, at least, to have avoided that avoided that decrease, which, because it lessened deposits diminished a form of credit that, according to recent statistics, is habitually utilized as a means of payment through banks, to an extent over ninety times greater than current money? The diminution from this source, in the ordinary facilities for exchange, suffered by July 12th, is apparently sufficient to account for the phenomenal depreciation in the market value of securities taking place. And is it not possible, since, at times, loans commanded a rate exceeding sixty per cent per annum, that even at the cost of a ten per cent tax, a temporary issue of notes, might have been more economical, in the emergency, than to have paid a premium for currency? As the adoption of any one of the means suggested would have rendered less necessary a resort to the others, the value of an association, through which all might have become available, seems beyond computation.

The leaders of the two political parties seem weary wrestling with the financial problem, which, though always up for settlement, never gets settled, and remains but to delay accomplishment of their most cherished plans. The party in power, too, exhibits a strong desire to repeal the tax on circulation in the hope of a settlement. It shows, also, a wish to sever the too intimate relations existing between the Treasury and the private financial interests of the country. An indication that the banks are able and willing to assume the entire burden of the latter, would meet, it is believed, a ready response.

The Secretary: Next we have a paper on

HOW TO PRESERVE THE NATIONAL BANKING SYSTEM.

BY HENRY BRUNNER, CASHIER OF THE COMMERCIAL BANK OF SAN LUIS OBISPO.

The National Bank act is beyond question the wisest financial measure ever passed by the Congress of the United States. Not only did it fully accomplish the immediate purpose for which it was enacted, namely, to create a home market for United States bonds, but it has given us a system of homogeneous banking such as no other country has ever had. This system has been of untold benefit to the whole Nation and has gained the undivided confidence of all classes of our people.

But the increased business of our great country has outgrown the usefulness of the wise law passed thirty years ago. A fundamental change is needed. The very principle upon which the system is established must be abandoned. The note issue secured by United States bonds is without profit to the bank, its customers, or the country, and has therefore forfeited its right to exist. In its place we need an elastic bank note circulation, *a circulation created for commerce and based upon commerce.*

Shall this change be made as a crowning improvement of, or shall it sweep from existence a banking system whose prestige is considered by thousands of bankers a sufficient inducement to submit to all the unprofitable requirements of the present law?

Upon this subject I published over five years ago an article in the *American Banker*. I have since followed closely the evolution of opinion in regard to this question and am convinced that, with a few alterations, my proposition of five years ago is superior to all those that have come to my notice, and I therefore take the liberty to submit my plan for your kind consideration.

The main features of this plan are:

I—That a NATIONAL BANK OF ISSUE be chartered by Congress for a term of fifty years, as an integral part of the National Banking System. The capital of this bank of issue to be equal to ten per cent of the total paid-up capital of all the National Banks and to be fully paid-up. The stockholders to be the National Banks; each National Bank to take shares of the Bank of Issue equal to ten per cent of its own paid-up capital stock. The liability of the stockholders to be the same as in the National Banks now existing. The maximum note-issue of said Bank not to exceed an amount equal to the total paid-up capital and surplus of all the National Banks. The act of Congress creating or chartering the said Bank, to limit its business to:

a. The issue of bank-notes.

b. The re-discount of commercial paper for the National Banks only and the collection thereof.

c. To act as financial agent of the United States.

d. To buy and sell gold and silver bars.

e. To receive legal tender gold and silver coin in exchange for bank-notes; but this is not to be an obligation.

f. To liquidate suspended National Banks.

The said act of Congress to prohibit the said Bank of Issue from engaging in the following branches of banking:

a. The receiving of deposits from and opening accounts for any person, firm, corporation, or bank, except from and for the Treasury of the United States; provided however, that it may, for the purpose of collecting foreign bills of exchange and establishing the equilibrium of trade, keep accounts with the leading banks of foreign countries.

b. To act as correspondent for any bank, National or other.

c. To buy, sell, or own stocks or bonds of any kind.

This National Bank of Issue to be under the control of the Comptroller of the Currency in the same manner as the National Banks now existing. Its principal place of business to be in the City of New York. The Bank to be under the management of a Board of seven Directors, to be elected annually by the stockholders, the National Banks; at least four new Directors to be elected each year. Said Board of Directors to have the same power as now exercised by the Board of Directors of a National Bank, within the restrictions of the charter, and it shall also have the right to establish branches in any part of the United States, and appoint the Cashier of such Branch, and assign the district or States to belong to each branch. The local management of such branches to be under the control of a Finance Committee of three, elected annually by the Presidents of the National Banks of the city in which such branch is established, the members of such Finance

Committee to be chosen from among the managing officers of the National Banks of such city, and at least one new member to be elected each year.

II—That Congress discontinue the issue and re-issue of gold, silver and coin certificates by the Treasury of the United States.

III—That Congress repeal such parts of the National Bank act, as make it compulsory for the National Banks to purchase United States Bonds and issue circulating notes.

IV—That the bank-notes issued by said National Bank of Issue be in denominations of $20, $50, $100, $500, $1,000, $5,000 and $10,000, and be secured:

a. By a reserve of legal tender coin and gold and silver bars, to an amount equal to at least thirty-five per cent of the notes in circulation.

b. By commercial paper, re-discounted from National Banks exclusively, having from 30 to 120 days to run, for at least sixty-five per cent of the notes in circulation. The domestic paper to be payable at the National Bank of Issue, or one of its branches, and all subject to protest, bearing interest from maturity only, if containing an interest clause. The foreign bills of exchange to be strictly documentary and subject to protest.

V—That the bank-notes so issued be not a legal tender, but have the legal character of a promissory note payable to bearer on demand. And that the same shall be received at par in all parts of the United States in payment of taxes, excises, public lands, and all other dues to the United States, except duties on imports; and also for all salaries and other debts and demands owing by the United States to individuals, corporations and associations within the United States, except interest on the public debt, and in redemption of the National currency. The Bank of Issue to pay to the United States the same tax on its circulation as is now collected on the National Bank circulating notes. Provided, however, that the act of Congress chartering this Bank, authorize the President of the United States to make said bank-notes full legal tender for all debts by proclamation in time of panic or war, upon the request of the Board of Directors of the Bank of Issue, for a term not exceeding one year at a time. During such term or terms the National Bank of Issue shall pay to the Government of the United States a tax of four per cent per annum on all its notes in circulation.

VI—That the rate of re-discount shall be uniform for the whole system; such rate to be determined from time to time by the Board of Directors of the National Bank of Issue; provided, however, that if the re-discounts of any branch or any bank exceed twenty-five per cent of the paid-up capital it represents (that is twenty-five per cent of the paid-up capital of the bank asking for re-discount, or twenty-five per cent of the paid-up capital of the National Banks belonging to the district of such branch) and if such re-discounts are above the average of the whole system, the rate of discount of such branch or bank shall be increased one per cent; and whenever the re-discounts of any bank or branch exceed fifty per cent of the paid-up capital represented by such branch or bank (as above specified), the Board of Directors of the National Bank of Issue shall have full power to fix a higher rate of discount for such bank, banks, branch or branches.

VII. That all the bank notes issued by such National Bank of Issue be signed by the President and Cashier of such bank. They shall also bear the signatures of two members of the Finance Committee, if put in circulation by the head office in New York, and the signatures of the Chairman of the Finance Committee and the Cashier of the local branch, if put in circulation by such branch. These bank notes shall be as nearly as possible of the same form and size as the present National Bank circulating notes. When redeemed by the National Bank of Issue, or any of its branches, they shall not be re-issued, but cancelled and destroyed under such regulations as the Board of Directors of the bank may establish.

VIII. Out of the net profits of the Bank of Issue, a dividend not exceeding six per cent per year may be declared annually by the stockholders, provided that not less than twenty per cent of the net profits shall be retained each year to create a surplus fund.

A careful study of the plan above outlined will convince you that it affords:

1. A bank note of unquestionable quality that can be created when it is wanted and cancelled when it has done its duty.

2. The largest and strongest Bank of Issue of any country, worthy of our immense resources, *and yet in keeping with our democratic institutions, creating no monopoly since every one is welcome into the system.*

3. The best organized and united system of independent banks.

I also believe that it commends itself to our political financiers in Washington, because it does not aim at special profit for the banker; it does not touch the rights of our laborers and farmers to free coinage of silver, new issue of greenbacks, issue of Government notes against farm produce and farm mortgages and whatever the great schemes may be. It simply proposes to create a currency suitable to the wants of our business men and their agents, the bankers, of such denominations that it will not go to the laborer for his wages and not remain with the farmer.

I do not know whether it is necessary to make the bank notes legal tender in time of panic or war, but thought best to mention the idea.

The proposition to stop the issue of coin certificates by the Treasury of the United States, is very important, *but not absolutely necessary.* This class of currency could be well replaced by the issues of the new bank note, to the advantage of all. It is also the partial solution of another problem which I have carefully avoided mixing with the question before us.

The rate of re-discount of the proposed Bank of Issue is a very delicate point. We all know that the rate of interest varies greatly in the different sections of our great country or even in the different portions of a State. A uniform rate for all re-discounts would therefore be unjust. But where are we to draw the line? I think that my solution of the problem is equitable and conducive to conservative management, but shall be glad to see it improved. It is but just to state that this difficulty is not greater for the proposed Bank of Issue, than for any plan of bank note issue not secured by bonds. You will also notice that the re-discounts of the individual bank are not limited, but that it is in the power of the Bank of Issue to make an effective limitation by the rate of discount.

When we consider that our best commercial paper in the grain, cotton, and provision trade goes to Europe for re-discount, taking away from us millions of profit and the finest business; that many conservative branches of industry and business suffer for want of low and regular rates of discount in this country; that every year at the time of moving crops and paying taxes we are suffering under a stringency of the money market; that at other times money so accumulates in the reserve centers, that our National Banks, under the conservative form of call loans, encourage gambling in stocks and produce; and when we add to this the helplessness of a local bank in case of a crisis, we must come to the conclusion that a change in our banking system is necessary. The country has reached this conclusion now and, unless the bankers by their superior experience, guide it in the right direction, the popular movement is likely to go wrong.

The Secretary: Next

A TALK ON THE FINANCIAL SITUATION.

BY JOHN M. C. MARBLE, PRESIDENT OF THE NATIONAL BANK OF CALIFORNIA, LOS ANGELES

Distrust, the cause of all panics, has been abroad in the land, and 1893 will be noted in the history of finance, as a panic periodic, only equalled by 1873-1857 and 1837, making four major crises, which have occured within the memory of men here present.

In this practical age, we should learn from experience, the great teacher, and evolve some plan to prevent the return of these great destroyers of wealth, and save the general Banking business of the country from degenerating, at times, into a simple calling of loans, curtailing of trade, and a rustling to get coin for those who want it to bury, or make dead to practical use.

The best authorities claim that Banks need not fail, and doubtless they are right; failure or success is simply the result of methods. Reliable reserves, up to approved rules, good loans at short dates, on valuable collateral, at a wide margin, will break a panic, before it can break a Bank.

The largest reserve the National Bank act requires, in any case is 25 per cent, of ordinary liabilities. Whenever such reserve drops under that per cent., the Bank must cease to loan until the required reserve is restored, which, with a portfolio filled with good short date obligations, should be a short matter. The late experience, of the New York Banks, is a good illustration of the great length of time it requires to exhaust such a reserve, even under the most trying circumstances, when Banks are united.

What we know, in financial affairs, as a crisis, is simply the culmination of what has gone before. Banks never have been, nor ever will be called on, for all their deposits in one day, It is the weakening of the banks by continued withdrawals in excess of deposits that brings the panic days. In the late pressure the National Banks of New York City reached their greatest volume of deposits September 3rd, 1892, $419,587,400. They then commenced to decline, and reached their lowest point September 9th, 1893, $299,816,400; a decrease in a year and a week of about 28½ per cent., which is a sum not greater than the average reserve of New York Banks. This means that for the year and a week the contraction was in progress, they could have maintained their payments without the collection of a loan or the help of a friend, thus proving—that all banks should maintain their credit in good times and bad—as some banks are always found to do.

It is not the province of Commercial Banks to furnish their customers permanent business capital. When they permit their assets to be absorbed in this way, their usefulness is largely paralyzed, and it were better that they retire from business. No credit should be better than those of banks, and it is not good form to excuse bank closing, at the expense of correct principles, by endeavoring to popularize the idea that banks can only be expected to keep their contracts in fair weather.

But over and above these preservative principles, the bank should, as the guardian of the money of the people, be hedged about by safe guards. In 1837 and 1857 the rotten condition of much of the State Bank currency was a prime factor in the distrust that caused those panics, and aggravated their losses. The National Bank Act, introduced by the necessities of the war, relieved the panics of 1873 and 1893 of all distrust as to losses on bank notes, as no one has lost a dollar by our currency since National Bank notes took the place of State Bank notes. Since it has been proven that one great function of our banks, i. e. currency, can be made absolutely safe, why not make the greater function, deposits, equally safe? Remove distrust, the prime factor in creating panics, by making deposits as reliable as bank currency is, and, so far as banks are concerned, panics will cease. In the line of this thought, the following amendments are suggested to the National Bank Act.

1. Authorize the Secretary of the Treasury to redeem all present issues of Government Bonds, not yet matured, and issue in their stead bonds payable at the pleasure of the government, bearing two per cent. per annum interest, whenever the substitution can be made with absolute profit to the government. (This would give over six hundred million dollars government bonds available to secure National Bank currency ; a sum more than three-fold greater than the volume now used for this purpose.)

2. Authorize banks to issue currency, to the par of all bonds deposited, to secure circulation.

3. Retain the present tax on circulation and set aside all profits therefrom, over expense of office of Comptroller of the Currency, as a safety fund to liquidate all obligations, (other than capital stock), of National Banks failing thereafter.

4. Prohibit National Banks from paying interest on deposits, except on recommendation of Clearing House of near by redemption city specifying rate and terms, the same to be approved by Comptroller of the Currency, with severe penalty for infraction of such rates.

5. Require said banks, at all times, to loan the government any amount of coin necessary to maintain its payments in coin, and thus insure the parity of our money. The rate of interest for all such advances not to exceed two per cent. per annum.

6. Authorize Clearing Houses, in redemption cities, to issue certificates (on good collateral) legal tender between banks, whenever, in the opinion of the Comptroller of the Currency, approved by the Secretary of the Treasury, a crisis

may warrant it ; such issues to be temporary, and to be promptly retired when emergency-has passed. This will overcome the lack of elasticity in our currency at vital moments in panic times.

7. All banks organized under these laws to be legal depositories, without bond, for all Federal, State, Municipal or other public or private funds. (This provision will prevent much of the inconvenience, which now results, at times, from taking out of use large volumes of money.)

Much of the financial trouble of the past year has been caused by the friends of silver unduly pushing their commodity forward as a measure of value. With more than six times as much silver (in value) as gold in the United States Treasury, with little demand for the white metal we had the spectacle of a great contention to further decrease the gold reserve to buy more silver. Such financiering, if continued, could have led to but one result, demonitization of gold and driving it out of use as a measure of value, thus contracting our money very largely in its best part. To a country, whose traditions favor bi-metallism, such a course could not be permanently satisfactory, and, since the country has declared itself on this question, a way will be found that will maintain the two metals, each as money, in use, and interchangeable at will of holder.

France is frequently cited as a country very successful in the use of silver. What France does, in that regard, the United States can do without awaiting the uncertainty of international agreement. This may require a change of ratio, or that the interchangeability should be maintained by limiting the coinage, and also by ceasing to coin any gold, under ten dollar pieces, or to issue any government or bank notes under denominations of five dollars.

A serious objection to bi-metallism is, that no two commodities are so fixed in value as to always prove precisely the same equivalents for declared ratios. Silver, being more base, may be a better protection against robbery, but the ideal measure of value is that most convenient in form, most steady in value, and most universally desired by the most enlightened people of the earth, gold, which, best of all, fills this measure.

Using the two metals has the advantage of giving more tools to measure with, and the detriment that an ounce of silver will sometimes exchange for more, and sometimes for less, of gold, can be overcome by the government taxing itself to maintain the cost of maintaining the parity. It will be found, that while the people will not tax themselves to buy the silver of the world at a price much greater than it is worth, they will cheerfully submit to a considerable tax to maintain the equality and use of gold and silver as measures of value.

The term dollar is a misnomer if it does not always indicate the same, and unless the parity of our money can be maintained it would be better to abolish the word dollar from our vocabulary, and cause people to contract for grains of gold, if they prefer gold, or grains of silver, if they prefer silver, rather than for a dollar of uncertain meaning.

With money, as with banks, legal status is of first importance, but even this, without honest methods and correct practices, can bring no true success.

There are times which demand a higher trait than selfishness. The spectacle of the New York Clearing House Banks in our late panic, rising to the occasion so splendidly, was an inspiration. In such times more is lost than gained by striving to make each tub stand on its own bottom.

Los Angeles recently presented a good object lesson in this. She should never have been the great calamity agitator.

I take it all members of this Convention are quite familiar with recent conditions; the pinch, last Spring and Summer, was quite severe in the East. The crisis, however, appeared to have largely spent its force, and things were pointing towards better conditions, when a small cloud appeared at Los Angeles. The sequel proves, that, with possibly one exception, every bank there had plenty of good collateral, and had the Los Angeles Clearing House Banks, when first called together to meet the crisis, concluded to pool their issues, as long as good collateral with ample margin was forthcoming, there certainly would not have been more than one failure there, if any, and the general liquidation and losses of the Summer saved. In fact, it is hardly probable that to have saved the failures would have required an issue of Clearing House Certificates one-fourth as large as the coin we were called upon to ship in in one fortnight. The denouement was sudden. Like a flash of lightning from a clear sky, in an unexpected quarter, it caused to go over the wires, "more than half the banks of Los Angeles have closed." This coming at a time when the public pulse was very sensitive, everybody was startled and became panicky. Los Angeles called San Francisco loudly for coin, San Francisco called New York more loudly, the epidemic spread, and soon it looked as if Satan had broken loose, everybody clamoring for coin they wanted, and for coin they did not want, and failure became the feature of the time. The fact that nearly all the suspensions were temporary, goes to prove that Los Angeles ought to have averted, not aggravated the calamity.

In this discussion no reference has been made to State Banks, which, in their various forms, have much the larger volume of business, but supply no circulation, appearing to be hedged about by a fear engendered by experience, in anti-bellum days, that they are not safe instruments to furnish currency. The conditions are now so different that it may be easy to overestimate the danger of State Bank currency. The National Bank system has proved so efficient and safe, and has been such an education to the people, that wild-cat banking would not be tolerated now. National Banks would have nothing to fear, even should some States be lax in their legislation. The rule of the survival of the fittest would prevail. Under the former State system there were State Banks that always honored their notes, and the present National Bank law is largely copied from State laws formerly in force. Let Congress reduce the present prohibitory tax on State circulation to that charged on National Bank notes, and it will be found, that such notes, if issued, will have a very limited home circulation, unless they are entitled to high credit from excellent security, and made redeemable at par in the great redemption centers of the country.

In conclusion, 30 years experience with the National Banking system, during a great war, under suspension of specie payments, and under specie payments, and with the vicissitudes of introducing a new and untried system, proves that a tax of one per cent. per annum exacted from National Banks on their circulation is more than ample to pay twice the losses on deposits made by failed banks, and that it is possible to make deposits in such institutions as absolutely safe as National Bank notes are.

So easy a remedy should not be deferred. The Chinese rule of chopping off a banker's head, when he fails, applies the remedy too late to help the depositor: better stop the trouble before the loss by establishing this sinking fund from taxes on circulation, and also by empowering business men to protect themselves by authorizing Clearing Houses or State Banking Associations, upon complaint, to investigate and wind up unworthy banking institutions before they can injure other than their shareholders.

The Chairman: Is there any other gentleman who desires to make any remarks?

Lovell White: Mr. Chairman, there was a matter of amending the by-laws of the Association. That would properly come up now, if the house is not otherwise occupied. It appears in the report of the Executive Council.

The Chairman: Very well; if there is no objection, the report of the Executive Council will be taken up.

The Secretary: The Executive Council, sir, recommended that a certain section of our by-laws, relating to the annual dues, be amended. The requirements of the Constitution as to amendments are as follows: " This Constitution may be altered or amended at any annual meet- " ing by a vote of two-thirds of the members present; notice of the " proposed amendment having been first submitted to the Secretary at " least ten days before the annual meeting, to be placed by him before " the Executive Council, that they may arrange for bringing it before " the Convention under the regular order of business "

All these requirements have been complied with, and the Execu- tive Council recommends that the By-Laws relating to payment of an- nual dues be amended as follows: The present By-Law reads: " Sec- " tion 1. The annual dues of the Association shall be considered due " at the beginning of the year, which year shall commence with the " regular annual meeting; it being understood that absent members " from such annual meeting shall not forfeit their membership nor the " right to become members, provided they comply with the Constitu- " tion and By-Laws, and remit the amount of the dues to the Secre- " tary within one month after such annual meeting."

It is proposed and recommended by the Executive Council that the entire section be stricken out and the following be substituted:

" The annual dues shall be due and payable at the commencement " of each calendar year."

By unanimous vote of the Convention, the amendment proposed and read was duly adopted.

The Secretary: Another recommendation of the Executive Council is that the president and vice-president of the Association be *ex-officio* members of the Executive Council. This is nowhere provided for in our Constitution as at present existing.

Upon vote being had, the proposed amendment to the Constitution, providing that the president and vice-president of the Association be *ex-officio* members of the Executive Council was duly adopted.

The Secretary: Mr. Chairman, here is a letter that was delivered yesterday after the adjournment of the Convention. It was evidently the intention of the writer that it should have been delivered before the adjournment.

> SOUTHERN CALIFORNIA BUILDING, ⎫
> MIDWINTER FAIR, ⎬
> SAN FRANCISCO, February 22, 1894. ⎭

R. M. Welch, Esq., Secretary Bankers Association, San Francisco, Cal.:

DEAR SIR:—The representatives of the Southern California Midwinter Fair Association respectfully invite the members of the Bankers Association of California to accept the hospitality of the Southern California Building on the Midwinter Fair grounds and inspect the golden products now on exhibition under the auspices of the Southern California Citrus Fair Association.

> Very respectfully yours,
> FRANK WIGGINS,
> Superintendent.

On motion, it was ordered that the invitation be accepted for Saturday, the 24th. the invitation having been received too late for its acceptance earlier.

The Secretary: Mr. Chairman, this resolution has been sent up to the desk:

"WHEREAS, Banks in the interior have no source of profit except " interest on their loans, and

" WHEREAS, The average deposits of individuals are too small to " justify the issuing of drafts free of charge and taking of exchange " at par; therefore, be it

" *Resolved*, That interior banks, in all cases, make a charge of " one-tenth of one per cent, to regular customers carrying a credit " balance, and one-fourth of one per cent to all others, on all drafts " issued, also on all exchange, whether cashed or placed for credit. " and on all collections of whatever nature."

This is signed by A. Tonn of the Farmers' and Merchants' Bank, of Hollister.

On motion of George H. Stewart of Los Angeles, it was ordered that the resolution read by the secretary be referred to the Committee on Resolutions and take the usual course.

The Chairman: Have the committees anything to report?

George H. Stewart: I do not think any committees will be ready to report to-day, Mr. Chairman.

The Chairman: I believe we have the California Bank Commissioners with us to-day, have we not? I see Mr. Knight and Mr. Dunsmoor. Mr. Knight, will you step forward? Gentlemen, I take pleasure in introducing Mr. W. H. Knight, Bank Commissioner.

Mr. Knight addressed the Convention as follows:

Mr. Chairman and Gentlemen:

I am entirely unprepared to say anything here before this Convention. I have just arrived from a long trip in the country, and I had no idea of saying a word, but there are one or two points that I might mention to this Convention and discuss a little.

First, I can say that the Bank Commissioners have always felt a great interest in this Association. I think the suggestion first came from the Bank Commissioners in our first report in 1890, in which we recommended that such an association be organized, and of course we have always felt and expressed much interest in it and its welfare. I desire to congratulate the California Bankers Association upon the practical steps that they have taken so far. I think that the papers that have been read here are very interesting and instructive, and are of much practical value to this Association. It would seem to me that that is the object of this Convention, to gain some practical good for the members themselves.

This subject that has been presented here, the overdraft system, and all the suggestions made in regard to the changing of the act governing the Bank Commissioners are of vital importance to the bankers of the State. There are a great many amendments that ought to be made to the Bank Commissioners' act. In the first place, there is a great deal of indefiniteness or uncertainty in regard to the intention of the act. It would seem as though it is incomplete. We have found it so practically in regard to the course that the commissioners are to take with reference to suspended banks. Those matters have all come up before the courts and they are matters which will have to be decided by the courts.

Some other alterations, as instanced in the suggestions made by

Mr. Ellioitt, should be made in the act. There is a great deal of uncertainty in defining what are savings banks, and in defining their position and their powers. Of course, the law should throw around savings banks all the safeguards that are possible; more so, of course, than in respect to commercial banks. The people that put their money in savings banks are the people who are entitled to have their interests guarded more safely than the patrons of commercial banks. They are supposed not to take the risk that other people may take. As has been stated here, these deposits are made, as a general rule, by poor people, and old people, and children, and the law should be very special and very guarded for the protection of savings banks. Practically, as the law now is, a savings bank may be incorporated as such and do a savings business, and when it has $300,000 capital, it can do a commercial business. We think that the distinction there should be defined more particularly.

I will mention that I think the act should be amended in regard to the expenses allowed for the commissioners. Now, they allow us no more money for traveling expenses than was allowed when there were only 85 banks. At present we have 235 banks, and we have to be very careful in the matter of the expenses of the commission. Very often we have to go out singly, and we have to make long trips, for instance, up the San Joaquin valley, and visit all the banks from one end to the other. As a matter of course—and as a matter of economy—we commence at one end of the valley, and the people at the other end know just about what time the commissioners will be around. We ought to have a larger amount of expense money for the commission, so that we may travel out, singly or altogether, as the circumstances require.

The matter of overdrafts is one in which this commission, from the beginning to the present time, has taken a very great interest. I think every banker in this Association will bear witness that the commissioners, from the very first, have expressed their opinion in regard to overdrafts. The custom of allowing overdrafts has been carried on throughout the State, especially in the country to a very great extent. Still, there are a great many bankers—and I think I can see some of them before me now—who still think that the overdraft system is all right. They say, "If a note is given and if a note is good, why is not an overdraft just as good?" But the commissioners have always taken very decided ground that the practice of allowing overdrafts is not in accordance with good rules of banking. It places the bankers in the hands of other people, and it is against the very best interests of sound banking. For instance, a farmer who draws a check, say, two or three or four or five times a year, why should he have an overdraft? There are some exceptions. For instance, you might have a flour mill as a customer, which gives a hundred checks a year, or much more, and makes frequent deposits; such an institution might have an overdraft. But, for farmers who have very little business, and draw but very few checks, to have overdrafts, is not proper. They have gotten into the habit, and have been for years in the habit of having these overdrafts, and it is hard to disabuse them of the idea that this should be allowed. I hope, after the suggestions that have been made here, and after hearing these papers on the subjects bearing on this question that have been read, that the banks will uniformly give up the system of overdrafts. This is the best time to discontinue the practice, now that the bankers in San Francisco and the bankers at all the large money centers are giving up the custom, and for all the country banks, without any exception, to come in under the general system that is being adopted.

There are a great many other subjects on which I might speak, but which I cannot recall to mind now. If I had had more time, I would like to suggest other things in regard to our commission.

There is a matter that comes to my mind just now, in regard to the capital stock that a bank should have. Under our present system a man can start a bank with $1,000, or even $500. Where they have but $5,000 of capital, we have almost always refused to issue them a license but, under the law we are powerless to prevent the forming of such banks, we cannot help it. There should be general laws governing the amount of capital stock that a bank should have.

The Chairman: You mean capital paid in, Mr. Knight?

Mr. Knight: Capital paid in; yes, sir. There are some localities where a bank might be conducted with a small capital, but we think it is against the best interests of the country that a bank be established with capital paid in of less than $25,000 at the least.

Mr. Elliott: Allow me to suggest, also, Mr. Knight, that when the capital is paid in, it should not be paid out again to the same parties who subscribed it. You will find it occurs in some cases that a person subscribes $1,000 and borrows $2,000 on the stock.

Mr. Knight: Yes, Sir.

We think that, as a rule, the state banking system is better adapted to the general banking business in the country than the national banking system. In the matter of loans, for instance, under the national banking system, while it is provided that not more than one-tenth of the amount of the stock can be loaned to any one person, there are some localities where capitalists put money into the bank, and they are the very persons who are the subscribers to the capital stock and are the persons who do the larger amount of business in the locality. Such persons, by throwing their business and their influence to the bank are entitled to larger loans, they think, they can give security, and they get larger loans than other persons would get. So there are a good many ways in which, under that system, a person is allowed to borrow more than one-tenth of the amount of the stock, and they take advantage of it. Then, again, there are the mortgage loans. In a great many portions of our State there is little commercial paper for the banks to loan money on. Consequently, they have to loan on mortgages. It is to their interest to do this, and it is a large amount of the country business. Of course, under the national banking system, loaning of money on mortgages is not done.

As to the matter of reports to the Bank Commissions, we think the law is defective. We have attempted to issue blanks for the banks to use in making reports at different portions of the year, but we have no authority to do it. The law should be amended so as to make it provide for the calling of reports several times a year.

I had no idea of being called upon to speak. If we had taken time to prepare for it, there are a great many other points that I could have given my views upon, but I think that is all I have to say at present. [Applause.]

F. T. Duhring of Sonoma: Mr. Chairman, bearing on the same point that Mr. Knight has been speaking of, we have Mr. Elliott's report or suggestions concerning certain changes in the banking laws. Now, that paper was read, and I do not know whether it was accepted or what was done with it. If it was accepted, what are we going to with it? Are we going to embody it in the form of resolutions, recommending that the Legislature make these changes? I believe it does not ask the Legislature to make any changes.

The Chairman: These papers have been read, but that does not signify that they are the acts of the Association.

F. T. Duhring: It does not mean that they have been adopted?

The Chairman: No, sir.

F. T. Duhring: These suggestions have been made, and I think that, now that they have been made, we should take some action upon them, either accept them or reject them, in whole or in part. That is one reason why we are assembled here to-day; to take some action in regard to questions brought up. Here is a suggestion made that a law should be passed that banks be required to keep on hand at least fifteen per cent of their deposits. Some think the proposition is a good one and others think it is not good. If the majority of us think that the law should be changed as suggested, we should take some steps to have the law so changed. We are the ones that will have to take the initiative, in having laws passed that we think are best for our business. These speeches that have been printed have been circulated, and I would like to see some discussion on them, and see the Convention adopt the suggestions of which it approves.

J. M. Elliott of Los Angeles: Mr. Chairman, I would say in that connection that this paper is not a report. It merely contains some suggestions that have come from me and which I have put upon paper, at the suggestion of some of the members of the Executive Council. I do not look for the adoption of any of them as the sense of this meeting. I do not care to have you do so. My experience with legislators has been, that if the bankers suggest anything, the legislators immediately assume that it is something for the benefit of the banker alone, and the idea then is to bury it immediately and kill it in committee. The way these changes should be brought about is by agitating the questions in such a way as to bring them before the Legislature in such a light that it will be seen that the changes are for the benefit of the community in general.

F. T. Duhring: Mr. Chairman, my idea in making these remarks is this: Mr. Elliott having prepared this paper, suggesting important changes that are supposed to be needed, it would seem that we should certainly take some action on them in order to produce results.

The Chairman: This Association does not father any paper that is presented here.

F. T. Duhring: I understand that, Mr. Chairman, but these papers have been read, and I think that something should be done in regard to them. They have been read, and that is all there is to it. There has been no discussion of them. I hope there will be some discussion of them later, if not now.

George H. Stewart of Los Angeles : Mr. Chairman, we have had the pleasure of listening to one of the Bank Commissioners, and I see there are two others here—Mr. Dunsmoor and the new Bank Commissioner, Mr. Fuller. I will state that as for myself I should like to make his acquaintance here. Those of us who are connected with State banks will have the pleasure of making his acquaintance later, probably, but I believe the members present would like to hear from him, and I call upon the chairman to ask Mr. Fuller to favor us with some remarks.

C. H. Dunsmoor, Bank Commissioner : I will take pleasure in bringing the gentleman to the front. Mr. Chairman and gentlemen of the Convention, I have the honor to introduce Mr. Fuller.

J. B. Fuller, Bank Commissioner, addressed the Convention.

Mr. Chairman and Gentlemen:

I feel very much flattered in being called upon to speak before this assembly, but regret that I am not capable, I fear, of making any suggestions whatever that will be of interest to you. I believe that this organization that you have formed, now only about two years old, will be one of the greatest sources of benefit to you, generally, and to the bankers throughout the State of California. I also know that the banking interests of our State are paramount to those of any other State in this Union. This has been shown by the crisis which has been passed within the year by all of you, proving that we have business men and men of principle at the back of our moneyed institutions.

I thank you very much, gentlemen, for calling upon me, and I hope I shall, and I probably will, during the years to come, have an opportunity of making you much better acquainted with me and of knowing you all more intimately.

John Reichman of Fresno: I think it was very nice for Mr. Dunsmoor to get out of addressing us by introducing Mr. Fuller. I think we should hear from Mr. Dunsmoor now.

C. H. Dunsmoor, Bank Commissioner:

Mr. Chairman and Gentlemen:

The bankers throughout the State are fully aware of the fact that I am not accustomed to making speeches. I have had the pleasure of listening to the addresses of others here. I was very much interested in the suggestions made by Mr. Elliott. I think the changes he suggests would be of much benefit. As the Bank Commission stands it is practically powerless. You thoroughly understand that. Some legislation should be had giving them greater powers, and it would be well that a committee be appointed for the purpose of bringing these matters before the Legislature, save and except that, as has been said already, the legislators would think that something was wrong, or that the changes proposed were for our own benefit, for the reason that they were favored by us.

We believe that not only fifteen per cent. of the amount of the deposits should be held in the banks, but that at least twenty per cent. should be held.

It has already been stated that there were only about eighty-five banks in existence when this commission was instituted, and to-day we have 247, including the private banks. It is practically an impossibility for the commissioners to visit every bank. The business of the last year has been most trying, and perhaps more so on us than on you gentlemen. Notwithstanding the stringency of the times, our last report will show that we have $4,000,000 more in the banks than we had in 1883. During the year we have lost $21,000,000 of deposits, and it will take a great deal of time and study to ascertain what has become of those deposits. Something must be done, and I think you, gentlemen, are more capable of devising means than are the commissioners.

I will state that during the three and a half years that I have been a commissioner, my visits among you have always been pleasant, and I hope that the new commissioner will have as pleasant a term as we have had. [Applause.]

The Secretary: Mr. Chairman, I have a letter here from Mr. William B. Wightman, National Bank Examiner for California, in reply to the invitation sent him to attend the convention, and explaining why he is not here.

LOS ANGELES, CAL., February 20, 1894.

Mr. R. M. Welch, Secretary California Bankers Association,
San Francisco, Cal.

DEAR SIR: Your letter of the 17th inst., enclosing programme of the Third Annual Convention of the California Bankers Association, and informing me that I have been enrolled as an honorary member thereof, is received, and I beg to express my thanks for the honor conferred upon me.

I regret very much that I cannot be present, for I know that I would be greatly benefitted thereby; But I cannot at this time leave this portion of the State.

Yours sincerely,

WM. B. WIGHTMAN.

The Chairman: Mr. Secretary, will you please read this dispatch which I have received?

The Secretary: Here is a telegram from Topeka, Kansas. The Kansas Bankers Association is in session there, on the same dates as our Convention is in session here. The telegram is as follows:

" Mr. I. W. Hellman, President California Bankers Association, " San Francisco: The bankers of the Sunflower State send greeting to " their brethren on the golden shores. H. W. Levy, President."

This telegram was sent yesterday.

Wm. Beekman of Sacramento: Mr. Chairman, I move that the communication be accepted and placed on file, and responded to by the secretary, the proper manner of doing which he knows better than I do.

Upon vote being had, the motion was duly carried, and the secretary was instructed to answer the communication.

The Chairman: Are there any other papers, Mr. Secretary?

The Secretary: No, sir.

The Chairman: Is there anything else to come before the meeting to-day, or any other gentleman who wishes to be heard?

George H. Stewart of Los Angeles: Mr. Chairman, unless there is some new business to be brought before the Convention, I believe it would be entirely in order at this time for us to adjourn, since the Fair, perhaps, would partake of the nature of new business to some of us, and I move that we adjourn until ten o'clock to-morrow morning, when we will take up the regular order of business, which, I believe, includes the reports of the various committees.

Mr. Stewart's motion to adjourn receiving second, upon vote being taken, the Convention took an adjournment until Saturday, February 24th, at ten o'clock A. M.

THIRD DAY.

SATURDAY—FEBRUARY 24.

The Convention was called to order at 10 o'clock A. M.

The Chairman: I am informed that Attorney-General Hart is present. He is a gentleman who has had a great deal of experience with banks, in one way and another, not often pleasant. With your permission, I will invite him to address this meeting. It seems that Mr. Hart is not present. Perhaps he will arrive later.

The Secretary: Mr. Chairman, here is a letter that has been handed to me, and which I will read:

" *President and Members of the California Bankers Convention:*

"GENTLEMEN: I respectfully request the favor of a few minutes' of your " time to read a paper that I feel will interest all interested in banking and " finances. Very respectfully,

" R. H. H. HUNT."

F. T. Duhring of Sonoma: Mr. Chairman, in view of the fact that we have a good many resolutions to consider this morning, I move that we accept the gentleman's communication, but excuse him from reading the paper, and refer it to the Committee on Resolutions.

John Reichman of Fresno: I second the motion.

Motion carried and Mr. Hunt's paper referred to Committee on Resolutions.

The Chairman: The next in the order of business is reports of special committees. None of the committees have yet reported, gentlemen.

The Secretary: I have here the report of the Committee on Resolutions.

The Chairman: The secretary will please read it.

Mr. President and Members of the California Bankers Association:

The Committee on Resolutions respectfully report action as follows on three resolutions herewith, viz:

No. 1—Mr. Tonn on Exchange.

No. 2—Mr. Miller on Time Notes.

No. 3—Mr. Lankershim on Savings Banks.

We recommend these Resolutions as containing valuable ideas but we recommend that they shall be published in the proceedings without any vote upon their adoption by the members of this Convention.

Respectfully,

H. W. WRIGHT,
H. H. HEWLETT,
C. S. BROOKS,
A. H. R. SCHMIDT,
FRANK MILLER.

On motion of Lovell White, seconded by John Reichman, the report of the Committee on Resolutions was adopted.

The Secretary: The other committees are ready to report, Mr. Chairman. Here is a report signed by two members, a majority of the

Auditing Committee. Mr. Gerber has not arrived this morning. It is as follows :

Mr. President and Members of the California Bankers Association:

GENTLEMEN : The undersigned appointed a committee to audit the books and accounts of the several secretaries who have served, and the treasurer, from September, 1892, to the date of the assembling of this Convention, beg leave to report as follows:

That we have examined the stubs of the receipts issued by the secretary for annual dues, and find that 174 have been issued, being 161 for dues to the end of 1893, and 13 for dues of 1894, representing in all $1,740, which amount has been paid to the treasurer.

That from all other sources there has been received by the treasurer $38.50.

That there have been drawn on the treasurer by the president and secretary 55 warrants, Nos. 67 to 121, both inclusive, aggregating $1,939.49.

That the balance in the hands of the treasurer September 5, 1892, was $1,081.22, and that the balance now in his hands is $920.23, as reported by him.

That for the warrants drawn on the treasurer we find the proper vouchers except No. 87, sundry telegrams for the former chairman of the Executive Council, $8.27; No. 90, Kingsley & Barnes, printing, $2.50; No. 93, Eisenhart & Kign, printing, $12.50, and Nos. 94, 96 and 97, $50 each, being secretary's salary for April, May and June, 1892.

Though the above-mentioned vouchers are missing, we believe that the money was properly expended for the benefit of the Association.

O. McHENRY,
J. M. ELLIOTT.

On motion of F. T. Duhring of Sonoma the report of the Auditing Committee was received, approved, adopted and placed on file.

J. M. Elliott of Los Angeles : Mr. Chairman, I will say that the Auditing Committee wish, verbally, to request the treasurer to keep a separate book from that of the secretary. We did not want to put that request in the report, because we had not been able to see the chairman whom we wished to consult about it. He is not here, so we will now make a request that for the benefit of the Auditing Committee the treasurer keep an entirely separate book.

The Chairman : You make that as a motion, Mr. Elliott?

Mr. Elliott : Yes, sir, if necessary.

The motion of Mr. Elliott, being seconded, was duly carried.

The Chairman : The report of the Nominating Committee is in order now.

John Reichman of Fresno : We have our report, Mr. Chairman. It is as follows :

To the President and Gentlemen of the Convention:

Your Nominating Committee would most respectfully submit the names of the following gentlemen for the several offices named:

For President—Lovell White, cashier San Francisco Savings Union,

For Vice-President—I. G. Wickersham, president First National Bank of Petaluma.

For Treasurer—G. W. Kline, cashier Crocker-Woolworth National Bank, San Francisco,

For Secretary—R. M. Welch, San Francisco Savings Union.

For Members of Executive Council—George H. Stewart, cashier Bank of America, Los Angeles; H. H. Hewlett, president First National Bank of Stockton; N. D. Rideout, president Rideout Bank of Marysville.

For Delegate to American Bankers Association—Edward Floyd Jones, vice-president First National Bank of Stockton.

Respectfully submitted,

ED. R. HAMILTON, Chairman.

JOHN REICHMAN, Secretary.

P. E. BOWLES,
L. W. BURRIS,
C. W. BUSH.

The Chairman: What is your pleasure, gentlemen? Shall a vote be taken for the adoption of the report as a whole, or shall each officer be voted for separately?

J. M. Elliott of Los Angeles: Mr. Chairman, I move that the secretary be authorized to cast the ballot of the Convention for the election of the various officers as nominated by the Nominating Committee.

Mr. Elliott's motion receiving second, was carried by the unanimous vote of the Convention.

The Chairman: Gentlemen of the Convention, I take pleasure in introducing Mr. Lovell White, as the next President of the California Bankers Association, and wish to say that there could have been no better nomination made, nor a better man for the position found. [Applause.]

Lovell White, President-elect.

Mr. Chairman and Gentlemen:

I thank the president for his courteous speech, and you gentlemen, for the election. I stated that I would not accept any official position, not because I was unwilling to do my part, but because I have been incessant in the discharge of duties connected with the Association since its organization, and I hoped to be let out. But my protest was unavailing.

I appreciate the compliment and thank you for it, although my election as President of the Association lays a burden upon me that I would rather escape. [Applause.]

The Chairman: The next matter in order is the selection of the place of the next Convention.

The question of holding another Convention this year has been brought before the Executive Council, and, if I understand them correctly, they are under the impression that we should not have another convention this year, that the next convention should be held in 1895. This Convention ought to have been held several months ago, but, for various reasons, it has been postponed until now. I do not know what place you will select for the next one. Fresno has been chosen twice before, and has given up for the time being its choice. If we could hold our Conventions in San Francisco or near this city, I think we would always have a larger attendance than if the Conventions be held in the country. But, that is a question that is left to you, gentlemen, to determine.

J. M. Elliott of Los Angeles: Mr. Chairman, I move that the matter of time and place of holding the next Annual Convention of this Association be left to the Executive Council.

Mr. Elliott's motion was seconded and duly carried, and it was so ordered.

F. T. Duhring of Sonoma: Mr. Chairman, if there is no other business of a pressing nature to bring before the Convention this morning, I would like again to make an effort to bring up the matter which I tried to put before the Convention yesterday, and that is the discussion of some of the suggestions made by Mr. Elliott, in regard to needed legislation.

Now, among those suggestions was one, that more powers be given to the Bank Commissioners as to controlling banks or taking steps to close up banks that they find to be in a weak condition. As the law stands now, it is optional with the Attorney-General whether he shall act upon the recommendations of the Bank Commissioners or not. The Bank Commissioners state that, during the excitement last summer, if they had had the powers they should have possessed, some of the failures would not have occurred at that time, and the banks that did close would have been closed before, and that would have prevented much of the panicky feeling which seized the whole country. Of course that would have helped matters to a great extent on this coast. Therefore, I would like to have some suggestions from the members here this morning in regard to what they think of the changes in the laws proposed by Mr. Elliott. Should the powers of the Bank Commissioners be enlarged?

Now, I know there are some people who feel this way, that any matter that comes before the Legislature that the banks want, the banks will have to pay for. Still, we who are most interested in these reforms should either appoint a committee to take hold of the matter or take some other measures that we believe will result in these bills being introduced, and, if possible, introduced in a way so that the pretorian part of the Legislature will not think we are the only inspiring spirits of them. It is certainly necessary that we make some reforms, and if we think that the commissioners ought to have these additional powers we ought to say so, and I believe that it would be well to appoint a committee to attend to such legislative matters at the next session of the Legislature.

Now, in regard to the commissioners being empowered to call for and cause to be rendered reports at any time, I think it is an excellent idea. Under the system of reports twice a year a bank that is in a weak condition can get ready and make a showing at these stated times that it could not make at other seasons of the year. I think it is in the interests of good banking for the commissioners to be able to cause reports to be made at any time. It is not a great deal of trouble to render these reports, because a cashier can make a report any night, and under the plan suggested he will be sure to make an honest report in each instance.

Then, in regard to the reserve. We know that all good, safe banks will carry 15 per cent. of their deposits on hand. To make a law requiring that this be done would have the same effect as the National Bank Act, requiring National Banks to keep that amount on hand. While I do not say that these laws are all absolutely necessary, I think we should discuss them here; I think it would be proper to get an expression of opinion on the subject from the bankers present.

Therefore, in order to bring the matter to an issue, I will move that it be the sense of this Convention that, in its opinion, it would be advisable to have a law enacted empowering the Bank Commissioners to close a bank if, after their recommendation to the Attorney-General that such bank be closed, he fails to do so. I make that motion in order to bring the matter before the Convention for discussion.

Mr. Duhring's motion was seconded and read to the Convention.

The Chairman: I suppose you mean that it be the sense of this Convention that such a law be enacted by the next Legislature?

Mr. Duhring: Yes, sir.

George H. Stewart of Los Angeles: Mr. Chairman, it seems to me that the resolution as presented is not sufficiently broad. I think, if I remember the expression in Mr. Elliott's paper, it was suggested that, upon an unanimous decision by the Bank Commissioners that a bank be closed, they have the power to close it. It does not seem to me that, in times of emergency, they should be compelled to report the matter first to the Attorney-General, but that, upon an unanimous vote by the commissioners that such action be taken, they immediately take the matter into their own hands. As I understand the National Bank law, the Bank Examiner, one single man, after inspection, has the power to close a bank.

The Chairman: I think Mr. Stewart is mistaken about that. The Examiner has to refer the matter to the Comptroller.

J. M. Elliott of Los Angeles: Yes, sir; Mr. Stewart has misunderstood it. It is necessary for the Bank Examiner to refer the matter to the Comptroller in Washington, who has the absolute power to close the bank up. I think this power should be given to the three Bank Commissioners, they acting unanimously.

My reason for making it unanimous was that, I think it might not be safe to place the power in the hands of less than three persons, without reference to anybody. Still, in times of emergency, they should be enabled to act, and act quickly.

The Chairman: Do you propose any amendment, Mr. Stewart?

Mr. Stewart: No, sir. My remarks were made merely in discussing that resolution.

J. M. Elliott: Mr. Chairman, I should be very glad if the Convention would discuss this matter and arrive at some conclusion in regard to it. There can be no question that, if the Bank Commissioners had had the power to close up two or three banks in the last few years, which they knew to be unsound, which they knew to be carrying on business in such a way as to be just ready to fall at the first blast of the financial tempest, it would have been done, and we would not have had anything like the amount of trouble that was experienced last year; these banks would have been closed up promptly, they would have been out of the way, and their failures would not have come at a time when it would have affected the general financial standing or credit of any other bank in the State, and by this time they would have been dead and forgotten.

I think it is very essential that the powers of the commissioners be extended, and I think that a committee should be appointed who will take steps to carefully look over the ground and see what can be done towards getting every man in this room to make himself a self-appointed member of a committee to see the members of the Legislature before they go to Sacramento and impress upon their minds the necessity of this legislation—and, not for the benefit of the banks, but for the benefit of the banks' customers. If we can impress it upon the legislators that we do not want it done for ourselves, but for the community, we may be able to get something done.

Lovell White: Mr. Chairman and Gentlemen: It seems to me, in connection with Mr. Elliott's valuable paper, what was said here yesterday by Mr. Knight should be taken into account. The changes suggested by Mr. Knight are in the same line and on the same subject. I also am of the opinion that the motion as made here this morning is not broad enough. I believe it would be well to refer the question to the Executive Council, with instructions to formulate an amendment to the Bank Commissioners Act, which will cover the whole ground. Now, Mr. Elliott has just suggested that we should use our influence with the legislators. But that will not prepare the bill. If anything is to be done, there is a proper way in which to do it. An important matter is the formulating of the law, making the bill. The Bank Commissioners Act was under discussion for a year and a half, and parties here in the city cogitated over the work and finally paid an attorney $250 for putting the bill in form, before it went to Sacramento, and Mr. Hamilton has the credit of making some needed changes in it before it went before the Legislature, though the Act was prepared, for the most part, in the offices of the banks in this city. It did not spring into being of itself. Now, the purpose is to supplement that Act and I think that our Executive Council, which represents all the banks, should take hold of the matter of formulating amendments to the Bank Commissioners Act. While it is in order for us to suggest what we wish to accomplish, we have not the time now, and we have not sufficiently studied the subject so that we can determine on just what we should do. That must be left to the Executive Council. I move, as an amendment to the motion now before the house, that the Executive Council be instructed to formulate amendments to the Bank Commissioners Act, and that it take measures to bring to bear the influence of the banks in support of the passage of those amendments at the next session of the Legislature.

Frank Miller of Sacramento : Mr. Chairman, the Committee on Resolutions had to consider several things yesterday and one or two to-day, in connection with which the question came up as to what was their authority. They thought they could not undertake to limit and mark out the policy of this convention; they could not decide whether some things were legal or illegal, whether some things were feasible or not, whether some things should be dictated to be done absolutely and literally, or left to general recommendation.

Now, this question is a very important one, and presented as a general motion or resolution, it would not be in a shape that would give it sufficient credit; it would not be given sufficient support. The wording should be carefully done, and the existing laws must be examined, and careful preparation made for presenting the matter, otherwise the entire effort would stop short of anything like success.

Mr. White's amendment would relieve the Committee on Resolutions of a great deal of work, and it would leave the labor in this matter exactly where it belongs—with the Executive Council. Then the Executive Council, with deliberation and with legal advice to guide it, would prepare something and submit it to the Bank Commissioners, or to other authorities, and as an outcome the ideas that are advanced here, perhaps crudely, would be in shape to receive considerable attention at least.

The Chairman : Do you second Mr. White's amendment?

Mr. Miller : I do, sir.

Mr. Reichman of Fresno : Mr. Chairman, I fully agree with Mr. White in the opinion that the working out of any change in the law should be left with the Executive Council, and that it certainly will be better done by them than by the Convention, because they will take more time, they have more time, to do it. But, at the same time, we are here to discuss matters of interest to banks, and we can express our views, so that the Executive Council will know what are the views of this Convention.

Now, I have read this article written by Mr. Elliott, and I find a great deal in it that would, if acted upon, benefit the banks very materially, but would benefit the depositors in the banks more, and I think that the suggestions contained in that paper should have the endorsement of the Convention, and that the Executive Council should be requested to draw up an amendment, or have drawn up an amendment to the present bank law, embodying the changes that are suggested in this paper, if approved by the Convention. Certainly there are several changes suggested in the paper that would be very good. For instance, that one of giving the Bank Commissioners authority in the matter of banks that are not being conducted properly. As a matter of course, under the National Bank act, the Bank Examiner has to report to the Comptroller of the Currency. That is because otherwise action would be left to one man. But under the system in California, where we have three Bank Commissioners, I think they should have authority, upon unanimous vote, to act in the matter.

There is another suggestion made which I think is an excellent one, and that is, as to the term of office of the Bank Commissioners, and that their term should not expire at the same time. I approve of this, because it is a political office, the appointees are usually friends of the Governor-elect, and are perhaps appointed as a reward for services in the campaign, and know very little of the banking business; so it would be much better, instead of having three new men go into office at the same time, under these conditions, if there could be a continuation of one or more of those serving until the new member or members become familiar with the duties to be performed.

All these are very good suggestions, and there should be an expression of opinion on them by this Convention, for the guidance of the Executive Council.

F. T. Duhring of Sonoma: Mr. Chairman, my object in making this motion was, not that the particular motion made by me should prevail, but to bring out an expression of opinion by the members of this Convention while we are assembled here. We could read these papers in our offices just as well as to do it here; but, it seems to me that the object of a convention is to have these thoughts expressed here and then hear them discussed. There has been no discussion in this convention until this morning. The papers have been read—when one was finished the next man has gone on reading, and we have forgotten about them; the report on resolutions was handed in and adopted, and we don't know what those resolutions are. There has been but little expression of opinion by the members assembled here, and I think that the convention utterly fails of its purpose unless there is an exchange of opinion. That is what we want to have. If we refer this matter to the Executive Council the way it stands now, the Executive Council will not know what the opinion is of the bankers here assembled. Now, some of them think that eight years is too long for the term of bank commissioners. Let them get up and suggest a shorter time, and give their reasons for favoring it. If they think fifteen per cent. is too much or too little for a bank to keep on hand, let them get up and say so. That is all we want: that the members get up and give an expression of opinion. To merely come here and read the papers is a waste of time, I think. The only advantage that has thus far accrued to us by reason of this convention is the making of the acquaintance of a great many very nice gentlemen; further than that we have done practically nothing, and we have gained very little information.

J. B. Lankershim of Los Angeles:

Mr. Chairman, I endorse the proposition to enlarge the sphere of the Bank Commissioners. About two years ago I was here, and at the close of the meeting, there having been no mention made of the matter, I asked that a resolution be passed thanking the Bank Commissioners for their able work during the two preceding years. Now, I think a resolution such as my friend here offers, and the discussion that he suggests to-day, is certainly a far better way of treating the Bank Commissioners than a mere vote of thanks. During the several years these gentlemen have been in office the banks have been prosperous, and I think this is due partly to their efforts.

They find that their powers are not as extensive as they should be, and I think that the endorsement by this Convention of the proposition to change the laws governing them will be just the thing.

The Chairman: If there is no further discussion, a vote will now be taken. Gentlemen, you have heard the amendment offered by Mr. Lovell White to the motion of Mr. Duhring; the amendment is seconded, and has precedence over the original motion.

Upon vote being had, the amendment was unanimously carried.

The Chairman: It is unanimously carried, consequently the original motion falls to the ground.

Frank Miller of Sacramento: Mr. Chairman, to the Committee on Resolutions was referred the article written by Mr. Hunt on the subject of "Money." Now, the Committee on Resolutions has not been assembled in full force since the paper was referred, and we have not had the necessary time—that is, we have had only half an hour, or an hour, say—to digest the article, which, from what I have seen of it, is what we might call a solid article, one which it would take some thought to read. In view of the circumstance that the gentleman is not a member of the Association, and considering the fact that he did not, as the rest of us have done, present his paper ten days in advance, and inasmuch as the time at our disposal now is short, I am compelled to report, for the Committee, that this paper should be laid on the desk for the action of the Executive Council.

The Chairman: If there is no objection it will be so ordered. Our rules require papers to be handed in ten days before the assembling of the Convention.

F. T. Duhring of Sonoma: Mr. Chairman, while not wishing to appear unduly persistent in the matter of discussion of papers presented, I would like to have it understood whether the adoption of the amendment to my motion offered by Mr. White, referring the whole matter to the Executive Council, precludes action on my motion.

Lovell White: Mr. Chairman, please allow me to say this: It seems to me very appropriate and perfectly proper that every gentleman present should join with the others in instructing the Executive Council or making suggestions for their benefit. It was not my intention in offering the amendment to cut off debate and an expression of opinion on all the points brought forward by Mr. Elliott in his paper, or those suggested by Mr. Knight in his remarks made yesterday. All these suggestions are very appropriate, and if they could be called out by the secretary, so as to refresh our minds on the different points made, and so as to get an expression of opinion from the Convention on the several questions, *seriatim*, it would help the Executive Council. My amendment was not intended to be antagonistic to the gentleman at all.

The Chairman: Mr. White's amendment was to refer the whole matter to the Executive Council; consequently, as the amendment was adopted, the original motion fell to the ground.

Lovell White: Mr. Chairman, I would suggest that the points in Mr. Elliott's paper be called out, so as to allow any one who wishes to do so to remark on them, one after another. Let there be a full expression of opinion. I make a motion that the points of Mr. Elliott's paper be read, in order, and opportunity given to the members here present to discuss them.

The motion was seconded and carried.

The Secretary: The paper is not lengthy. I will read the introduction and then stop after the first proposition.

"The following suggestions as to the enlarging of the powers of "the Bank Commissioners are made in the hope that some law may "be adopted which will put that body into a better position than it is "at present for controlling certain banking elements within the State.

"The writer feels satisfied that if the State Bank Commissioners "had powers that should have been granted to them by law, several "failures of State banks could have been prevented.

"The time to stop poor banking is in its incipiency; but, unfor- "tunately, as the law now stands, Bank Commissioners are powerless "after having reported the matter to the Attorney-General, who may "or may not, as he sees fit, carry out the suggestions made to him by "the Commissioners.

"The first change suggested is that the law requiring the banks "to make reports be amended so as to abolish that part requiring "them to report separately the amount of their capital stock."

J. M. Elliott: That is a mistake on my part. That has been repealed already, Mr. Chairman. There is no necessity for discussion of that point.

The Secretary: The next proposition is:

"Second, that published reports be called for five times during "the year at a date which is already past, just as the Comptroller "of the Currency calls for reports from the National Banks. If the "dates as called for by the Comptroller could be adopted it would "be an improvement."

Mr. Elliott: Mr. Chairman, may I say a word in explanation? Being an officer of a National Bank, I have been asked by two or three members why I should write of this matter in regard to State banks. I will say that I am also president of a State bank, and even if I were only an officer of a National Bank, I would feel that it was a matter in which all the bankers in the State are interested to a suffi- cient extent for me to feel at liberty to write and make these sugges- tions in regard to changes of the law.

F. T. Duhring of Sonoma: Mr. Chairman, while not wishing to put this in the form of instructions to the Executive Council, I would like to make a motion to this effect: that it is the opinion of this convention that the change suggested in regard to reports, as made by Mr. Elliott, would be to the advantage of the whole community that has to do with banks or with banking interests.

George H. Stewart of Los Angeles: Mr. Chairman, I beg to second that motion.

H. W. Wright of San Jose: Mr. Chairman, as this whole matter is in the hands of the Executive Council, I move that it remain there; that the whole matter be referred to the Executive Council for their careful consideration and that it be left with them. That is, I do not know that there is any need of a motion, as it is already with them, but I suggest that it simply be discussed and the whole matter left with them for their determination.

L. W. Burris of Santa Rosa: Mr. Chairman, I certainly do not see any good reason for making so many reports. It would entail a great deal of extra work on the bank officers, especially in the country where we have not many clerks. Of course, four or five reports a year from a small institution would require considerable time to make. I do not think there is any necessity for the Bank Commissioners coming around more than once or twice a year, and the banks rendering their regular reports twice a year. I think that is sufficient.

C. S. Brooks of Marysville: I am opposed to this multiplication of reports. I think, as the gentlemen has very aptly remarked, it will be enough to attend to the regular work of the banks as we now have it to do. We have other reports to make besides reports to the commissioners—reports to the directors, reports to the stockholders. I think this would be adding to our duties without any compensation whatever for it.

L. W. Burris of Santa Rosa: I don't see any real reason for the banks making any reports, if the commissioners come around and make their reports. As it is now, including the reports that the banks are required to make and the commissioners' reports, there are four reports a year. If you require a bank to make four or five reports a year, it must be specified when, or a time set for these reports. If a banker wants to do anything to shield himself in any way, I see no real good in requiring him to make any report, or having any reports made, except those made by the Commissioners themselves.

H. W. Wright of San Jose: Mr. Chairman, I think Mr. Duhring's motion is improper. This matter, as I understood, was to be taken up for discussion and not for the purpose of instructing the Executive Council as to what they should do. It is merely for discussion. Now, as I understand, Mr. Duhring makes a motion to suggest to the Executive Council to embody certain things. That seems to be taking the matter out of their power. I think his motion is out of order. If he wants to express his views or hear the views of others, that is proper enough, but I don't think it is proper for him to make a motion instructing the Executive Council to do a thing when the matter has been left to them to decide.

F. T. Duhring of Sonoma: I probably did not correctly express my thoughts in this matter. I wish to say that I did not make this motion with the idea of instructing the Executive Council, or anything like that, but merely to get the ideas of the members present, to ascertain whether they were in favor of such a thing or opposed to it. I am perfectly willing to withdraw my motion and let this matter come up, and, when the matter comes up, call a rising vote from those who are either in favor of or opposed to this suggestion. I do not want to instruct the Executive Council. I do not want the action taken here now to be final. In order to facilitate matters, I will withdraw my motion, with the consent of my second.

George H. Stewart: Yes, sir.

John Reichman of Fresno: Mr. Chairman, I think we are a little mixed on this proposition. First, we referred the matter to the Executive Council for their action; then, upon the motion of the Chairman of the Executive Council, we bring the matter up for discussion. Now, if any subject is to be discussed without any termination, without coming to a vote, without taking the sense of the meeting, then we had better not discuss it at all. What do you mean by discussion? To simply get up and express views on the subject? How do we know that the members here are in favor of those views? How is it possible to get the sense of this meeting without putting the matter to a vote? It seems to me that it is necessary to take some action to determine the sense of the Convention. We should either not say anything on the subject, and leave it in the hands of the Executive Council, or discuss the subject, and, after the discussion, make a motion that the recommendation proposed be approved, so that a vote can be taken and the sense of the meeting can be ascertained. Those are my views on the subject.

The Chairman: There is no motion before the meeting.

H. W. Wright of San Jose: We can hear the expression of opinions by the members. It can easily be ascertained how the Convention feels in regard to the matter.

Frank Miller of Sacramento: I think we might take the sense of the meeting by standing up here, without making a record. Let those who are against the proposition stand up and be counted, and those who are in favor of it stand up and be counted, and then the members of the Council can take note of the expression for what it is worth. I think the Convention would permit that, and I would like to stand up and be counted on one side or the other, and I should be counted in favor of it.

The Chairman: What is the proposition? Shall I put the vote on the proposition that five reports or that two reports a year should be made?

L. W. Burris of Santa Rosa: Mr. Chairman, I move that it be the sense of this convention that three reports per annum should be required of banks, at such times as may be designated by the Commissioners.

George H. Stewart of Los Angeles: Mr. Chairman, I trust that the Chair will declare that motion out of order, because the action of the convention on this matter heretofore has been to leave the matter to the Executive Council, and that all action in connection with these subjects contained in Mr. Elliott's paper shall be simply advisory.

L. W. Burris of Santa Rosa: I do not mean to instruct. As the gentleman said with reference to his motion, we will simply express our opinions here. If the Executive Council see fit to go contrary to our opinions, they have a perfect right to do so. The matter is in their hands and they are supposed to know what to do and to be able to arrive at an equitable conclusion. But I think it is highly proper that we should express our views here. I do not think it is advisable to relegate everything to the Executive Council. An expression here would be appropriate, I think.

J. B. Laukershim of Los Angeles: Mr. Chairman, I second that motion. They come around and take two reports, and I can see no harm in our approving that way of doing business.

Motion put by the Chairman. Division called and rising vote asked for.

C. E. Palmer of Oakland: Mr. Chairman, I would like to ask

what they refer to as reports; whether they are reports that are to be filed or recorded, or what is to be done with these reports?

J. B. Lankershim: As I understand it, it is not compulsory for the banks to publish their reports now. As I understand, these reports would be of the same kind.

Rising vote being had, the majority of the convention were shown to be adverse to the proposition.

The Chairman: If there is no further discussion on this point, the secretary will read the next proposition.

The Secretary: The next is as follows:

" Another provision similar to that of the National Bank law I " think would be very serviceable. Many of the interior banks of " really good reputation and management were until lately, at least, " in the habit of keeping in their own vaults a very small pro- " portion of cash, depending entirely upon a correspondent in the " nearest large city for supplies when needed. A provision of the law " requiring, say fifteen per cent. of cash to be kept on hand in the " case of the Commercial Banks and a much smaller proportion in the " Savings Banks would, I think, to some extent, remedy this evil."

L. W. Burris of Santa Rosa: I move that that particular clause be approved—that is, requiring the banks to keep in their vaults at least 15 per cent of cash for the commercial banks. I think that 20 or 25 per cent is not too much. It has been one of the great evils of the country banking system that they have been in the habit of keeping too small an amount on hand.

Frank Miller of Sacramento: Mr. Chairman, I would like to call the attention of the Convention to this fact: I have not had occasion to operate very much under that provision, so I am not very sound on the law, but my impression is that while the National Banks are required to keep 15 per cent on hand, in our smaller towns, like Sacramento, they may be said to carry 15 per cent; still part of it is not there. I do not remember the exact wording of the law. I do not suppose that any one wants to put the State banks under more stringent laws than those that apply to National Banks. With that implied understanding, I should vote for that proposition.

L. W. Burris of Santa Rosa: Perhaps I was mistaken as to that, but I think that any bank, it matters not whether it is a

State bank or National Bank, or any other, should at any time carry not less than 15 per cent in its vaults, and I am really in favor of their always keeping 20 to 25 per cent on hand. They might keep a portion of that with a reserve agent, but in case of a panic or pinch it is better to keep it at home. It is best to keep 15 per cent in the vaults; then the bank is secure, beyond question.

A rising vote was had upon the question, and the proposition approved.

The Secretary: The next proposition is:

"Further, the law should be amended so as to enable the Bank "Commissioners themselves to commence an action against any "banking institution which is violating the law, or whose methods "of banking are such as to render it plain to them that disaster "would be the result of its continuance; also, that in cases of emer-"gency the Commissioners, by a unanimous vote, could close any "banking institution."

The Chairman: Have you any opinions to express on that question?

L. W. Burris of Santa Rosa: Mr. Chairman, I think that the Commissioners' power ought to be extended. At the same time it is dangerous politics to concentrate too much power in any one individual or any small body of men. That point should be looked to. Their power should be extended to a greater extent than it is at present, at the same time this matter should be carefully guarded, for any man with a great deal of power has also much human nature about him and is liable in some cases to be disposed to punish his enemies and reward his friends. Such things might happen, and therefore there might be some danger in extending these powers to a great extent. However, I do not object to anything that has been proposed. There has been no suggestion made yet that is anywise in that direction. Still, I will say that when a change is suggested it is as well to guard against future evils in one direction as in another.

J. M. Elliott of Los Angeles: Mr. Chairman, I would ask to say a few words in explanation. I will say that this does give the Bank Commissioners a very great power. It would seem that they are too great. I think, however, that men who have great powers and are obliged to use them feel the responsibility of them, and I do not think that Bank Commissioners who have eight years to serve, each one of whom is appointed at a different time, and by a different Governor, would have any collusion among themselves and dare to put themselves in the position of commencing an action against a reputable bank or try to do a reputable bank any harm. I think it is a great power, but, as I said before, I think it would be used only in cases of emergency, and I think that power ought to rest with somebody. As. it is now, the power is supposed to rest to a certain extent with the Attorney-General, one man. I suggest that the power be placed with three men, each of whom is to be appointed by a different Governor, at a different time, and then I think we will be better off and in a safer position than we are at present.

B. U. Steinman of Sacramento: We will then be in the same position that we are now, because the Bank Commissioners would have an attorney and they wouldn't do anything without his advice: they would do just as he did, anyhow. Then the Constitution of the State would have to be changed, because the Bank Commissioners are elected for four years, the Constitution provides for their election for four years. It would take some time to get to this.

F. T. Duhring of Sonoma: As far as that question is concerned, as to whether the Bank Commissioners shall serve four or eight years, that comes in the next proposition suggested by Mr. Elliott. The question now under discussion is merely the question as to whether the Commissioners, by unanimous vote, shall have power to close any bank which they deem to be in an unsafe condition. If this is to be done, the Bank Commissioners must have their powers enlarged: if this is not done, they will fail to do that for which they are appointed and for which a provision was made for them in our Constitution. As the law stands now, they have their powers so limited that they can do very little good and be of very little assistance to the people of this State whose interests they are supposed to protect, for they can merely make a recommendation to the Attorney-General and he can act as he pleases: therefore it is all in the hands of the Attorney-General. Now, we propose to leave the power in the hands of three people, who are to be unanimous in their decision before they can take any steps. I think it would be a protection to everybody, so no honest and sound bank need fear.

B. U. Steinman: Wouldn't they have to go him to have the suit commenced? I think it would come right back to where it is now.

George H. Stewart of Los Angeles: If I understand it correctly, the Comptroller does not have to enter suit to close up a National Bank.

He goes and shuts it up, and I don't think that there is any necessity for the Bank Commissioners to get a lawyer to close a bank. So far as Mr. Steinman is concerned, he is living there under the shadow and amongst the wisdom of our legislators, but still I think he is mistaken in the impression he has that the Bank Commissioners are a creation of the Constitution. There is an Act of the Legislature creating the Board of Commissioners, and that would not require a constitutional amendment to modify.

J. M. Elliott of Los Angeles: I wish to say that the different legal points of these propositions did not occur to me. There may be a great many legal objections. I merely expressed my general ideas in regard to the matter.

Frank Miller of Sacramento: I do not wish to discuss this matter in regard to the State Bank Commissioners, because I am not interested, but I would like to suggest to you that the Comptroller is an autocrat. The National Bank Examiner is without authority except to demand to count your cash and examine your accounts. His authority that far is simply clerical. He can overhaul the loans, etc., but, if he should ever make any suggestions, he would be told to mind his own business. But that one man, working on a small salary, who travels over the country looking into the accounts of National Banks, can send a note to Washington that you have a note on hand with interest unpaid, report it as a bad debt, that you have a good many such notes, in other words that the bank is insolvent, and then, nine times out of ten there comes back a telegram for him to take charge of the bank. If he finds the conditions about as I have stated, he has authority, under his instructions, to report it to Washington, and usually the result is as I have stated. I simply refer to this to show you that it is a one man power which exists with the National Banks.

John Reichman of Fresno: I think that the suggestion made is a very wise one, and I think that we should approve it. There is no question but that, if we have Bank Commissioners who are supposed to have the supervision of the banking system of this State, they should have some power. Now, under this proposition, that power is left with the three, who can only by unanimous vote close a bank. As to the question of the legality of such a transaction, we cannot of course pass upon that. If we approve of this recommendation at this meeting, then it is for the Executive Council to take the matter in hand and embody this provision in the law, provided they find it can be done. I don't see any objection to it. I don't think that the Attorney-General is necessary for the purpose of bringing suit against a bank for the purpose of closing it, because it is not necessary to sue. The idea is that the Bank Commissioners, upon investigation of the affairs of the bank, and finding that it is not being conducted honestly, or upon business principles and sound financial principles, may call the attention of the bank officers to the discrepancies, suggest corrections, and then, if these suggestions are not complied with, they can have a meeting of the three Commissioners, discuss the subject, and, if they conclude that the evil has gone too far, they can say, "Gentlemen, we will close this bank unless you put it in better condition." That is all. Now, if this meeting votes that it is in favor of such an amendment to the law, very well; let the matter remain in the hands of the Executive Council for the purpose of putting it into legal shape. I certainly favor the recommendation.

Motion to approve the last recommendation read was voted upon and carried.

The Chairman: Read the next, Mr. Secretary.

The Secretary: The last one is as follows:

" Lastly, that the term of office of all the Commissioners be in-
" creased to, say eight years, and that at least two political organiza-
" tions be represented in the personnel of the Board, and that the dates
" of the commissions of no two members should expire within twelve
" months of each other."

The Chairman: What is your pleasure as to this, gentlemen?

F. T. Duhring of Sonoma: As to this last proposition, there may be some legal objections raised against it, as to our proposing any changes of the Constitution. Of course we are discussing these questions with a view to arriving at what we think would be best to do, if it can be done. We may have the opinion that a change would be best, nevertheless, it may be that it cannot be done. I think that is all this suggestion means.

John Reichman of Fresno: Mr. Chairman, as to this last recommendation, I must say that I am opposed to it. We have just been discussing the subject, and the opinion has been expressed that the terms of the different Bank Commissioners should not expire at the same time, but that each succeeding Governor should have the opportunity to appoint one Bank Commissioner. The term of the Governor, as I understand it, is four years. Now, if the present Governor appoints one commissioner, and the next Governor appoints another commissioner, and the next Governor appoints another commissioner, and so on, so that the term of office is four years for each one, and there are always two remaining in office when the other's term expires, I do not see that there can be any objection to that. Eight years is a very long term. As to there being two political parties represented on the Board, I don't think that cuts any figure. The positions will be for the political parties to fight for. If a Democratic Governor is elected, he will appoint a Democratic commissioner, and if a Republican Governor is elected he will appoint a Republican commissioner.

C. S. Brooks of Marysville: I must say that I am opposed to this proposition. I don't think it would be difficult to find good Bank Commissioners, but I think eight years is altogether too long a time, if we happened to get a bad one. If we get a bad one for eight years it would be very hard to get rid of him. While it might be an advantage to have a good one serve eight years instead of four, I really believe that it is easier to get a good Bank Commissioner for four years than to get rid of a poor one who is in for eight years.

J. H. Jewett of Marysville: I would like to ask, for my own information, whether this law is an act of the Legislature, or is founded upon the Constitution of the State?

The Chairman: It was originally passed as a law, long before the new Constitution was adopted. That I know, because I took a great interest in having it passed.

F. T. Duhring of Sonoma: I would like to make this motion, that it is the sense of this Convention that no two Bank Commissioners be appointed within less than twelve months of the same time.

L. W. Burris of Santa Rosa: I second that motion.

J. M. Elliott: I wish to say, Mr. Chairman, that the reason why I suggested eight years was because I think it has been a matter of general knowledge that the Governor has appointed men for the position who are not bankers, and it takes them a good while to get their duties well learned, and then, just about the time they get the work well in hand, and get acquainted with the personnel and general inclinations of the bankers and banks throughout the State, they are relegated to private life, and some man who is entirely new to the business is put on the Board, and then it takes him a year or two, if it don't take him the whole four years, to learn what he ought to do.

L. W. Burris of Santa Rosa : The office of Bank Commissioner being filled by political appointment, I think there is likely to be an individual appointed that is not desirable. In case we should get in a bad Commissioner, we would be compelled to keep that bad one for the eight-year term. You can't regulate the matter exactly. I think the proper way would be for each Governor to appoint one Bank Commissioner. Then we would have two old Commissioners and one new appointee every four years.

The Chairman : Gentlemen, the proposition before you is as to the extension of the term of the Bank Commissioners from four to eight years. That is what I understand is before you, and nothing else.

J. H. Jewett of Marysville : As to this clause that Commissioners are not to be appointed within twelve months of each other, how would it be in case of the death of a Commissioner and an appointment for the unexpired term ? It might be that it would be necessary to make an appointment, then, within less than twelve months after the last one had been made.

The Chairman : Are you ready for the question ?

A Delegate : Question.

Upon vote being taken, the motion was not carried.

George H. Stewart of Los Angeles : Mr. Chairman, now that the members of the Executive Council have had an opportunity of arriving at pretty nearly the sentiment of this Convention on the propositions discussed, I move that all votes as to these matters be stricken from the record.

N. D. Rideout of Marysville : Mr. Chairman, I am very glad to have these expressions here, but, really, I do not think that the votes express fully the sentiment of the Convention. There was one vote on which there were only fifteen on one side and eleven on the other. I don't think that would give a very good idea of the sense of the whole Convention.

The Chairman : What is your motion, Mr. Stewart ?

George H. Stewart : That all of the record of the votes on this matter, since the reference of Mr. Elliott's paper to the Executive Council, be stricken from the record.

Lovell White : I second the motion, Mr. Chairman.

Motion put to a vote and carried.

The Chairman: Is there anything else before this meeting?

The Secretary: Mr. Chairman, here is a resolution that has been handed to me by the Committee on Resolutions:

To the Members of the California Bankers Association: GENTLEMEN:—

WHEREAS, It has pleased Divine Providence to remove from us by the hand of Death, Hon. E. F. Spence, former Vice-President of this Association and one of its most ardent supporters,

Resolved, That we appreciate the sterling qualities of our departed friend as a successful banker, as a man of thoughtful mind and broad views and as a friend whose loss we keenly feel.

Resolved, That a copy of these resolutions be transmitted to family of deceased, to the American Bankers Association, of which he was an executive officer, to the First National Bank of the city of Los Angeles of which he was for many years the President, and that the same be spread upon the records of this Association.

FRANK MILLER,
H. W. WRIGHT,
C. S. BROOKS,
Committee on Resolutions.

J. H. Jewett of Marysville: Mr. Chairman. I move that the resolution be adopted by a standing vote.

The resolution was adopted by a unanimous rising vote of the convention.

L. N. Breed of Los Angeles:

Mr. Chairman, and Gentlemen of the Convention:

We, of Los Angeles, who have known Mr. Spence's good qualities and appreciated them so long, miss him more than we can tell, and by his death we feel that our city has sustained an irreparable loss. Mr. Spence was one of Nature's best and truest noblemen. He was a true and loving husband, a kind and indulgent father, he was straightforward and strictly honest in all his business transactions, and a man who commanded the respect of all who knew him. From such men it is very hard to part. Let us hope that, when we shall have crossed the River, we shall all be permitted to make his acquaintance in that "house not made with hands, eternal in the Heavens."

Frank Miller of Sacramento: Mr. Chairman, since our Association last met in convention other prominent bankers of the State have passed away, notably, L. Gottig, President of the German Savings and Loan Society, R. C. Woolworth, President of the Crocker-Woolworth National Bank, John McKee, Cashier of the Tallant Banking Co., Edward S. Hast, Secretary of the Bank of California. They were all worthy men, eminent in their calling, and should not be forgotten. The Committee on Resolutions therefore desires to offer the following:

Resolved, That this Convention recognizes with sorrow that the hand of Death has removed from our view several members whose abilities and virtues made them conspicuous among us.

Resolved, That the roll of our dead is an honorable roll and the secretary is hereby directed to print it in full as a record of the past and as a page from which the living may profitably read.

> FRANK MILLER,
> H. W. WRIGHT,
> H. H. HEWLETT,
> A. H. R. SCHMIDT,
> C. S. BROOKS,
> Committee on Resolutions.

On motion, duly seconded, the resolution was unanimously adopted by a rising vote:

The Secretary: We have here a resolution of thanks from the Committee on Resolutions:

Resolved, That the thanks of this Association are tendered to the Chamber of Commerce for the use of these rooms; to the Union Lithograph Company for the artistic programs furnished with its compliments; also, that we appreciate the efforts and courtesies of the press in making our proceedings public.

On motion the resolution was adopted by a unanimous vote.

J. B. Lankershim of Los Angeles: I desire to offer a resolution, to which I think there will not be a dissenting voice. Our discussions of many things brought before us have been very profitable, the weather has been pleasant, and everything has been favorable to a pleasant session. I think, gentlemen, that the unanimous action that we have had in the meeting has been largely attributable to the efforts of our presiding officer, Mr. Hellman, and I move that the thanks of the convention be tendered him for his very able conduct of the proceedings.

Lovell White: I will relieve him by officiating in his stead during the vote on the motion. I hear the motion seconded by several. (Motion carried by unanimous vote.) Motion to tender thanks to Mr. Hellman is unanimously carried. It is so ordered.

I. W. Hellman: Thank you, gentlemen.

The Secretary: Before the adjournment, I would like to call the roll of counties, and ask for nominations for vice-presidents of the counties, so as to ascertain if all the counties have elected vice-presidents. I will call the roll of counties, and take the names of vice-presidents nominated.

The Secretary proceeded with the calling of roll of counties, in alphabetical order. Nominations being made as follows:

Alameda—J. E. Baker, Cashier Bank of Alameda, Alameda.
Butte—Charles Faulkner, Cashier Bank of Butte County, Chico.
Colusa—W. P. Harrington, Cashier Colusa County Bank, Colusa.
Contra Costa—Nomination passed.
Fresno—H. D. Colson, President Fresno National Bank.
Glenn—B. H. Burton, Cashier Bank of Willows.
Humboldt—Nomination passed.
Kern—Nomination passed.
Lake—Nomination passed.
Los Angeles—I. N. Breed, President Southern California National Bank of Los Angeles.
Merced—C. Landram, Vice-President Merced Bank, Merced.
Monterey—T. J. Field, Vice-President Bank of Monterey.
Napa—Nomination passed.
Nevada—E. M. Preston, President Citizens Bank of Nevada City.
Orange—Nomination passed.
Placer—D. W. Lubeck, Vice-President Placer County Bank, Auburn.
Riverside—Nomination passed.
Sacramento—W. E. Chamberlain of the National Bank of D. O. Mills & Co., Sacramento.
San Benito—T. W. Hawkins, Cashier Bank of Hollister.
San Bernardino—Nomination passed.
San Diego—R. M. Powers, President Bank of Commerce, San Diego.
San Francisco—Nomination passed.
San Joaquin—Nomination passed.
San Luis Obispo—R. E. Jack, Cashier County Bank of San Luis Obispo.
Santa Barbara—Nomination passed.
Santa Clara—J. W. Findley, Vice-President Commercial Savings Bank, San Jose.
Santa Cruz—W. T. Jeter, President Bank of Santa Cruz County.
Shasta—Nomination passed.
Siskiyou—Nomination passed.
Solano—R. D. Robbins, President Bank of Suisun.
Sonoma—L. W. Burris, Cashier Santa Rosa Bank.
Sutter—George W. Carpenter, President Farmers Co-operative Union, Yuba City.
Tehama—Nomination passed.
Tulare—S. Mitchell Cashier Producers Bank, Visalia.
Ventura—J. S. Collins, Cashier Wm. Collins & Sons, Ventura.
Yolo—C. W. Bush, Cashier Bank of Yolo, Woodland.
Yuba—J. H. Jewett, President Decker, Jewett & Co. Bank, Marysville.

When Sacramento was called Mr. Frank Miller spoke as follows: Mr. Chairman, I would like to nominate for Vice-President for Sacramento County Mr. W. E. Chamberlain, and, in making that nomination, I wish to express the wish that you all will attain to something that Mr. Chamberlain has. He has one qualification as a banker that everybody connected with a bank ought to have. You may think it is money. Money does not stay with you, but this qualification does stay with him, and that is he is ninety-two years of age; and may you all live to be the same.

The Chairman : Is there anything else to come before this meeting, gentlemen ?

The Secretary : There is nothing on the secretary's desk, sir.

W. P. Harrington of Colusa : Mr. Chairman, I think it is very proper that we return our thanks to the secretary for the able manner in which he has conducted the duties pertaining to his office. I move that the thanks of the Convention be extended to Mr. Welch the secretary.

Motion seconded and was duly carried.

The Chairman: Before adjournment, I wish to say that the San Francisco Clearing House people will meet as many of you gentlemen as desire to confer with them this afternoon, at half-past one o'clock, here in this room.

Motion to adjourn was then made, it received second, and was carried. The Chairman declared the Convention adjourned, *sine die.*

MORTUARY RECORD.

SPENCE—E. F. Spence, President of First National Bank of Los Angeles and Vice-President of the California Bankers Association, died September 19th, 1892, aged 59 years. A native of Ireland. He came to California in 1852 and was engaged in mining, mercantile business and banking, successively, in Nevada City, San Jose, San Diego and Los Angeles, in which latter place he settled in 1875. Genial, but firm and energetic, he had warm friends among all classes, and held creditably numerous public positions.

WOOLWORTH—Ralph C. Woolworth, President of the Crocker-Woolworth National Bank of San Francisco, died June 10th, 1893, aged 52 years. Mr. Woolworth was born at Lowville, Lewis County, New York, which place he left in the early years of his manhood for California. On his arrival at Sacramento he secured a position as clerk in the bank of D. O. Mills & Co., and continued in their employ until he was elected cashier of the Capital Savings Bank. In May, 1875, he removed to San Francisco and was elected cashier of the First National Bank, which office he held until February, 1876, when he became its president. In 1883 Mr. Woolworth and Charles Crocker established the bank of Crocker, Woolworth & Co., which was changed in 1886 to the Crocker-Woolworth National Bank, of which institution Mr. Woolworth was president until the date of his death. Through his long, active and successful connection with banking, Mr. Woolworth won for himself a high position among the leading bankers of San Francisco. His methods and earnest application to business, his genial nature and unswerving integrity enlisted the respect and admiration of all with whom he was associated.

HAST—Edward S. Hast, Secretary of the Bank of California, San Francisco, died October 19th, 1893, in the 58th year of his age. He was a native of London, England, and came to California in 1871, representing a syndicate of English capitalists. In 1871 he entered the service of the Bank of California, and in January, 1890, was elected secretary.

GOTTIG—Lawrence Gottig, President of The German Savings and Loan Society, San Francisco, died November 10th, 1893, in the sixty-seventh year of his age. He was born in Flensburg, a town in Schleswig-Holstein, Prussia. In 1851 he came to the United States and soon after found his way to California where he engaged in merchandising in Gibsonville, Sierra County. Later he was agent of the Pacific Mail Steamship Company at Benicia. He was one of the incorporators, and a member of the first Board of Directors, of the German Savings and Loan Society and in 1869 became its President, which position he held continuously until the day of his death. His activity in business matters and his tall form served to make him well known in the community, and his absence from California street will be long noted and regretted.

McKEE—John McKee, Cashier of the Tallant Banking Company, San Francisco, died December 17th, 1893, aged 67 years and 16 days. A native of Wheeling, West Virginia, in 1850 he came to California and located in the northern part of the State, in the vicinity of Mount Shasta. He engaged principally in mining until 1857 when he moved to San Francisco and connected himself with the private bank of Tallant & Wilde, established in 1850. Mr. Wilde dying in 1863, Mr. McKee became associated with Mr. Tallant as partner, under the firm name of Tallant & Co. The firm incorporated in 1891 as a State bank, Mr. McKee becoming the cashier. At the time of his death he was also President of the San Francisco Clearing House Association, a director of the California Powder Works and of the Central Gas Company of Sacramento, Treasurer of the Pacific Union Club and a member of the Boards of Trustees of the Protestant Orphan Asylum and the Young Men's Christian Association. He was a man of strong religious convictions and zealous in good works, with manners exceedingly gracious and pleasing.

DUNN—John Dunn, an old and highly respected employee of the Bank of California, San Francisco, died January 6th, 1894, in the sixty-eighth year of his age. A native of England. He became connected with the Bank of California in 1866 and continued in its service, filling a number of responsible positions, until his death.

———

NOTE: This Mortuary Record is prepared in accordance with resolutions adopted at the Convention of which this pamphlet contains the proceedings, and records the only deaths that have been reported to the Secretary.

It is hereby requested that every member of the Association notify the Secretary of the death of any banker, or officer or director of a bank, belonging to the Association, that may occur before our next annual Convention, that this record may be complete hereafter.

INDEX.

www.ingramcontent.com/pod-product-compliance
Lightning Source LLC
Chambersburg PA
CBHW022258280326
41932CB00010B/902